Global Aging

Suzanne R. Kunkel, PhD, is the director of the Scripps Gerontology Center and professor in the Department of Sociology and Gerontology at Miami University. She has been principal investigator or co-investigator on local, state, federal, and foundation grants totaling more than $3 million. Kunkel is a fellow of both the Gerontological Society of America (GSA) and the Association for Gerontology in Higher Education (AGHE). She received the Hiram Friedsam Mentorship Award from AGHE, and is currently treasurer of the GSA. Kunkel is coauthor (with Leslie Morgan) of *Aging, Society, and the Life Course*, a textbook now in its fourth edition. With Frank Whittington and Erdman Palmore, she coedited the most recent edition of the *International Handbook on Aging*, and coedited with Frank Whittington the spring 2013 edition of *Generations*, focusing on global aging. She has published more than 40 articles, books, and book chapters, and more than 30 research monographs on the aging network, innovations in the delivery of home care, population projections, global aging, and gerontology education.

J. Scott Brown, PhD, is an associate professor and director of graduate studies in the Department of Sociology and Gerontology and research fellow with Scripps Gerontology Center at Miami University. His research interests are focused on wealth and health inequalities across the life course with particular emphasis on gender and race differences in physical and mental health. He has authored or coauthored more than two dozen articles and book chapters across multiple research areas including mortality and disability, mental health life course trajectories across age, variation in race and ethnic measurement and its social and health implications, and cross-national investigation of the initiation of and changes in welfare state policies. Dr. Brown is currently working on a National Institutes of Health–funded multiyear research project investigating the life course effects of region of residence in early life on a variety of subjective and objective health outcomes. He serves as an associate editor for the *Journals of Gerontology: Social Sciences*.

Frank J. Whittington, PhD, is professor of gerontology and senior associate dean for academic affairs in the College of Health and Human Services at George Mason University. His research interests focus on the social dimensions of health and health care of older persons, especially African Americans. His publications include 10 books and more than 60 articles and chapters on health behavior, long-term care, and global aging. With five colleagues in the Georgia State University Gerontology Institute and based on research funded by the National Institute on Aging and the AARP Andrus Foundation, he coauthored *Communities of Care: Assisted Living for African Americans*. His most recent project was the *International Handbook on Aging*, coedited with Erdman Palmore of Duke University and Suzanne R. Kunkel of Miami University. Dr. Whittington has served as president of the Southern Gerontological Society, which selected him to receive the Gordon Streib Academic Gerontologist Award in 2009. He also received the 2010 Clark Tibbitts Award for outstanding contributions to academic gerontology from the AGHE.

Global Aging

Comparative Perspectives on Aging and the Life Course

Suzanne R. Kunkel, PhD

J. Scott Brown, PhD

Frank J. Whittington, PhD

with

Jasleen K. Chahal, MGS

SPRINGER PUBLISHING COMPANY

NEW YORK

Springer Publishing Company, LLC
11 West 42nd Street
New York, NY 10036
www.springerpub.com

Acquisitions Editor: Sheri W. Sussman
Production Editor: Shelby Peak
Composition: Amnet Systems Pvt. Ltd.

ISBN: 978-0-8261-0546-2
e-book ISBN: 978-0-8261-0547-9

14 15 16 17 / 5 4 3 2 1

The author and the publisher of this Work have made every effort to use sources believed to be reliable to provide information that is accurate and compatible with the standards generally accepted at the time of publication. The author and publisher shall not be liable for any special, consequential, or exemplary damages resulting, in whole or in part, from the readers' use of, or reliance on, the information contained in this book. The publisher has no responsibility for the persistence or accuracy of URLs for external or third-party Internet websites referred to in this publication and does not guarantee that any content on such websites is, or will remain, accurate or appropriate.

Library of Congress Cataloging-in-Publication Data

Global aging : comparative perspectives on aging and the life course / Suzanne R. Kunkel, J. Scott Brown, Frank J. Whittington; with
Jasleen K. Chahal.
 p. ; cm.
Includes bibliographical references and index.
ISBN 978-0-8261-0546-2 (print) — ISBN 978-0-8261-0547-9 (e-book)
 I. Kunkel, Suzanne. II. Brown, J. Scott (James Scott). III. Whittington, Frank J.
IV. Chahal, Jasleen.
[DNLM: 1. Aged. 2. Aging. 3. Cross-Cultural Comparison. 4. Internationality.
 5. World Health. WT 100]
RA427.8
362.1—dc23

2013040371

Special discounts on bulk quantities of our books are available to corporations, professional associations, pharmaceutical companies, health care organizations, and other qualifying groups. If you are interested in a custom book, including chapters from more than one of our titles, we can provide that service as well.

For details, please contact:
Special Sales Department, Springer Publishing Company, LLC
11 West 42nd Street, 15th Floor, New York, NY 10036-8002
Phone: 877-687-7476 or 212-431-4370; Fax: 212-941-7842
E-mail: sales@springerpub.com

Printed in the United States of America by Edwards Brothers.

Contents

Contributors   ***xi***

Preface   ***xiii***

1. Our Aging World   *1*

More, Less, and Least Developed Nations   *3*

Culture, Population Aging, and Social Change   *4*

    China: One-Child Policy   *6*

    Germany: Inverted Pyramid   *8*

    Kenya: Health Challenges   *11*

Aging and the Welfare State   *12*

    Development of the Welfare State   *13*

    The Welfare State and Role of the Family   *14*

International Initiatives on Aging   *17*

The Study of Global Aging   *19*

    1. To Get Educated   *19*

    2. Self-Interest   *19*

    3. The Smart Move   *20*

Summary   *21*

Discussion Questions   *22*

Key Words   *22*

Essay: Gender, Aging, and Power in Rural Bangladesh:
    Getting Older as the Priming of Women   *23*
    Fauzia E. Ahmed

2. The Study of Global Aging   *27*

Types of Investigation   *27*

Cross-National Comparative Research   *29*

    The Importance of Comparison: From Description to
        Explanation   *30*

The Challenge and the Promise of Comparative Research   *33*
     Challenge #1: Unit of Analysis   35
     Challenge #2: Conceptualization and Measurement   40
     Challenge #3: Getting Valid Data   42
     Challenge #4: Respecting Participants   43
Summary   *45*
Discussion Questions   *45*
Key Words   *46*

Essay: An American in Havana: Observations About
   Aging in Cuba   *47*
   Frank J. Whittington

3. The Welfare State and Global Aging   53

Retired and Living the Good Life?   *53*
Defining the Welfare State   *55*
     History of the Welfare State   *55*
     Program Types and Eligibility   *58*
Distribution of Program Types   *62*
The Recent Trend: Retrenchment   *63*
The Future of the Welfare State and Global Aging   *64*
Conclusion   *68*
Discussion Questions   *69*
Key Words   *69*

Essay: Older Swedes: Living in the "Role Model of
   Welfare States"   *71*
   Kathrin Komp

4. Demographic Perspectives on an Aging World   75

Demographic Transition Theory   *77*
Demographic Divide   *81*
Speed of Population Aging   *82*
Demographic Dividends   *83*
Measures of Population Aging   *84*
     Population Pyramids   *84*
     Proportion Aged   *89*
     Median Age   *90*
     Life Expectancy   *91*
     Aging Index   *92*
     Dependency Ratios   *93*
     Prospective Age   *95*

Interpreting and Using Demographic Data   *95*

Summary   *97*

Discussion Questions   *98*

Key Words   *99*

Essay: Income Inequality and Heterogeneity in Mortality
Patterns   *100*
  Scott M. Lynch

5. **Disability and Active Life Expectancy**   *109*

Why Is Disability an Important Topic for Global Aging?   *111*

Defining Disability for Global Comparisons   *112*
  Measuring Disability Comparatively   *114*
  The Difficulties of Data   *117*

Disability Around the Globe   *118*
  The Developed World   *118*
  The Developing World   *120*

Future Trends: Adding Years to Life and Adding
Life to Years?   *120*

Discussion Questions   *123*

Key Words   *123*

Essay: Methodological Problems Related to the Measurement
of Psychiatric Disorders in International Surveys:
An Example Comparing the United States and Nepal   *124*
  Mark Tausig and Janardan Subedi

6. **Health and Health Care Systems**   *129*
  Jasleen K. Chahal, Suzanne R. Kunkel, Janardan
  Subedi, Sree Subedi, and Frank J. Whittington

Patterns of Health and Aging   *129*
  From Acute to Chronic Diseases   *130*
  Differences Within Older Populations—Does Age Matter?   *132*
  The Role of Culture in Health Patterns   *133*

Health Systems: A Global Perspective   *134*
  Types of Health Care Systems   *134*
    Folk Medicine   *134*
    Traditional Medicine   *135*
    Modern Medicine   *137*
  Models of Organizing and Financing Modern Medicine   *138*
    The Bismarck Model   *140*
    The Beveridge Model   *141*

The National Health Insurance Model **142**
The Out-of-Pocket Model **143**
Health Systems and Older People **144**
Health Behavior of Older People **145**
Complementary and Alternative Medicine **145**
CAM and Aging **146**
Health Promotion and Self-Care **148**
Health Literacy **149**
Self-Directed Care **150**
Summary **151**
Discussion Questions **152**
Key Words **152**

Essay: Palliative Care: A Global Public Health Initiative
to Improve Quality of Life **154**
Jasleen K. Chahal

7. **Long-Term Services and Supports** **163**
Robert Applebaum, Emily Robbins, and Anthony Bardo

Defining Long-Term Services and Supports **164**
Typologies of LTC Services and Supports **165**
A New Typology **166**
Group 1 **166**
Group 2 **171**
Group 3 **173**
Group 4 **177**
Group 5 **179**
Cross-Cutting Issues for an Aging Planet **183**
Financing **183**
Support for Family **184**
Need to Develop an Efficient and Effective LTC
System **184**
Need for Prevention **184**
Conclusion **185**
Discussion Questions **185**
Key Words **186**
Appendix A: Country List **186**
Appendix B: OECD Country List **186**

Essay: Aging in Nicaragua **187**
*Milton Lopez Norori, Carmen Largaespada Fredersdorff, and
Keren Brown Wilson*

8. **Work and Retirement** *193*
   Phyllis Cummins, J. Scott Brown, and Philip E. Sauer

   Defining Work and Retirement *195*
   What Gives Rise to Retirement? *197*
   What Drives Individual Retirement? *198*
      Bureaucratic Rules *199*
      Functional and Health Limitations *199*
      Financial and Personal Reasons *201*
   Private Pension Systems *202*
   Different Forms of Retirement *204*
      Early Retirement *205*
      Delayed Retirement *206*
      Partial Retirement and Return to Work *209*
   Retirement in Developing Nations *210*
   Conclusions *212*
   Discussion Questions *212*
   Key Words *212*

   Essay: Retirement in China *214*
      Jiayin (Jaylene) Liang

9. **Families, Caregiving, and Community Support Systems** *219*
   Jennifer M. Kinney, Suzanne R. Kunkel, Jasleen K. Chahal, and Frank J. Whittington

   An American Family *220*
   The Universal Concept of Family *220*
   Evolving Definitions of the Family *221*
      Kinship Ties *223*
      What Do You Call Your Grandmother? *223*
   Aging Families *225*
      Household Structures and Living Arrangements *225*
      Intergenerational Transfers *228*
      Older Adults as Caregivers *229*
   Cultural Values About Older Adults and Family Relationships *230*
      Interdependence *232*
      Filial Piety and Filial Responsibility *232*
      Intergenerational Solidarity–Conflict *233*
      Family Integrity *233*
   Who Provides Care for Older People? *236*

Informal and Formal Systems of Support   *237*

Variations in Systems of Support and Care   *238*

Community Care: NGOs   *240*

Expanding Role of NGOs: The Madrid Plan   *241*

Families and Social Support Today: Updates to
the Madrid Plan   *245*

Conclusion   *247*

Discussion Questions   *248*

Key Words   *248*

Essay: Social Support Systems for Rural Older Adults in Kenya   *250*
Samuel M. Mwangi

10. Global Aging and Global Leadership   255

Themes Worth Remembering   *257*

Becoming a Global Leader   *262*

About the Expert Panel   *265*

Web Resources for Further Information   *267*

References   *275*

Index   *301*

Contributors

Fauzia E. Ahmed, PhD, Assistant Professor, Department of Sociology and Gerontology, Miami University, Oxford, Ohio

Robert Applebaum, PhD, Professor, Department of Sociology and Gerontology, Miami University, Oxford, Ohio

Anthony Bardo, MGS, Research Assistant, Department of Sociology and Gerontology, Miami University, Oxford, Ohio

Jasleen K. Chahal, MGS, Research Assistant, Department of Sociology and Gerontology, Miami University, Oxford, Ohio

Phyllis Cummins, PhD, Postdoctoral Fellow, Scripps Gerontology Center, Miami University, Oxford, Ohio

Carmen Largaespada Fredersdorff, PhD, Representante Residente, Organización de Estados Iberoamericanos, Managua, Nicaragua

Jennifer M. Kinney, PhD, Professor, Department of Sociology and Gerontology, and research fellow, Scripps Gerontology Center, Miami University, Oxford, Ohio

Kathrin Komp, PhD, Postdoctoral Fellow, Department of Sociology, Umeå University, Umeå, Sweden

Jiayin (Jaylene) Liang, Doctoral Candidate, Department of Sociology and Gerontology, Miami University, Oxford, Ohio

Scott M. Lynch, PhD, Professor, Department of Sociology, Princeton University, Princeton, New Jersey

Samuel M. Mwangi, PhD, Kenyatta University, Nairobi, Kenya

Milton Lopez Norori, MD, MPH, Program Coordinator, Global Aging and Health Program, Jessie F. Richardson Foundation, Managua, Nicaragua

Emily Robbins, PhD, Guest Scientist, Institut für Psychologie, Goethe-Universität, Frankfurt am Main, Frankfurt, Germany

Philip E. Sauer, MGS, Research Assistant, Department of Sociology and Gerontology, Miami University, Oxford, Ohio

Janardan Subedi, PhD, Professor, Department of Sociology and Gerontology, Miami University, Oxford, Ohio

Sree Subedi, PhD, Professor, Department of Sociology and Gerontology, Miami University, Oxford, Ohio

Mark Tausig, PhD, Associate Dean, The Graduate School, The University of Akron, Akron, Ohio

Keren Brown Wilson, PhD, President, Jessie F. Richardson Foundation, Clackamas, Oregon

Preface

Population aging is now a universal phenomenon. In fact, for the first time in human history, people age 60 and older now outnumber children younger than age 5. We can foresee a day when older adults will be more numerous than children younger than age 15. This truly revolutionary situation—expected to occur within the next four decades—will demand a completely different political, economic, and social response from all national governments.

As a result, the field of gerontology is expanding in every corner and is becoming increasingly internationalized. The inclusion of cross-national content in gerontology curricula and the development of gerontology education programs in many countries speaks to a growing worldwide interest in aging. This interest is driven, in part, by the undeniable demands an aging population places on a society—for policies and programs designed to meet the unique needs and utilize the potential contributions of an older population; for a workforce trained to fulfill those needs; and for citizens educated about the issues of an aging world.

First, the intended audiences for this text are faculty teaching undergraduate and graduate courses in global aging and their students. Second, many of the topics addressed in this book will be of interest to faculty and students in undergraduate and graduate courses in the demography of aging and sociology of aging, as well as courses in gerontology taught with a comparative, international focus. We hope also that it will serve to focus the attention of all gerontologists on the growth and value of the research and teaching going on in countries outside the United States and Europe. The value of cross-national research is another important theme of this book. Until we incorporate findings from research on non-Western, non-white samples of aging people, we will not have a deep or accurate understanding of how people and societies age.

This book provides an overview of major issues associated with societal and global aging, paralleling the structure of many introductory social gerontology textbooks. However, unlike existing textbooks in the field, the discussion of each topic in this work is explicitly comparative, focusing on similarities and variations in the aging experience across nations. The text is organized thematically, with examples from around the world embedded throughout the narrative where they are available and appropriate. The comparative perspective is enhanced further by topical essays and country-specific descriptions of policies, programs, and experiences of aging.

The volume opens (Chapter 1) with an overview of aging in global perspective to orient the reader to the topic. Chapter 2 follows with a description of what comparative research is and how it is done. Chapters 3 and 4 present discussions of the political and economic policies that surround aging issues in many nations and how demographic forces behind population aging are affecting the welfare state in both developed and developing nations. We devote three chapters to the substantial issue of aging and health. Chapter 5 focuses on disability in old age and the various ways countries measure and track disability. Chapter 6 features an in-depth discussion of different models of providing health care and the major public health issues in both the more- and less-developed countries, whereas Chapter 7 presents a typology of the different national policies and programs that provide long-term care for older adults with significant chronic health conditions. In Chapter 8, we turn to another vital concern of older people in every country—the issue of work and retirement. Chapter 9 discusses another universal topic: how families address the aging of their members and struggle with the issues surrounding caregiving, as well as—on the other hand—the active, productive role that older adults continue to play in family life. The chapter concludes with a description of how communities and, indeed, the world community—through nongovernmental organizations (NGOs)—are responding to the burdens that economic and demographic changes are imposing on family support and caregiving. Finally, in Chapter 10 we summarize 13 major themes of the book and conclude with a call to readers for global leadership—in both aging issues and beyond.

We began to write this text with considerable experience as gerontological researchers and educators and with an equal confidence that we were up to the task. However, we quickly learned that the content of an adequate book on this subject was already far beyond our expectations. We realized that the scope of work would be much broader—and take longer—than we had first imagined. Without the wonderful assistance of many, many people, we could not have completed it. First in line for our deep appreciation is our energetic and insightful "assistant author," Jasleen Chahal. As a doctoral student in gerontology at Miami University, with family roots in India and Canada, Jas gave us the perfect combination of critical opinion and careful judgment. We are indebted also to several colleagues who undertook leading or sharing authorship with us on some of the chapters: Oliver Hautz for his help with Chapter 2 ("The Study of Global Aging"); Jas Chahal and Janardan and Sree Subedi for their assistance on Chapter 6 ("Health and Health Care Systems"); Bob Applebaum, Emily Robbins, and Tony Bardo for authoring Chapter 7 ("Long-Term Services and Supports"); Phyllis Cummins and Philip Sauer for Chapter 8 ("Work and Retirement"); and Jennifer Kinney and Jas Chahal for Chapter 9 ("Families, Caregiving, and Community Support Systems").

We believe the nine essays illustrating special issues in a specific country, one per chapter (except for Chapter 10), are distinctive additions to the text. We appreciate the essay authors' cultural insight and their patience as we labored to fit all the pieces together; the book would not have been complete without the contributions of the following essay authors (and the ideas and countries they write about): Fauzia Ahmed (Bangladesh); Frank Whittington (Cuba); Kathrin Komp (Sweden); Scott Lynch (inequality); Mark Tausig and Janardan Subedi (Nepal); Jasleen Chahal (palliative care); Milton Lopez Norori, Carmen Largaespada Fredersdorff, and Keren Brown Wilson (Nicaragua); Jaylene Liang (China); and Samuel Mwangi (Kenya). In addition, we extend deep appreciation to the three global aging experts—Zach Zimmer, Dorly Deeg, and Karel Kalaw—who allowed us to interview them about their views and to incorporate their thoughts on both the present and the future of an aging world into Chapter 10.

The work of all these contributors has made this a much better book, but the assistance of several other people who have supported our efforts along the way has made it possible. We acknowledge and thank Amanda Baer at George Mason University and a long list of graduate assistants, support staff, and colleagues at Miami University for their valuable help with this project. Finally, we want to express our heartfelt gratitude to Sheri W. Sussman, our editor at Springer Publishing Company, for helping us bring this volume to press. Sheri's patience is matched only by her determined persistence. When she commits to people or to a project—and for Sheri that often is the same thing—it is for the duration. Sheri, this one's for you.

To the rest of you who have known of our work and waited patiently for its conclusion, we offer apologies for its long gestation and thanks for waiting. In the words of Penny Wharvey McGill—a character in one of our favorite Homeric classics, the American movie, *O Brother, Where Art Thou?*—people should be, must be, *bona fide*. We agree and we think books should meet that standard too. We have done all we can to ensure this one is bona fide, authentic, certified, *pukka* (Hindi), *echt* (German and Yiddish), and *dinkum* (Australian and New Zealand). We hope it meets your expectations. If not, we are anxious to hear about its shortcomings, with the aim of improving our effort on a second try. Of course, if you do think we have done justice to your region or country and captured the essence of aging around the world, we will be just as grateful—and far more satisfied.

Suzanne R. Kunkel
J. Scott Brown
Frank J. Whittington

CHAPTER 1

Our Aging World

The world's population is growing older, leading us into uncharted demographic waters. There will be higher absolute numbers of elderly people, a larger share of elderly, longer healthy life expectancies, and relatively fewer numbers of working-age people. . . . Population aging does raise some formidable and fundamentally new challenges, but they are not insurmountable. These changes also bring some new opportunities. (Bloom, Boersch-Supan, McGee, & Seike, 2011, p. 2)

The world's older population is growing more than twice as fast as the world's total population (United Nations, 2009). More than 1.2 million people join the ranks of the older population *per month*! In countries like Nigeria, India, Italy, Japan, and China, the proportion of population that is aged 65 and older will more than double between 2000 and 2050. Other countries will have even higher growth: India's proportion aged will nearly triple, and Kuwait will experience a ninefold increase in the proportion of its population age 65 or older during those 50 years. The phenomenal rate at which global aging is occurring—along with the far-reaching social, cultural, and economic impacts within countries, across regions, and around the world— is the focus of this book.

The aging of the world's population, and the issues that each nation is facing as its aging citizens increase in number, is receiving increasing attention from the media, government and policy-making officials, international organizations such as the United Nations, and researchers. The growing numbers of older people in developing nations are especially noteworthy. Today, more than 60% of all people age 65 and older live in developing nations (a term to be discussed in greater detail); that proportion will exceed 75% by 2040 (Kinsella & He, 2009). These numbers may seem surprising, given the relatively low proportions aged today in many of these countries, as well as lower life expectancies and median ages in developing nations (as can be seen in Chapter 2). But consider that about 82% of the world's total population in 2010 lived in the developing nations of the world (Population Reference Bureau, 2010a). Take India as an example. Although only 5% of India's 1.21 billion people are currently aged 65 or older, that 5% represents more than 60 million older people. Because so much of the world's population is concentrated in these developing nations, and because these regions are beginning to experience rapid population aging, it is easy to see how three-fourths of the world's older people will be living in these areas in only a few decades.

Population aging in developing nations (such as India, Thailand, Kenya, Chile, and Guatemala) poses unique challenges to the governments, families, and individuals in those countries. Their populations are aging quickly, but they are less likely to have in place programs, policies, or health care systems prepared to meet the needs of older people. This structural lag in the development of options to deal with coming older populations in those nations can be explained by a combination of factors, including relatively poor economies without revenues to invest in new programs or services; pressing concerns about general nutrition and maternal and child health; traditional value systems that emphasize norms of family care; and the very rapid pace of demographic and health transitions—giving countries little time to adjust to the new realities of an aging society. Many nations in the developing regions of the world are simultaneously dealing with relatively

Source: Dr. Sukhminder S. Bhangoo.

high fertility, problems of poverty and hunger, population aging, and new demands for chronic health care.

Although of quite a different nature, challenges related to aging are also significant in the more developed countries around the world, such as the United States, Japan, and Germany. In particular, existing pension programs and formal long-term care systems in such countries are already inadequate, or likely to become so, as the proportions of older people continue to grow. At the risk of oversimplifying a complex situation, the general pattern is that nations in the less developed regions of the world are faced with the dilemmas of devising new programs, policies, and services for aging populations, whereas more developed regions are dealing with the problems of funding, adapting, or expanding existing policies and programs. It has been said that developing nations get old before they get rich; however, today's developed nations got rich before they got old (World Health Organization, 2010b). Given what we know about both economic development and aging, it may also be true that poor countries beginning to age may never get rich.

The intersection of demography, culture, politics, and economics comes into play as countries around the world plan for and adapt to their aging populations. Each nation is unique in its configuration of these social, economic, and cultural factors. Throughout this text, the specific situation of different countries is described to illustrate similarities and variations in the realities of aging. However, it is also useful (and common in the global aging literature) to compare across regions of the world. Since many of those comparisons are based on the categorization of more, less, and least developed regions, a discussion of those designations is necessary.

MORE, LESS, AND LEAST DEVELOPED NATIONS

Although classifying countries or regions is complicated, the categorization is based generally on the area's level of economic development. The United Nations Statistics Division cautions that such designations should be understood as a "statistical convenience" rather than a judgment, and that there is no single, established standard for classification (United Nations Statistics Division, 2010). For our purposes, think of the designations as the result of a two-step process. First, the World Bank calculates a gross national income per person for each country and then places each into one of four categories: low income, lower middle income, upper middle income, and high income. In the next step, high-income countries are defined as developed countries, and all remaining (low- and middle-income) countries are classified as developing countries. As a point of reference, the threshold for high-income (developed) countries in 2010 was a gross national income per person of US$12,196; at the other end of the continuum, low-income countries were at or below $995 per person, with the other groups in between (World Bank, 2010). Even though these categorizations are only statistical conveniences, they do provide a general sense of the level of resources available in a country to address important needs, including those related to having an aging population.

A commonly used alternative to the World Bank categorization comes from the United Nations, which currently designates all of Europe and Northern America plus Australia, New Zealand, and Japan as **more developed countries**; all others are **less developed** (or sometimes referred to in shorthand as developed and developing). Within the group of less developed countries is a special designation for **least developed countries** (LDCs). Several criteria are used to distinguish the nations in that category: (a) very low income per person, (b) economic vulnerability, and (c) poor human development indicators (population nutritional status, mortality, literacy, and education). LDCs currently include 33 African nations, 15 Asian countries, and Haiti (United Nations Office of the High Representative for Least Developed Countries, 2010). For our exploration of global aging, these designations help to differentiate countries and regions of the world on a number of dimensions, including the current age of the country. More developed countries currently have a much higher proportion of older people than do less or least developed countries. However, the populations of the less developed nations are aging much faster than did the populations of the developed nations, as can be seen in Chapter 4. Consequently, the nations in these categories differ in the types of challenges they face related to population aging. Each of these issues is explored in greater depth throughout this volume.

CULTURE, POPULATION AGING, AND SOCIAL CHANGE

Although we can agree that population aging is a truly global phenomenon—happening in every nation in the world—the experiences and realities of aging unfold very differently in different places. This book is committed to

Source: The World Bank.

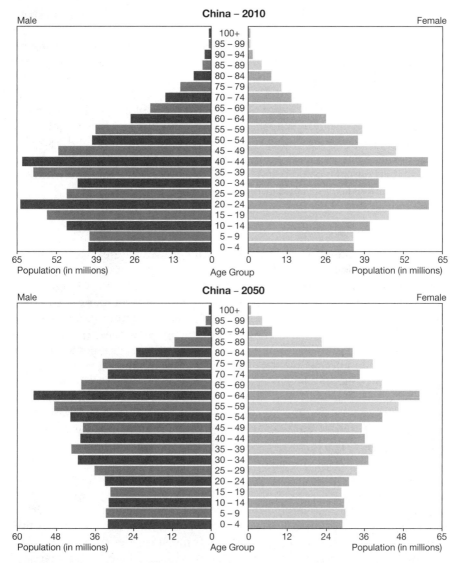

FIGURE 1.1 Population pyramids for China, 2010 and 2050.
Source: U.S. Bureau of the Census International Data Base (2013).

exploring those different realities of aging. But it is also committed to uncovering and dispelling stereotypes about other countries, and about what it must be like to grow old in those countries. The essay for this chapter offers a unique view into the life of older women in rural Bangladesh that raises interesting issues about age, gender, and power in a developing nation, and may well surprise you.

Ahmed's essay beautifully illuminates the importance of culture in shaping the experiences of aging. Here, three case studies are offered to further illustrate this point. China, Germany, and Kenya—countries with quite dissimilar demographic, cultural, and social situations related to population aging—are described. These examples illustrate the intersections of population aging with social change and cultural traditions within each unique context, and they present an idea of the types of issues that are explored in the remainder of this book. You also can compare each case study to what they might know about aging in the United States to inform their understanding of the specific dynamics that have shaped aging there. These comparisons, as well as the essay in this chapter, should begin to shed light on the distinctive influences at work in different societies and cultures.

China: One-Child Policy

As noted in Chapter 4, **population pyramids** provide a great deal of information about population aging. Comparisons of pyramids—either across different countries or over time for the same country—reveal significant demographic shifts and hint at the social changes that accompany such shifts. The population pyramid of contemporary China (shown in Figure 1.1) has a very distinctive shape, reflecting its unique age structure. This structure is the result of China's well-known **one-child policy**, implemented in 1979 to stem a very high and unsustainable rate of population growth in favor of long-term economic development and improved standards of living for China's people. Prior to 1980, China's fertility rate averaged about 2.9 children per woman; during the two decades after implementation, the rate fell to around 1.8 children and has fallen even further in the past 5 years to just over 1.5 children. The impact of the one-child policy can be seen in the much smaller size of the base of China's population pyramid in 2010. As a result of this very rapid decrease in fertility, combined with low mortality, the proportion of China's population age 65 and older is increasing very rapidly. China has, through policy, accelerated the normal decline in fertility that is part of the demographic transition. The population pyramid for 2050 illustrates this reality: The base of the pyramid (children) is much smaller than all the other age strata, except for the very oldest (age 80 and older). By 2050, the first generation of parents who were affected by the one-child policy will be in their 60s and 70s; these cohorts will be significantly larger in number than those just behind them—including their children. In a culture that highly values traditions of respect, care, and honor from children to parents and grandparents, this age structure will be culturally and socially challenging.

Another notable challenge to the traditional systems of kin support of older adults is the migration of young and middle-aged Chinese citizens from rural areas to cities, where economic prospects are better. The situation has become so bad for millions of the rural older population that they are being called "the left behind." For the upcoming generations of older people, the combination of very small family size and migration patterns will challenge the traditional system of norms and expectations about the responsibilities of children to provide care for older kin. "The huge transient labor force renders a severe blow to the traditional Chinese type of family support for the elderly," as do unresolved issues regarding how one-child families should support parents (Du & Yang, 2009, p. 146). One married couple, for example, both employed and living in a city many miles from their family homes, would share the responsibility for caring for as many as four aging parents—with no siblings to share that obligation.

Aging and changes to family structure pose another challenge to China because of its limited infrastructure for programs and services to older people. Although the traditional family system for care is vulnerable to demographic changes, there is a shortage of facilities and trained professionals ready to step in to provide formal care. For example, China is only now developing nonfamily alternatives for long-term care needs of older adults. It has been suggested that this lack of a formal care system essentially "pushes the burden of long-term care back to the family" (Du & Yang, 2009, p. 154). Because of the limitations in the availability of family caregivers and the growth of the older population, scholars who study aging in China are calling for the development of a formal long-term care system supported by public funding and overseen via government regulation (Du & Yang, 2009; Flaherty et al., 2007). Changes in social structures and public policies have not kept pace with the rapid transformation of China's age structure. Retirement is also an emerging institution in China, with few norms or opportunities for meaningful use of time after leaving the work role. There is mandatory retirement for men at age 60 and for women at age 55. With increasing longevity, Chinese retirees face decades of life without work and, at the moment, without meaningful alternatives to work. In addition, the Chinese pension system is inadequate to provide income security for the majority of its retirees (Population Reference Bureau, 2010b). The public pension system is funded in the same way as the U.S. Social Security system (pay as you go). That is, current tax receipts are used to pay current benefits; no money is saved, in the traditional sense, to pay workers' benefits when they retire. So, in the very near future, China will face the same fiscal challenge as the United States—too many retirees and too few workers. Shifting age structures require some change to the pension-financing mechanism. Just as in the United States, China faces hard choices—either an increase in taxes, a decrease in benefits, an exception to the strict pay-as-you-go model to allow accumulation of funds today (although the number of people paying into the system is still relatively high) to be used in the future (when the number of workers paying in will be much lower and beneficiaries will be numerous), or some combination of these strategies. The United States actually has pursued a combination of all three strategies over the past two decades, raising taxes substantially and curbing benefits slightly to create a trust fund that now holds a significant surplus. It now appears, however, that due to life-expectancy extension and economic stagnation, the surplus will be depleted much sooner than planned. So a fiscally sound and politically viable new plan must be developed.

China's health care system also will be moving away from a focus on maternal/child health and infectious diseases and toward inclusion of care for chronic conditions and health care needs of an older population. This change requires retraining health professionals to understand geriatric medicine and the special challenges of aging, just as Europe, Japan, and the United States are struggling to do. The challenge is great, but the health care system clearly needs to adapt in many ways. The medical reality created by an aging Chinese society is stark: "By 2030, older adults will account for two thirds of the total disease burden in China" (Population Reference Bureau, 2010b, p. 4).

Germany: Inverted Pyramid

Germany's population pyramids for 2010 and 2050 show the classic pattern for developed nations with little population growth. Evidence of a baby boom in the 1950s and 1960s is seen in the large numbers of people between the ages of 40 and 55 in 2010; by 2050, that bulge will have moved upward in the pyramid, and its social and economic weight will rest on smaller numbers of young people. Germany has had sustained low fertility (about 1.4 births per woman) for several decades and has enjoyed high life expectancy for many decades. The projected result of these trends is an inverted population pyramid, as illustrated in Figure 1.2.

One of the obvious results of such an age structure is a shrinking labor force. Labor force declines are a hallmark of countries that are old. Decreasing size of the working-age population has implications for the sustainability of pension programs and for the ability of a country to fill jobs to keep the economy vibrant. Aged dependency ratios (an idea explored further in Chapter 4) compare the size of the working-age population to the older population; this measure is called a dependency ratio because of the assumption that the working-age population will, to some degree and in some way, have to support the older population (usually through taxes to pay for programs and public pensions for older people). Germany, Japan, and Italy have the most challenging aged dependency ratios in the world— three working-age people for every one person age 65 and older (Population Reference Bureau, 2010a). The viability of Germany's well-established and generous pension program is already threatened by the inverted pyramid. At present, Germany spends about 13% of its gross domestic product on the pension system, one of the highest percentages in the world (Kinsella & He, 2009). The proposed solutions to the public pension problem in Germany include increasing the tax rate or the age at which a person is eligible to receive the pension and expanding immigration from other countries to admit more workers. The political viability and economic wisdom of any of these solutions is under heated debate in Germany (Haub, 2007), just as in other nations.

In addition to a long-standing public-pension program, Germany has a well-developed system of services and programs for older people, including

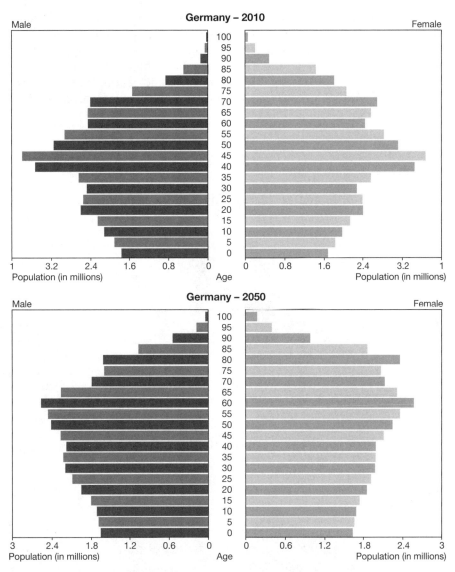

FIGURE 1.2 Population pyramids for Germany, 2010 and 2050.
Source: U.S. Bureau of the Census International Data Base (2013).

formal long-term services offered in institutions and in the community. Even so, the significant size of the older population poses challenges for the future. Germany's response to, and planning for, these challenges reflects basic cultural values, as illustrated in a recent national report on aging policies. These values include a shared responsibility and solidarity, generational equity, lifelong learning, and disease prevention (Kruse & Schmitt, 2009). In its focus on promoting healthy, active aging, and lifelong opportunities for learning and civic engagement, Germany is very similar to the United States. Developed nations in general have the luxury of such a focus as long as their economies permit sufficient funding, but may find them challenged when the population pyramids are inverted. In contrast to this picture, some developing nations are struggling with poverty and significant health challenges, even without a very large aging population. Kenya is an example of such a country.

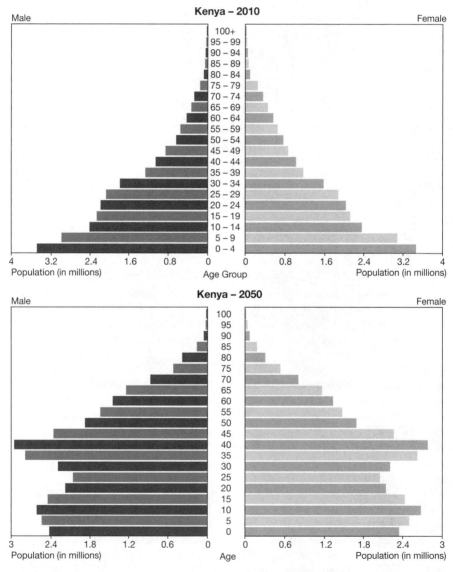

FIGURE 1.3 Population pyramids for Kenya, 2010 and 2050.

Kenya: Health Challenges

Kenya's population pyramid for 2010 is a good example of a young society, with a true pyramid shape. By 2050, however, that shape will change dramatically, becoming thicker in the middle and growing noticeably broader at the top—signs of the demographic transition. That altered age structure is illustrated in Figure 1.3. Between 2000 and 2050, the proportion of Kenya's population that is aged 65 and older will triple—from 2.8% to 8.6%. Although still low in comparison to other nations, Kenya's circumstances reflect those of a number of countries in the less-developed category.

Kenya's story is not simply one of economic development and aging, since other health-related trends are contributing to the challenges it faces. As Kenya anticipates its growing aging population over the next decades, older Kenyans today already face some pressing realities. The HIV/AIDS epidemic has "eroded hard-won progress in health and mortality, and has led to a decline in life expectancy from 59 years in the 1980s to 53 years in 2007" (Yin & Kent, 2008, p. 2). However, this added mortality is not affecting the older population as much as adults in their prime years of productivity. For many older people, the HIV/AIDS epidemic translates into loss of their adult children and the necessity to care for their orphaned grandchildren. The HIV/AIDS epidemic in Africa is broad-based, involving both women and men. This means that both marital partners may contract the disease and, without expensive (and sometimes unavailable) medications, both may die. Whereas the majority of older people in Kenya live with family, some are now living in **skipped-generation households,** with the middle generation missing and grandparents acting as surrogate parents. Of course, many countries (including the United States) face this problem, created by several factors including parental addiction, incarceration, and serious illnesses. In the United States in 2010, 7% of children lived in a household headed by a grandparent. For more than one half of these children (numbering 2.9 million), the grandparents were the primary care provider (Population Reference Bureau, 2012). Africa, however, has the highest proportion of older people living in such a situation (12.2%), which is most often related to HIV/AIDS mortality of the middle generation (United Nations Department of Economic and Social Affairs, 2005).

In addition to the vast implications of HIV/AIDS mortality, older persons in Kenya face problems with poverty, illiteracy, poor nutrition, limited housing options, lack of income security, and few social service programs (Mwangi, 2009). As in many nations across Africa, the Kenyan legal system has not specifically recognized the rights of the older population and does not provide them with equal access to health care, social services, and income security or much protection from age discrimination, especially in matters of inheritance and property rights. (HelpAge International, 2008)

Kenya recently adopted a national policy on aging and older persons that identified priority issues consistent with the already-listed problems.

The policy focuses on health, nutrition and food, income security, poverty reduction, and healthy family culture. Financial support for the most vulnerable older adults in the form of small retirement benefits was authorized in this 2008 legislation, one of the first steps in Kenya's development of government support for older people (Mwangi, 2009). Eligibility for Kenya's old-age pension is age 55; however, life expectancy at birth is just age 56. About one third of African countries that offer some old-age insurance benefit have life expectancies lower than the pensionable age (NIA/NIH/Department of State, 2007).

Although challenged significantly by a relatively low level of economic development, Kenya is currently seeking to amend its constitution to guarantee the rights of its older population to receive protection from discrimination, life with dignity and respect, and reasonable care and assistance from family and the government (Mwangi, 2009).

These three countries—all with old or aging populations—illustrate a wide range of demographic, cultural, and social characteristics. It is instructive to see how each of these nations is planning for, and responding to, its aging population. Clearly, many cultural, economic, demographic, and political forces are at work shaping the ways these—and all—countries view old age and deal with their older people. To help understand the development of public policies and programs in particular, the concept of the welfare state is a useful tool to assist in analyzing the similarities and differences among nations. The welfare state is applicable to issues of work, retirement, economic security, family relationships, caregiving, and long-term care. Because it is referred to throughout this text, basic ideas are introduced here.

AGING AND THE WELFARE STATE

In the United States, the term *welfare* usually connotes the safety-net programs for citizens who, for a variety of reasons, require public support for basic necessities such as shelter, food, and health care. However, the **welfare state** is much broader than just a system of safety-net programs. The concept is most often thought of as the collection of social-assistance policies and programs provided by a nation–state that takes the place of support traditionally provided by the family or by religious institutions. Such policies often include public old-age pensions, health care programs, family allowances, sickness and maternity/birth benefits, and unemployment compensation. Policies and programs that focus specifically on the needs of the older population comprise an **old-age welfare state,** which is described in detail in Chapter 3. Whereas most industrialized nations have fairly well-developed welfare states, they vary considerably in how policies are applied. Many developing nations, like Kenya, are at the early stages of forming national policies for aging populations.

Development of the Welfare State

A few ideas are important, as more is learned about how, when, and why old-age welfare states emerge and what they look like in different parts of the world. In general, changes related to economic development, industrialization, and urbanization produce social conditions that no longer mesh with traditional sources of social and economic support: the family and religious institutions. Because these traditional social institutions have become less able to address the majority of needs for social and economic support, many countries have looked to the nation–state for help with the challenges of assisting dependent persons and groups.

One of the most important social changes influencing the development of a welfare state is industrialization, which requires large concentrations of workers for factories and thus often induces a substantial migration from rural farmland to urban areas. This migration introduces a new way of life: Individuals are separated from the land and frequently from their extended families. Whereas rural farmers often have kin for neighbors, ensuring others nearby who can provide social and economic assistance when necessary, urban dwellers typically find themselves among strangers, separated from their traditional social-support networks. This new social living condition requires some mechanism to replace that lost family support, and this mechanism becomes the welfare state. This process that unfolded for Western Europe and the United States in the late 19th and early 20th centuries is similar to what is happening in the developing nations of the world today. As described in the case of China, the migration of young people to cities in search of better jobs, and the resulting isolation of older people in rural areas, is one factor undermining the traditional system of family care.

Pensions programs, health insurance, unemployment benefits, coverage for long-term care, and compensation for workplace injuries are all specific aspects of the welfare state that relate to the needs of older adults in many countries. In light of global aging, the current status and future development of welfare-state programs and policies are topics of great interest to researchers, advocates, and decision makers working in the realm of public policy and aging. The balance of family, community, and government involvement in supporting an aging population underlies much of the explorations in the remainder of this volume. From the earlier discussion of the different situations in China, Kenya, and Germany, it should be clear that welfare-state programs develop as part of a whole fabric of social change, including both shifting cultural values and economic development. A recent report advises caution when making international comparisons of social security systems, noting that all such systems "are embedded in economic and demographic realities and in cultural expectations about who cares for the elderly" (Population Reference Bureau, 2009, p. 3). No single model of the welfare state, or even for a particular aspect of the system, would work well or be culturally appropriate across the diverse set of aging nations in the world.

Source: Lawrence Downes.

If one model were to fit every country, it would be reasonable to expect a **welfare state convergence,** in which the welfare-state programs in all nations would mirror each other as all countries modernize and their economies become more developed. This assumption is problematic for many reasons, including lack of evidence for such convergence and the underlying Western-dominated perspective. Ample evidence for questioning it is provided by one study of the convergence hypothesis (Montanari, 2001). Among 18 countries with advanced economies (including Germany, Italy, Japan, the Netherlands, and Australia), the United States provided one example of a notable exception toward convergence: It lacked a national health policy. Another example of the lack of uniform welfare-state models can be seen in Montanari's description of significant variations among the 18 countries in the proportion of the population that is covered by social insurance programs. Whereas recent health care legislation in the United States may (or may not) negate that exception, there is every reason to question the path and destination of old-age welfare state evolution, especially in the developing world. Just as the demographic transition is unfolding differently for those countries, the welfare state, too, will emerge in distinctive, culturally shaped patterns.

The Welfare State and Role of the Family

In considering the evolution of the welfare state in developing nations, the role of the family deserves particular attention. The definition of the welfare state at the beginning of this section suggests that such a system emerges when societies develop economically and their social structures modernize. The assumption within that description is that government-sponsored programs and policies are necessary to supplant, or at least complement, some of the roles that had been traditionally filled by families in earlier times. Although this general pattern—in which a welfare state accompanies economic growth—has been well documented for currently developed nations, it is dangerous to make dogmatic predictions about what will happen in today's developing nations. As noted earlier, such changes are the result of social change, economic development, *and* cultural values. It cannot be easily predicted that a welfare state will replace the role of the family in the lives of older adults in all currently developing regions, as occurred in already-developed nations.

Cultural values play an extremely important role. The United States places great value on independence in family relationships across the life cycle, which translates into patterns such as "intimacy at a distance" and older adults not wanting to "be a burden" on children. This value is reflected in contemporary living arrangements. As in other developed nations, in the United States the most common living arrangement for older people is alone or with a spouse. In contrast, co-residence of multiple generations is the most common living situation for older people in most developing nations, where norms of family caretaking are strong (Kinsella & He, 2009).

China's strong tradition of filial piety is a clear example of such family norms. According to Charlotte Ikels (1993), China's traditional culture of the early 20th century (pre-Communism) was based on Confucianism, "an ethic of familism that not only served as the standard to guide proper family organization for many centuries but was also codified into law" (p. 124). This system emphasized vertical family ties—those between the generations—as more important than horizontal ties, such as those between spouses, which were viewed primarily as a means by which to continue the lineage (or vertical line) through offspring. It seems unlikely that this deeply rooted value system could be completely replaced by an old-age welfare state in China anytime soon, even in the face of formidable demographic pressures. Can China somehow integrate these values into its need to adapt to a rapidly aging population, widespread migration, and the high levels of pressure on younger generations with large numbers of older parents, for whom a cultural sense of responsibility continues?

If China follows the pattern of other modernizing and industrializing states, it might happen. Support for such a scenario can be found in the long-recognized phenomenon of "value stretch," first described by Hyman Rodman (1963), who was seeking to explain how the African American community could continue to profess a preference and value for childbirth only within marriage and also tolerate and even embrace increasing numbers of unwed mothers. Rodman argued that members of the Black community had "stretched" their values to accommodate and redefine the meaning of "family." Similarly, it can be imagined that pressures of a modern economy might simply force the Chinese to redefine filial piety by changing how an adult child might take care of older parents. A model of co-resident, direct care might well evolve into one of support from a distance, where the employed child pays for direct care, both through taxes to support a welfare-state solution and, where necessary, by hiring local caregivers to provide direct services to the parents. In this way, the employed child would be able to fulfill the demands of the modern industrial state—and individual social ambitions—although the value and responsibility of providing for the parent in old age is preserved through modern, nontraditional means.

Over the next several years, research on the evolution of China's welfare state will surely provide insights into how rapidly aging countries manage to balance public programs, traditional values, shifting family patterns, and the needs of an unprecedented number of older people.

In a study of old-age homes in India—another developing nation that strongly endorses co-residence and family caregiving—Liebig (2003)

Source: Tomoko Brown.

surveyed managers, supervisors, and board members of nearly 50 old-age homes and day-care centers for older adults. Responses to questions about the proper role of old-age homes reveal several diverse perspectives: (a) government involvement in meeting such needs for older people will erode the family responsibility; (b) such care options should be seen as a last resort for older populations who have no family support; and (c) old-age housing is necessary because older persons sometimes fall through the safety net of family care (Liebig, 2003). This range of responses nicely captures the tension between a desire to preserve traditional, family-based systems of care and the pressure to recognize that those systems may be increasingly less viable due to changes in family structure and growing numbers of older people who need assistance. This tension between traditional values and modernization embodies the transition to some type of welfare state.

Public pensions, government-sponsored old-age homes, and other aspects of the welfare state will continue to emerge in some form in developing nations; both the growing size of the older population and changing family structures in many of these countries seem to demand some government response. However, cultural values will play a crucial role in the development of public policies in these nations. Families provide the vast majority of long-term care in many nations throughout the world (just as in the United States) and are quite likely to do so in the future as well. The balance of traditional values against changes in economic structure, availability of kin, and population aging in vastly different cultures is not likely to produce the same type of government response or welfare state convergence.

INTERNATIONAL INITIATIVES ON AGING

In recognition of the many complex and momentous issues, opportunities, and challenges raised by global aging, the United Nations convened the First World Assembly on Ageing in Vienna in 1982. This congress, attended by representatives from countries around the world, resulted in the first international document intended to guide research, planning, and policies related to aging: the Vienna International Plan of Action on Ageing. The plan sought to strengthen government and community commitments and capacities to address the needs of older people, their ability for continued growth and development, and their right to such opportunities. More than 60 recommendations were included in the plan, covering issues related to health and nutrition, income security, employment, and housing. The Vienna conference action plan generated a series of other international initiatives, including the International Year of Older Persons in 1999. In 2002, a Second World Assembly on Ageing convened in Madrid, with participation from 156 countries, to review progress and challenges that had occurred since the 1982 world assembly and to refine the original plan of action. One of the most important features of the Second World Assembly on Ageing was the focus on, and involvement of, developing nations. At the time of the first world assembly,

Source: U.S. Bureau of the Census.

"many developing countries did not consider the issue of ageing to be a pressing concern" (Huber, 2005, p. 3). In contrast, the second world meeting emphasized the rapid aging occurring in less developed nations and the challenge for those nations to simultaneously address issues of poverty as well as aging. The implementation plan resulting from the second assembly—the Madrid International Plan of Action on Ageing (MIPAA)—addresses concerns and contributions of older people around the world. MIPAA emphasizes full participation of older people in every society, as did the first action plan. However, the MIPAA placed this goal in the context of overall economic development goals; the plan notes that societal participation of older people rests on the assurance that basic necessities of an adequate income and access to health care are provided. In addition, nations were called upon to provide opportunities for fulfillment, well-being, and empowerment of older people to participate in all aspects of society. Summing up the ideology that is the foundation of the international plan of action, the Madrid world assembly offered that: "A longer life provides humans with an opportunity to examine their lives in retrospect, to correct some of their mistakes, to get closer to the truth, and to achieve a different understanding of the sense and value of actions. This may well be the most important contribution of older people to the human community" (United Nations, 2003, p. 1).

Progress toward the specific goals of these international action plans is monitored via periodic reports to the secretary-general of the United Nations. The 2010 follow-up report provides a snapshot of a wide range of efforts by individual nations to move toward these goals. Initiatives undertaken in support of the MIPAA include: a program in Mexico providing tax incentives to employers who hire older workers; a government-sponsored program in Thailand in which volunteers are paid a small stipend to take older people to health clinics and make sure they receive the proper medication at home; a long-term care insurance policy adopted into law in the Republic of Korea; and a meals program for older people in Ecuador. Kenya's new constitutional provision for the protection of the rights of older people (mentioned earlier) was another highlight of the 2010 follow-up on the Second World Assembly on Ageing (United Nations General Assembly, 2010).

THE STUDY OF GLOBAL AGING

Thus far in the overview of this book, the dramatic demographic emergence of an aging world has been acknowledged; case studies showing how the experiences of aging unfold differently across nations have been considered; and the concept of the welfare state in aging societies has been explored. These three topics give a small glimpse into the exploding literature on global aging. Still, none of this explains clearly why an aging world population is important to everyone and, therefore, why we should learn about it.

As Whittington and Kunkel (2013a) have argued elsewhere, studying global aging is important to everyone for three main reasons.

1. To Get Educated

Aging is a new, powerful social force—never seen before in human history—that already is changing the way Western societies are structured and how their citizens will live out their lives. For the first time in history, large numbers of the human species are living beyond their working years and confronting the personal and family issue of what to do with their time. Retirement is a concept that was unknown to most of our ancestors living during the first 70 centuries that civilized societies have been on earth; now it must be designed and adapted to by more and more people. Part of being an educated person is having knowledge about this revolution in longevity.

2. Self-Interest

The world is globalizing, becoming, in the words of Marshall McLuhan (1962), a "global village." The twin revolutions in technology and communication that allow people in one part of the world to know what is happening in all other parts—and to go there quickly, as tourists or as permanent migrants—mean that we are not only connected but *collected* with each other in important ways. If the economic and political well-being of the United States (or any other nation) is heavily dependent on the work and consumer behavior of 1.4 billion Chinese, or the technical knowledge of 1.1 billion Indians, or the religious tolerance of 237 million Indonesians, or even the political aspirations of 75 million Iranians—attention must be paid to what is going on in their countries. In the 2012 campaign for the Republican nomination for U.S. president, one of the candidates, Herman Cain, famously denied that it was of any importance that he should know the name of the president of Uzbekistan (he didn't). But Uzbekistan is an important part of the connected world, and what happens among its 29 million residents may not remain isolated there. It can be quickly communicated, transmitted, or migrated to a neighborhood near you.

As aging transforms developing nations demographically and socially, it will create profound economic and developmental changes in these emerging world powers, along with exciting opportunities for the realization of human potential. Whatever is happening to the smallest, least-visible countries will affect the developed world in ways we can hardly imagine today. It is in the interest of all people that such far-reaching and fundamental changes be understood sooner rather than later.

3. The Smart Move

Each of us has a perspective on life and the world that is limited and shaped by our experience. Such limited perspectives can have unpleasant (even destructive) consequences when the nature, motives, and intents of others are misinterpreted by some—leading to prejudice, discrimination, racism, war, and even genocide. It is an article of faith of most educated people that expanding one's experience and broadening one's perspective can reduce such misunderstanding and negative behavior. Learning about global aging will not, by itself, lead to world peace. However, it could contribute to a fuller, more accurate picture of how other people live, raise their families, care for their parents, and live out their lives. If that knowledge impresses us with the realization that aging is a universal experience, that all families, communities, and societies—no matter how different they may seem from our own—struggle as we do to cope with its results, and that many older people find it a productive, fulfilling time of life, we may begin to perceive our commonalities as greater than our differences. That would be the beginning of wisdom at least.

Final thoughts: As the experience of aging in different countries or comparing countries on important dimensions is examined, a word of caution is required against a tourist approach to the study of global aging. Careful investigation of global aging requires thinking beyond an interest in the **exotic other.** This concept derives from a rich tradition in anthropological research that seeks to understand other cultures from a wholly authentic point of view, not reducing people who live in other societies to cultural objects. It can be argued that a fascination with the exotic other is preferable to disdain for anyone different from us; however, a deeper understanding of the meanings and experiences of aging around the world requires commitment to seeing realities of aging deeply woven into an entire fabric of history, culture, and social structures from the point of view of those within that culture. What makes aging in another culture interesting and important is not that it is merely different from our own experiences, but that there are both common-alities and unique patterns to uncover—and appreciate.

SUMMARY

The demographic reality of global aging is undeniable; clearly, the aging of a society is accompanied by, and is a catalyst for, enormous social reform. These changes are the driving force of a set of "trends that represent a trans-formation of the world" (NIA/NIH/Department of State, 2007). In addition to the revised patterns of fertility and mortality, global aging is associated with changing family structures, adjustments in work and retirement pat-terns, shifting burdens of disease away from infectious to chronic illness, new economic challenges, and the development of social welfare systems. Global trends in longevity and population aging are heralded as a success story, but the challenges posed are also widely acknowledged (Kinsella & Phillips, 2005). How these issues play out in specific countries or major regions of the world will vary, depending upon a host of factors including demographics, economics, and cultural values.

Each region and each nation face both the challenge and the promise of aging societies. There has never been a clearer mandate for gerontology education and research. In response to this mandate, gerontology programs are beginning to appear in countries worldwide. In some places, such as the United States, Germany, and the United Kingdom, gerontology is a well-developed discipline, with credentials offered at several levels of higher edu-cation. In other places such as China, Israel, and Mexico, gerontology is a specialty within other professional programs such as medicine, nursing, and social work (Carmel & Lowenstein, 2007; Kunkel, 2008; Pichardo, 2009). In still other countries such as Kenya, gerontology education is offered primarily as training for direct-care workers. In recognition of the need for data about aging populations, many national and cross-national efforts are underway. Examples of such research initiatives include a survey of aging, health, and well-being conducted in Argentina, Mexico, Barbados, Uruguay, Chile, and Brazil; a lon-gitudinal study of aging in India; the Survey of Health, Ageing, and Retire-ment in Europe (SHARE); a massive study of the oldest old in China; and the World Health Organization (WHO) longitudinal study of global aging and adult health. These are but a few illustrations of the educational and research efforts underway to meet the challenge and the promise of global aging.

This volume is not simply a compendium of facts about aging around the world, although facts abound in its pages. Instead, it provides a framework for understanding the broad array of issues, challenges, and opportunities associated with global aging. Our plan and our hope for this book is that you will find your own challenges; that you will begin to feel the same excitement as students in Malaysia, in Brazil, in Kenya, and in Sweden are feeling right now as they learn about aging in their own countries; and that you will catch a sense of the promise of longer life spans for all people, everywhere.

DISCUSSION QUESTIONS

1. Why is it important to understand global aging?
2. Do you live in a developed or developing country? How can you tell?
3. What are the worst and best things about living where you do?
4. What is so important about population aging?
5. How are Germany, China, and Kenya being affected by the aging of their populations? What are they doing about it?
6. Why is it said that poor nations may never get rich?
7. Which nation do you think is likely to have the best environment for its older citizens 50 years from now?
8. How does the family benefit from the welfare state?
9. Do you think the welfare state was a wise invention, or should nations have developed different solutions to their changing economies and work structures? In what way?
10. Do you think students in your school should study global aging? Why or why not?

KEY WORDS

Exotic other
Least developed countries
Left-behind generation
Less developed countries
More developed countries
Old-age welfare state
One-child policy
Population pyramid
Skipped-generation household
Welfare state
Welfare state convergence

Gender, Aging, and Power in Rural Bangladesh: Getting Older as the Priming of Women

Fauzia E. Ahmed

> *I am running (for public office) because I see the injustice. And I saw that things could get even worse. We (women) have been repeatedly pushed and shoved (by society), let us see what happens if we push back just once.*
>
> Alveera, Muslim woman

Illiterate and low-income, Alveera is a middle-aged Muslim woman in rural Bangladesh who is running for public office in a local-level election. Like many older women I interviewed during my ethnographic study of gender power and aging in a sharecropper village community, she is considered a leader and exercises considerable power. In a gerontocratic culture, aging for women is also priming for power. It is a process of getting ready to accept the mantle of leadership (to be a role model) and to act as a spokeswoman for other women in the community. Alveera looks forward to the future with determination, courage, and hope; opportunities, hitherto denied, are just beginning to open up for her.

In most Western societies, aging—especially for women—is seen as a general decline. Growing older is synonymous with the shrinking of opportunities. Older women are seen as less employable, less attractive, and less deserving of respect. This is even truer if they are less educated and have lower income. Furthermore, women who are running for public office need to look as young as they possibly can.

Why are things different in Bangladesh? I explore the various dimensions of the answers to this question through an analysis of the nexus of gender, aging, and power in the village (meso) and the national (macro) contexts (see Ahmed, 2006).

AGING IN THE VILLAGE: TRADITIONAL PATHWAYS TO POWER

Rural society in Bangladesh is gerontocratic: It is organized around a hierarchy based on age. Villages comprise *paras* (neighborhoods) and each *para* consists of several households (*baris*). A *bari* constitutes several dwellings built around a courtyard. Although one extended family occupies a *bari*, the entire neighborhood is considered kin. When a bride first enters the *bari* as a daughter-in-law, she occupies the lowest rung on the social ladder. Her mobility is restricted by *purdah* (a custom that defines relationships between men and women through segregated boundaries.) Her conduct is regulated and prescribed by the *shalish*, an indigenous village court system consisting of a jury of all men. Young and inexperienced in the ways of her *shoshur bari* (in-laws' household), she knows that she must please everyone in the entire neighborhood, especially her mother-in-law. She also knows that as she ages, she will climb the ladder to one day gain a position of authority, just like her mother-in-law.

Although *purdah* is oppressive to women in many ways, restricting access to education and jobs, opportunities for gaining authority exist even in this traditional system. From the time she enters her in-laws' household, the young bride is primed for leadership through two pathways, both of which increase as she ages. First, she can look forward to greater geographic mobility. *Purdah* restrictions decrease with age. This resulting physical freedom is linked to increased kin ties, considered a tangible source of social capital in rural society. As a woman ages, her network expands to go beyond the neighborhood. Although they originally entered as outsiders, older women become insiders with increased kin ties: They not only arrange marriages for their own children, but they arrange marriages for other young people in the village.

Second, in gerontocratic culture, increased equity in gender relations is an inevitable result of growing older. If, as the young daughter-in-law, Alveera kept quiet when addressed by male relatives, as a middle-aged woman, there are now a number of younger men, including her son(s) and nephews, who occupy a lower status. Aging also means that older women are addressed with an honorific that specifically signifies the status that can only come with age. When she speaks, younger men must listen respectfully, even if they do not agree with her. If, as the young bride, she was compelled to be subservient to older people, as an older person herself, she can now expect subservience and *seva* (service) from those who are younger. In return, she is in the privileged position of conferring her blessings on the next generation.

Some older women like Alveera are also midwives; bringing children into the world is viewed as holy in village society. This status that emanates from her is also conferred on her husband. Such men are often willing to take on household responsibilities—a switch in gender roles because they know that their wives are compelled to leave the household at short notice and without any definite indication of when they will return. Linked to the greater physical mobility allowed for midwives is the increase in kin ties. As they deliver babies, women create a permanent relationship with the infant and its parents. A younger woman who serves as an apprentice can look forward to the day when, as she grows older, she can also "do work that gains Allah's blessings."

In addition to being a midwife, Alveera also runs her own grocery store. She earns income through her entrepreneurial activities, has savings in the bank, and serves as the treasurer in the women's collective, where she has been a member for the past 10 years. She argues with male relatives in her village about gender wage equity and the need for women to run for public office—something that no woman, of any age, would have been able to do in the past. This transformation has taken place because of structural changes in the national (macro) arena (United Nations Development Programme, 2005).

THE NATIONAL CONTEXT: MODERN ROUTES TO POWER

Today, 40 years after its birth, Bangladesh is a two-party democracy where both the head of state and the opposition leader are middle-aged women. Improvements in the status of women in the country as a whole have changed this nexus of age, gender, and power. The fertility rate has decreased from 6.1 to 3 (Jahan & Germain, 2004); girls' enrollment in primary school has increased so that for every 100 boys there are 104 girls (U.N. Development Programme, 2005); and women's entrepreneurial activities have increased their mobility and their household income (Pitt, Cartwright, & Khandker, 2006). Women can now become microcredit borrowers with no collateral. With loans as small as $40, they can increase their entrepreneurial skills and improve household welfare. Defying oppressive notions of *purdah*, women now leave the *bari* for entrepreneurial activities, work in the fields alongside men, and run for public office. Non-governmental organizations (NGOs), a characteristic of a vibrant civil society, have worked in conjunction with the government to achieve these goals.

These dramatic improvements underscore an even more dramatic reality: a tenacious and visionary women's movement that has effectively forged alliances with all sectors of civil society. Few know that older women like Alveera constitute its popular leadership base. The success of the family planning program is a result of the continuing discourse that older women led all over Bangladesh about Islamic principles and reproductive health. The reach of the movement is best understood by the effervescence of the *adda* (discussion) of such older village women; their vitality continues to change a masculine-dominated society on a daily basis. Leaders of a widespread movement for social change, their *adda* goes beyond reproductive health to gender wage equality; more profoundly, village women now want to define Allah in their own terms.

How does Alveera express her authority when she argues with older village men? The shape and form of this new women's leadership combine oral traditions of village culture with modern perspectives. These women challenge patriarchal beliefs and make men understand (*boojhano*) through sheer eloquence and wit. In fact, *boojhano* was repeatedly mentioned by men as an important mechanism in how they reframed masculinity and became more aware of gender injustice. Villagers respect and see these qualities as evidence of forensic ability and leadership. Discussion or *adda* is not only a traditional way of resolving dispute; it is a forum for reflection. Villagers learn through a dialogue in a town-meeting format that is rich in metaphor.

The level of analysis that these women leaders use, however, is entirely modern. It is a systematic analysis of village patriarchy, or the masculine-dominated system, that leads them to challenge patriarchal Islam by reframing religion. In particular, these older women reframe traditional notions of sin. They refer to the Islam preached by the mosque establishment as "a long list of don'ts." Such women use their gerontocratic authority to castigate a husband who refuses to allow his wife to have property in her own name as "having sin in his heart." In fact, men who commit such infractions, along with those who are violent, can be tried in a reformed *shalish* that now includes women jurors—yet another innovation of a traditional system.

To summarize, modern transformations at the national level have built on traditional village mechanisms to give older women power, thereby priming poor women, at the lowest rung of society, for leadership. Growing older still has its problems: After years of hard labor, Alveera complains of back problems, and the fees of the nearest doctor who lives in the city are too high for her. Notwithstanding, fundamental improvements at the national level, combined with the traditional respect for age, have given poor women opportunities for leadership that they could not even have imagined 40 years ago. It is not surprising that, happy and proud to be considered old, Alveera feels she is in the prime of her life.

CHAPTER 2

The Study of Global Aging

Chapter 1 gave some sense of the exploding interest in, and literature on, global aging. To sort through the growing number of reports and research articles on this topic, and to start thinking about what it really means to investigate aging around the world, it helps to consider that the study of global aging actually encompasses at least three different categories of investigation.

TYPES OF INVESTIGATION

First, there are broad questions about the aging of the globe as a whole. The focus for this type of **descriptive global patterns** research is macro-level, aggregated depictions of major demographic, economic, and social trends in many countries. Chapter 4 (on the demography of global aging) takes this general approach, offering illustrations of demographic conditions and trends in different countries and regions. Two very good reports that exemplify this kind of research on global aging are *Why Population Aging Matters* (NIA/NIH/U.S. Department of State, 2007), and *An Aging World: 2008* (Kinsella & He, 2009). Both publications describe important trends related to population aging, such as increasing life expectancy, increasing burden of chronic rather than infectious diseases, and living arrangements among older people in a wide range of countries.

This type of research relies on international data sets, or a compilation of national data sets, that include information on demographics, health, economic development, and characteristics of the population in a given country, such as labor-force participation, income, and educational levels. The Luxembourg Income Study is a good example of an international comparative data set; this resource provides standardized income, poverty, and inequality data from 30 countries, enabling researchers to easily draw comparisons. Some countries have participated for 30 years or more, also permitting comparisons over time for developing or developed nations (Luxembourg Income Study, n.d.). In subsequent chapters, there are references to other international data sets in the discussion of work and retirement status of older people (Chapter 8); common health problems of older people in different countries (Chapter 6); family caregiving and living arrangements (Chapter 9); and long-term care systems (Chapter 7).

A second area within the study of global aging focuses on questions about aging *within* a country. This type of scholarship contributes to the literature on global aging by illuminating the policies, social structures, cultural practices, and experiences of older people in a particular location. Examples of **single-nation global aging research** include a study of depression among older women in South Korea who live with adult children (Do & Malhotra, 2012); an analysis of the productivity of older women and men in rural Bangladesh (Cameron, Kabir, Khanam, Wahlin, & Streatfield, 2010); and an investigation of the prevalence and portrayal of older adults in prime-time television in Taiwan (Lien, Zhang, & Hummert, 2009). This type of inquiry is unique in its focus on what aging is like for people within one particular place. It is different from the first category because it does not compare people in different countries or regions of the world and because it focuses on individuals rather than countries as the entity of interest (unit of analysis). These in-depth explorations of aging within a culture or within a nation are growing in number, as are the outlets for such publications, pointing to the increasing prominence of this component of global aging research. Research that focuses on aging within a particular culture or society relies on the same range of methods used by social scientists in general. The specific within-nation examples mentioned here used interviews and surveys and analyses of **secondary data** (data already collected for other purposes). These articles follow the same rules of conceptualization, measurement, sampling, and analysis already familiar to those who have learned about social science research methods. These methods take on a new dimension when **cross-national comparative global aging research**, the third type of global aging research, is considered.

Comparative global aging studies in some ways combine characteristics of the first two categories; this type of research looks at similarities and differences across two or more countries (as is true for the category classified, for our purposes, as descriptive global patterns), but looks in depth at a particular topic related to aging such as pension plans, quality of life, or family caregiving (as does the within-country research already described). Comparative global aging research seeks to understand the nature of differences and degree of similarity in the experiences of aging across locations. Four recent issues of the Journal of Cross-Cultural Gerontology (vol. 24, 3/4; vol. 25, 1/2) included some good examples of comparative studies of aging: satisfaction with intergenerational communication in Bulgaria and the United States; hospice development in Japan, South Korea, and Taiwan; meaning and measurement of social support across four ethnic groups; and comparison of self-perceptions of aging in France and Morocco. All these studies include the two important features of comparative global aging research: they have looked in depth and across countries at topics related to the experiences of aging. Comparative research presents extraordinary opportunities to get at the heart of what is universal and what is unique in our "ageways." These opportunities

Source: U.S. Bureau of the Census.

are accompanied by some challenges in attempting to sort out the complex interactions of policies, cultures, economic development, and other unique aspects of nations being compared.

CROSS-NATIONAL COMPARATIVE RESEARCH

All good research requires a clear statement of the problem, an explicitly stated research question with strong conceptual grounding, and rigorous methods. The same is true of cross-national comparative research, but the design of these studies contains added features. To understand the distinctive goals, challenges, and value of comparative research, consider why it might be of interest to compare the life satisfaction of older people in Bangladesh to that of older adults in the United States. Are older adults in these two countries the same? If not, how do they differ? If life satisfaction is different for older people in these two places, why is this the case?

That is the essence of comparative research on aging: to discover patterns of similarity and difference in the experiences of aging across settings or circumstances. Writing specifically about comparisons of aging across cultures, Palmore succinctly states, "Cross-cultural research is essential for two purposes: separating universal processes of aging from culture-specific processes, and understanding how cultural factors influence aging" (1983, p. 46). Thus, comparative research is appropriate for answering questions such as: Is aging the same in different countries? Does any particular experience of growing older hold true across those settings? If not, what explains the differences? Answering any of these questions requires enough depth of understanding about the uniqueness of specific locations and a conviction that patterns in those unique locations do exist and can be identified.

The question about life satisfaction in the United States and Bangladesh points to an interesting challenge in research across different cultures. To know how people in these two countries are similar or different regarding their life satisfaction first requires finding out whether the concept of life satisfaction is shared by both cultural contexts, and if it can be measured in meaningful—and comparable—ways in both places. This unique facet of comparative research is one example of the ways in which good comparative research forces us to question our assumptions, confront our own cultural biases, and carefully consider the design and purpose of our study. These distinctive features of comparative research are more fully explained later in this chapter.

Scholars who specialize in studying the experiences of people in different places debate about whether there is greater value in first seeking an in-depth understanding of one place, or whether a better understanding of human experiences can be attained by beginning with comparisons across settings. To continue with the life-satisfaction example, a case-study approach would require deep exploration into the definitions, meanings, and components of life satisfaction in one country or the other. A comparative approach would lead a researcher to seek a measure of life satisfaction that could be used in both locations. As with most such debates, there is common ground in the middle. There is value—and disadvantage—in both perspectives. The former one-case approach focuses on the uniqueness of one culture and the experiences of people living in that location, giving depth and richness of understanding. The latter multicase perspective calls for a comparative approach, sacrificing an in-depth focus on uniqueness for the ability to observe, and measure, similarities and differences. The essay in this chapter, "An American in Havana," is a very good example of an in-depth look at one case. Frank Whittington discusses the historical, economic, and social conditions that help to explain the circumstances of older people in Cuba, providing a case-study perspective. Notice, however, that the essay concludes with observations about the ways in which aging in Cuba is the same as, and different from, aging in the United States. Whittington is applying a multicase comparative analysis in the second half of his essay, moving from a description of Cuba to a comparison between Cuba and the United States.

The Importance of Comparison: From Description to Explanation

In many ways, comparative research is the logical next step after an in-depth, one-case study of a single culture. Whereas a one-case study can describe the way things are and how the pieces of the puzzle seem to be connected, full explanation of similarities and differences requires comparisons. As a next step after a descriptive case study and toward explanation, the researcher might conduct (or look at results from) another case study and then organize the descriptive information from these two rich examinations of different places or cultures. From that categorization of descriptive elements, the investigator would develop a set of variables that might help to explain similarities and differences between the two settings. In this final step, the research is moving from descriptive questions about what things look like to relational questions about why things are the way they are; the latter type of research question "ask(s) how traits are related to other traits" (Ember & Ember, 2009, p. 37).

We can illustrate the path from a one-case description to categorization across cases to explanation with a hypothetical example about the social status of older people in society. Imagine studying a society where agriculture is the basis of the economy and life expectancy is low. Based on observations of daily life, conversations and reading about cultural traditions, and discussions with residents of this society, researchers can document the interactions, roles, and respect accorded older people in this one place. With careful analysis, this information could yield a rich understanding of the ways in which traditional cultural values and economic realities coincide with a reverence for age. Reasonable connections might be drawn among the facts that, in this fictional society, not many people live to be old, old age is believed to be a sign of favor from the gods, and older people hold valuable knowledge about planting cycles. It would make sense that older people have high status in this culture. However, we could not conclude that all societies with similar values and economies hold older people in high esteem, nor could it be inferred that those values and economies are the explanation for the status of older persons.

For a better understanding of the connection between economic development and social status of older people, it would be necessary to look at another, and then another, and then another case. The research design would require measurement of important aspects of culture that might be related logically to the position of older people and then analyses of the extent to which those connections hold true across different cultures. At this point, cross-national comparative research is being conducted.

The particular example of the link between economic development and status of older people is one of a much larger set of propositions put forth by **modernization theory**. This early theory in gerontology was rooted in cross-cultural foundations and cross-national comparisons. The authors (Cowgill & Holmes, 1972) argued that as societies "modernize," the shift from agricultural to industrial economies devalued the knowledge and skills held by older people; new jobs require new skills and tend to be concentrated in growing urban areas. As a result of their exclusion from the new economy, the migration of younger people to urban areas, and away from traditional living arrangements, the status of older people is hypothesized to decline. Modernization theory (highly simplified here) generated a great deal of literature and a great deal of controversy. Although it has received very little empirical support, it remains an important stimulus to the study of global aging and has generated significant comparative research over the past four decades.

Current social science literature is full of examples of research that compare two or more groups of people (e.g., age groups, income groups, people who participated in a program and those who did not), two or more countries, or two or more points in time. These studies seek to learn something about the similarities and differences among groups, locations, or time periods, and the causes of those patterns. The global aging literature is similarly replete with research on factors associated with similarities and differences in the experiences of aging. For example, in an earlier section describing single-nation global aging research, a study by Do and Malhotra (2012) was mentioned. Although these authors were interested in the experiences of aging within South Korea, the strength of their study came from making some comparisons across groups of older people within South Korean culture. The authors were interested in levels of depression among older South Korean widows who live with children. But they did not simply describe the level of depression among these women. They wanted to know whether depression is higher or lower, depending on living arrangements. And it was: Living with an adult child had a protective effect against depressive symptoms for the widowed women in this study. Because Korean culture places value on children caring for their aging parents, the widows living with an adult child were compared to those *not* living with an adult child. The participants in this study are presumed to share an important cultural value: that living with adult children is preferred. If such a study were done in the United States, the comparisons might be different, based on the cultural values or concerns held about aging. Perhaps widows living alone might be compared to those who live with relatives, assuming that the most important factor for depression is not whether the widow lives with children but whether or not she lives alone.

This example illustrates the value of comparative research within one culture, but one of the great promises in comparative studies of aging is looking across countries or cultures. Another example of current global aging research does just that. Nguyen and Cihlar (2013) explored the differences between older adults in Vietnam and Germany with respect to physical fitness and self-rated health. The authors were interested in sorting out how much decline in physical health is due to aging and how much might be due to differences in lifestyle. Citing possible cultural differences such as labor-force participation of older adults in the two countries, the authors wondered whether the longer working life of Vietnamese compared to older Germans would have a positive or negative effect on health. They found that older Vietnamese in their study maintained higher levels of physical fitness than did the older Germans. Whereas it is not possible from this one study to isolate exactly which factors might be responsible for these differences, the research makes a significant contribution to the global aging literature by identifying some variations across culture in the impact of aging on

Source: Dr. Sukhminder S. Bhangoo.

health. Interestingly, these authors also found that there was no difference in the self-rated health of the two groups, even though the performance measures suggested that the older Vietnamese were healthier (Nguyen & Cihlar, 2013). The value of, and need for more, comparative research seems clear.

The Challenge and the Promise of Comparative Research

Comparative studies accomplish two important objectives: (a) distinguishing between culturally specific and universal behaviors and experiences (Ember & Ember, 2009; McDonald, 2000), and (b) isolating the cultural or location-specific factors that explain differences. The underlying premise of comparative research is the possibility of universals. "If you want to say something about [aging] in general, there is no substitute for a worldwide cross-cultural study" (Ember & Ember, 2009, p. 20). Obviously, a worldwide cross-cultural study is not feasible, given the resources and time it would take. But even if the goal is comparison across two or three cultures or locations, some significant challenges must be kept in mind.

The search for similarities must allow for the possibility of differences and must consider why these differences might exist. Therein lies one of the most important assumptions of comparative research: Something about setting (geographic place, culture, or historical time) might make a difference. Ideally, research questions should be explicit about why variations might be found. By identifying the features of a culture or place that might reasonably be expected to produce different experiences, a stronger case for universality can be built if we find similarities; if we find differences, there can be some explanation for those variations. For example, the article discussed earlier by Nguyen and Cihlar (2013) offered some ideas about why a difference in physical health might be observed between older adults in Vietnam and those in Germany (sedentary lifestyle in Germany; longer working life in Vietnam). Too often, however, comparative research looks for similarities and then uses culture or location as a way to explain away observed differences (Chi, 2011). To avoid the use of culture or location as nothing more than the residual explanation for differences, it is much more desirable, and much more scientifically sound, to identify the particular aspect of culture or place that might make a difference. These features should, in fact, be treated as variables in a study.

In our earlier example of the relationship between age and life satisfaction in the United States and Bangladesh, the focus would be on the extent to which age does or does not affect life satisfaction and whether those effects are the same in these two countries. To answer these questions (what is the same and what is different), the researchers could not simply look at a sample of people in Bangladesh and a sample in the United States and compare the correlation between age and life satisfaction. That would tell only part of the story. Instead, they need to include other variables that might help to explain any differences between the two countries in their degree of life satisfaction–age correlation. If this study revealed that life satisfaction increases with age in both countries, there is no problem: Perhaps the pattern of improved life satisfaction in later life is universal (at least in these two countries). However, if there is a decrease in life satisfaction with age in Bangladesh but no decrease in the United States, we would want to know more. Had the research included some cultural or economic variables that might be important, there would be the possibility of accomplishing two objectives with this study: (a) illustrating the extent to which a change in life satisfaction universally occurs with age, and (b) isolating some of the reasons that this might be a culture- or place-specific experience rather than a universal experience.

But what are those variables, and are they features of a country, a culture, a group, or a sample? These questions illustrate some of the challenges inherent in comparative research.

Challenge #1: Unit of Analysis

In the Bangladesh/United States comparison, the first task for a careful comparative researcher would be an attempt to clarify the "unit" of study. Are countries, cultures, or different subcultures within a country being compared? The answer to this question immediately raises another: What are the boundaries of the units to be compared? For countries, recognized geographic boundaries are generally appropriate, but those boundaries are sometimes political and contested. Geographic boundaries may define a single cultural group, or they may include multiple cultural groups. For example, many readers of this book are accustomed to thinking about the United States as a geographically defined country. However, within this nation are numerous groups that are culturally distinct from each other despite sharing a national identity. There is abundant literature in gerontology that explores the differences in experiences of aging across racial and ethnic groups in the United States. Jackson (2002) draws linkages between the methodological

Source: Dr. Sukhminder S. Bhangoo.

and conceptual issues that underlie studies of racial and ethnic minorities in the United States to those that are important in cross-national research: considering how different groups "traverse the individual life course as they age" (p. 827), "removing cultural blinders . . . and focusing on what makes a difference and what does not" (p. 826).

So far, this chapter has referred often to country and sometimes to culture. This is one of the unique trials of comparative research—deciding, defending, and following through with the geographic or otherwise bounded aggregations intended for study. Hantrais (2009) offers a list of the units that might be the focus of comparative research in the social sciences and humanities: "societies, countries, cultures, systems, institutions, social structures, and change over time and space" (p. 2). Since each of these units could be a valuable focus for a comparative study of aging, it is essential to be clear (despite the fact that this chapter thus far has taken liberties with this rule).

Location

It is common to use location as the unit of analysis in comparative research, sometimes as a shorthand for culture. Studies of global aging often make comparisons across countries, especially in demographic research. Geographic units are relatively easy to define and draw boundaries around. Depending on the research question, geographic units of analysis may be most appropriate. Some social indicators, such as proportion aged, literacy levels, and health status are collected at national levels, making broad-scale comparisons possible.

Beyond the convenience and feasibility of national (or other geographic) comparisons, it is reasonable to think that geographic boundaries help to define, at least at a general level, shared values, norms, and behaviors. However, even if we decide that a geographic location is the unit of analysis for the study, this immediately raises another concern: What are the boundaries of the units to be compared? In addition to the mutability of political boundaries, border regions might be characterized by large populations of people from one country commuting to the other country or even living in the other country for economic, political, or security reasons.

The meaningfulness of geographic borders raises the question of whether there might be, in fact, an ultimate interest in the role of culture, rather than location. Even when location is a more convenient (and often appropriate) unit of analysis, it is worthwhile to consider the extent to which location and culture intersect and to clarify whether location is being used as a proxy for some aspect of shared cultural experiences.

Culture

Clarity about whether the unit of analysis is location or culture requires an understanding of what the term culture might refer to. There are many complex, sophisticated, and varied definitions of **culture**; however, for our purposes it is adequate to define it as the values, practices, beliefs, and behaviors shared by a group of people in a particular place or time, exhibited in ways of life and everyday existence. For example, Chapter 9 discusses **filial piety**— the idea that the older generation is to be revered and cared for by younger generations. This belief, often associated with Asian cultures, is translated into expectations and behaviors related to living arrangements and long-term care for older adults. In contrast, in the United States, independence is a dominant cultural value—reflected in the general preference among older adults to live close to, but not with, children. Many more examples of cultural values and practices that help to create variability in the experiences of aging are presented in subsequent chapters of this volume.

Culture is transmitted in many ways, including by family, religious institutions, and education systems. It is apparent how geographic proximity makes it easier for a culture to become shared. However, if we want to study culture, how do we determine who belongs to which culture? For countries, geographic boundaries are generally appropriate. Depending on the specific research question, a situation might arise where data are collected from people who live in the same area (possibly even neighbors), but who grew up in very different cultural contexts and thus might hold very different perspectives on the world. This is particularly true in a globalized world in which people relocate to other countries for better jobs.

Nation–state

Given the complexity of defining and measuring culture, comparative researchers often use stand-ins to conduct meaningful studies involving multiple cultural contexts. As noted at the beginning of this discussion about the unit of analysis, geographic locations are often used as a proxy for culture. The proxy that is used most often is the nation–state (Miller-Loessi & Parker, 2003). Using the nation as a proxy for culture seems to be recognized as feasible, although fraught with limitations; indeed, this practice continues to stimulate academic debate about the difference between cross-cultural and cross-national research.

Kohn (1987) defines cross-national research as research that "is explicitly comparative . . . using systematically comparable data from two of more nations" (p. 714). He further distinguishes four different kinds of cross-national research: (a) cross-national research where nation is the *object* of study; (b) cross-national research in which nation is the *context* of study; (c) cross-national research where nation is the *unit of analysis*; and (d) cross-national research that is *transnational* in character. Table 2.1 summarizes the main characteristics of the four different approaches as described by Kohn (1987).

In describing these categories of cross-national research, Kohn notes that the distinctions are not always clear, but he offers a convincing discussion about the differences in emphasis in each of these categories. Where nations are the objects of study, the focus is on the nations themselves, or on particular social institutions within those countries. A comparison of the pension systems in the United States and Germany is a good example (as can be seen in Chapter 8). When nation is context, the research becomes a bit richer in

TABLE 2.1 Types of Cross-National Research

1. Nation is *object* of study	Investigator is primarily interested in the specific countries (i.e., how does country A compare to country B?).
2. Nation is *context* of study	Investigator is mainly interested in how the social structure within a nation affects the individuals.
3. Nation is *unit of analysis*	Investigator attempts to find similarities and differences between types of nations without reference to a specific nation. Nations are classified along certain characteristics and are compared on the basis of these characteristics.
4. *Transnational*	Nations are treated as part of larger systems (e.g., the financial system, regions, or the European Union).

Adapted from Kohn (1987).

its exploration of how particular social arrangements help to explain similarities or differences in the experiences of people in those countries. The last two categories move to higher levels of abstraction about what characteristics of nations, or interrelated international systems of countries, make a difference in the topic of interest. When nations are the unit of analysis, researchers are interested in how categories of countries (e.g., developed and developing) compare to each other. Comparing the long-term care systems of developed nations to those of developing nations would be an example of this kind of research. **Transnational** is a term that is becoming increasingly common in the globalized world. Chapter 9 discusses the idea of transnational families in which family roles and relationships are affected by the fact that family members may live and work in different countries for part of the time. In transnational research, countries are treated as components of larger international systems; there is presumed to be an observable connection among those nations. In the case of families whose lives are affected by workers who spend some time overseas, the connectedness of the sending and receiving nations can be measured in terms of migration patterns; the impact of such connectedness is the topic of transnational research. While Kohn's very sophisticated classification of types of cross-national research is beyond the scope of this chapter, it serves to illustrate how carefully these issues are considered within the field of comparative research.

Units of observation

Once the unit of analysis that is to be the basis for the comparison is decided, the next big question is how to obtain information about that unit. This is the problem of the unit of observation. Denton (2007) defines **unit of analysis** as "the object on which behavioral relations among theoretical constructs are conceptualized" and **unit of observation** as "the object on which a measurement is made" (p. 4). In other words, the unit of analysis is the entity about which information is sought (such as individuals, households, countries, states, cultures), whereas the unit of observation is the element on which data is gathered. Units of observation can be the same as the unit of analysis, but they do not have to be. A brief example from educational research on school systems might be helpful. Hypothesizing that school systems with bigger budgets produce better outcomes for students, data would be collected about the schools' budgets and about the average performance of students from those schools. The unit of analysis is the schools, but some of the data is collected from students who attend those schools. Students are units of observation for the study of schools.

For those who are most familiar and comfortable with research on individuals, this issue of unit of observation versus unit of analysis may seem quite impenetrable and unnecessarily complicated. We seek information about individuals (the unit of analysis); therefore, individuals are asked questions (they are also the unit of observation). However, some comparative research focuses on questions about countries or cultures. For example, Mwangi (2010) was interested in why some countries have developed systems of palliative care and others have not. (Palliative care is designed to provide care and comfort, rather than cure, for people living with terminal illnesses; Chapter 6 provides more information about this kind of care.) Mwangi analyzed several national-level factors that might explain this variation. He considered overall level of economic development, assuming that the resources for this specialized care might not be available in the poorest countries. His study also included the major causes of death in each country—reasoning that countries where infectious diseases are predominant might not consider palliative care a priority, as the period between onset and death is relatively short—while countries in which chronic diseases such as cancer or HIV/AIDS are prevalent will typically see much longer dying processes and thus might be more focused on end-of-life care. He also researched the proportion of the population that was older and the level of government expenditures for health care. These variables (economic development, population aging, health care expenditures, and major causes of death) were features of the countries themselves, not individuals. In this case, nations are the unit of analysis (he wanted to compare countries) and the unit of observation (he collected data from and about countries).

In some studies, the unit of observation and the unit of analysis are not the same, as briefly described in the earlier schools example. For a study of global aging, data might be collected on individuals living in two different countries, but these data would be aggregated for a comparison of the two countries themselves. In this case, the unit of analysis would be different from the unit of observation. Consider a study of intergenerational transfers of money within multigenerational households. In this study, individuals are asked about their living arrangements, household structures, and intergenerational exchanges. Individuals have provided the data (they are the unit of observation), but the study focuses on household characteristics and practices (households are the unit of analysis).

The distinction between unit of analysis and unit of observation is important in all research, but the issue is at the forefront in comparative research, which assumes that some entity beyond the individual (country, culture, or tribe) may play a role in individual experiences.

Challenge #2: Conceptualization and Measurement

At the core of every research project are the concepts that investigators seek to understand. In comparative research, as in all research, the first task is to clarify the research question and the variables that researchers want to include. The special challenge in comparative research is to find or devise concepts that are meaningful across cultures and across languages.

In the United States/Bangladesh example, the possibility was raised that the very concept of life satisfaction may not mean the same thing at all in those two countries. How do investigators handle this situation? If they really want to compare life satisfaction among older adults in both of those countries, they need a measure that is standardized enough so it can be compared. Asking entirely different questions in the two locations is not an option, but asking exactly the same questions might not work either.

In an attempt to gather data on the functional health of older adults in Nepal, and then to compare the rates of functional impairments across Nepal and the United States, two researchers (Kunkel & Subedi, 1996) set out to use the standard U.S. measures of functional ability with a sample of older adults in Nepal. These two scales (discussed thoroughly in Chapter 5), Activities of Daily Living (ADL) and Instrumental Activities of Daily Living (IADL), ask about whether the person is able to independently accomplish the things necessary for everyday life: bathing, preparing food, shopping, dressing, eating, and the like. The researchers encountered two significant problems. The first was with the basic premise of the ADL/IADL scale; the questions center on whether the respondent is still able to do a particular task independently, without help or supervision of another person. As it turned out, the very idea of *independence* in getting daily tasks accomplished was simply not meaningful, or even translatable, in Nepal. Especially in rural areas where this study was being conducted, life is organized around the ideal of **interdependence**, not independence. All do what they can, and they help each other. This is quite different from the U.S. cultural context, where the loss of independent functioning is an unwelcome marker of physical decline, frailty, and old age itself.

The second problem encountered by these researchers was related to the specific activities they asked about. Again, using the standard U.S.-based ADL/IADL scale, they wanted to know whether the participants still were able to—on their own—bathe, dress, prepare meals, shop for groceries, and so forth. In the United States, the ability to bathe without help is typically related to whether the individual can safely get in and out of the bathtub and stand or sit safely while bathing. In rural Nepal, bathing involves hauling water and heating it over a fire. Clearly, "impairment in bathing" means entirely different things in the two countries. Similar challenges were encountered with understanding what is involved in shopping for food, and, importantly, with activities that *were not* included but were meaningful to everyday living for rural Nepalese (such as getting to prayers, and freshening up the walls with a new coat of specially prepared mud).

In Chapter 5, the essay by Tausig and Subedi addresses this fascinating challenge of conceptual comparability. Their research on mental health among adults produced results very different in the United States from results in Nepal. (Tausig, Subedi, Broughton, Subedi, & Williams-Blangero, 2003). For example, nearly one half of the U.S. respondents reported that they had felt sad, empty, or depressed for several days in a row at some time in their life, but only 12% of the Nepal respondents said they had this experience. Tausig and Subedi suggest that perhaps the question was not understood in the same way in the two locations, or that cultural values were at work in helping to shape the answers the respondents gave.

Comparative research in global aging has come a long way since that somewhat misguided early attempt to import a U.S.-based measure of health status to a very different location and culture. Numerous cross-national research projects on aging have been implemented, allowing scholars to address the very issues raised here regarding conceptualization and measurement. The Survey of Health, Ageing, and Retirement in Europe (SHARE) is an excellent illustration of these collaborative, coordinated, well-designed cross-national research initiatives. SHARE is a multidisciplinary and cross-national database of information on health, socioeconomic status, and social and family networks of more than 85,000 individuals aged 50 and older from 19 European countries and Israel (Survey of Health, Ageing, and Retirement in Europe, 2013). The SHARE survey is designed so that the measures, coding, and analyses can be directly compared with those in the Health and Retirement Survey (one of the most extensive ongoing studies of aging in the United States), and the English Longitudinal Study of Ageing, allowing for endless possibilities to compare and understand the experiences of aging in many different countries (Borsch-Supan et al., 2013). This rigorous process of standardizing measures, coding, analyses, and study design to maximize comparability across different locations is called **harmonization**.

Another illustration of remarkable progress in the design and implementation of culturally sensitive research about aging is the World Health Organization's Quality of Life (WHOQOL) project. This initiative responded to two important needs in research on aging: (a) holistic measures of health that go beyond disease, mortality, and functional status, and (b) instruments that are truly cross-cultural, not merely translations of existing measures (often developed in Western nations). "The WHOQOL is a quality-of-life assessment developed by the WHOQOL group with 15 international field centres, simultaneously, in an attempt to develop a quality-of-life assessment that would be applicable cross-culturally" (World Health Organization, 2013). The measure has been used extensively to study the factors

Source: United States Bureau of the Census.

related to quality of life for older adults in a range of locations, including the positive impact of social support on quality of life among older men in Kenya (Campbell, Gray, & Radak, 2011), and differences in the way quality of life is described by Nepalese women who live with family compared to those who live in an old-age home (Shrestha & Zarit, 2012).

Challenge #3: Getting Valid Data

Having a well-conceptualized and compelling research question—with culturally appropriate measures—is the first step in any project. Once the topic, the concepts, and the unit of analysis have been decided, the researchers must turn their attention to decisions about how to get the information they need. Secondary data (data that has already been collected) can be the most appropriate source of information for some questions related to global aging; earlier in this chapter, the description of global patterns research gave some examples of secondary data. Researchers who are interested in, for example, comparing the level of literacy and proportion of older people with a decent standard of living across different countries could use data from the Human Development Index, constructed by the United Nations.

Very often, however, the topic of study will require the collection of new data. In this case, researchers must grapple with sampling—selecting and reaching the right people to interview, survey, or observe. Sampling strategies are key in every social science discipline, whether research is being done *across* or *within* societies or cultures. The basic questions related to sampling are: Who should be talked to (or observed) in order to understand the topic being studied? How many and which people should be included in order to result in a good representation of an entire group and a valid understanding of the topic? The art and the science of sample design are far beyond the scope of this book, but the ideas behind them are not. Since social science researchers virtually never have the option of communicating with every member of a population, there must be a plan for choosing the appropriate subset of people to include. In some studies, this subset might be *key informants*—people who possess specialized and in-depth knowledge about the topic being studied. For example, if investigators want to learn about the everyday lives of grandmothers in Swaziland who are raising their grandchildren, it would be essential to talk to some of those women. After all, they are the experts on this topic; hearing directly from them will help build a rich understanding of the shared joys and challenges they face.

In other types of studies, the sample will not focus on key informants, but rather on a group of people who, taken together, can accurately represent a much larger group. This representative group would be selected through sampling techniques that ensure the right number and type of participants. If, for example, researchers were interested in the prevalence of certain health conditions among grandmothers raising grandchildren in Swaziland, it would NOT be sufficient to interview 10 or 12 women. Although the stories of those 10 women would be highly enlightening, investigators could not conclude that their experiences (or health conditions) were generalizable to the whole population of women in this situation. In order to generalize, researchers need larger samples of people who can, through careful selection techniques, represent the whole group.

Challenge #4: Respecting Participants

Whether based on key informants or a representative sample (or some combination), comparative research adds interesting new twists to the strategies for selecting, and reaching, participants. The establishment of trusting relationships with research participants is a cornerstone of ethical and valid research no matter where it is being conducted. When differences in language and cultural values are in play, the responsibility for researchers to learn how to appropriately interact with participants is significantly heightened. Challenge #2 addressed one part of this concern—assuring that concepts are translatable and that the translations capture meanings correctly.

At one level, these may appear to be very pragmatic concerns that make cross-cultural research more challenging. But they are more than that: They speak to the profound opportunity afforded by such research—to deeply understand the experiences of aging in other cultures. They also speak to the ethical issues related to the fairness, justice, and respect due to all research participants. In the United States, as in many other nations, both professional associations and the government have formal processes and written standards for the ethical conduct of research (cf., U.S. Department of Health and

Source: Lawrence Downes.

Human Services, n.d.). In cross-cultural studies, researchers are obligated to think carefully about how the ethical principles apply in different settings. Marshall (2006) discusses the challenges in getting informed consent from participants. This universally accepted idea rests on two foundations—that potential participants fully understand the research in which they are being asked to take part, and that they are free to say no. Marshall (2006) cites a variety of factors that can make informed consent difficult in cross-cultural research, including comprehension of information, understanding of risk, and perceptions about the authority and power held by the researcher. U.S. institutional review boards (IRBs), are charged by federal law to oversee and approve researchers' plans to study human subjects. Many IRBs have shown great concern about—and, in fact, on occasion have blocked—investigators' offering cash to potential participants as compensation and incentive for agreeing to be interviewed. They are especially concerned that—to the poor in less developed countries—even a modest amount of money ($25–$50, say) might be coercive, practically forcing them to consent to be studied. This ethical dilemma represents a truly thorny problem for cross-cultural researchers.

The WHO offers a casebook with numerous illustrations of, and guidance for, applying principles of ethical research in cross-cultural studies (Cash, Wikler, Saxena, & Capron, 2009). To highlight the issue of voluntary informed consent with older populations, the authors describe a situation in which researchers sought to understand traditional health practices among the older adults of the community. Respecting the local system in which the oldest adult son is recognized as head of household, the researchers first sought permission from the son before approaching the older adults in the household. However, the interviews were conducted only with the elders; no other family members were present. One of the older adults became agitated during the interview, and his son accused the researchers of making his father ill in order to force him into the hospital. The complicated situation described in this case example illustrates questions of trust, cultural misunderstanding, whose consent and comfort is in play, and even the voluntariness of the consent given by the older person once his son had agreed.

SUMMARY

With all of these challenges, why should we try? Each challenge is actually an essential feature of the enormous opportunity afforded by comparative research. For example, thinking through the principles of ethical research and how these principles must be applied in a culturally respectful way requires researchers to learn a great deal about the group or society they seek to study before they even begin; the knowledge gained in this way is apart from, but foundational to, truly understanding the specific topic of interest. It simply doesn't work for researchers to take their own assumptions, definitions, and research practices into a culturally unique setting. Doing so would inevitably result in mistakes, potentially create misunderstandings, and ultimately undermine attempts to gain the valid knowledge that is sought.

Comparative research requires investigators to be better than they might otherwise be, taking nothing for granted and focusing on the underlying principles of good design and respect for participants, not just the pragmatics. In addition to the heightened awareness about the research enterprise that can be gained in comparative research, there are many other good reasons to conduct such studies. In an elegant summary, Baistow (2000) identifies four ways that we can learn from comparative research: learning about others, learning from others, learning about ourselves, and learning with others.

Perhaps there is no more compelling statement of the value of comparative research than American political scientist Seymour Martin Lipset's succinct claim that, "[A person] who knows only one country, knows none" (Diamond, 2007). This is an era of unprecedented opportunity to expand the depth of knowledge about *ageways* in some countries, thanks to the perspective that may be gained from learning about many other countries. It is the obligation of researchers—and readers—to apply the highest standards of rigorous and culturally respectful comparative research to ensure the validity and utility of that new knowledge.

DISCUSSION QUESTIONS

1. What are some of the benefits of cross-national research?
2. What are some of the barriers to doing research in other countries?

3. In what ways does cross-cultural research differ from regular research? In what ways are they the same?
4. How is aging in the United States similar to that in Cuba?
5. Can you learn more about aging from talking with older people in Bangladesh or in the United States?
6. Why is getting valid data so important?
7. Is it a good idea to compensate research subjects with money?

KEY WORDS

Cross-national comparative research
Culture
Descriptive global patterns
Filial piety
Global patterns research
Harmonization
Interdependence
Modernization theory
Secondary data
Single-nation research
Transnational
Unit of analysis
Unit of observation
Within-country research

An American in Havana: Observations About Aging in Cuba

Frank J. Whittington

Cuba represents an interesting case for aging and the older population. As Jim Sykes and Enrique Vega point out in their chapter on Cuba in the *International Handbook on Aging* (Palmore, Whittington, & Kunkel, 2009), Cuba has a less developed economy but an age structure that resembles a developed nation. In fact, Cuban life expectancy stands at about age 76.5, only 1.4 years less than that of the United States (age 77.9), and very close to many of the nations of Western Europe. The proportion of the population older than age 65 is actually higher than in the United States (13.7% vs. 12.8%), due mainly to the higher birthrate among immigrant populations in the United States.

CUBAN–UNITED STATES HISTORY

Understanding how a very poor nation could achieve such a good result for its people probably requires some historical and political background. In the 1950s, Fidel Castro led a guerilla-style war against the dictator Fulgencio Batista, overthrowing him on New Year's Eve, 1959. Initially, most of the people in the United States and even the U.S. government were supportive of Castro's revolution—until it was learned that he and most of his *compadres* were Communists and were supported by the Soviet Union.

As Castro took over the country, he nationalized all land holdings and most businesses, causing many of the wealthy and middle class to leave Cuba for the United States. The large Cuban American population in Florida today—descended from those immigrants—wields a disproportionate amount of political power, especially where our government's policy toward Cuba is concerned.

Several other events, including the Bay of Pigs invasion (1961), the Cuban Missile Crisis (1962), and the hypothesized role of Castro in the assassination of President John F. Kennedy (1963), created a relationship between the United States, Cuba, and the Cuban people that was actively hostile, tense, and difficult in the early days. Then the political relationship settled into an uneasy, passive hostility that gradually faded from public consciousness, except for the Cubans in Florida and Havana. Because they were connected by blood and by history, these communities worked daily to keep the issue—and the hostility—alive. The Cuban Missile Crisis was resolved ultimately by a naval blockade of the island, pitting American warships against Soviet warships in the waters around Cuba; this 1962 crisis brought our nation closer to catastrophic war than any other time in our history. The naval blockade evolved into a permanent, full-scale economic embargo and a political shunning that we have not used against any other country—not even with Vietnam following that war, or North Korea in the 57 years after the Korean War.

The boycott, as it is often referred to, continues: keeping U.S. goods away from Cuba; Cuban products out of U.S. markets; and, more importantly, the Cuban and U.S. governments from exchanging views directly or engaging each other for mutual benefit. Most damaging have been the tight restrictions imposed on Americans traveling to Cuba and Cubans coming to the United States. Although these restrictions have loosened in recent years, the flow of visitors between the two countries is still meager.

It was in this context that I was invited to join a delegation of American gerontologists who traveled to Cuba in December 2010 to learn about aging and health care in that country. The trip was sponsored by the National Council on Aging (NCOA). The people in our group were all either members of NCOA or friends of members; they included local service providers, college professors, advocates, a senior center director, a health care administrator, an entrepreneur, a geriatrician, and an attorney. The delegation was led by Jim Sykes, a retired gerontologist from the University of Wisconsin, who has traveled and studied extensively in Latin America and had visited Cuba more than 20 times.

One of the constant themes of our trip was the American economic boycott of Cuba. We learned that the impact of the boycott has produced significant hardship for Cubans. Their country remains one of the poorest in the Western Hemisphere. Its communications infrastructure is at least 20 years behind that of the United States; consumer goods for the average Cuban are in very short supply; and their housing stock and commercial buildings are inadequate, shabby, and in some places crumbling.

The country's economy is not vibrant, and development is slow. Yet Cuba has an antique feel and patina that are attractive and even charming to an American tourist. Some would attribute this stagnant economy to the Communist system, whereas others would blame the boycott for keeping Cuba out of the economic mainstream. It is probably due to a little of both. Recent reports suggest that Cuban President Raul Castro, Fidel's younger brother, is seeking to introduce capitalist-like incentives for entrepreneurs and eliminate the tight government control of all economic activity. President Obama already has loosened some of the government's restrictions on travel and scientific and cultural exchanges. Some speculate that a dramatic shift in our policy may yet happen—perhaps even a lifting of the boycott.

Despite the boycott, Cubans enjoy two advantages that Americans do not: free education (from kindergarten through college) and free health care. Cubans pay nothing for a visit to a health clinic, nothing for delivery of their children, nothing for dental care, and nothing for hospital or nursing-home stays. One might assume that such free health care must take a huge chunk out of the country's gross domestic product (GDP), impoverishing every other sector of the economy. Well, to the contrary, whereas the United States spends about 17% of its GDP on health care, Cuba spends only 2%.

My preconceived notion about the Cuban system was that the combination of free care and small expenditures must produce overuse and low quality. I can't speak to overuse, since such data are not collected and not deemed worthy of concern. However, I can testify that the clinic buildings, examination rooms, waiting rooms, and medical offices we saw were all of low quality, old, small, poorly furnished, and poorly maintained. None of us would want to work or be treated there. However, the results—in very low infant mortality and length of life—are hard to argue with. Cuba is an outlier in the relationship of economic well-being and health status of its population—one of the poorest nations in the Western Hemisphere is enjoying one of the highest levels of health and longevity.

A VISITOR'S OBSERVATIONS

I learned several things from my observations and discussions with Cuban health care and aging professionals during our visit to Cuba in late 2010.

1. Population aging is a well-understood reality for those in both government and academe, and most policy makers are at least thinking about how Cuba is changing as the age structure shifts away from youth toward maturity. It is understandable that countries with a higher proportion of older citizens would have the most advanced gerontology programs and research. Yet the increase in proportion aged has slowed recently in the highly developed countries, and it is the less developed nations like Cuba that are facing the most rapid growth—in both size and proportion—of their older populations, with all of the accompanying challenges. Perhaps the less developed nations have the greatest need to develop gerontological capacity and to rapidly create programs for their older people so that they can anticipate and minimize some of the problems of aging experienced by industrialized countries.

2. Geriatrics is now recognized and supported in Cuba, and, although still few in number, gerontological researchers and educators are engaging their nation's aging issues as best they can—often with insight and scientific rigor. I was especially impressed that an epidemiologist was located and engaged in applied research in a local health center (referred to as a polyclinic because of its multidisciplinary team approach). Whereas his physical tools and technical support were rudimentary, his methods

were classic and effective. He could show how the clustering of rural immigrants living in his catchment area correlated closely with the reported cases of dengue fever in the community. He, like all the staff of the clinic, wore a white lab coat, conveying to all—patients and visitors, alike—the sense of serious, scientific medicine being practiced there. Most members of our group were quite impressed with both the strong commitment and the sophistication of the staff in practicing community medicine. Prevention appeared to be their default mode and daily operating principle.

3. A third obvious lesson from my visit is that many of the phenomena we would label as problems of aging and that we struggle with in the United States are also found in Cuba. In fact, Cuba appears to not be very different in this regard from many other nations of the world, developed or not. In Palmore and his colleagues' handbook (2009), the authors describe their own aging populations and policies in terms that could pass for those of an American observer—and very similar to my observations in Cuba. Our hosts at the geriatric medicine program of the University of Havana gave a stimulating (if familiar) lecture on the ravages of physical decline with age and the shortage of good medical care and long-term care arrangements; a weakening of the family and social network of support for older adults; the serious negative effects of old-age poverty in Cuba; exploitation or outright abuse of vulnerable older people; and the psychological and mental health problems besetting older Cubans. Does that list sound vaguely familiar?

I was quite impressed with these geriatricians' descriptions of their decades of study, clinical experience, and research with older patients. Though they do not have easy access to the books, journals, and conferences available to scientists in developed nations, they nevertheless have managed to keep up with most modern geriatric knowledge and understanding. Their clear grasp of the needs of their patients and an informed approach to care suggest that any of us would be as well treated in Havana as in Atlanta, although admittedly we would receive fewer tests, shorter stays in the hospital, and fewer medications, but, because of the free care system, we also would receive no bill.

During our visit we witnessed an amazing performance by a senior drama group of an original play highlighting aging and intergenerational themes. The group's director did not refer to it as *drama therapy*, as we might have done in the United States. Such experiences in the United States often teach us that older people are capable of far more than most of us suspect. We expect an older person to be sick, weak, and disengaged; when we see evidence that, at least for some, the opposite is true, we are struck by the contrast between our age stereotype and the reality before our eyes. Similarly, these Cuban older adults said they were especially gratified by their grandchildren's reactions to seeing them in the play: Grandma and Grandpa were suddenly *cool*, and the seniors knew that the kids' ageist biases would never be the same.

4. Differences do exist. We in the United States differ from Cuba and many other less developed countries of the world, mainly in the widespread challenges of an aging population and the well-developed support programs designed to ameliorate them. For all the surface similarities between the United States and Cuba's aging populations and issues, I did notice some jarring differences in where we are and where they are. In some cases, it appears that where they are is where we have been. Because we are a much richer nation, our poverty is less widespread and probably less an actual burden on aging lifestyles in the United States than it is in Cuba, at least in absolute terms. However, because Cuba is a Socialist country and the wealth (or lack of it) is much more equally distributed, relative deprivation is likely felt more acutely here than there.

Although we saw one large and amazingly vibrant senior center with day health services and treatments onsite, we could not verify how common these are. The therapy equipment proudly displayed consisted of electromagnetic field devices attached to cots, where seniors could rest while receiving a low dose of magnetism. Because magnet therapy is scientifically unproven and actively rejected by most Western physicians, such treatments likely delivered only a placebo benefit that, of course, is not to be completely discounted. Center participants were lively, welcoming, and apparently healthy; however, the director also gratefully accepted our small gifts of soap, shampoo, and toothpaste, commodities not readily available to many Cuban seniors.

CONCLUSIONS

I am aware my observations are limited, having visited Cuba for only a short time. Nevertheless, Americans visiting Cuba for the first time bring many years of distance education about this island nation, its people and culture, and its political and economic system. I was not surprised, therefore, to conclude that Cuba is not totally free, totally open, or totally modern.

However, I was struck by the facts that Cuba also seemed freer and more open than I thought it would be; more advanced than I thought, especially in medical care and the promotion of health among people at the community level; and its population is older than I thought, owing to its low infant mortality rate and relatively high life expectancy. Most importantly, its national policy toward aging appears to value age and older people in authentic and meaningful ways.

Despite five decades of political and economic boycott by the United States and its allies, Cuba is far less isolated than I had imagined. I met professionals who had studied and worked in Africa, China, Russia, and Western Europe. I met citizens who had traveled to Europe, the United States, and Asia; and I met and saw hundreds of people from the United States, Canada, Europe, and Asia who were visiting Cuba while we were there. I even heard several Cubans describe their favorite contemporary American television shows (*House* and *Grey's Anatomy*) and movies (*The Godfather* and *Spiderman*). Clearly, a significant volume of cultural and economic exchange is going on here that undermines all attempts to impose economic and political isolation.

We hope our visit and new understanding will contribute to the growth of a truly international science and professional practice in gerontology. In this way, the study of global aging—in all of its forms—can provide the foundation for improved quantity and quality of life for the hundreds of millions of people already older in the world and those soon to be.

CHAPTER 3

The Welfare State and Global Aging

RETIRED AND LIVING THE GOOD LIFE?

Tooncie lives alone in a modest apartment in a small city in the southeastern United States. At age 87, she has been a widow for almost 20 years. Although she worked all her life in the furniture manufacturing industry, *Tooncie* has no employer-sponsored pension. Indeed, she never really thought much about retirement until she was nearing later life. As a young adult, she notes, *"You didn't think about it. Nobody really thought that they were going to live that long."* The combination of her relatively low wages, her late husband's modest income, and her fairly large family (*Tooncie* has four daughters) allowed little opportunity to accumulate any personal savings. Therefore, all of her income now comes from public support.

Tooncie retired at age 62 and has been receiving Social Security (SS) income payments for about 25 years. With cost-of-living adjustments over that period, her monthly SS check in 2012 was $1,155. That equates to an annual income of less than $14,000. Despite this small monthly payment, *Tooncie's* total SS benefits received to date far exceed the amount that she paid into the system as a worker. When asked about how she felt about this fact, she replied without any hesitation regarding her benefits. *"That's my money!"* she declared. *"I paid into Social Security so the government would take care of me when I am old, and that's what they are supposed to do."*

At age 65, *Tooncie* also began receiving Medicare health insurance coverage. Whereas all former workers in the United States receive Medicare Part A (hospitalization insurance), many also elect to receive Part B (physician and outpatient coverage) by paying a monthly premium for this coverage (currently about $100 per month). Because her monthly SS benefit is below $1,200, *Tooncie* is not required to pay this premium. Nevertheless, *Tooncie* purchases a private-market Medicare supplement insurance policy that, except for prescription medications, covers the co-pays (generally 10%–20% of all health care bills that Medicare requires recipients to pay themselves) and other out-of-pocket medical expenses not covered by Medicare. This policy costs her quarterly payments of $356. Additionally, although greatly reduced in cost through the Medicare Part D prescription drug program, she pays monthly co-pays of about $16 for the three medications she takes regularly.

With her relatively low income, one would think that *Tooncie* would qualify for several low-income welfare programs such as food stamps (financial assistance for food costs) or Medicaid (health care coverage for low-income persons). However, her income is actually too high for almost all of these programs. Indeed, the only assistance she receives is through Section 8 of the Housing Act of 1937, which subsidizes her apartment rent payment. *Tooncie's* apartment rent normally would be $400 per month, which is already quite low compared to most properties in her area. With Section 8 (government housing) assistance, this expense is reduced to $225 per month.

Initially, *Tooncie* refused to apply for Section 8 assistance because she did not think of herself as being at an income level where she deserved to receive the benefit. However, once she became aware of some friends and neighbors—a bit better off than she—receiving this assistance, she decided to apply to Section 8. *"I didn't want it at first, but I like getting it now,"* she notes.

When her housing and health expenses are paid, *Tooncie's* already modest monthly income is reduced to less than $800 per month. With that, she must pay her other typical expenses such as food and utilities. Once those necessities are paid for, almost no money is left over. To deal with these financial limitations, *Tooncie* has had to make sacrifices in other areas of her life. For example, although she would usually host the family Christmas gathering, she is only able to give small gifts to her ten great-grandchildren. Her four daughters and seven grandchildren receive no gift. *Tooncie* might be more anxious over this financial reality were it not for the fact that her situation is quite typical of working-class women in retirement under the U.S. social insurance system.

This brief view into Tooncie's life provides a very good example of how much the state is involved in the lives of older adults around the world. Depending on where one resides, the state may be involved in providing income security, medical benefits, food and housing allowances, or even **in-kind benefits**. This collection of state-sponsored programs and policies is often referred to in aging research and popular media as the **welfare state**. In this chapter, we examine the role of the welfare state in the lives of elders and explore the substantial variation in these policies and programs around the world.

DEFINING THE WELFARE STATE

Although one of the most commonly used terms in social science today, the welfare state is not particularly easy to define. Some scholars have included within the welfare state any government policies established for the public good. Such a broad definition would include things such as the interstate highway system in the United States or public education systems. Most, however, would limit the welfare state to policies that address individual risks that were traditionally addressed by support provided by the family or by religious institutions, particularly those that arise in modern industrial/ capitalist societies. Such policies include assistance to the poor, public health care/insurance, and public pensions; they are intended to provide a kind of social insurance against various life risks such as poverty or poor health for what are usually considered to be vulnerable populations such as children, the poor, or older adults. Whereas most industrialized nations have rather well-developed welfare states, there is considerable variability in how policies are applied across countries. Why welfare states emerged and why there is such cross-national variability in their policies is a complex story that unfolded across two centuries, originating in the industrial and economic revolutions of the 19th century.

History of the Welfare State

Issues such as poverty and need for medical care that are addressed by modern welfare state policies are certainly not new, and the seeds of welfare policies have premodern roots. Indeed, the social well-being of the individual before the 19th century was typically looked after by two social institutions: religious organizations and the family.

For centuries in Europe, a major role of the Catholic Church was attending to social issues that today would fall under the purview of the welfare state. For example, relief for the poor was long a part of Catholic practices in the Middle Ages. In other parts of the world, similar roles for religious institutions evolved, as with Islam in west and central Asia. Indeed, charitable work, especially that focused on the most financially needy, continues to be a major part of the religious activities of many faiths today.

Whereas religious organizations focused on the poor, the family was responsible for almost all other areas of life that are currently addressed by the modern welfare state. Almost all caregiving (including a fair portion of medical treatment) was historically provided within the family. Children were cared for by relatives living within an extended family household or otherwise in close proximity. Elders were cared for by younger family members, and, indeed, children were viewed as a resource for older age. Remnants of these long-held practices remain in modern societies, and these are discussed in more depth in Chapter 9. For example, it is still quite common in Japan for the oldest male child to remain in the family home, even after marriage and fatherhood, ultimately becoming both the caretaker (along with

Source: Jiayin (Jaylene) Liang.

his wife) of his parents and the owner of the family home. The family and religious organizations remained the primary institutions addressing issues of social risk until the onset of the Industrial Revolution in the 19th century, which fundamentally changed the way people lived.

Prior to the 19th century, most individuals lived on family-owned and -maintained farmland with little migration of more than a few miles. Industrialization, however, required a centralization of population to maintain factory operations. Thus, many people began migrating from farms to urban industrial centers. In doing so, the ability of the family to provide some buffer against social risks failed; family members who might have assisted with such things as childcare or temporary financial hardships now lived simply too far away to provide assistance. Similarly, the support network of the church was either broken by such distance or, even when available, overwhelmed by the massive influx of new migrants. For example, the British poor law, which was originally established during the reign of Queen Elizabeth I in the 16th century and administered in local parishes, was revamped in 1834 into a more centralized system of workhouses—a precursor to the establishment of a welfare state in the United Kingdom. These population shifts resulting from economic industrialization and related processes such as urbanization (described in more detail in Chapter 4) produced social conditions that no longer meshed with such traditional sources of social and economic support. As these traditional social institutions proved inadequate in a rapidly changing social environment, people began to look to the nation–state for assistance with various aspects of individual social welfare. Thus, the emergence of the welfare state unfolded across the 19th and 20th centuries.

More specifically, industrialization, through its need for large concentrations of workers for factories, induced a substantial migration in various nations from farms to urban areas. This migration, however, was no mere mobilization of populations. Rather, it introduced a new way of life where individuals were separated from the land and frequently from their extended families. Whereas rural dwellers often had kin for neighbors who could provide social and economic assistance, urbanites typically found themselves among strangers and, thus, separated from their traditional social support networks. This new social living arrangement was in need of some mechanism to replace the lost family support, and this mechanism was to be the welfare state.

Although some welfare state-like phenomena existed even prior to the Industrial Revolution (e.g., Britain's poor laws, various military pension programs dating as far back as the Roman Empire), the first modern welfare state emerged in the newly formed German Empire in the 1870s and 1880s. Under Otto von Bismarck's **"state socialism,"** a collection of programs was established to provide for the social and economic welfare of German workers. These included policies on health insurance, accident insurance, and old age and disability pensions. Over the next six decades, such programs spread across most European nations as well as to several industrialized former European colonies such as the United States; by 1950, almost all industrialized nations had well-established welfare programs in place. In addition to the ongoing diffusion process across nations, the welfare state also expanded in the types of programs enacted during the 20th century. Beyond just old age pensions and health/accident programs for workers, state-based social and economic support was added in many countries, providing assistance with expenses related to maternity and childbirth, periods of unemployment, and health care more generally (U.S. Social Security Administration, 1999).

Whereas these extensions of the welfare state continued throughout the second half of the 20th century, the post-1950 period also included a new diffusion of the welfare state into developing nations (Brown, 2005). The 30 years following 1950 witnessed the rapid formation of new nation–states from former colonial holdings, especially in Africa, parts of Asia, and the island colonies in the Caribbean and the Pacific. These new nations, however, often had only limited industrialization, and thus their experience with welfare programs was quite different from that of the developed world. In particular, policies were frequently in place on paper, but the reality of program implementation was far from complete (Hsiao & Shaw, 2007). Commonly, actual welfare state benefits in these developing contexts were available only to government employees or to individuals residing in major urban areas. In some cases, welfare policies were official law, but the programs to fulfill these policies never were established or funded.

The 20th century also witnessed rapid global aging, a demographic reality resulting from reductions in family sizes in industrial societies (see Chapter 4), and this demographic process came to dominate welfare state issues in the latter half of the century. **Public pensions** were among the first types of welfare state programs and by the 1970s were easily the most widespread social assistance programs. Indeed, more than 160 nations had some form of public pension system as official law by the end of the 20th century. This breadth of policy adoption coupled with the rapid aging of many national populations resulted in the overwhelming majority of global welfare state spending (about 70%) being devoted to public pension programs by the 1980s (Pampel & Williamson, 1989). More recently, this proportion has declined, largely due to the substantial increases in the funding demands of health care policies. In many nations, increases in the size of the aged population as well as increases in longevity have heightened demand for medical care programs such that in many countries the annual cost of health care programs rivals the public pension system.

Beginning in the 1980s, the increased financial burden on these programs created by population aging resulted in financial crises in many nations. Many democratic nations elected conservative governments about this time, and efforts to reform welfare state programs were undertaken; welfare states ceased expansion, and in many cases actually began to contract. Often, changes to social insurance programs resulted in significant reductions in benefit levels, more stringent program eligibility rules, and in some cases complete reworking of the program. Frequently, in the latter case, the retooling of a program resulted in a significantly more privatized and individualized approach to social welfare. For example, in the late 1990s several European nations (e.g., Sweden) introduced **privatized public pension systems** (essentially government-mandated savings accounts) that replaced their previously universal systems that had paid flat-rate benefits to all citizens. This process of welfare state contraction is often referred to as *retrenchment* and is still occurring today as populations continue to age and welfare programs continue to experience financial pressure (see Leibfried & Obinger, 2000).

Program Types and Eligibility

National variation in welfare state programs and in who qualifies for them is considerable. As noted earlier, the five types of welfare programs include public pensions, health care, family allowances, sickness and maternity/birth benefits, and unemployment compensation. These different programs obviously address a myriad of social support needs across the life course, as can be seen in the story of *Tooncie* at the beginning of this chapter. Additional variation is also considerable within any of these policy areas. Since public pensions are the most common of these policies, they provide an excellent example of this variation.

Source: U.S. Bureau of the Census.

First, public pensions vary significantly in how they are funded. In the United States, for example, the largest portion of the public pension system, **Social Security**, is funded via a payroll tax specified for this use. In other cases, such as the remaining portion of the U.S. system (Supplemental Security Income [SSI]) or the universal pension program in Iceland, funds are drawn from general revenue. Beyond this broader distinction, systems of all types are funded in varying proportion by workers, employers, and the government. The variability in these proportions is substantial, with a range from 0% to 100% from each of these three sources, depending on which nation one is examining, regardless of the separate fund or general revenue distinction.

Second, public pensions vary by policy entitlement. In other words, whether an individual has a right to a particular program or benefit varies from nation to nation. In many Scandinavian countries, **universal programs** have historically been applied to all citizens and even long-term noncitizen residents. This type of entitlement is often referred to as **citizenship entitlement**. In the United States, on the other hand, entitlement to public pensions is an **earnings-related entitlement** and depends either on being a program contributor (i.e., a worker who has paid into the system) for a period of time and a particular salary level, or on one's relationship to such a worker (e.g., a spouse, a minor dependent, etc.). Whereas these two forms of entitlement are the most common for all welfare programs globally, others do exist. For example, entitlement to some programs in the Netherlands is dependent on being a nonworking mother.

Program eligibility is another area of variation in public pensions, although this is often confused with entitlement. Whereas entitlement refers to a right to benefits, eligibility refers to the criteria required to qualify to receive those benefits. U.S. Social Security policy demonstrates this distinction nicely. One is entitled to a SS benefit based on years of workforce participation that is taxed for the program. Eligibility for SS benefits, however, is based on reaching a certain age—age 62 for reduced-benefit early retirement and (soon) age 67 for standard benefits. In general, two types of eligibility criteria dominate social policies: **age eligibility** and **need-based eligibility**. Age eligibility is fairly straightforward: One becomes eligible for benefits upon reaching a certain age. Across nations, however, what age must be reached varies greatly, with some set as early as age 55 and others approaching age 70. Of course, life expectancy also varies greatly from one country to the next; if the pension age is geared (or even indexed) to life expectancy in a country, total pension benefits may be more or less equal. Furthermore, age eligibility can vary across programs within the same nation. To illustrate, the old age health care system in the United States, Medicare, requires one to be age 65, which is different from either early or standard retirement age for SS.

Need-based eligibility (also known as the income-tested or means-tested criterion), on the other hand, is eligibility based on an income (or wealth) threshold such that one must have income under the threshold to be program-eligible. Generally, these thresholds are at or near a country's poverty level, with programs intended as a form of poor relief. However, some exceptions exist. For example, Australia's means-tested public pension system has an income threshold set at such a high level that the overwhelming majority (more than 70%) of its aged citizens are eligible for public pension benefits. It is also, as in this last example, not uncommon for welfare programs to have both need-based and age-eligibility requirements.

In order to bring some understanding to this international variability, in the 1990s the U.S. Social Security Administration began to include a constructed typology of seven public pension types in their biannual publication, *Social Security Programs Throughout the World* (U.S. Social Security Administration, 1999). Table 3.1 shows how these seven program types vary in funding, entitlement, and eligibility. Of note, this work and its publication have been contracted to the International Social Security Association since 2000, and that organization has altered the titles of some of these categories (new category titles are included in parentheses).

In addition to the variability in public pension systems already discussed, Table 3.1 shows differences across program types in the source of funding. Essentially, all public pensions are funded in three ways: taxes on individual employee salaries, employer taxes, and other government revenues. What is not shown in the table is the variability in how much each of these sources provides. In New Zealand, the entirety of funding for the means-tested pension

TABLE 3.1 Types of National Public Pension Systems

Program type	Funding type	Funding source	Entitlement basis	Eligibility criteria
Contributory earnings-related (Earnings-related)	Specified tax fund	Shared by employee and employer	Employment-based	Age (often with minimum years of contribution)
Contributory flat-rate universal (Flat-rate)	Specified tax fund	Shared by government and (sometimes) employer	Citizenship or residence-based	Age and length of residence
Noncontributory flat-rate universal (Flat-rate universal)	General tax revenue	Shared by government and (infrequently) employer	Citizenship or residence-based	Age and length of residence
Noncontributory means-tested (Means-tested)	General tax revenue	Government only	Citizenship or residence-based	Income level
Mandatory private pensions (Occupational retirement schemes)	Industry/ occupational fund	Employer only	Industry-based	Age and (sometimes) years of employment
Mandatory private savings (Individual retirement schemes)	Individual fund	Employee (sometimes with employer-matched funds)	Employment-based	Age (sometimes with minimum years of contribution)
Mandatory public savings (Provident funds)	Individual fund	Shared by employee and employer	Employment-based	Age

Source: U.S. Social Security Administration (1999).

system comes from the government, with no contributions from individuals or businesses. In Belgium, on the other hand, most of their earnings-related system comes from a 7.5% tax on employees and an almost 9% payroll tax on employers. Different still is the Chilean mandatory private savings system, where employees must provide a minimum 10% contribution (a higher percentage is allowed), but employers make no contribution at all.

One additional element of Table 3.1 is noteworthy regarding eligibility. The difference between age-based and need-based eligibility has been noted previously, but other criteria are sometimes also relevant for public pensions. These typically take the form of a minimum period prior to eligibility being obtained, regardless of age. These include minimums in length of residence within a nation, length of time making contributions to the pension system, or length of years of service within a particular industry. Regardless of which of these criteria are used, it is important to note that in several nations an older individual, despite reaching retirement age, might still be ineligible for a public pension due to a lack of years of residence, contribution, or service.

DISTRIBUTION OF PROGRAM TYPES

Earlier discussion is focused on individual program types and the variability across those programs individually. However, one further area of variability in public pension systems is the number of programs a nation has in place. For example, the United States actually has two public pension programs: SS and SSI. The former is an earnings-related system where beneficiaries are either former workers or have some important relationship to that worker (e.g., a spouse). The latter is a means-tested system that provides minimum benefits to low-income individuals regardless of their work history. Figure 3.1 shows a map of the world with the number of public pension systems noted for each country at the turn of the 21st century.

The map shows that although a majority of nations provide only a single type of public pension, a substantial minority of nations utilize more than

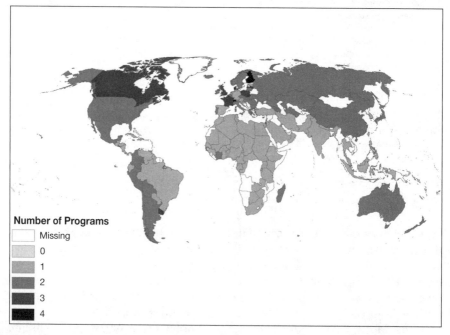

FIGURE 3.1 Number of old age security programs in 1999.

one system. Indeed, a few countries (Denmark, Finland, and Switzerland) have as many as four different types of public pensions; although given varying eligibility rules, older citizens of those nations may not be eligible for all (or any) of these programs. For example, France employed three public pension systems in1999: earnings-related, means-tested, and mandatory occupational pensions. In this case, workers in certain industries are eligible for both the earnings-related and occupational pensions, but workers outside of these industries may only receive the earnings-related benefits. In Uruguay, on the other hand, earnings-related, means-tested, and mandatory private savings (i.e., individual retirement accounts) are all public pension options, but how these are applied varies by cohort. Workers who were older than age 40 in 1996 have an opt-in choice for the private savings program, but more recent cohorts of Uruguayan workers are required to participate in a mixture of the earnings-related and private savings systems.

THE RECENT TREND: RETRENCHMENT

Whereas most of the history of the welfare state has been one of expansion of programs and benefits, the last two decades of the 20th century and the first decade of the 21st century have been a period of welfare state contraction. It is somewhat ironic that this period of contraction is occurring at the same time that, due to rapid population aging, the needs of older adults are perhaps higher than at any time in history. In the welfare state literature, this program and benefit contraction is referred to as **retrenchment**.

Karl Hinrichs (2000) provides an excellent overview of these trends in the European context in his article, "Elephants on the Move: Patterns of Pension Reform in OECD Countries." The OECD is the Organisation for Economic Co-operation and Development. He notes six specific reforms that have been ongoing. First, the formula by which public pension benefits in a given nation is calculated has been made more stringent, typically penalizing higher income individuals' benefit levels and more severely curtailing the benefits of workers with less than full employment records. To illustrate, in Sweden, public pension benefits are now indexed for rising longevity gains in more recent cohorts, resulting in a reduction of recurring payouts (i.e., Sweden's programs now anticipate life expectancy gains and reduce monthly benefits accordingly). Kathrin Komp discusses the details of this Swedish system and the challenges inherent to rising Swedish longevity for its welfare provisions in the essay at the end of this chapter.

Second, changes in the age for (especially full) retirement benefits have been increased to postpone entry into the public pension system and lengthen the period in which workers pay into the system. For example, the United States will soon complete the process of gradually increasing the retirement age for full SS benefits from age 65 to age 67. In the European context, welfare states had frequently employed a different retirement age for men and women (with women usually having a lower age threshold). These reforms have moved toward equalizing these gender differences by increasing the pensionable age for women.

Third, contributory programs have experienced an increase in subsidized funding from general tax revenues. This change has often been enacted to avoid increasing the payroll taxes on employers in contributory pension systems. The fourth change has been the incorporation of unpaid family care into benefit calculations. Whereas on the surface this might seem to be an expansion of benefits, Hinrichs suggests caution, noting that **pronatalist** considerations may be the driving force behind these changes (i.e., such changes encourage women to stay home and raise families).

A fifth change regards the benefits of national civil servants as well as local government employees. Civil servants were historically the first group to receive public pension benefits and other welfare programs as welfare states developed, and often these initial programs remained separate from national-level policies as the latter were established and expanded. The recent trend, however, has been either to reduce the differences between these civil servant programs and standard national programs or to abolish the separate systems and unify all pensioners, both public and private, into a single system.

The final change noted by Hinrichs regards privatization of previously universal basic pensions in much of Europe. Several European nations, especially the Nordic countries (Norway, Sweden, Denmark, and Finland), often utilized a universal flat-rate pension as at least a part of their overall public pension programs. During retrenchment, however, some of these countries have begun to eliminate these universal plans and replace them with individual retirement schemes, and this trend is apparent in other regions in Europe (e.g., Baltic Sea states like Poland, Estonia, and Latvia) and in other areas of the world (e.g., Latin America). Rather than having a flat, state-guaranteed (and funded) pension, a system of nonguaranteed, individually funded accounts is becoming more common.

Table 3.2 shows the global distribution of privatized savings systems (both **provident funds**—defined as a fund into which the state, employer, and/or employee pay money regularly, so that upon retirement the employee receives a sum of money—and individual retirement schemes) in 1960 and 2010. In 1960, the only such systems were provident funds clustered mostly around the Indian Ocean rim. By 2010, however, substantial expansion of privatized programs is readily apparent. Although a handful of these new national programs are provident funds (mostly in Africa and the Pacific), the expansion in Latin America and Europe represents the replacement of earnings-related systems (Latin America) and flat-rate universal systems (Europe) with individual retirement schemes. Figure 3.2 shows the global distribution of these private savings systems in 1960 and 1999.

THE FUTURE OF THE WELFARE STATE AND GLOBAL AGING

What then is the future of the welfare state in this time of rapid global aging? Will retrenchment in the developed nations continue and steadily erode public benefits, or will these policies and programs rebound? Will some new form of welfare come to dominate old-age assistance? And what will be the

TABLE 3.2 Global Distribution of Privatized Public Pension Systems

Provident funds		Mandatory private savings	
1960	2010	1960	2010
Haiti	Brunei	None	Bolivia
India	Fiji		Bulgaria
Indonesia	Gambia		Chile
Iraq	India		China
Malaysia	Indonesia		Colombia
Singapore	Kenya		Costa Rica
Sri Lanka	Kiribati		Croatia
	Malaysia		Dominican Republic
	Nepal		Ecuador
	Samoa		El Salvador
	Singapore		Estonia
	Solomon		Hungary
	Islands		Kazakhstan
	Sri Lanka		Kyrgyzstan
	Swaziland		Latvia
	Uganda		Mexico
	Vanuatu		Nigeria
			Panama
			Peru
			Poland
			Romania
			Russia
			Slovak Republic
			Sweden
			Taiwan
			Uruguay

fate of the emerging welfare states in developing nations? Will these nations follow in the footsteps of their developed predecessors, or will they blaze their own unique trails in welfare policy?

Muir and Turner (2011) offer four distinct directions for the welfare state in the 21st century that provide answers to some of these questions. Their recommendations apply more directly to developed nations but have implications for developing nations. First, these authors suggest that one solution for benefit retrenchment in public pension programs is to increase the overall coverage of work-related private pensions (see Chapter 8 for a more detailed discussion of private pensions). Indeed, as they note, the range of private pension coverage even among the industrialized nations of Europe is substantial, with the highest coverage rates in places like Switzerland (90% of workforce covered) compared to the lowest private pension coverage in places like Poland (only 2%). Different nations have adopted a range of strategies to increase this private pension coverage, from mandating it to providing incentives for private pensions for workers and their employers (e.g., through tax incentives). Muir and Turner, however, suggest that the best

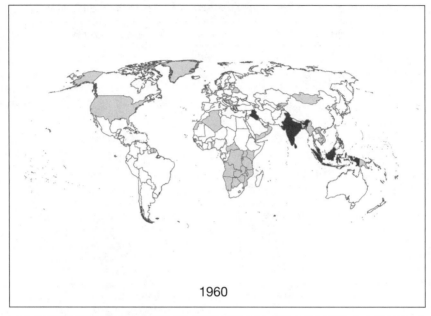

FIGURE 3.2 Mandatory savings programs, 1960 and 1999.

approach may be to make work-related pension participation the default, but to allow for opt-out options. This direction is more likely to be followed in developed nations. In many developing countries, the dominant employment sector is agriculture (often family-based), so it is difficult to envision how private pensions could be applicable there.

Second, Muir and Turner discuss the need to more evenly share social and economic risks between the public and private sectors than is the current practice in many nations. The recent global financial crisis has demonstrated quite clearly that no retirement investments are completely safe. Indeed, in the United States, the loss of home values has been devastating for American retirees and those near retirement, since much of the wealth of current and future retirees is found in those homes. These authors suggest that governments should extend some of the guarantees of government-funded pensions to the private pension in the form of formal insurance programs, especially if their first point regarding extended private pension coverage is to be undertaken. Muir and Turner also note that political risks are tied to economic risks for pensions; the turmoil in 2012 and 2013 in Greece regarding voter approval of new financial austerity measures is an excellent example of such political risk. When the financial system collapses (or comes close to collapse), governments must often make major cuts in welfare program spending, causing further economic hardship and deep voter resentment. No European government in power since the beginning of the Great Recession of 2008–2009 has been reelected. However, the suggestion of greater risk-sharing is much more viable in the developed than in the developing world. Where such nations have difficulty funding and providing public pensions to large segments of their populations, it is difficult to see how these governments are capable of guaranteeing even more risks for the private sector.

Third, Muir and Turner suggest that programs will need to address the issue of providing adequate benefits; indeed, even defining what adequate benefits are. Throughout most of the 20th century, adequate benefits have been defined in terms of **replacement income** (the income level needed by a retiree to maintain preretirement lifestyle). This is often thought to be about 70% of preretirement income. These authors note that governments in the face of financial crisis are now questioning what is meant by replacement income and whether to use this notion at all. Indeed, should the percentage be 70% or something else? Should the percentage, whatever it is, be calculated based on average lifetime wages, last wage, or (as France has done) on current prices? Muir and Turner see these questions as driving much of the change in pension systems, and in the welfare state more generally, in the near future. Again, however, these questions seem more focused on the developed rather than the developing world. Yet, recent work by Muruthi (2012) may suggest some developing world options in this vein. In his work on how older adults view retirement in Kenya, Muruthi notes that many individuals would prefer an income generation source (e.g., a goat or a cow) be provided by the government rather than cash payments. As such, rather than a replacement income percentage, a replacement income *source* might be more applicable in such settings.

Finally, Muir and Turner note that all programs will need to address the issue of increasing longevity. As discussed in chapter 5, life expectancies have risen drastically over the last 100 years, and despite regular declarations by various scholars that a maximum life expectancy has been achieved, expectancies continue to break through these supposed maximums. Nations will need to respond to this trend. The most obvious solution is to index benefits for longevity (i.e., adjust payments for the rate of increase in longevity), and some nations have already begun doing so (e.g., Sweden; see Kathrin Komp's essay at the end of this chapter). Other possibilities include the elimination of payout options that do not mesh well with increasingly longer life for older adults; in this scenario, retirees would not have the option of receiving a lump sum payout, but would be required to receive their benefits as a regular annuity payment. This strategy would prevent early exhaustion of individual retirement savings. Here, again, such reforms are less applicable to developing nations, where aging is occurring at a much more rapid rate than in the developed world; therefore, indexing benefits to longevity is akin to trying to index them to hyperinflation. Trying to adjust to the hyperlongevity change soon to be experienced in many places like China and Thailand may well be impossible.

Muir and Turner also note the importance of culture in understanding current and future pension system variation, and this point may be the most relevant, especially for developing nations. Developing nations are experiencing aging quite differently from their developed counterparts. Aging is occurring at a much more rapid pace than has ever been seen before. This rapidity of change has resulted in unique combinations of expanding government programs and widespread continuation of traditional family and religious modes of support in these countries. What might be seen from these developing contexts, therefore, is a synthesis of welfare state, family, and/or church supports, rather than a replacement of the latter two by the former. What is woefully apparent, however, is the scarcity of welfare state research in the developing world and the strong possibility that research findings from the developed nations will be (at least partially) inapplicable for these emerging welfare states.

CONCLUSION

The story of *Tooncie* opened this chapter's discussion of the welfare state and its importance in global aging. One might wonder what her older adult life would be like under a welfare state regime different from that of the United States. In Sweden, she would have experienced a very different retirement where she would have been guaranteed a basic universal pension that was supplemented by progressively applied earnings-related payments, and if she had persistent health problems, government-funded long-term care services as are noted by Komp in her essay. In Canada, she would have been covered by a national health care plan with substantially lower out-of-pocket expenses. In both these nations, however, she would have paid larger portions of her working income to taxes to support these systems. On the other hand, in Gambia she would not have had any public pension coverage available to her for most of her life. Gambia's provident fund system was not established until 1981 (and subsequently changed to an earnings-related system in 1987), when *Tooncie* was 56 years old, which would have left little time for her to accumulate retirement savings, assuming that she lived in an urban area where the coverage could be obtained. Clearly, the welfare state has substantial impact on how we age, no matter where on earth we do that aging.

On a final note, although the welfare state includes both income maintenance and health care programs for older adults, this chapter has focused predominantly on the former. The welfare state literature is dominated by research on income maintenance programs (especially public pensions), which should not be surprising given that they (a) are the oldest welfare state programs, (b) are the most widespread welfare state policies, and (c) to date have accounted for the overwhelming majority of welfare state spending. This is changing, however, as more nations address health care issues for older adults and as the expense of such systems rises with increasing medical costs and booming old age populations. Discussions of health, long-term care, and health care policies are provided in Chapters 6 and 7.

DISCUSSION QUESTIONS

1. What is the *welfare state*?
2. What institutions were most commonly associated with maintaining the social well-being of individuals before the 19th century?
3. How did the Industrial Revolution change the provision of care for those in need?
4. Why did developing nations begin to establish welfare states?
5. How did the demographic shift of aging populations place a significant burden on welfare states in the latter half of the 20th century?
6. What is the difference between entitlement and eligibility?
7. What are the need-based eligibility requirements for some welfare state programs in your country? Are there any requirements of age eligibility or minimum period prior to eligibility that may prevent certain individuals from participating in these programs?
8. If you could help a country start over, how would you design a good pension system?
9. What is welfare state *retrenchment*?
10. Can you explain some welfare state retrenchment strategies? What retrenchment strategies are evident in your country?
11. Why do some countries adopt pronatalist policies?
12. Why might the state want to privatize pension systems?
13. How has increased life expectancy affected welfare states?
14. How might developing and developed nations respond differently to population aging?

KEY WORDS

Age eligibility
Citizenship entitlement
Earnings-related entitlement

In-kind benefits
Need-based eligibility
Privatized public pension systems
Pronatalist
Provident funds
Public pensions
Replacement income
Retrenchment
Social Security
State socialism
Universal programs
Welfare state

Older Swedes: Living in the "Role Model of Welfare States"

Kathrin Komp

Populations around the globe are aging, and northern Europe is currently one of the oldest regions in the world (United Nations, 2009). Sweden is the largest country in this region, covering a surface of 450,000 sq km (about 174,000 sq mi), and containing a population of about nine million people (U.S. Central Intelligence Agency, 2013). It is well known for its extensive forests, harsh winters, and vast population of elk. Among scholars, Sweden is also well known for its welfare state. The Swedish welfare state is famous for the wide range of support it offers its citizens and for its ability to even out social inequalities. Many scholars and policy makers, therefore, look to Sweden for inspiration on how to design social policies. Some scholars even go so far as to refer to Sweden as the "role model of welfare states." Whether it can be maintained that one type of welfare state is better than another is debatable. After all, welfare policies reflect the culture, history, population, and geography of a country. However, Sweden's prominent position in debates about welfare states warrants taking a closer look. This essay (a) describes the state of population aging in Sweden; (b) outlines the key features of the Swedish welfare state; (c) portrays what the Swedish welfare state does for its older citizens; (d) shows how older Swedes participate in their welfare state; and, finally (e) discusses challenges and opportunities for the welfare state in an aging Sweden.

HOW GRAY IS SWEDEN?

The Swedish population has already aged considerably, and this demographic shift is still continuing. In 2012, one in four Swedes was aged 60 and older, and one in five Swedes was aged 65 and older. These numbers put Sweden in the group of the oldest countries in Europe, although not at the absolute top (that distinction belongs to Germany and Italy; Eurostat, 2013). Sweden reached this stage of population aging through slow changes that took place over more than a century—a characteristic that sets Sweden apart from many other countries that experienced a more recent and dramatic increase in the age of their populations. Chesnais (1992) argues that possible reasons might be that Sweden had a rather stable economy and did not suffer major losses in wars during that time. Expressed in numbers, the proportion of Swedes aged 65 and older doubled from 1960 until today, and it is expected to increase to almost one in three persons by 2050 (Eurostat, 2013; United Nations, 2001). Interestingly, Sweden not only has a large number of older citizens, but its typical citizens reach the impressive age of almost eighty years. Once Swedes reach the age of 65, they can look forward to 14 more years in good health, followed by 5 years in poor health (Eurostat, 2011b). These numbers mean that Swedes can look forward to long lives and to many years of health and activity after retirement.

WHAT IS THE SWEDISH WELFARE STATE LIKE?

If countries were compared according to the size of their welfare states, then Sweden would be a giant. In 2012, the Swedish government spent 28% of its budget on social issues, ranking it 5th among both the OECD (the 34 most developed countries in the world) and European countries; and this is 9% higher than the 19% spent by the United States (OECD, 2013). The reason for Sweden's high welfare expenditures is not only the range of welfare provisions there. In addition, the high level of state involvement in welfare provisions boosts welfare budgets. Esping-Andersen (1990, 1999) explained that the Swedish government is active in many social areas that in other countries are left to families, companies, or welfare associations. Because of this engagement, the Swedish government manages to drastically reduce social inequalities. Moreover, it creates a densely knit safety net that effectively helps people faced with social risks, such as unemployment or poor health (Esping-Andersen, 1990; Korpi & Palme, 1998). The bottom line is that the Swedish welfare state is very well developed, active, and supportive of its citizens.

WHAT DOES THE SWEDISH WELFARE STATE DO FOR ITS OLDER CITIZENS?

The Swedish welfare state supports its older citizens, but it does not favor them over younger ones. Lynch (2001) studied how much welfare states spend on older citizens compared to younger citizens and found that Sweden is much less biased toward its older citizens than, for example, Greece, the United States, or Italy. Instead of explicitly focusing on older citizens, the Swedish welfare state emphasizes programs that support young or middle-aged people, such as childcare services and unemployment benefits, and it is very active in supporting programs that benefit all its citizens equally, such as universal health care that is accessible to anyone in need of help, regardless of their income (Trydegard & Thorslund, 2010).

Some governmental support programs that are particularly important to older Swedes are pension benefits (similar to Social Security [SS] in the United States), health services, and long-term care services. The Swedish pension scheme sets age 65 as the mandatory retirement age. However, Swedes can transition into early retirement from the age of 55 on, and they do have the legal right to continue working until the age of 67, if they wish (International Social Security Agency, 2010; OECD, 2011b). If older Swedes experience health problems, they can call on the help of public health care services. These services are available to all Swedes, without the need to purchase supplementary health insurance (Paris, Devaux, & Wei, 2010). Finally, if health problems persist, then older Swedes can use publicly funded long-term care services. These services are provided both in the home of the frail person and in institutions (OECD, 2011a).

HOW DO OLDER SWEDES PARTICIPATE IN THEIR WELFARE STATE?

Older Swedes generally are quite active, thanks to their good health. They use their time and capabilities to engage in various activities—several of which affect the welfare state. Older Swedes are politically active, voting in governmental elections more often than their younger counterparts (Komp, 2013), so they have a strong influence on what their government is like. Additionally, older Swedes participate directly as members of parliament, having an immediate impact on what their welfare state does. For example, in 2011 almost one half of the members of the Swedish Parliament were aged 55 or older (Eurostat, 2011a).

On the other hand, older Swedes also engage in activities that are important for welfare states, such as working for pay, volunteering, and helping their kin (Komp & Aartsen, 2013). The workforce participation among older citizens in Sweden is higher than in many other countries. In fact, in 2009 Sweden reached the highest workforce participation rate in Europe for people age 55 to age 64. In that year, 70% of the Swedes in this age group worked for pay (DeStatis [Federal Statistical Office of Germany], 2011). Similarly, Swedes aged 50 and older also are more likely to volunteer in organizations, to provide care to kin, and to help their kin and friends than many other Europeans (Hank & Stuck, 2008). Only in their participation in religious organizations do we find older Swedes to be less active than most of their European peers (Sirven & Debrand, 2008).

CHALLENGES AND OPPORTUNITIES FOR THE WELFARE STATE IN AGING SWEDEN

Sweden changes as its population ages. The number of older people increases, and Swedes are living longer. This trend challenges the Swedish welfare state to cater more and more to the needs of older people. For this reason, the Swedish government has already begun to change some welfare provisions, such as pension schemes and long-term care services (Hinrichs, 2000;

Trydegard & Thorslund, 2010). At the same time, a second type of change is occurring within Sweden. Due to the increasing healthy life expectancy, old age is more and more associated with an active lifestyle and social opportunities. This trend is particularly well pronounced in Sweden, because retirees experience a longer period of healthy life than in many other countries. This change opens up new opportunities for the Swedish welfare state. The Swedish government could, for example, try to prolong working lives even more, or they could try to increase social cohesion by encouraging older citizens to volunteer (Komp & Béland, 2012). The aging of the Swedish population is, therefore, more than a simple pressure point for welfare states; it is a qualitative shift that requires policy makers to rethink what it means to be old. Consequently, it is also a shift that allows policy makers to develop a new type of old age policy. The next few decades will show whether the Swedish government is able to seize this opportunity.

CHAPTER 4

Demographic Perspectives on an Aging World

Population aging may be seen as a human success story. . . . But the worldwide phenomenon of aging [brings] many challenges . . . concerning the ability of [nations] and communities to provide for [an] aging population (Kinsella & Phillips, 2005, p. 5).

The challenges presented by an aging world are hinted at in the quote above. New reports and articles appear almost weekly, describing the issues facing aging societies on all continents. Work, housing, retirement, transportation, technology, health care, and intergenerational relationships are being transformed by **population aging**. No doubt, you can see signs of these changes all around you within your own country. In the United States, baby boomer aging is discussed on news programs, reflected in a seemingly endless array of new products to make old age easier and better, and is even the subject of a growing number of websites. Down the road, an aging workforce, with a short supply of younger workers, will cause citizens of the United States, Canada, and Europe to rethink their attitudes about older workers and retirement. In China, concern is on the rise about the impact of the one-child policy on traditional family caregiving values and the lack of formal care alternatives.

The significance of worldwide population aging is nicely summarized in a United Nations publication on the subject: "Population aging is unprecedented, pervasive, enduring, and has profound implications for many facets of human life" (United Nations, 2002, p. xxvii). *Population aging* refers to the social and demographic processes that result in the aging of a population—the transition to an age structure with increasing numbers and proportions of older people and decreasing proportions at the youngest ages. The specific

Portions of this chapter have been adapted from *Aging, Society, and the Life Course* (4th ed.), by L. A. Morgan and S. R. Kunkel, 2011, New York, NY: Springer Publishing. Copyright 2011 by Springer Publishing. Adapted with permission.

forces involved in societal aging, along with its measures, are discussed later in this chapter. For now, the focus is on the general impact of population aging on a society.

The size and composition of the older population influences the most basic features of social life; for example, the aging of the U.S. baby boomers has sparked the emergence of more and more active adult communities, widespread marketing campaigns for so-called lifestyle pharmaceuticals (hair-growth drugs, antiwrinkle cream, and sexual stimulants), and ethical debates about end-of-life medical treatment (see the essay by Chahal in Chapter 6). Families, the labor market, education, government, health care, media, and consumer goods are all affected by the age of a population; however, the nature of the changes facing an aging society depends on a number of different factors. A brief example will help to illustrate this point.

Think about the differences between India and the United States. India is a relatively young society: Only 5% of its population is aged 65 or older, and average life expectancy is about 64 years. The United States is considered to be an aging society, with more than 13% of its population in the age 65+ category and an average life expectancy in 2009 of 78.5 years. As can be seen in the discussion of population pyramids, young societies have high birthrates (fertility) and high death rates (mortality), whereas aging societies have low fertility and low mortality. Many aspects of social life (such as the type and availability of housing, the level of economic development, and the status of women) are related to these patterns of birth and death that produce population aging. For example, health care in India is focused largely on maternal and child health, family planning, and immunization. In contrast, the United States spends its health care dollars very differently: Medicare, the government-sponsored health insurance program for older people, is the nation's largest health insurer (U.S. Department of Health and Human Services, n.d.).

The availability of public education, access to safe water and sufficient food, and the demands that compete for limited government resources are very different in the two countries. In the United States, we take clean water for granted (although there is increasing evidence that perhaps we shouldn't do so); education through age 18 is guaranteed as a basic right of all citizens; and nearly 90% of the older population is eligible for a public pension (Social Security). In India, all the major causes of death in children are directly linked to the lack of clean water and food; about one half of older men and about 80% of older women are illiterate (United Nations, 2002); there is no national system of health care for older people (Kumar, V., 2003); and about 40% of older adults live in poverty, whereas only 10% are covered by pensions (Kumar, S., 2003). Older adults typically live with and are economically dependent on kin to meet their needs. Although the different age of the Indian and American populations does not fully explain their basic and profound differences, it certainly is a contributing factor. The aging of India is occurring amid enormous social and economic change. One Indian scholar summarizes the promise of population aging this way: "The aging of society reflects the triumph of civilization over illness, poverty, and misery, and the decline in human fertility" (Goyal, 1989, p. 19).

Population aging can produce major benefits for a society, even as it presents significant challenges. The short quiz in Exhibit 4.1 will test your understanding of the basics of population aging as well as both positive and negative outcomes. In this chapter, we will provide answers to all these questions or give you the tools to make educated guesses. Go ahead and take the test now, or at least read through the questions to prepare yourself to find the answers as you read the chapter. If you can't wait, the answers to the quiz are in Exhibit 4.2, at the end of this chapter.

Given the importance of population aging (we hope that you are convinced by now!), it is logical to ask how populations grow old. The simple answer is that societies grow older when both the fertility and mortality rates are low. In short, population aging occurs when large numbers of people survive into old age and relatively few children are born. In such societies, life expectancies are high and the proportion of the population aged 65 and older is high. But how does mortality decline? Under what circumstances does a whole society of people decide to have fewer children, lowering the fertility rate? An important framework for understanding these changes is the demographic transition theory.

DEMOGRAPHIC TRANSITION THEORY

The **demographic transition** is a set of interrelated social and demographic changes that result in both rapid growth and aging of a population. The prototypical transition pattern occurred throughout Western Europe in the 19th and early 20th centuries. The first stage of the transition is related to mortality (the rate of death in a society). During the European transition, the economies of these countries went through enormous shifts, changing from an agricultural base to an industrial mode of production, requiring and enticing large numbers of rural farm workers to migrate to the cities to work in factories. At the same time, as a by-product of economic and scientific development, these countries experienced significant mortality decline. They gained control over infectious diseases, improved the availability of clean water, and saw the emergence of more advanced medical technology. This shift from high and somewhat variable mortality (variable because of epidemics) to lower mortality is shown in Figure 4.1.

As you can also see in this graph, fertility remained high longer than did mortality as these societal changes unfolded; but fertility then began to decline when people realized that large families were no longer necessary for agricultural labor and in fact were a financial drain in a wage economy. This second transition phase, the lag between mortality decline and fertility decline, set the stage for rapid population growth. Mortality was not

EXHIBIT 4.1

Ten Questions About Global Aging

1. True of false? The world's children under age 5 outnumber people aged 65 and over.

2. The world's older population (age 65 and over) increased by approximately how many people each month in 2008?
    a. 75,000
    b. 350,000
    c. 600,000
    d. 870,000

3. China has the world's largest total population (more than 1.3 billion). Which country has the world's largest older population?
    a. China
    b. Germany
    c. Russia
    d. India

4. True or false? More than one half of the world's older people live in the industrialized nations of Europe, North America, Japan, and Australia.

5. Which country had the world's highest percentage of older people in 2008?
    a. Sweden
    b. Japan
    c. Spain
    d. Italy

6. True or false? Today, average life expectancy at birth is less than 45 years in some countries.

7. There are more older widows than widowers in virtually all countries because:
    a. Women live longer than men.
    b. Women typically marry men older than themselves.
    c. Men are more likely to remarry after divorce or the death of a spouse.
    d. All of the above.

8. What proportion of the world's countries have a public old-age security program?
    a. All
    b. Three fourths
    c. One half
    d. One fourth

9. In which country are older people least likely to live alone?
    a. The Philippines
    b. Hungary
    c. Canada
    d. Denmark

10. True or false? In developing countries, older men are more likely than older women to be illiterate.

Source: Kinsella & He (2009).

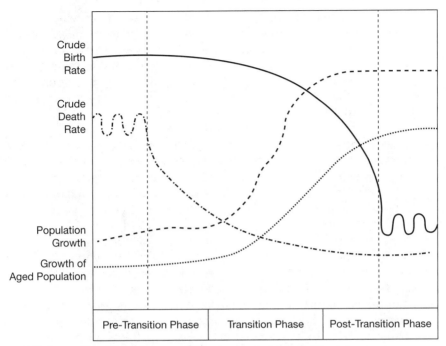

FIGURE 4.1 Simplified diagram of the demographic transition.
Source: Myers (1990); Yaukey (1985).

removing nearly as many people from the population as before, and continued high fertility was adding many additional people. Finally, with sustained low mortality and low fertility, population aging occurs. Figure 4.1 shows the curves for population growth and for growth in the aged population that result from the demographic transition.

Thus far, the demographic transition as a pattern of change in mortality and fertility that accompanied industrialization has been discussed. Yet the demographic transition *theory* has not been mentioned. A theory goes beyond description to search for explanations and ultimately to make predictions. *Why* did mortality and fertility decline accompany economic development in Western Europe? Is the pattern of decline consistent? What will happen in nations that are just beginning to enter the transition phase? Will Bangladesh and El Salvador experience the same demographic patterns as France and Canada? Data on the consistency of the prototypical pattern suggest that even in Western Europe there were variations in the timing of fertility and mortality declines.

More importantly, *causal* connections between the demographic trends and industrialization are not well established. In Western Europe, the stages of the demographic transition are related to "and in part caused by, industrialization, urbanization, and the spread of literacy and education" (Matras, 1990, p. 27). An industrial economy created, for the first time, an economic surplus; all members of a society could be supported by a smaller number of workers. For this reason, it was not necessary for families to have large numbers of children to work the family farm or to ensure that at least some survived. It may seem unusual to imagine that people decide how many children to have based on such a rational calculation. However, there is extensive literature in demography about the many factors, including the "costs and benefits" of having children, that go into such a personal and emotional decision. Keep in mind as well that the means of birth control were limited and unreliable prior to the past six decades. Yet, fertility patterns tend to follow economic cycles in many countries: Parents have more children when economic times are good and manage, somehow, to suppress family size when the economic outlook is worse. It has been said that the most effective birth control is the wish not to have children.

More about the strengths and weaknesses of the demographic transition theory can be understood by looking at how well the pattern and predictions are holding for the developing regions of the world that are still young. The declining mortality rates in some of these countries are characteristic of the beginning of the second stage of the demographic transition. Whether, when, and how quickly declining birthrates will follow mortality declines remains to be seen, because fertility patterns are affected by a whole host of factors, including religious beliefs and the status of women. Such a decline is necessary, however, for these and other developing nations to move into the third (posttransition) stage, characterized by an older population, a lower rate of population growth, a stable low mortality rate, and a fluctuating but low fertility rate.

When and how any given country reaches the posttransition stage depends on an array of cultural and social factors that are not thoroughly understood. Some evidence suggests that mortality in developing nations is having a greater impact on population aging than it did in developed nations. This departure from the classic demographic transition model (Coale, 1964), in which fertility has the primary impact on population aging, points to the caution that must be exercised in applying existing models of change to developing nations. The essay by Scott Lynch in this chapter presents another reason to be cautious about oversimplifying the nature of mortality changes that take place as countries move through the demographic transition. Lynch shows that improvements in life expectancy (decreases in mortality rates) within a country are sometimes unequal, especially when that country has a high level of economic inequality. Furthermore, in North America, Western Europe, and Japan, population aging proceeded along with economic development. In developing nations today, partly because of the rapid importation of technology to control fertility and mortality, population aging is occurring ahead of economic development, and these forces very likely will continue to have an impact on the timing and nature of both phenomena in the developing regions of the world.

DEMOGRAPHIC DIVIDE

The nature, scope, and importance of global aging far exceed simple descriptions of economic or demographic patterns. However, such information sets the stage for—and is an integral part of—a deeper discussion of social and cultural changes associated with global aging. For example, the concept of the demographic divide captures some significant patterns in population aging and social change. The **demographic divide** refers to the distinction between countries with low birthrates and high life expectancies (aging populations with slow or no growth), and those with high birthrates, significant growth, and comparatively young populations. This divide is defined by demographic patterns, but it coincides with the more/less/least developed designations discussed in Chapter 1.

The less developed nations, characterized by high fertility and young populations, will contribute virtually all of the population growth that will take place in the world over the next four decades (Haub, 2007). They will also contribute the vast majority of new older people to be added to the world, since life expectancy is increasing, in some cases rapidly, in most of the less developed countries. Some of these societies will be addressing the challenges of nearly simultaneous population growth and population aging. The countries already on the old side of the demographic divide are, in contrast, facing labor force pressures that arise from low birthrates and low fertility, resulting in little or no population growth. These countries may not have enough workers to sustain economic productivity or to nurture the support programs necessary for an older population—discussed in several later chapters of this book. The demographic divide is one of many ways to think about global patterns of aging and how those patterns relate to the economic and social challenges of population aging.

Table 4.1 provides some information about the three major regions of the world (developed, less developed, and least developed) on the indicators related to the demographic divide: life expectancy, fertility, and proportion age 65+. The information on fertility helps to illustrate how countries on the young side of the demographic divide—those in less developed regions— will contribute virtually all of the coming growth in the world's population. It is easy to see that, with an average fertility rate of 2.7 children per woman and a 2010 population of more than 5.6 billion people, the less developed region of the world will be contributing a much higher proportion of new global citizens. In contrast, the more developed region already has low fertility, longer life expectancies, and older populations. Although today there are a wide array of age profiles when viewed across the two sides of the demographic divide, that gap will be closing very quickly—making aging a worldwide challenge, not simply an issue for the richer countries of the world. Currently, it appears that the less and least developed nations will face this challenge without adequate resources or infrastructure, leading to risks of serious, negative outcomes for their health and long-term care systems (see Chapter 7).

TABLE 4.1 Population Data for Regions of the World

Region	Mid-year population in 2010 (in millions)	Total fertility rate	Percent of population age 65 and older	Life expectancy at birth
World	6,892	2.5	8	69
More developed	1,237	1.7	16	77
Less developed	5,656	2.7	6	67
Least developed	857	4.5	3	56

Source: Population Reference Bureau (2010a).

SPEED OF POPULATION AGING

Aging is occurring much more rapidly in less developed regions than it did in the United States and other already aging countries. This pattern may seem counterintuitive, since developing regions have much higher fertility and younger populations than the developed nations. How is it possible that they can grow older so much faster? The major explanation is that the improvements in mortality (that is, the extension of life expectancy that is part of the demographic transition) happened more slowly in the developed nations, and typically followed a decline in fertility. Developing nations today are slower to lower their fertility than was the case in Europe and the United States but are more quickly getting control over mortality. The medical and public health advancements necessary to reduce mortality, such as immunizations and cleaner food and water, became more rapidly and widely available to the developing world than they had been in today's developed nations. For example, it took France 115 years for the proportion of its population age 65 and older to increase from 7% to 14%; Sweden took 85 years for this change; and, in the United States, this increase will be completed in 59 years. For Thailand, this same doubling of the proportion of older population will take place in barely 22 years, and in South Korea it will take a mere 18 years (Kinsella & He, 2009).

Figure 4.2 shows the speed of population aging for selected countries and the time period during which the transformation has taken (or will take) to move the population of older people from 7% to 14%. France completed its 115-year transition by 1980; the United States very likely reached the 14% mark in 2013. South Korea only began its aging transformation in 2000 but will have completed the change by 2018, only 5 years after the United States! It is easy to imagine the magnitude of the challenges facing countries within which populations will age so rapidly. Systems to serve the unique health, housing, social, and economic needs of older people continue to be at issue

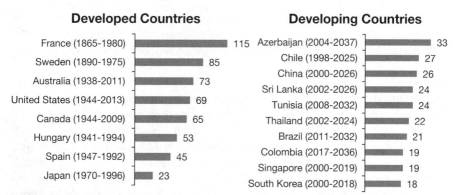

FIGURE 4.2   The speed of population aging in selected countries.
Source: Kinsella and He (2009).

in countries such as the United States, which have had a considerably longer time to prepare for this change. The less developed countries are having or will have significantly less time and fewer resources to face these challenges, making the development of culturally appropriate adaptations even more difficult.

DEMOGRAPHIC DIVIDENDS

So the demographic transition and, ultimately, population aging are proceeding at varying speed in different countries around the world. All countries are experiencing, or are on the cusp of, significant demographic shifts as part of population aging. In contrast to the challenges of the demographic divide, the **demographic dividend** is a different and interesting perspective on these changes. As the name implies, this term refers to the positive economic impacts and potential benefits a nation might experience during the demographic transition. Fertility rates decline, and the young people already born are very likely to survive to become part of the adult labor force—a change that may enhance progress toward economic development. At this stage, the older population remains relatively small, because changes in fertility and mortality have not yet produced their long-term result—an increasing older population. So, not only is the labor force larger than the younger population that depends upon it (that is, a favorable youth dependency ratio), the old age dependency ratio is also low. At this point, "the labor force grows more rapidly than the population dependent on it, freeing up resources for investment in economic development and family welfare" (Lee & Mason, 2006, p. 1). Thailand and Vietnam are examples of countries currently in the midst of this phase in their transitions (Goldstein, 2009; Wongboonsin, Guest, & Prachuabmoh, 2005). Whether the shifting age structure, resulting in a large labor force and low dependency ratios, will produce a positive impact on economic development in any particular country depends on a host of factors, including policies about the larger economy (e.g., wages and taxation rates), as well as social norms about consumer spending and saving (Kinsella & He, 2009).

Some scholars postulate a second demographic dividend, as countries move into later stages of the demographic transition. As a society ages, the population becomes concentrated in the older working ages, as is the case today in the United States and many European countries. Since these older workers (people in their 50s and 60s) can look forward to a long life after retirement, they have strong incentives to save and invest for their later years. These savings, in turn, contribute to individual economic well-being (which can encourage both midlife investment and later life spending, both of which benefit the economy), and to total national income. As with the first demographic dividend, whether the shifting age structure will result in the full potential gains depends on complex economic and policy factors, including tax incentives and disincentives for work and for investment, policies about mandatory retirement, and patterns of consumption across the life cycle (Lee & Mason, 2006). The potential for demographic dividends illustrates the importance of connecting changes in fertility and mortality and shifting population age structures with their consequences for all aspects of social life, including the vigor of a nation's economy.

The third—and perhaps most important—dividend of more years for individuals is an extended opportunity for personal experience, growth, wisdom, and productivity. Although such qualities are hard to measure, the personal value each individual might place on a longer, healthier life and the social benefits to families and communities that could accrue must be acknowledged.

MEASURES OF POPULATION AGING

How can we show whether a population is aging? The seven commonly used indicators of population aging are *population pyramids, proportion aged, median age, life expectancy, the aging index, dependency ratios,* and *prospective age.* Although using seven different tools or measures to describe the same phenomenon may seem like overkill and somewhat confusing, each is actually a simple, elegant piece of arithmetic that tells an important part of the story of a society's "age," and together form a powerful national narrative. Each is described and compared in the following sections.

Population Pyramids

A **population pyramid** is a graphic illustration of the age and gender structure of a population. It shows the percentage or number of people within a total population that falls into selected age and gender categories. Population pyramids are truly pictures worth a thousand words. They capture and illustrate at a glance many past, present, and future demographic trends. Only three demographic forces directly determine the shape of a pyramid: fertility, mortality, and migration. The numbers of people being born, dying, and moving into or out of a location will affect the relative size of all the age and gender groupings for that population, whether it is a town or a country. The impact of fertility, mortality, and migration in shaping a population structure is discussed in the following examples of population pyramids.

Figure 4.3A shows the population pyramid for the United States in 2010. The bulge of people in the 45- to 65-year-old range is the baby boom generation (the large number of people born after World War II, between 1946 and 1964). Thus we can see the powerful impact of a past fertility trend reflected in the shape of today's pyramid. The slightly lopsided top of the pyramid that shows the greater number of older women than men is also evident. This imbalance is a manifestation of past and current trends in mortality: Women live longer than men. This phenomenon is covered in greater detail later in this chapter.

Based on the age/gender structure illustrated in the 2010 pyramid, we can make some predictions about the shape of the U.S. population pyramid in the future. The most significant feature of that shape will be the movement upward of the baby boom generation. Demographers sometimes refer to this as the "pig-in-the-python," conjuring up the earthy image of watching a whole pig move slowly through the digestive tract of a large snake. So, too, the baby boom bulge moves slowly upward through the population pyramid of the United States. The midlife baby boomers of today are the older generations of tomorrow, and young adults today are the middle-aged of the near future! Figure 4.3B shows this very phenomenon, with projections for the population in 2050.

In contrast to the U.S. pyramids, the population pyramid for the United Arab Emirates (UAE; Figure 4.4) has a very unusual shape. Working-age men far outnumber women of the same age. Why would this be so? As noted earlier, there are only three possible influences on the shape of a pyramid: fertility, mortality, and migration. In this case, the imbalance in the numbers of working-age men and women is due to the immigration of thousands of people from Asia and other parts of the Middle East to work in the oil fields. These workers are nearly always men who migrate into the UAE without their families (McFalls, 1998), skewing the gender distribution in these age ranges.

For most countries, migration does not currently play such a big role in the age and gender structure; fertility and mortality are by far the more powerful influences. However, for smaller geographic units, such as states and counties within the United States, migration can be an important factor. Think about what the population pyramid would look like for a small county that builds a 500-unit, state-of-the-art, low-cost retirement community that can accommodate 1,000 older people. This desirable location would attract people from all around the area, including neighboring counties; the relative size of the older population for the receiving county would be affected immediately and significantly. If the receiving county had a small, rural population, a large number of new, older residents could create a T-shaped population pyramid, with a concentration at the top age ranges.

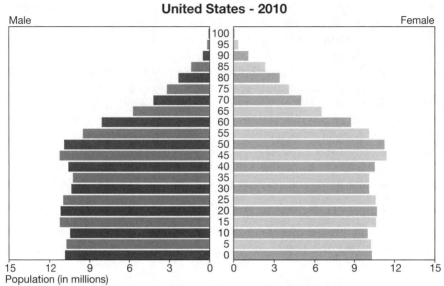

FIGURE 4.3A Population pyramids for the United States, 2010.
Source: U.S. Bureau of the Census, International Data Base (IDB; 2013).

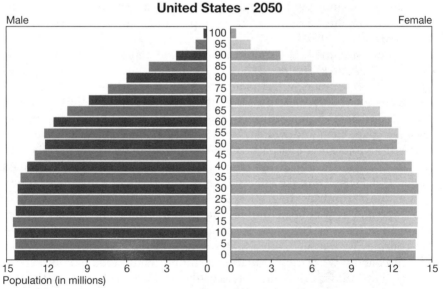

FIGURE 4.3B Population pyramids for the United States, 2050.
Source: U.S. Bureau of the Census, International Data Base (IDB; 2013).

The shape of a population pyramid thus relates something about the past, present, and future of a society—not only the fertility, mortality, and migration trends but also something about life in that society. Population pyramids often take on one of three basic stylized shapes, each of which

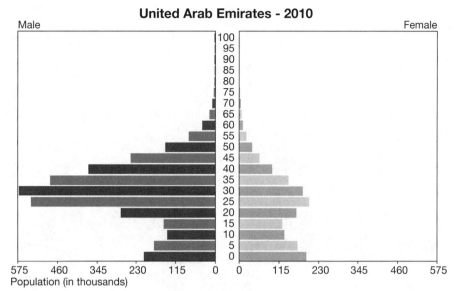

FIGURE 4.4 Population pyramid for the United Arab Emirates, 2010.
Source: U.S. Bureau of the Census, International Data Base (IDB; 2013).

distinguishes, in a general way, demographic patterns and other aspects of social life, such as a stage in the demographic transition and level of economic development. Figure 4.5 shows two of the three basic shapes. The true pyramid, or fast-growth shape, is characteristic of young countries with high fertility and high mortality such as Swaziland, a small nation in southern Africa. The rectangular, or no-growth, pyramid shows the effects of sustained, very low fertility and very low mortality, as is projected for Germany.

The third classic pyramid shape is a slow-growth, beehive-shaped pyramid; it represents a transition stage between the true pyramid and a rectangular pyramid. This shape was seen for the United States in Figure 4.3B, reflecting a pattern of low mortality and fertility. Some demographers have suggested a fourth pattern: the collapsing or inverted pyramid, which is narrowest at the base. The bottom half of the pyramid for Germany (in Figure 4.5B) has this shape, and it is possible that Germany will eventually have an inverted pyramid, if current levels of extremely low fertility continue.

Students are often curious about which pyramid is most desirable for a society. That question has no simple answer: Each pyramid shape represents a different set of challenges. For example, a pyramid with a wide base and narrow apex describes a society with many children, large families, and high rates of mortality. In such a society, the major focus of public policy probably will be on maternal and child health, schools, and family planning—as in India today. In a society with a rectangular pyramid, the relative size of the older population is large and in many ways likely to dominate public attention and concern. It is fairly certain that significant public

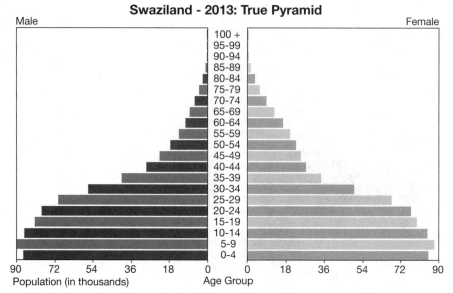

FIGURE 4.5A Example of a true pyramid.

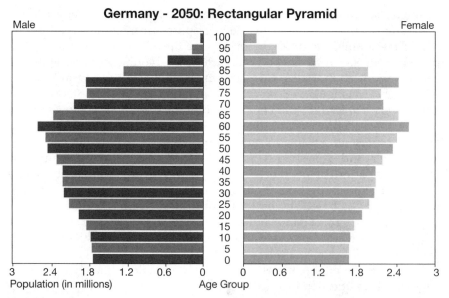

FIGURE 4.5B Example of a rectangular pyramid.

policy and tax resources will be devoted to caring for this society's older members. The society in between—transitioning from a child-centered to an older adult-focused society—may have the most difficult challenges: recognizing and tracking the trends and gearing national policies and spending accordingly. So, there is no best shape for a population pyramid; views on the most acceptable set of challenges are determined by economic development, cultural and social values, political will and adaptability, and, perhaps, age of individuals.

Population pyramids are elegant, informative, intuitively useful representations of the age and gender structure of a society. They give information about how old or young a society is and provide an indication of the level of economic development, the state of advancement in medical technology, and the nature of the resource allocation dilemmas faced by a society. Their weaknesses, however, are their complexity and clumsiness when comparisons among countries are desired.

Proportion Aged

A very straightforward measure of population aging that does allow for easy comparisons is the proportion of a society that is older. "Older than what?" might be asked. Good question! Most reports of *proportion aged* use age 65 as the marker, but some, especially those comparing countries around the world, use age 60 as a cutoff point. So it is wise to be attentive to the precise definition of proportion aged. The last two columns in Table 4.2 show the proportion of population that is age 65 and older for a broad selection of countries, as of 2012 and as projected for 2050. These proportions for 2012 range from lows of less than 1% for the UAE and 3% for Swaziland to a high

TABLE 4.2 Measures of Population Aging in Selected Countries (2012 and Projected for 2050)

	Median age	Life expectancy at birth		Proportion age 65 and older	
		Men	Women	2012 (%)	2050 (projected %)
Swaziland	20.5	49	48	3	6
Thailand	34.7	71	77	9	21
China	35.9	73	77	9	23
United Arab Emirates	30.2	76	78	<1	20
United States	37.1	76	81	13	21
Germany	45.3	78	83	17	31
Japan	45.4	80	86	24	36

Sources: All data except for the last column are for 2012 and are taken from Population Reference Bureau (2012), World Population Data Sheet. Projections for proportion age 65+ in 2050 are from United Nations (2002).

of 24% for Japan. The average proportion of the population age 65 and older for the more developed world is 16%—for less developed nations, it is 6% (Population Reference Bureau, 2012).

As noted, the proportion aged is easily used to make comparisons among nations or across historical time periods within a country, state, or city. Proportions aged are both less complicated and less informative than population pyramids, which give a more detailed picture of the age structure of the population. Nonetheless, trends in the proportion aged in a society are a very important, widely used indicator of population aging. For example, the final column in Table 4.2 projects dramatic growth in the proportion aged 65+ in selected countries. Although Swaziland will still have a relatively small proportion aged, in the next few decades that proportion will double. The UAE is projected to go through enormous demographic (and cultural) transformation, from a proportion aged that is less than 1% (primarily due to in-migration of working-age men), to a population in which one in five citizens will be age 65 or older. By 2050, Japan is predicted to have a population that is more than one-third older people.

Median Age

Like the proportion aged, median ages are single numbers that are often used in conjunction with other measures of population aging. The **median** (from the Latin word for middle) is the midpoint of a range of numbers—the

Source: Dr. Sukhminder S. Bhangoo.

point at which one half of cases falls above and one half falls below. The first column of Table 4.2 shows quite a range of median ages. Japan, by many measures the oldest country in the world, has a median age of 45.4. Swaziland, among the youngest countries in the world, has a much lower median age of 20.5. There are some countries with an even lower median age, including Afghanistan (17.9 years) and Niger, with an amazingly low median age of 15.2—one half the people in this landlocked African nation just north of Nigeria are children! Curiosity about these patterns would lead to an investigation of the recent history, fertility patterns, political turmoil, natural disasters, and food shortages that might have befallen a country with such unusual demographic patterns.

Life Expectancy

Another measure of population aging included in Table 4.2 is life expectancy. **Life expectancy** refers to the average length of time the members of a population can expect to live. It is not the same as **life span**, which refers to a theoretical biological maximum length of life that could be achieved under ideal conditions. There are calculations for the life span of different animal species that can be raised in those optimal conditions, but for humans it is neither ethical nor practical to control the environment. For humans, the maximum possible life span is gauged by using the most recent reliable data on how long a single individual has actually lived. Currently, the life span for humans is estimated to be about 120 years, based on the documented experience of a French woman, Jeanne Louise Calment, who died in 1997 at the age of 122 (Gerontology Research Group, 2006; Russell & McWhirter, 1987).

Life expectancy, then, is the *average* experience of a population. It is calculated from actual mortality data from a single year and describes what would happen to a hypothetical group of people if they moved through their lives experiencing the mortality rates observed for the country as a whole during the year in question. It is probably not surprising that among the countries in Table 4.2, those countries with the lowest percentages of aged persons and lowest median ages are also those with the lowest life expectancies. These various measures of societal aging are all related; Germany and Japan have the highest median ages and highest life expectancies. However, because of the many factors that shape the health and age structure of a population, there is not a perfect correlation between life expectancy and other measures of population aging. For example, Swaziland and Thailand have relatively low median ages; however, Thailand's life expectancy is considerably higher than that for Swaziland (age 77 for women in Thailand, but only age 48 for women in Swaziland). Swaziland is one of the world's nations hardest hit by the HIV/AIDS epidemic, along with many other countries in sub-Saharan Africa.

A gender difference in life expectancy is readily apparent in Table 4.2. In every country except one (Swaziland), women have higher life expectancy than men. At least two questions come to mind: Why do women live longer than men in most countries? Why do women *not* live longer than men in only a few countries?

The general pattern of higher life expectancy for women comes from the fact that, in general, at every age, men are more likely to die than women. How can this "excess male mortality" be explained? Readers probably have some ideas on the subject. Whenever this question is presented in classes, in talks, or in casual conversation, there is never a long wait for responses. Explanations for the gender differential fall into two major categories: biological and social/behavioral. Biological explanations are based on the premise that women have a physiological advantage that results in greater longevity, whereas social/behavioral explanations focus on lifestyle choices, socialization, risk taking, stress, and occupational hazards. There is evidence supporting both types of explanations. For example, women have lower mortality than men *at every age*, even *in utero* and during early infancy before cultural and environmental influences have had a chance to affect the genders differently. However, by the childhood years, boys rather than girls in nearly all cultures are being socialized to seek more dangerous lifestyles and assume more life-threatening occupations—producing a further negative impact on masculine longevity.

The same pattern of "excess male mortality" holds true for most countries, but the size of the gap is different. In more developed nations, the gender gap has been about 7 years but is decreasing. In less developed nations, the gap is currently smaller (about 3.5 years), but is expected to widen with increased education and economic growth (United Nations Department of Economic and Social Affairs, 2009). In a few places, men currently outlive women. For example, in Southern Africa (the region that includes the countries of Botswana, Lesotho, Namibia, South Africa, and Swaziland), life expectancy for men is age 55, compared to age 54 for women (Population Reference Bureau, 2012). The smaller or reversed gender difference in longevity in the developing nations is due primarily to maternal mortality—deaths among women during pregnancy and childbearing. This same pattern in the United States was seen in the late 19th century, when knowledge of infection, sterile practices, and medical care during childbirth was less widely available.

Aging Index

The **aging index** is the ratio of older people (age 60+) to children under the age of 15. It is a straightforward measure of the age structure of a population, showing how many older people there are for every 100 children. By 2030, nearly all of the more developed countries of the world will have an aging index of 100 or more (Kinsella & Phillips, 2005), indicating that there will be one older person for every child under age 15. As might be expected, more developed countries have a much higher aging index than less developed countries. In 2000, Europe had an aging index of 116, more than ten times higher than that of Africa. In Africa, the aging index of 12 per 100 describes a very young population. Nigeria has fewer than 11 older adults for every 100 children, whereas Italy has 168 older people for every 100 children. The aging index is an indicator of the pressures that societies may face in allocation of resources.

Dependency Ratios

Dependency ratios are, as the term suggests, measures of the proportion of a population that falls within age categories traditionally thought to be economically dependent: traditionally those under age 15 (the youth dependency ratio) and over age 64 (the aged dependency ratio). Issue can be taken with the definition of anyone under age 15 or over age 64 as automatically being economically dependent, especially in countries where people enter the labor force long before age 15 and sometimes stay long after age 65. In some calculations of dependency ratios in Western nations, age 18 is used instead of age 15 but international comparisons still use age 15. Other scholars have challenged the dependency assumption by pointing out that some older people fuel economic growth through their taxes and income and that some working-age people may be unemployed (Kinsella & Phillips, 2005). Despite this limitation, however, dependency ratios are useful as comparative indicators of the relative proportions of working-age versus non-working-age people. As such, they point to different patterns of demand on economic and social resources across states or nations, for such social needs as health care, tax dollars, and the educational system.

The aged dependency ratio is similar to proportion aged and to the aging index but is calculated and interpreted in a different way. The proportion aged in a society is simply the number of older people divided by the total population (including the old). The aged dependency ratio is the number of older people divided by the number of people ages 15 to 64. It is interpreted as the number of older people for every working-age person (sometimes stated as the number of older people per 100 working-age people). Most often it is translated into the number of workers in a society it takes to support each older person.

Figure 4.6 shows the youth, aged, and total dependency ratios for the same selection of countries as in Table 4.2. Among these, the country with the highest total dependency ratio is Swaziland, which has 121 children and older adults for every 100 working-age citizens. Swaziland has more dependents than workers. Countries such as the United States, Japan, and Germany have roughly 10 working-age people for every 6 or 7 dependent persons. Looking at the two components (aged and youth) of the total dependency ratio for countries with very high total dependency ratios and those with relatively low total dependency ratios shows a pattern: Most often the youth dependency ratio contributes disproportionately to high overall ratios. This pattern would be predicted by the demographic transition theory. As noted, high fertility and high mortality are typical of a country in the pretransition

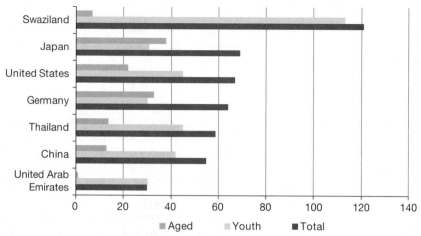

FIGURE 4.6 Dependency ratios for selected countries, 2010.
Source: United Nations Department of Economic and Social Affairs (2011).

or early transition phase. Many children are born and many people die: producing a low proportion of older people and a high proportion of children relative to the working-age population. The relative sizes of the youth and aged dependency ratios also are demonstrated by the shape of a country's population pyramid.

One final point about dependency ratios is important to keep in mind. Although the numbers and patterns may be interesting in and of themselves, they are based on some assumptions that bear careful inspection. First, the ages used to categorize people as dependent (or not) must be standardized so that countries can be compared to each other over time. However, just considering the United States, it is clear that not everyone age 65 and older or age 15 and younger is out of the workforce. It is not very difficult to find cultures where many children and older adults are working; even if it is informal unpaid labor such as work in the family fields, these efforts contribute to the economic well-being of the household and the nation. Compared to more developed countries, older people in the developing regions of the world remain economically active longer, partly because pensions are less likely to be available, and, if available, they provide relatively little income (United Nations, 2009). Hence the idea of dependency is problematic, as are the ages that define the category.

The second problem with dependency ratios, despite all their usefulness and value, is that they sometimes are used to make an argument, defend a position, or influence public policy. In the United States and in some other older developed societies, the increasing proportion of older persons, and the accompanying increase in the aged dependency ratio, has "prompted concern and even alarm about society's capacity to pay for pensions, to finance health care, and to provide the personal assistance that disabled older adults need in their daily lives" (Treas, 1995, p. 6). However, it is well to remember that the ability of a society to meet the needs of its aging population—indeed, its entire population—depends not simply on numbers of old people in relation to working-age people, but also on the productivity of the economy, the continued contributions of older adults, and the conscious, values-driven decision making on the part of politicians and voters (Friedland & Summer, 2005).

Prospective Age

As a final note in this section on measures of population aging, consider the expression that "50 is the new 40." This statement makes some intuitive sense—the average 50-year-old today often seems as young as a 40-year-old of earlier times. We are likely thinking of overall health and vitality when we make such an observation. Some very innovative demographers (Sanderson & Scherbov, 2008) are shedding scientific light on the notion that 50 is the new 40 by analyzing prospective age rather than chronological age. **Prospective age**, based on life expectancy, is the average number of remaining years of life for a person. These researchers suggest that this measure can be more meaningful than chronological age (how many years a person has already lived) for understanding population aging. Sanderson and Scherbov illustrate this idea by comparing data on French women born in 1922 and those born in 1975. The 1922 cohort had a life expectancy at birth of 74.7 years, whereas the younger group, born more than half a century later, had a life expectancy of 84.4 years. If the focus becomes how many years of life each cohort has left, it is seen that the older group had 44.7 years left by the time they reached age 30; however, the younger group would be age 40 (in 2015) before their remaining life expectancy is 44.7 years. For this younger group, their prospective age can be used to say that 40 is the new 30. These scholars go on to show the significant implications of using prospective age instead of some of the measures of population age that have been discussed in this chapter. Their work offers a scientific and provocative look at new ways to measure, think about, and respond to population aging.

INTERPRETING AND USING DEMOGRAPHIC DATA

Demographic data provide an important foundation from which to visualize, illustrate, and compare (across time and across nations) important features of the age structure and composition of a society. In using such data about the older population, it is extremely important not to overgeneralize—not to make blanket statements about all older people or about the typical older person. This caution takes on even more weight when comparing major regions of the world encompassing countries that may be quite different from each other. So, although the use of demographic data is encouraged as a valuable tool to summarize and illustrate the aging experiences of a country or a group of older people, we caution you to use these data ultimately as a way to uncover the complexities and varieties of aging.

One common trap is to assume that the demography of aging, as compelling as it might be, will attract popular attention and spur policies and planning for aging populations. This is known as the **fallacy of the demographic imperative**. One key to avoid this fallacy is to keep in mind that "demography is not destiny." Larger numbers of older people do not compel a particular course of action. In fact, those numbers can be used to promote very different courses of action. Friedland and Summer (1999; 2005) illustrate various interpretations of even commonly accepted demographic wisdom. The general public has probably heard and read a great deal about the baby boomers and what their aging will mean to individuals and to society. Friedland and Summer point out that everyone can get a different sense of the magnitude of the "baby boom problem" if they consider not just the total number of people in that birth cohort but also the additional people born solely because of the higher birthrate. During the 18 years of the baby boom era, the higher birthrate added about 12 million additional children beyond the number that would have been born if the pre-World War II birthrates had continued. In 1957—the peak year of the American baby boom—4.3 million babies were born; in 2008, 4.25 million babies were born in the United States, very nearly the same number (Hamilton, Martin, & Ventura, 2010). If we think about it in this way, the baby boom does not seem as large. These authors reiterate what has been emphasized throughout this chapter: Although they may seem compelling, numbers are only part of the picture. What any society decides to do about the aging of its population depends not simply on how many older people it has but also on the political, social, and moral values of the society. Demography contributes to but is not, by itself, destiny.

The warning against invoking the demographic imperative certainly applies to those who use the dependency ratio to foretell impending economic disaster. The implication of the numbers describing a coming "age wave" is a matter of interpretation. Choices about which numbers to present are critical and often very ideologically based. Some critics have suggested that language such as the "silver tsunami" should be avoided because of the destructive, negative image it portrays. So, whereas demographic information should be considered as a useful resource, it is important to be aware of the social and political context (and organizations) that generate the numbers and direct their uses.

Although demographic information provides an essential framework from which to understand the aging of societies, it is equally important to remain aware of the powerful influence of culture and the overarching impact of other social institutions (the economy, politics, family systems) when considering how best to deal with the challenges of aging. "We need not believe ourselves to be at the mercy of blind forces such as demographic and economic imperatives, as if these existed outside the realm of public discussion and debate" (Robertson, 1991, p. 147).

SUMMARY

This chapter illustrates that the increase in the size and proportion of the older population has an impact on every aspect of social life. In the United States, the number of older people is projected to exceed 70 million by the year 2030, at which time all the baby boomers will have reached age 65; older people will represent about 20% of our population by then—one in every five people on the sidewalks and in the grocery store will be old! Even more dramatic is the extent to which population aging is changing the world. At the beginning of Chapter 1, we noted that the world's older population is increasing by about 1.2 million persons *per month* (Kinsella & He, 2009). The charts and tables discussed in this chapter (Chapter 4) illustrate in more detail the dramatic change that will be taking place in countries around the world over the next 40 years. For all the countries in Table 4.2, the minimum increase seen is a near doubling of the older population by 2050. In the United States, the proportion aged will rise from 13% in 2012 to more than 20%. Other countries will have significantly higher growth. Swaziland's proportion of older people will double; Thailand's proportion aged will more than double; and the UAE will go through a profound shift from virtually no older adults to a population that is 20% older adults. Germany and Japan will have median ages of 54 and 53, respectively. The aging index for every country will increase significantly by 2050, signaling a greater number of older people per 100 children than was the case in 2000. China will change dramatically over these 50 years, from 40 to 183 older people per 100 children. Japan and Italy will have more than three times as many older people as children under age 15—an aging index of more than 300! "This trend may lead to compelling demands for changes in the way society's resources are shared between generations" (United Nations, 2002, p. 16). The demographic patterns of global aging and the specific ways in which population aging is affecting life in every society around the world have never been of greater importance.

The causes, consequences, and measurement of population aging are large-scale issues. Powerful forces, such as fertility and mortality, alarmist warnings about the consequences of global aging, and assumption-laden measures of dependency ratios may seem far distant from your life. However, we hope that you have begun to see that population aging affects each of us as individuals and our families. On a more macro level, it is influencing the government, public policy, health care systems, and the economy of every nation. As seen earlier in this chapter, a large proportion of all older people will live in developing nations by the year 2020. The challenges facing the nations where rapid population aging will compete with maternal and child health concerns are enormous. Of equal magnitude are the challenges for the global community to plan for their aging societies and to propose and implement culturally relevant solutions to the challenges of health care and economic security.

EXHIBIT 4.2

Answers to the Global Aging Quiz

1. **True.** Although the world's population is aging rapidly, children still out-number older people. Projections indicate, however, that in fewer than 5 years, older people will outnumber children for the first time in history.

2. **d.** The estimated change in the total size of the world's older population between July 2007 and July 2008 was more than 10.4 million people, an average of 870,000 each month.

3. **a.** China also has the largest older population; it currently numbers about 120 million.

4. **False.** Although industrialized nations have higher percentages of older people than do most developing countries, 62% of all people aged 65 and over now live in the developing countries of Africa, Asia, Latin America, the Caribbean, and Oceania.

5. **b.** Japan, with 22% of its population aged 65 and over, has recently supplanted Italy as the world's oldest major country.

6. **True.** In some African countries (e.g., Malawi, South Africa, Zambia, and Zimbabwe) where the HIV/AIDS epidemic is particularly devastating, average life expectancy at birth is less than 45 years.

7. **d.** All of the above. Older women are more likely to be widowed because they marry men older than they are, they live longer, and they are less likely to remarry after the death of their husbands.

8. **b.** As of 2004, 167 countries/areas of the world (74%) reported having some form of an old-age/disability/survivals program. In many cases, program coverage is limited to certain occupational subgroups.

9. **a.** The Philippines. The percentage of older people living alone in developing countries is usually much lower than that in developed countries; levels in the latter may exceed 40%.

10. **False.** Older women are less likely to be literate. For example, data from China's 2000 census revealed that 26% of older women could read and write, compared to 66% of older men.

Adapted from Kinsella & He (2009).

DISCUSSION QUESTIONS

1. How has population aging affected your country?
2. How do you think the population in your country will age in the future?
3. Do you think Bangladesh and Cambodia will experience the same demographic transition as Canada and France?
4. Japan is currently the world's oldest country. What does that mean? How does it affect Japan's families, economy, and health care system?
5. Do you think aging will be good or bad for your country? Why?
6. What are some of the demographic dividends of an aging population?

7. Which of the various measures of a population's age seems most useful to you?
8. Is there any basis for the claim that "50 is the new 40"?
9. What is the fallacy of the demographic imperative?
10. How do you react to the statement that "demography is destiny"?

KEY WORDS

Aging index
Demographic divide
Demographic dividend
Demographic transition theory
Dependency ratio
Fallacy of the demographic imperative
Life expectancy
Life span
Median age
Population aging
Population pyramid
Prospective age

Income Inequality and Heterogeneity in Mortality Patterns

Scott M. Lynch

The study of mortality was the foundation of demography. In the mid-1600s, John Graunt, a largely self-taught and successful London merchant, developed the first life table showing how long a person could expect to live, given the prevailing rates of mortality/survival in England at the time. The interest in mortality continued, and two centuries later (1825) another London businessman and self-taught mathematician, Benjamin Gompertz, developed his famous law of mortality. His law can be stated very succinctly: A person's risk of dying increases exponentially across age. That is, it increases at an ever-increasing rate.

Mathematically, Gompertz's law can be stated as: $h(t) = ae^{bt}$, where $h(t)$ is the hazard (or risk) of dying at a particular age (t), a is the risk of dying at some base age, e is the exponential function (the base of the natural logarithms), and b is the rate at which the risk of death increases per year of age. Although this formula may seem intimidating, it has a corollary in banking. Consider a savings account, where b is the continuously compounding interest rate and a is the initial deposit at the opening of the account. In that context, $h(t)$ is the amount in the account at time t. Thus, if I start a savings account with a $100 deposit (i.e., $a = \$100$ and $t = 0$), and the interest rate is 2% per year (i.e., $b = .02$), my balance will be $122.14 after 10 years. If the interest rate were 7% instead, my balance after 10 years would be $201.38, roughly twice as much as my initial deposit.

This savings account example shows how quickly something will double, given a particular annual rate of growth. To apply this example to mortality, we need to switch gears a little bit and think about growth in the risk/rate of dying per year of age. Indeed, in both demography and banking the "rule of 70" (also known as the *doubling rule*) provides a rough guideline to estimate doubling time, whether referring to savings account growth, population growth, or hazard rates. The rule is simply that we divide the rate of growth (b) into 70 to estimate the number of years required for doubling, such as in the banking example above in which a 7% interest rate roughly doubled the account balance over 10 years (i.e., 70/7 = 10 years). Thus, under Gompertz's law, if the rate of growth in the hazard of dying is 8% for each year of life, then the risk of dying doubles every 8 or 9 years older a person becomes (i.e., 70/8 = 8.75 years).

The b in the Gompertz formula has historically been considered a "senescence parameter," where senescence refers to the biology controlling aging, and it has been assumed to be relatively constant within animal species, including humans. That is, senescence refers to the rate of physiological deterioration of individuals across age, largely due to accumulations of harmful aging processes. Similarly, prior to the 20th century, the base rate of mortality, a, was also assumed to be constant *within* a given society, but it was assumed to vary *across* societies due to international differences in disease rates, health care, and other factors.

Figure E4.1 shows the Gompertz model applied to U.S. mortality rates from ages 65 to 105 in 2005. The circles are actual mortality rates at each age, whereas the solid line shows the prediction of the rates based on the Gompertz model. The best estimates for a and b were *.013* and *.098*, respectively. In

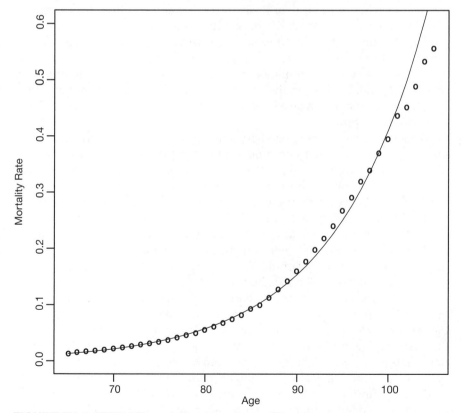

FIGURE E4.1 2005 U.S. mortality rates at ages 65+.
Source: Human Mortality Database (2011).

other words, the estimated mortality risk at age 65 is .013 (13 deaths per thousand "person-years" lived between age 65 and age 66, where a person-year is the amount of time during a year of age that a person is alive). For example, a person who reaches age 66 has lived one person-year since age 65, whereas another person who died exactly 6 months after the 65th birthday has lived only one-half a person-year from age 65 to age 66. In Figure E4.1, mortality risk doubles about every 7 years of life (70/.098). In general, the model fits the data quite well, but it fits less well after age 85 than before, first underpredicting mortality risk and then overpredicting it.

During the mid-20th century, as life expectancies at the oldest ages began to increase rapidly, the poor fit of the Gompertz model at advanced ages became more apparent, suggesting that an alternative model should be developed. One model that received considerable attention beginning in the 1970s was the "gamma-Gompertz" model (Beard, 1963; Vaupel, Manton, & Stallard, 1979). The premise of the gamma-Gompertz model is that, just as there may be cross-country variation in the value of a in the original Gompertz model, there may also be variation in this parameter across subpopulations *within* a country. Heterogeneity in a within a country produces an overall mortality rate curve for the country that deviates from the Gompertz curve because of *selective survival*. Selective survival occurs when persons with higher mortality rates at earlier ages (frailer individuals) die at faster rates than those with lower rates (robust individuals), leaving an increasingly robust surviving population at successive ages. As a result, mortality rates begin to slow down in their rate of increase at advanced ages and thus deviate from Gompertz's law. In other words, at the oldest ages the doubling rule no longer applies.

This principle of heterogeneity and its effects can be illustrated by thinking about the frailer and more robust members of a population as different colors of M&Ms in a jar. Let's say that the frailer people are the red M&Ms and the more robust people are the green M&Ms. If you eat the red M&Ms more often than the green M&Ms, you will eventually run out of red M&Ms, leaving only green ones. Just as the jar of candy will be changing in composition as you overeat the red candies, a population's composition—in terms of mortality rates—will also change as the frailer members die. Thus, the overall risk of dying will decline because the most vulnerable members will have already died.

The gamma-Gompertz model handles this type of heterogeneity in mortality risk within populations by making an adaptation to the Gompertz model: it allows a to vary within a population rather than treating it as a single number. The model's notation differs from the original Gompertz model only slightly: $h_i(t)=z_i ae^{bt}$. Here, a is constant for everyone, just as in the original Gompertz model, but z_i—a frailty term that follows a gamma probability distribution from which the name of the model derives—is added, showing how much each individual's mortality risk differs from the average risk. The technical aspects of the gamma distribution do not need to be understood in order to understand what the model accomplishes: The model allows different subpopulations within the larger population to have different base age mortality rates, and so it allows the overall risk of death in the population to deviate from an exponential curve.

The frailty term—or, more specifically, the variance in frailty within a population—can tell us important things about mortality within and between countries. For example, are countries similar in terms of the heterogeneity in their mortality risk? If not, is heterogeneity in mortality risk within a country related to the level of income or wealth inequality in a country? Put another way, some studies have shown that countries with higher levels of inequality have higher base *rates* of mortality (i.e., a is larger), but do they also have greater heterogeneity in mortality (i.e., bigger variance in frailty)?

In order to address these questions, I use mortality data from 30 countries primarily in North America and Europe. The data come from the Human Mortality Database (2011) and consist of numbers of deaths and measures of exposure (person-years lived, on average) in 1-year age intervals. For the purpose of these brief analyses, I use only mortality data from 2007 for adults ages 30 to 100. I use 2007 data because it is the most recent year for which all countries have complete mortality data. The countries investigated are noted in Table E4.1.

For each of these countries, I estimated a gamma-Gompertz model. I then examined how the elements of this model differ across countries and how they relate to income inequality. Inequality data were obtained from the World Bank (World Bank Development Group, 2012). Inequality is measured using the gini coefficient, which is a measure of the cumulative proportion of total income made per cumulative proportion of the population. Countries in which the majority of the population makes little income and a tiny minority makes most of the income have larger gini coefficients than countries in which the proportions are more equal (i.e., in countries where most income is not made by a small minority of wealthy individuals). Gini coefficient data for the countries investigated here are from 1985–2009. Most countries have data for only 1 year; those with multiple years of data were assigned a single measure by averaging measures across years.

RESULTS

Figures E4.2 and E4.3 display the key results of the analyses. Figure E4.2 presents estimated intervals for each country that reflect the extent of variability in mortality rates at age 30. For Figure E4.2, I sorted the intervals from the widest to the narrowest. Russia has the broadest interval, indicating that age 30 mortality ranges from close to 0 to about .015. Japan has the narrowest interval, ranging from close to 0 to about .001. Interestingly, the countries with the broadest ranges appear largely to be Eastern European and former Soviet Bloc countries (note the triangles vs. circles in Figure E4.2), whereas those with the narrowest ranges are Western countries. The exceptions include the United States, which has the sixth widest interval, and Bulgaria, with the tenth smallest interval.

TABLE E4.1 Countries Included in Mortality Analyses

Western countries		Former Eastern Bloc countries	
Country	**Abbreviation**	**Country**	**Abbreviation**
Australia	AU	Belarus	BY
Austria	AT	Bulgaria	BG
Belgium	BE	Czech Republic	CZ
Canada	CA	Estonia	EE
Denmark	DK	Hungary	HU
Finland	FI	Latvia	LV
France	FR	Lithuania	LT
Ireland	IE	Poland	PL
Italy	IT	Russia	RU
Japan	JP	Slovakia	SK
Luxembourg	LU		
Netherlands	NL		
New Zealand	NZ		
Norway	NO		
Portugal	PT		
Spain	ES		
Sweden	SE		
Switzerland	CH		
United Kingdom	UK		
United States	US		

Figure E4.2 also shows the mean mortality rate at age 30 for each country. The means do not appear to show as much variation as the upper bounds on the intervals. However, the pattern in the means seems to be fairly consistent with the pattern evidenced by the intervals: The greater the variation in mortality at age 30 within a country, the higher the mean mortality at age 30 for that country. Although previous research has found that countries with higher levels of inequality tend to have higher *levels* of mortality, the results here suggest that higher levels of inequality may be related to higher levels of *heterogeneity* in mortality as well.

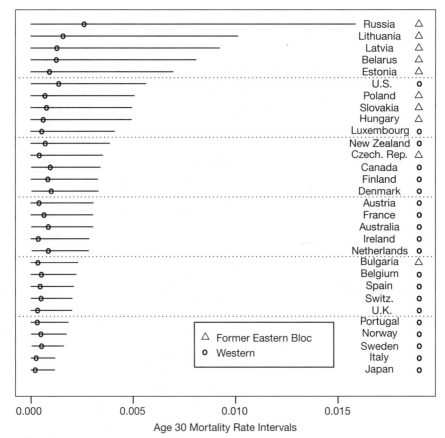

FIGURE E4.2 Interval estimates for mortality rates at age 30 by country.

Figure E4.3 is a plot of the variance in frailty against inequality by country. The overall pattern in the relationship between inequality and heterogeneity in mortality appears to be negative, as indicated by the solid (correlation) line: Countries with higher levels of inequality tend to have lower levels of mortality at age 30. However, the pattern differs between Eastern and Western countries. Eastern countries (marked with larger letters) follow the general pattern; however, for Western countries, those with higher levels of inequality have greater heterogeneity in mortality. The negative pattern among Eastern countries seems to be driven primarily by Russia and to a lesser extent by the Czech Republic. Russia has high levels of inequality but modest frailty, whereas the Czech Republic has low inequality but very high frailty. The general pattern appears negative because of compositional differences between the East and the West. Inequality tends to be somewhat greater in Western than Eastern countries, although frailty tends to be higher in Eastern than Western countries.

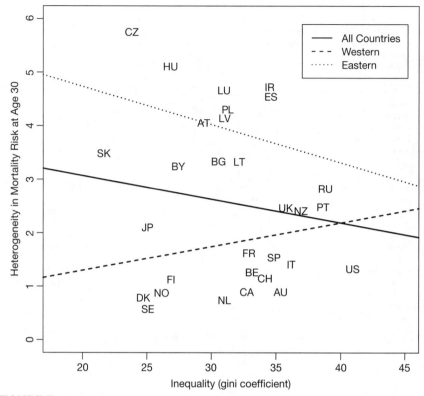

FIGURE E4.3 Inequality and heterogeneity in mortality by country.

Overall, the results suggest that Eastern and Western countries have very different mortality patterns, perhaps to the extent that they should be examined separately. Eastern countries tend to have much higher levels of mortality at age 30, and they tend to have higher levels of frailty. The consequence is that they have a very broad range of mortality rates at age 30, despite having relatively low levels of inequality. In contrast, Western countries have low levels of mortality at age 30 and somewhat lower levels of frailty than Eastern countries. The consequence is that intervals capturing the range of mortality at age 30 are relatively narrow in these countries, despite their having high levels of inequality.

CONCLUSIONS AND LIMITATIONS

These very brief analyses have provided an illustration of how mortality demographers think about and conduct international research on mortality. Understanding mortality differences across countries is a fundamental starting point for improving health and life conditions for populations. Research has shown fairly consistently that countries with higher levels of income inequality tend to have higher levels of mortality. Here, I asked whether income inequality is also related to inequality in mortality rates. In other words, does income inequality possibly produce disparities in the risk of dying within populations? The answer based on the brief analyses presented here suggests this is true, at least for Western countries.

However, we should consider the limitations of the current analyses before concluding that the best way to improve mortality conditions within countries is to reduce income inequality. The analyses presented here have some significant limitations, as almost any international demographic research does. First, I used mortality data from only a single year for all countries, which requires that we assume mortality rates are unchanging across birth cohorts. If this assumption is not met, then deviations of the aggregate mortality pattern from the usual Gompertz pattern may reflect differences between cohorts and not differences within a cohort. In that case, the theory underlying the gamma-Gompertz model is inconsistent with the process that is generating the data. Ideally, then, I should use data from a single birth cohort over a broad age range. However, it would be difficult to obtain data from multiple countries for the same birth cohort over a long period of time. Additionally, it would difficult to decide which cohort to examine. Cohorts may vary considerably in their mortality experience within a country and between countries, given the unique history of each nation. For example, mortality rates for American and European men in their 20s during World War II were quite high compared to other cohorts whose young adulthood happened during more peaceful periods. Moreover, given the geography of combat and destruction, the pattern in the United States differs dramatically from that of Poland, for example, which was in the center of the fighting and experienced increased mortality in the general civilian population of both men and women, and because of the Holocaust, it was especially high among Jewish people.

The inequality data used in the analyses here are also problematic. Of the countries examined, only two had measures of inequality in 2007 (the same year as the mortality data), and only four had measures of inequality in 2008. Measures of inequality for most countries came from earlier years, as far back as 1985. Only one third of the countries had more than one measure of inequality since 1985. Although economic inequality may not change considerably over a short period of time, tremendous political and economic changes have occurred in the United States and in Europe over the last three decades. Notably, the economies and political systems of Eastern Europe and Russia collapsed in the 1990s! Furthermore, economic inequality has exploded in the United States over the last three decades, and Japan's economy has been troubled since the early 1990s. Thus, using inequality measures from different years for different countries is far from ideal.

If possible, I would use data on mortality for multiple cohorts across a broad age range and measures of economic inequality from multiple years. Unfortunately, ideal data are not usually available for demographic analysis. As a result, demographers generally use the data they have available and acknowledge its limitations.

CHAPTER 5

Disability and Active Life Expectancy

Disability sounds pretty bad. It conjures up images of wheelchairs, artificial legs, white canes, and guide dogs. Disabled people are often thought of as not being whole, as missing a crucial piece of anatomy. Because of this, it is assumed they cannot participate completely in their own lives—or in ours.

Another word for **disability** is **handicapped**, as often seen in the signs "Reserved for Handicapped and Elderly Persons" that dot American public places. In some parts of the world (e.g., the United States) it has become common (and even legally required) to make special provisions (e.g., convenient parking spaces, accessible bus and theater seats, Braille signs) for those deemed unable to function fully. The fact that in many such circumstances older people are grouped with the disabled or the handicapped should not be taken as an insult; the intent is to help, to support, to provide compensation. But it certainly does reflect an unhelpful stereotype of older adults—that simply because of their age, they are disabled. In fact, age by itself is often seen as a handicap, although of course it is not. Whereas many older people are disabled, it is the result of physical or mental impairment that causes a functional deficit for which the social and physical environment cannot compensate. The following vignette provides but one example.

In a scrubby bush area of western Kenya, outside the city of Kisumu and not far from the shores of Lake Victoria, stands a smallish hut-type house belonging to an 83-year-old woman who we shall call Miriam. The house contains no more than 60 square meters of dirt floor but is home to Miriam and her 13 grandchildren, ranging in age from about 3 to 18. Each of the children is an AIDS orphan, left in Miriam's care by the death of her four sons and four daughters-in-law. Miriam's family receives a small amount of financial aid and social support from HelpAge Kenya, a Nairobi-based nongovernmental organization (NGO) affiliated with the parent organization, London's HelpAge International.

Miriam appears to have a number of physical infirmities typical of old age, including muscle weakness and arthritis, and she is nearly blind. She has difficulty standing and requires assistance to rise from her chair and to remain upright. She appears completely unable to carry out normal

Source: Tomoko Brown.

household chores such as cooking, washing, cleaning, and childcare, and her capacity for self-care seems very limited. By any measure, Miriam is physically disabled.

Yet Miriam is the acknowledged head of the family, and each of her grandchildren shows her the filial respect and devotion due one who is credited by the local authorities as "raising 13 grandchildren." Several female neighbors who live nearby, although not within sight, function as her support system, making sure each of the children is fed, clothed, and able to get to school. As the children have become adolescents, each has taken on more family responsibilities. Miriam's disability is real, and life in this isolated, rural Kenyan community is hard, but neither she nor her family is overwhelmed by it. The African proverb, popularized by Hillary Clinton's book of similar title (1996) "It takes a village to raise a child," is vividly illustrated by Miriam's family.

In earlier chapters, we introduced several important topics in global aging and several of these areas have focused on health and health-related topics such as mortality rates and causes of death. We now turn attention to another significant area of aging and health research: the study of disability and active life expectancy (ALE). Briefly stated, disability represents a combination of an individual's health and social circumstances that determines one's ability to function within a given social context. ALE is one of a multitude of ways by which disability can be measured and, importantly, is the most common way that disability is measured in a comparative and global context. In this chapter, we show how central disability is to the understanding of global aging and how social and demographic forces have led to its rising importance. Definitions of disability and related concepts like ALE are considered, including discussion of difficulties in measuring these concepts comparatively. We also examine the current state of knowledge about disability and global aging in both the developed and the developing world, and we end the chapter with a discussion of current and future directions in the global study of disability.

WHY IS DISABILITY AN IMPORTANT TOPIC FOR GLOBAL AGING?

In order to understand the importance of disability for global aging, we must first understand the historical circumstances that have given rise to it. As mentioned in Chapter 4, fundamental changes in global demography and health have led to a drastic change in the age structure of many national populations. Specifically, the demographic transition from high-fertility/high-mortality societies to societies with low fertility and low mortality has led to a rapid aging of the population for many, if not most, nations. Additionally, the 20th century witnessed the **epidemiological transition** (or transitions) where public health initiatives, accompanied by development of effective vaccines and other medical advances, changed the nature of potentially deadly diseases from being mostly communicable in nature affecting all ages to being mostly chronic conditions among older adults. In other words, much of the world experienced a shift from contagious (acute) disease mortality to chronic disease mortality, resulting in a shift of death and impairment from early to late life. This is not to say that disability did not exist prior to these transitions or does not exist among children and young adults currently. Indeed, in any preindustrial society of the 18th century, one certainly would have met many disabled individuals, and a visit to the children's ward of any modern hospital would easily demonstrate the reality of disability for many younger persons today. However, the result of the demographic and epidemiological transitions is that, unlike during any other period in history, most individuals born today can expect to live into later life—indeed the world's population today includes about one-half million people age 100 or older (United Nations, 2010)—and to experience chronic disease-related disability of some type before death.

However, we still have much to learn about global trends in disability. For example, some have suggested that a second epidemiological transition occurred in the 1960s (Myers, Lamb, & Agree, 2003). This second transition, the result of increased attention to chronic illnesses by medical researchers and improved medical treatments, led to substantial drops in mortality rates from most late-life diseases, including the leading cause of death among all people—heart disease. This second transition could lead to reduced disability rates if the interventions have a similar effect on morbidity; however, if they do not, nations that have experienced this second epidemiological transition would find themselves with an increasingly large disabled older population. The importance of comparative work on this matter is paramount given that a global examination of disability would include nations that have experienced none, one, or both transitions. As a result, disability trends may be moving in different directions in developed versus developing nations as well as in the more and less developed nations of the developing world.

These different directions for disability trends have tremendous potential policy ramifications for many nations in both the developed and developing world. If disability rates are indeed declining, coupled with increasing **life expectancy** (as described in Chapter 4), this would result in an increasingly large segment of populations that are older and relatively healthy. National policies in many countries, especially in the developed world, would need to be adjusted to reflect this new population distribution. For example, given the financial strains on public pension systems noted in Chapter 3, understanding that the older population will become less disabled over time would be invaluable for planning changes in retirement ages for public programs or for targeting work-incentive programs to increase the pool of workers paying into such pension systems. On the other hand, if disability rates are *increasing* along with rising life expectancy, this would increase the overall health care burden on individuals, families, and the state. In other words, if longer life is coupled with a larger portion of life lived with a disability, then policy makers need to plan for the increased burden on families and prepare for a rising tide of long-term care needs and costs, especially in the developing world where family care for older kin is the norm, and formalized public and private sector infrastructure for such care is sparse or nonexistent. These policy concerns are examined in detail in Chapter 7, but now we turn to measuring and comparing disability across nations.

DEFINING DISABILITY FOR GLOBAL COMPARISONS

Whereas disability is clearly an important topic, defining and measuring it are not easy tasks. Indeed, researchers have been working on this problem for at least half a century. The focus of earlier work was on defining disability and developing measures to accurately capture those definitions. As definitions and measures became widely accepted and utilized in many nations, research has shifted to examinations of how to assess disability globally and how to measure disability in a way that can be used in comparative work.

The earliest work on defining and measuring disability was done by Katz and his colleagues (1963), who created what has become the most widely used set of disability measures to date—**activities of daily living** (ADLs).

Source: Lawrence Downes.

ADLs (as the measures are called) assess the abilities an individual needs to live independently on a day-to-day basis. That is, if individuals could not perform one of these tasks, they would need some form of assistance (e.g., special devices or the help of another person) to survive. Katz included six items in his original conceptualization of ADLs, among them, the ability to (a) feed oneself, (b) dress oneself, (c) bathe oneself, (d) toilet oneself, (e) transfer from a bed or chair to a standing position, and (f) remain continent. Since that time, continence was removed from the list since it more accurately describes a symptom than a disability status, and a within-the-home locomotion item (often referred to as the walking ADL) was added. Additionally, the ability to groom oneself (brush teeth, shave, comb hair, clip nails) has been included as an ADL in a significant minority of studies. Often researchers have referred to these as *basic activities of daily living*, given the relatively simple nature of each task. Inability to do any one of these tasks would necessitate the use of an assistive device, assistance from another person in one's home, or institutionalization in a care facility.

Following the development of ADLs as measures of basic disability, desire for more nuanced measurement of differences in disability in the community setting led to the creation of other tools. The most prominent of these is the **instrumental activities of daily living** (IADL) scale, developed by Lawton and Brody (1969), which measures the ability to perform more socially complex tasks than the basic ADL, such as the ability to do laundry, use the phone, shop, manage money, and prepare meals. Such tasks make independent living easier, although they are not necessary to live independently. Unlike ADL, which usually is measured with the six fixed items noted, IADL measures are used by researchers in various combinations (often mixed with ADL items).

At about the same time that the IADL scale was developed, other researchers began focusing on functional limitations as measures of disability (Nagi, 1976; Rosow & Breslau, 1966). Unlike ADL and IADL, **functional limitation** items are more abstract. That is, ADL and IADL refer to abilities to do concrete tasks such as bathing oneself or managing money. Functional limitation measures, on the other hand, refer to abstract tasks such as being able to walk one-quarter mile or lift a five-pound object above one's head. Thus, these limitation measurements have quite a different orientation from ADL or IADL. Indeed, it is quite possible that any individual might be able to perform an ADL, yet be unable to perform a number of functional limitation tests, or vice versa.

Verbrugge and Jette (1994) brought some clarity to this issue when they described disability as a *process* of disablement. Specifically, they described disablement as "impacts that chronic and acute conditions have on functioning of specific body systems and on people's abilities to act in necessary, usual, expected and personally desirable ways in their society" (p. 3). Verbrugge and Jette further described the disablement process from disease to disability, tracing a path beginning with disease diagnosis (pathology), followed by specific body system dysfunction (impairment), physical and mental restrictions (functional limitations), and ending in difficulty doing daily activities (disability). Their model clarifies the relationships among health status, impairment, limitation, and disability, and thereby measurements of these concepts such as those noted above. Importantly, Verbrugge and Jette clearly place disability within social context, clarifying the often blurred line between more abstract functional limitations and more socially concrete disabilities.

Measuring Disability Comparatively

While measures of disability were being created and tested, demographers interested in comparative health and mortality began using them to compare countries on health and disability, particularly in the developed world. These demographers introduced a classic tool of demographic research into discussions of disability—the demographic life table. Thus, comparative work on disability frequently has taken on the language of mortality demography, especially using the demographic notion of life expectancies.

Life expectancy is a relatively straightforward demographic concept. Put simply, **life expectancy** is the number of years that an average individual of a certain age in a given population can expect to live. It is usually generated within a life table where death due to all causes is the usual end state. Historically, life expectancies produced from life tables have been used to examine gender and race/ethnic differences as well as differences in life expectancy

TABLE 5.1 The Relationship Between Total, Disabled, and Active Life Expectancies

Total life expectancy (TLE)	=	Disabled life expectancy (DLE)	+	Active life expectancy (ALE)
The number of years that an average individual of a certain age in a given population can expect to live.		The number of years that an average individual of a certain age in a given population can expect to live disabled.		The number of years that an average individual of a certain age in a given population can expect to live free of disability.

by specific diseases. As more advanced versions of the life table developed,[1] it was a fairly natural extension of these tables to focus on transitions into and out of disability and other health states.

When constructing life tables in which different states are disaggregated, overall life expectancy is referred to as **total life expectancy** (TLE). When producing such a life table with disaggregated disability states, the TLE is divided into a life expectancy for the disabled state and a separate life expectancy for the nondisabled state, which necessarily sum to the TLE (as is shown in Table 5.1). The former disabled state expectancy is referred to as **disabled life expectancy** (DLE); the latter nondisabled state expectancy is referred to as **active life expectancy** (ALE), or *disability-free life expectancy* (DFLE). From the active part of the name, one might easily (and correctly) deduce that ALE (or DFLE) is produced by dividing life expectancy into disabled and nondisabled segments using ADL. Specifically, the disabled state in such life tables is typically determined by the number of years a person lives with any one or more ADL limitations. That is, if individuals indicate at a particular age that they are living without the ability to perform independently any of the six ADL tasks already noted, they would be classified as being in the disabled portion of their TLE for their given population. Thus, such a life table for a population can break down TLE into the average number of years lived active and the average number of years lived disabled.

One can easily see how well this type of measure might be applied in cross-country comparisons. First, a standard measure is being used to define disability—ADL impairment. Second, a standard metric is used to measure disability—average expected years of disabled life versus active life. Third, the data requirements to obtain comparable data are relatively low. One simply must have data that follow a population across time, recording individual ages, individual ADLs, and perhaps some basic demographic characteristics (e.g., gender) with which to further disaggregate the life table. Fourth, the outcome of such an analysis is easily translated into the language

---

[1]For example, multiple decrement life tables that examine death due to multiple causes and multistate life tables that allow individuals to transfer back and forth between predeath states such as from married to divorced and back to married.

Source: Jiayin (Jaylene) Liang.

of policy makers and other stakeholders within any given nation or cross-national organization (i.e., changes over time in average years of expected disabled life for one nation or differences in such expectancies between two nations). Indeed, ALE (or DFLE) has become the most common comparative measure of disability.

However, this life table approach to examining disability comparatively is not limited to ADL status and, therefore, has given rise to several alternatives to ALE in comparative work. The most common of these alternatives is **healthy life expectancy** (HLE), which differs from ALE only in that the healthy state is defined as being in good or better health using a self-rated health measure[2]

---

[2]Self-rated health is usually measured using five ranked categories of health: excellent, very good, good, fair, and poor. The three best health categories are usually combined to define the healthy state, and the lowest two categories are combined for the unhealthy state in analyses of HLE.

rather than the absence of ADL impairment. Although commonly used in the same manner as ALE, it is important to note that HLE captures an earlier segment of the disablement process as described by Verbrugge and Jette (1994). A measure similar to HLE is **health-adjusted life expectancy** (HALE)[3], a measure commonly used by the World Health Organization (WHO). HALE differs from HLE as well as ALE in that it considers severity of health impairments in defining healthy and unhealthy states rather than using a simple healthy/unhealthy or disabled/nondisabled dichotomy. As such, the data requirements to measure HALE are considerably more demanding. Finally, another comparative measure of disability of note is the **disability-adjusted life year** (DALY). Whereas the other measures noted here are measures of health expectancy, the DALY is a health-gap measure. Specifically, the DALY quantifies the gap between a population's actual health and a defined health goal—an especially helpful piece of information for policy makers. However, much like HALE, the DALY has more stringent data requirements than either HLE or ALE.

The Difficulties of Data

Data requirements are especially important when attempting to measure disability in comparative work. Detailed data to measure health impairment and condition severity required for HALE have been generally available in industrialized nations for some time; however, obtaining such data from most developing nations is next to impossible. For example, a WHO analysis of HALE, using data from the year 2000 for 191 nations, required the use of estimated data in one third to one half of nations examined (Mathers et al., 2001). Indeed, even when examining the relatively simple constructs of ALE or HLE, developing nations often lack the vital-statistics data required to distinguish between disabled and nondisabled states. Efforts by methodologists and statisticians have solved some of these problems by allowing for the incorporation of health data from national surveys as substitutes for vital-statistics information (see Sullivan, 1971), but only recently have such techniques offered the opportunity for more than the simplest health comparisons (e.g., Lynch & Brown, 2010).

Whereas the focus of most researchers has been understandably on the lack of detailed data across (especially developing) nations, less attention has been given to the validity and comparability of the disability measures themselves across national contexts. In other words, although efforts have been made to collect data on ADL in either vital statistics or in national surveys in numerous developed and developing nations, little attention has been given to the question of whether ADLs are actually equally valid measures of disability across widely varying social contexts. For example, one

---

[3]A measure of *disability-adjusted life expectancy (DALE)* has also been used, although far less extensively than the other measures described here. DALE essentially compares to HALE in the same manner as ALE compares to HLE.

of the commonly used ADL items refers to an individual's ability to get out of (transfer from) a bed. Within the context of the United States and many countries in western Europe, this ADL involves the underlying functional ability of being able to move oneself from a prone position on top of a platform about two feet (or two thirds of a meter) above the floor to a standing position. In Japan, however, where many people sleep on futons (padded mats that are laid directly on the floor), the functional limitation underlying the bed transfer ADL involves a different process of elevating oneself to standing from an initial position of lying on the floor. Yet, the inability to get oneself out of bed in each context may have very similar social ramifications. Whether and how such cultural differences operate has not been fully examined in the comparative disability literature.

DISABILITY AROUND THE GLOBE

Given the considerable challenges regarding data on disability in the developing countries of the world, the amount and detail of knowledge varies considerably from nation to nation. Therefore, an examination of what disability looks like globally is done best by discussing the developed and developing world separately.

The Developed World

Considerable work has been done examining disability across the developed world. In particular, comparisons of DFLE (ALE) across European nations have been examined extensively thanks to the work of scholars involved in the Joint Action European Health & Life Expectancy Information System (JA:EHLEIS) and its predecessor, the European Health Expectancy Monitoring Unit (EHEMU). These scholars have assembled an online database (www .eurohex.eu/index.php?option=welcome), including health expectancy information on 27 European nations over the last decade.

From such extensive data collection and analysis, questions regarding disability in developed nations have moved well beyond basic documentation of ALE or HLE across nations. Instead, given that substantial differences have been noted in *healthy life years*[4] *(HLYs)*, attention has turned toward understanding these gaps and toward policy initiatives that can reduce them. For example, Denmark and Malta lead all other European countries in HLY for men, with an average number of HLYs at birth approaching 70 years. On the other hand, the Baltic states of Estonia, Lithuania, and Latvia have average HLY for men at birth of only about 48 years to 50 years (Jagger & Fouweather, 2012). What makes this 20-year gap even more remarkable is the fact that the differences in average TLE for men at birth are only about 10

---

[4]HLY is essentially the same as HLE, but HLY has become the preferred term in Europe.

years, ranging from the mid- to upper 60s for the Baltic states to the mid- to upper 70s for Denmark and Finland. These trends are mirrored in data on European women, although values for both TLE and HLY are greater for women than for men.

Table 5.2 shows the heterogeneity among the European nations in later life health and function and suggests more complex relationships between health and longevity. For example, both Sweden and France have longer TLEs for women at birth compared to Denmark (by about 2 years to 4 years), although living standards in these nations are nearly identical. Yet, women of both nations experience fewer years of healthy life at age 50 than women in Denmark. The patterns for European men are also quite heterogeneous. Thus, extra years of life do not directly translate into additional years of health, even in the relatively similar social and economic contexts of the European countries. Whereas socioeconomic measures may have some utility in explaining this heterogeneity (e.g., nations with higher gross national income per capita tend to also have higher TLE and HLY), more investigation is needed to understand the surprisingly substantial differences in healthy life observed in the developed world.

TABLE 5.2 Healthy Life Years at Age 50 for "Good" Self-Rated Health in Selected European Countries

Country	Men	Women
Austria	18.34	18.94
Belgium	16.71	17.38
Denmark	18.3	19.46
Finland	10.32	12.63
France	16.39	16.59
Germany	12.46	11.4
Greece	20.34	16.03
Italy	15.05	12.05
Luxembourg	18.3	17.42
Netherlands	18.68	20.85
Portugal	7.43	5.33
Spain	18.16	16.6
Sweden	18.53	17.31
United Kingdom	15.73	17.73

Source: Eurobarometer (www.eurohex.eu) Survey (2002).

The Developing World

Our knowledge and understanding of disability and HLE in the developing world are even less. Indeed, it is only within the last decade that *estimates* of health expectancies have been available for many developing nations, and in many cases, these values are estimated from combinations of data and simulation techniques rather than through direct observations via vital-statistics records. Nevertheless, several insights have come from the limited data in developing countries.

It is generally known, for example, that more economically advantaged nations have longer average healthy life expectancies than their less economically fortunate peers. This relationship, however, is not perfectly linear. For example, some less economically advantaged nations, like the Philippines and Malaysia, have greater HALE at age 60 than some more economically advantaged nations such as Russia and the Ukraine. Such differences, which are similar to those noted in developed nations, show clearly that socioeconomic status, although an important predictor of comparative differences in disability, is not the only driving force behind disability and health heterogeneity among nations.

HALE data from developed and developing nations also reveal global patterns that are important in understanding disability around the world. Not surprisingly, HALE values at age 60 are the highest and relatively similar in western Europe, the United States and Canada, Australia and New Zealand, and Japan, with healthy life exceeding 17 years at age 60 in these locations. The worst HALE at age 60 can be found in sub-Saharan African nations and war-ravaged areas like Afghanistan where average healthy life at age 60 is less than 8 years. Other nations around the globe fall in between these extremes, with nations such as Argentina, China, and Thailand approaching the age 60 HALE values of the developed world, but other nations such as Bolivia, India, and the Ukraine faring only marginally better than the sub-Saharan nations in Africa. Despite the usefulness of these patterns in comparing developing nations with each other and with the developed world, more detailed data are needed to truly understand the tremendous heterogeneity of health and disability across the developing world.

FUTURE TRENDS: ADDING YEARS TO LIFE AND ADDING LIFE TO YEARS?

In 1980, James Fries proposed that mortality and morbidity, including disability, were compressing into an ever-shortening period in late life. In other words, Fries proposed that medical advances and other factors were moving death, illness, and related impairment into only the last few years of life in the oldest ages. The implications of Fries's hypothesis were profound. A reduction of morbidity, limiting and "compressing" it into the very latest years of life, would mean that most people would enjoy good health and remain active well into old age (see Figure 5.1). Whereas the idea of a compression of

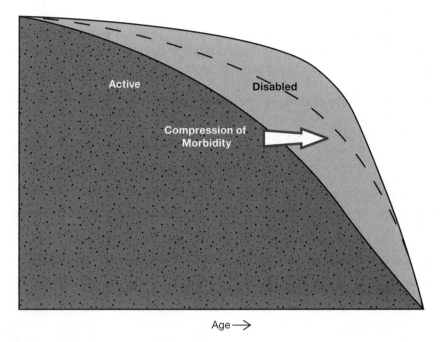

Age $\longrightarrow$

FIGURE 5.1 Compression of morbidity.
Source: Matthew Cable.

morbidity has not been the focus of comparative work in disability, data from cross-national studies may be telling. Data on the TLE of Japanese women have shown that mortality is not compressing, where mortality compression is defined as narrowing of the age range in which most deaths occur (i.e., complete compression of mortality would imply that all individuals would die at exactly the same age). Indeed, recently, TLE of Japanese women at birth exceeded 85 years, which is well beyond the maximum that Fries proposed. Data on whether disability is compressing is mixed at best. The key question to be resolved is whether TLE is increasing at a more or less rapid rate than ALE. If the former is true, then not only would morbidity and disability not be compressing, but disabled years would actually be expanding. Given the heterogeneity in life expectancies and disability across various national contexts, it is quite possible (if not probable) that compression and expansion may both be occurring. Comparative work on disability, with its focus on heterogeneous context, is particularly well positioned to address this question.

A related matter regards the question of whether disability rates have been declining in recent years. Some studies in the United States have noted a decline in ADL disability over the last couple of decades. Other studies using different U.S. data have noted the opposite trend (see Freedman et al., 2004 for an overview). Suggested answers to the question that these contradictory findings bring forth revolve mostly around the populations surveyed (i.e., community surveys vs. those that include both community-dwelling and institutionalized older adults). Once reliable longitudinal data are more widely available, comparative work will likely contribute to this debate. In particular, it will be quite interesting to see trend data from some developing countries where, due both to underdeveloped institutional care and stronger familial obligations of care, the line between community dwellers and institutional populations is less relevant.

Finally, it is important to note that this chapter has been focused almost exclusively on issues of **physical impairment**. This focus is not accidental, since the overwhelming majority of comparative global research has largely ignored other types of disability. This is unfortunate, since evidence from developed nations suggests that cognitive impairments such as Alzheimer's disease and stroke-related dementia are a growing area of disability within these countries. How such **cognitive impairment** compares across nations is largely unknown and even less so regarding how these impairments translate into disabilities. Given the apparently rapidly growing rates of cognitive impairment in nations like the United States, the need for more comparative work, especially in developing countries where virtually no research has been done, is urgently needed. Similarly, mental-health problems can be equally disabling and even more difficult to measure in comparative research. Tausig and Subedi demonstrate this in describing the measurement of psychiatric disorders in their comparative work examining the United States and Nepal in their essay at the end of this chapter.

Likewise, other non-ADL-type disabilities are often ignored in comparative disability research. Vision and hearing impairment can lead to significant disability, especially in a developing nation where assistive devices are rarer and often cost prohibitive. Comparative work on levels and trends in vision and hearing difficulties is also urgently needed. The last few decades have seen a great deal of growth in our knowledge regarding disability globally, especially in the developed world (e.g., Rubin, Roche, Prasada-Rao, & Fried, 1994), but much remains to be understood about the disablement process internationally.

Aging in every country is difficult, both physically and socially. Whether the physical and mental impairments that are a normal part of aging become disabling and whether disabilities become handicaps depend in large part on the social and economic resources of the society and the mental fitness of the individual. Nowhere is the difficulty of assessing and measuring healthy life and disability any clearer than in the case of Miriam, the Kenyan grandmother described at the beginning of this chapter. Anyone seeing a close-up picture of Miriam would deem her disabled; however, a wider angle view, encompassing her family, her neighbors, her community, and her culture, certainly would assess her situation differently. Miriam struggles to stand but maintains her role as matriarch of a large, needy family because she possesses both the personal will and the social supports to keep going. Clearly, her healthy, active life has ended. Yet disabled she is not.

DISCUSSION QUESTIONS

1. What is disability? By your definition, is age a disability?
2. What are some of the driving demographic forces behind population aging? What demographic forces do you recognize in your country as leading to population aging?
3. How would you describe the second epidemiological transition? When did this occur?
4. How have the demographic and epidemiological transitions affected public policy where you live? How have they affected policy elsewhere?
5. Who are the policy makers in your country? How do policies impact the lives of people with disability? Who influences policy makers in your country?
6. What is the difference between ADLs and IADLs? How might each of these measures be used to tell us something useful about the older population?
7. What are functional limitation measures? What is their use?
8. What are some barriers for collecting health data in developing nations? How might these barriers be compared to those in developed nations?
9. How does the prevalence and experience of disability differ between the developed and developing world?
10. What is the difference between physical and cognitive impairment? What are some issues with comparing cognitive impairment internationally?

KEY WORDS

Active life expectancy
Activities of daily living
Cognitive impairment
Disability
Disability-adjusted life year
Disabled life expectancy
Epidemiological transition
Functional limitation
Handicapped
Health-adjusted life expectancy
Healthy life expectancy
Instrumental activities of daily living
Life expectancy
Physical impairment
Total life expectancy

Methodological Problems Related to the Measurement of Psychiatric Disorders in International Surveys: An Example Comparing the United States and Nepal

Mark Tausig and Janardan Subedi

In order to understand any social phenomenon in a cross-national comparative context—be it aspects of aging, older care, or mental illness—it would seem obvious that the same information from each national source is needed. This is simple: Just ask the identical questions in each country and compare the answers. Alas, the reality is far from simple. In order to make the needed comparisons, it is important that (a) the same questions are being asked, (b) the questions are understood in the same way, and (c) the answers are recorded accurately. Only after each of these problems has been addressed do researchers have confidence that the information can be compared across different countries and cultures. These concerns are technical aspects of the method used to collect data but they are also crucial to understanding cross-national differences and similarities.

Cultural, linguistic, material, geographic, and social differences among countries may make it difficult to know if the same questions are being asked in different societies. This type of difficulty refers to the validity of the construct the investigators are trying to measure and compare. As an example related to aging, consider the concept of IADL skills that are measured by assessing the following (among other skills): ability to use the telephone, use transportation, and ability to manage medication. Whereas these questions are perfectly sensible in the United States, they are not reasonable in a country like Nepal. Residents in Nepal very often have no telephones, no motorized vehicles may exist in a rural village, and modern medicine is not available. How can we compare the answers given by U.S. citizens to those given by Nepal citizens? Indeed, we simply cannot ask the same questions to assess IADL skills in the United States and in Nepal. And if we change the questions we ask in Nepal to fit the circumstances, can we compare the answers we get from a modified list of IADL skills (can you ride a water buffalo?) with the list used in the United States?

The measurement of psychiatric symptoms using a survey format can be similarly difficult. Even if we suppose that it is possible to ask the same questions about an individual's feelings and emotions in the United States and Nepal, we need to assess the extent to which survey respondents in both the United States and Nepal understand the questions being asked and the extent to which they will answer accurately. Notice that the problem is true for data collected both in the United States and Nepal. This is because the challenges are related to the method for collecting the information and they occur because of the method—in this case, a survey.

From 2002 to 2003 identical large-scale surveys of psychiatric disorders in adults in the United States and in Nepal were conducted using a survey called the World Health Organization–Composite International Diagnostic Interview (WHO-CIDI). This survey is designed to diagnose up to 23 psychiatric disorders using standard diagnostic criteria and has been shown to agree with diagnoses done by clinical interviews conducted by trained psychiatric personnel. The objectives of the studies included the ability to compare rates of disorder between countries.

Of course the interview needed to be translated into Nepali and interviewers needed to be trained. The translation was done using standard procedures and the quality of the translation was extensively checked to make sure it was accurate. Similarly, the interviewers were trained for several weeks to assure the quality of their work. Because of all this work, we thought we had asked the same questions in the United States and in Nepal.

The results, however, raised some concerns about whether the questions were understood in the same way and whether the recorded answers were accurate. In the United States, for example, looking at a series of 16 questions that were designed to screen respondents for possible disorders, the average respondent reported 3.74 symptoms; in Nepal the average respondent reported 1.22 symptoms. There were also big differences in the percentages of respondents who reported particular symptoms. In the United States, 49% of respondents reported having felt sad, empty, or depressed for a period of several days sometime in their lives; in Nepal only 12% said they had ever felt this way.

Possibly the questions were misunderstood by respondents in the United States or Nepal. Maybe respondents didn't give accurate answers. Indeed, these are common concerns when conducting surveys and there are ways for checking on them and for estimating their effects on observed answers. To see if respondents understand the questions being asked, surveys often ask the interviewer to evaluate the respondents' comprehension of the survey questions. Overall, respondents in the United States were rated as having poor understanding of the survey 7% of the time; in Nepal this figure was 13%. We also found that when respondents have a good understanding of the question, they tend to report fewer of the symptoms being asked about.

In both the United States and Nepal, respondents reported a statistically significantly lower likelihood of having ever felt sad, empty, or depressed during their lives when they understood the question.

What about accuracy? Again, this is a common concern when using surveys to collect information. It isn't that we think respondents will lie to survey interviewers (although they probably do sometimes). Rather, it is not unusual for respondents to worry if they give answers that might cast some shame or embarrassment or disapproval on themselves. Hence, they are more likely to give the socially desirable answer; the answer they think the interviewer expects and that will seem normal. The survey had a series of questions that measure social desirability, which we can use to compare the type of answer we get from respondents who may be giving socially desirable answers that don't reflect their true feelings versus respondents who do give us true answers. In this instance we found that U.S. respondents were answering from the social desirability perspective 15% of the time; in Nepal the figure was 36%! In both the United States and Nepal, persons answering from this perspective reported much lower symptoms. Since symptoms of mental illness are socially undesirable, respondents who are sensitive to that idea were less likely to report feelings of sadness, emptiness, or depression.

Another factor that affects the accuracy of reports is whether someone else in the household is present when the interview occurs. Particularly when the interview discusses feelings and emotions, it might be expected that having someone else in the room when questions are being asked would cause the respondent to withhold information. As it turns out, it was the opposite. Respondents reported more symptoms when someone was present during the interview. This was true in both the United States and Nepal, but the effect on symptom reports was larger in the United States. That is, United States respondents rather than Nepalese were more likely to report symptoms when someone else was present at the interview.

So, what are the overall conclusions? When we adjust the survey responses in the United States and in Nepal to account for these common sources of misreporting, misunderstanding, and social desirability, we find that the rates of psychiatric symptoms reported are still much higher in the United States than in Nepal. The adjustments made in both surveys give us a more precise count of symptoms that can now be compared across these two countries. They show far more psychiatric disorder in the United States than in Nepal. How true is this conclusion? We don't think the differences are as dramatic as the adjusted data suggest. We think that the cultural differences between the United States and Nepal are such that the Nepal respondents vastly underreported their feelings. Nepalese are not accustomed to thinking about how they feel emotionally and, when they do, may not think in the same terms as people living in the United States. In addition, people in Nepal are almost never surveyed and they are very suspicious of revealing information to strangers (our interviewers). We also found that Nepalese are sensitive to the stigma associated with mental illness and are also very likely to ignore or self-deny symptoms when they occur. In this instance, asking the same questions in two different countries (even after adjusting for the methodological biases that can affect survey results) may not give us a good basis for comparing the levels of psychiatric disorder in these two countries. Not so simple!

CHAPTER 6

Health and Health Care Systems

*Jasleen K. Chahal, Suzanne R. Kunkel, Janardan Subedi,
Sree Subedi, and Frank J. Whittington*

The health status of an older person is influenced by many factors, including lifelong health habits (such as diet and exercise), genetics, and exposure
to occupational and environmental hazards. The quality and availability of
health care throughout life also play a role in health in later life. Most of these
influences on individual health are, in large measure, socially and culturally
shaped. Health behaviors are affected by societal values, cultural traditions
and beliefs, and by the practices and habits of the people in one's immediate
social world, such as family members and peers. For example, a person's food
preferences and eating habits clearly are affected by family preferences and
cultural traditions. Variation across culture and occupation in the amount
of physical activity an older person typically gets is another example of the
impact of social and cultural factors on health behaviors. Sorting out the puzzle of how the personal, behavioral, social, and cultural pieces fit together to
produce a particular health outcome in an older individual is a compelling
challenge and well beyond the scope of this book. Rather, this chapter focuses
on the cultural and social issues that come into play. A broad view of three
topics is provided: patterns of health and disease across world regions, variations in health care systems, and the importance of personal responsibility
and self-care for successful public health initiatives for aging populations.

PATTERNS OF HEALTH AND AGING

The adage "When you have your health, you have everything" may be a
Western overgeneralization that simply does not apply in all cultures. However, it is certainly true that health is a universal good and a lifelong concern.
Because aging is a marker for some physiological changes, the link between
old age and health status is a topic of considerable research. However,

We gratefully acknowledge the contributions of Mark Tausig to sections of this chapter.

Chapter 4 presented the harsh reality of countries in which life expectancy is so low that only a relatively small proportion of people have the opportunity to experience later life health concerns. In these societies, infectious diseases (including HIV/AIDS) and childhood mortality are of greatest concern. On the other hand, in many places (such as North America, western Europe, Australia, and the developed nations of Asia), the benefit of greater longevity brings with it the challenges of chronic diseases and burgeoning populations in need of long-term care.

From Acute to Chronic Diseases

The preceding chapter on disability and active life expectancy described the sweeping changes that gave rise to the emergence of disability as a growing later life concern. The **epidemiological transition** describes successive societal shifts in the major causes of mortality. As originally put forth by Omran (1971), in the early stages of the transition, mortality is high, life expectancy is short, and infectious diseases are responsible for the majority of deaths. As societies progress, they develop strategies to improve public health, including advances in medical treatment, greater availability of clean food and water, sanitation, and immunizations against infectious disease. With these changes, mortality is better controlled, death occurs later in life, and it is largely attributable to **chronic noncommunicable diseases** (CNCDs). CNCDs are conditions that cannot be passed from person to person; they generally progress slowly and have a long duration. Heart disease, diabetes, hypertension, respiratory disease, and cancer are the major examples of CNCDs (World Health Organization, 2013).

Recalling the demographic transition discussed in Chapter 4, it is easy to see how all of these changes fit together. In the early stages of development, societies are young, fertility and mortality are high, and infectious diseases dominate health and mortality statistics. As infectious diseases are controlled, survival rates improve, fertility declines, populations grow older, and chronic diseases become more prevalent. Of course, this general pattern varies greatly, and the interactions among economic development, globalization of medical advances, and demographic change are complex. Yet the overall picture of health, aging, and economic development persists: In 2011, in high-income countries, 70% of all deaths occurred among people age 70 and older, whereas nearly 40% of the deaths in low-income countries were among children under age 15 and were attributable to infectious disease (World Health Organization, n.d.).

The fact that infectious diseases are more common in developing nations, and chronic diseases are responsible for the majority of deaths in economically developed countries can lead to an incorrect assumption—that CNCDs are a problem of affluence. The reality is more complicated. Although infectious diseases do indeed continue to take a heavy toll on developing nations, 80% of deaths due to CNCDs in 2008 occurred in low- and middle-income countries (World Health Organization, 2011).

To compare health and disease more easily across nations and across time, the concept of **burden of disease** was introduced in 1990 by the World Health Organization as part of an ongoing project to quantify and track the effects of various diseases in different regions of the world. This elegant concept measures the impact of specific diseases on years of life spent in poor health and years lost due to premature death. Figure 6.1 illustrates differences in the burden of diseases in high- , middle- , and low-income countries, and across time. In 2008, noncommunicable diseases were responsible for virtually the entire burden of disease in high-income countries, about two thirds in middle-income countries, and about 40% of the health burden in low-income countries. By 2030, more than one-half of the burden of disease in low-income countries will be attributable to chronic diseases; the remainder of the burden will come from infectious and parasitic diseases (Kinsella, Beard, & Suzman, 2013).

In rapidly aging nations, rising chronic disease prevalence combined with unresolved problems related to child health and infectious diseases will present at least a double burden. If we add the fact that childhood health plays a strong role in later life well-being, the health prospects for aging adults who did not grow up with adequate nutrition or medical care suggest that the burden may be more than double (Lloyd, 2012, pp. 17–18). Illustrating the challenge facing rapidly aging, developing countries, Duda and colleagues (2011) document the prevalence of hypertension and obesity among

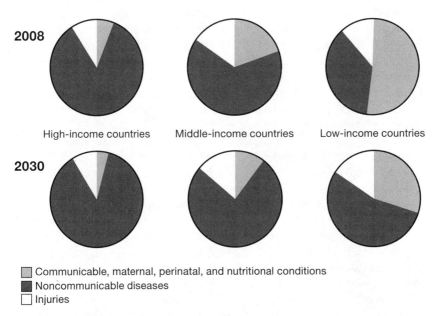

2008 — High-income countries   Middle-income countries   Low-income countries

2030

☐ Communicable, maternal, perinatal, and nutritional conditions
■ Noncommunicable diseases
☐ Injuries

FIGURE 6.1 Global burden of disease, 2008 and 2030.
Source: World Health Organization, Global Health and Aging (www.who.int/ageing/publications/global_health/en; 2011).

women age 50 and older in Ghana—a country in which reproductive health remains high priority. Compelling and perhaps competing priorities related to infectious disease, maternal and child health, and chronic diseases present significant challenges to the evolution of health care systems in developing nations with limited resources and infrastructure.

Differences Within Older Populations—Does Age Matter?

These burden of disease patterns generally compare younger, less developed nations to older, more economically developed ones. Despite differences across these two types of countries, we have seen that chronic diseases are of concern everywhere, partly because every country is seeing an increase in the size of its older population. But, does this mean that aging causes disease? Is there an inevitable increase in illness and poor health that accompanies age? To answer these questions, the health status of older people overall could be compared to that of younger cohorts; a definite increase in the prevalence of chronic conditions such as heart disease would be seen with age. However, variations within the older population should also be examined.

Indeed, the degree of diversity in health among older people suggests that age itself may not be a very strong predictor of health problems. Variations in health status across cultures, resulting probably from food and life-style choices, provide further evidence for the idea that age is not the most powerful influence and that environment can play a much larger role. For example, Americans experience a progressive age-related increase in blood pressure; however, in Japan and China resting blood pressure changes very little well into old age (Alessio, 2001). It should be kept in mind that aging is accompanied by normal physical changes, such as a reduction in collagen that results in wrinkling of the skin and decreased elasticity of veins and arteries, which can reduce the ease and efficiency of blood flow through the body. The timing and extent of such changes are highly variable among individuals, and they do not inevitably produce disease or disability.

Some diseases do become more common as people grow older—arthritis, heart disease, and Alzheimer's disease (AD). It is true that age is highly correlated with the prevalence of chronic diseases, and age can be a marker for physiological declines, but its role as a *cause* is not entirely clear. AD provides a good case in point. The risk of developing this condition increases with age. In the United States in 2013, 11% of people age 65 and older had AD, as did almost one-third (32%) of those age 85 and older (Alzheimer's Association, 2013). Because the chance of having AD increases so markedly with age, older countries (especially those with higher proportions of people in their 80s) have a higher prevalence rate than do younger countries. For example, an estimated 7.2% of the older population in western Europe are affected by the disease, whereas only 2.1% of older adults in southern Africa are affected (Alzheimer's Disease International, 2010). It is not yet clear whether people in developing nations will show the same patterns of prevalence of AD in advanced old age as seen in developed nations. Variations in the prevalence of any disease are related less to age and more to a wide range of cultural factors, such as environmental or lifestyle risks that may increase the chances of getting AD, availability of medical technology and training to diagnose the disease, and cultural norms related to how people with the symptoms of AD should be treated.

The Role of Culture in Health Patterns

We must take care not to assume that age-related diseases are solely or even primarily caused by age. Some older adults get them; others do not. Age is therefore not a universal or inevitable cause, or almost everyone would get these diseases as they aged. Beyond this, the patterns of illness do not necessarily hold true across all cultures, as mentioned previously regarding high blood pressure. Compare, for example, the lower prevalence of breast cancer among Japanese women to its exponential increase with age among American women. In the United States in 2000, an average of 29.2 women per 100,000 died of breast cancer. The mortality rates of this type of cancer increase markedly with age, from 59 per 100,000 women age 55–64 to 151 per 100,000 for the age 75 and older group (World Health Organization, 2006). Based on these numbers, it might be concluded that something about the passage of time—simply living a certain number of years—increases the likelihood of breast cancer. However, in Japan in 2000, only 14 women (of all ages) per 100,000 died of breast cancer (World Health Organization, 2006), less than half the rate for all American women. Although a noticeable difference in breast cancer rates still exists between the two countries, recent research suggests that breast cancer incidence is on the rise in Japan; observers speculate that this increase may be due to Westernization of lifestyles, including consumption of more calorie-dense foods and greater inactivity (Jemal, Center, DeSantis, & Ward, 2010). Such changes suggest that cultural factors—the context in which both aging and the passage of time are taking place—are at least as important as age. This conclusion could be further strengthened if ongoing research confirms the impact of Westernized lifestyles on breast cancer incidence in Japan.

We could cite many other illustrations of international variations in the prevalence of health conditions of older people, suggesting that culture matters a great deal. In the comparison between Japan and the United States, lifestyle factors related to diet and exercise were emphasized. In the case of AD mentioned earlier, variations in prevalence rates across countries might be explained by a host of cultural differences—in levels of exposure to risk factors, in how the disease is understood by older people and their families, or in how and when the disease is diagnosed and treated by medical practitioners. A society's health care system itself plays an important role in the health of older people. Access to and availability of modern, scientifically based health care makes a difference, as do cultural beliefs about disease and medical care, and public awareness about health problems and solutions.

HEALTH SYSTEMS: A GLOBAL PERSPECTIVE

According to most Western conceptions, the medical/health care system comprises a single, institutionalized, bureaucratic system of hospitals, clinics, and agencies providing health care services—the Western biomedical model, or as it is generically called, the modern medical system. The reality is that, although the modern medical system is the dominant form of health care around the world, other approaches to health care coexist and, in some cases, are preferred. This phenomenon is referred to as **medical pluralism**, which is the coexistence of two or more institutionalized forms of health care delivery that are available to and can be utilized by a population. Research in societies with medical pluralism indicates that these competing systems may be used simultaneously or alternatively, or a particular system is used exclusively (Subedi, 1989; Subedi & Subedi, 1993). However, in many societies, modern medicine is promoted above the other forms of medicine, and its practice is upheld by the law (Helman, 1984). Thus, the way that medical pluralism operates within a society can be affected significantly by public policy.

Types of Health Care Systems

Various classification schemes have been used to describe health systems around the world, but F. L. Dunn's (1976) classification scheme (Table 6.1) is well referenced. He describes three types of health care services or systems: (a) the local system of primitive folk practitioners and health care services, which can be called folk medicine; (b) the regional system, involving codified, traditional health care services—for example, Ayurvedic, Unani, and Chinese medicines delivered by trained professionals in the area, which can be called traditional medicine; and (c) the professional, bureaucratic, or modern system of health care services, so-called modern medicine. Health care systems in different parts of the world can be categorized into one of these three broad types: folk, traditional, and modern medicine.

Folk Medicine

This type of medicine has existed since earliest times. Limited knowledge and control over what exists beyond the present, visible world appear to be the basis of folk beliefs. **Folk medicine** comprises a belief-based system that is informal and passed down through families from one generation to the other by word of mouth, observation, and experience. Since this system is belief-based, the explanations for illness causation and its subsequent treatment do not fit within the framework of scientific medicine but are shaped by the social and cultural realities of the indigenous groups from which they are derived. Therefore, this body of beliefs and practices usually involves cultural, religious, and often supernatural explanations for illnesses and treatment options designed for individuals but often targeted to, and intended for, the health of the entire family, or even the community.

TABLE 6.1 Dunn's Health Care System Classification

Folk medicine (Belief-based)	Traditional medicine (System-based)	Modern medicine (Symptom-based)
Astrologer	Ayurveda	Physicians
Medical palmist	Acupuncture	Nurses
Christian Science	Acupressure	Hospitals/clinics
Curanderismo	Chiropractic	Pharmaceuticals
Faith healing	Homeopathy	Technology
Susto	Meditation	Medical equipment manufacturers
Herbalists	Naturopathy	Nursing homes
Navajo/Cree	Nutritional therapy	Public health
Psychic healing	Osteopathy	Hospice
Shamanism	Vitamin therapy	
Vodoo	Unani	
Yin and Yang	Yoga	
Spiritual/wise women		

Source: Dunn (1976).

Folk medicine practitioners are recognized by many names: *shaman* (originally used in Russia but also applied to many other cultures), *curandero* (Mexico), spirit medium, native healers, *kahuna* (Hawaii), *dhami-jhankri* (Nepal), and so forth. As with modern medical practitioners, each folk practitioner has a different and specific treatment approach based upon the etiology and explanation for each illness. Thus, folk treatment may involve prayer, healing and cleansing ceremonies, religious rituals, cultural rites, medicinal herbs, hot and cold foods, and other belief-based practices. Animals (such as snakes, toads, eels, and earthworms) and animal parts or byproducts are often believed to have healing properties and are used to treat certain illnesses and conditions (Huff, 2002).

Traditional Medicine

The term traditional medicine has been used differently by writers and researchers. Many have used this term incorrectly to discuss all medicine other than or prior to modern medicine. The use of traditional medicine in this chapter refers to what Dunn's (1976) classification calls regional or scholarly traditional (folk medicine being nonscholarly traditional). This form of medicine also dates back centuries and to the earliest societies (such as Ayurveda in India and Chinese herbal practices, both of which originated

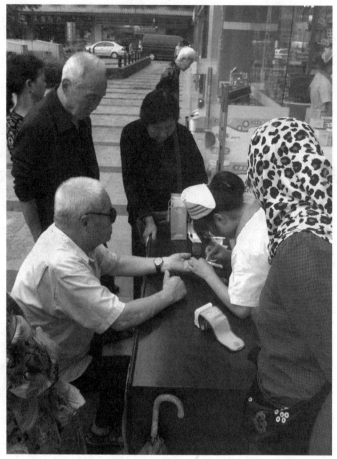

Source: Jaylene Liang.

before Christ [BC]), whereas others (e.g., homeopathy, chiropractic, osteopathy) are much more recent developments, originating in the 18th and 19th centuries. In fact, the founders of homeopathy and osteopathy were doctors trained in modern medicine.

According to the World Health Organization (2008) **traditional medicine** refers to health knowledge, skills, and practices based upon explanations indigenous to a culture (whether explicable or not) that are used to prevent, diagnose, and treat a wide variety of illnesses. Traditional medicine covers a diverse range of practices and therapies that vary not only from country to country but within countries. These may include special diet, plants and herbs, minerals, animal-based medicines, lotions, ointments, and a wide array of other therapies (including music and massage).

Traditional medicine is developed around a body of beliefs and explanations in which illness and disease are seen as natural products of bodily imbalances (system-based). Therefore, treatment involves restoring the body's system to its natural equilibrium or balance and, in doing so, preventing future occurrences of the same illness and other illnesses as well.

Unlike folk medical practitioners who learn their skills through informal sources or claim special powers by birth or religion, most practitioners of traditional medicine are educated and trained in specialized educational institutions offering degrees in the particular type of traditional medicine. In these institutions, although the instruction does not follow the framework of scientific medicine per se, it does have its own understanding and rationale about the body and the elements that help maintain balance and health (e.g., "humors," magnetic fields, dislocation of bones and viscera, loss or lack of adequate naturally occurring chemicals and water to maintain the body's optimal system).

Although traditional medicine is not based on belief alone, it can be closely related to the local culture from which it emerges and may often include elements of belief derived from religion and the host culture. Unlike folk medicine, however, traditional methods of treatment are considered by their advocates and practitioners to have a scientific (broadly defined) basis (Dunn, 1976). For example, acupuncture has an ancient history, dating back thousands of years to the use of sharpened stones and bones and officially documented as early as 100 BC (White & Ernst, 2004). The continued refinement and codification of the philosophy and practice of acupuncture has resulted in increasingly precise understanding of the acupuncture points. This more formalized and clinical approach to medicine differentiates it from folk medicine; the focus of acupuncture on balance and flow of energy within the body, rather than on germs, clearly distinguishes it from modern medicine.

Modern Medicine

According to Weiss and Lonnquist (2012), one of the most significant events in the development of modern, scientific biomedicine was the discovery of Louis Pasteur's germ theory of disease in the late 1800s. This theory postulated that diseases could be traced to specific causal agents, such as bacteria, viruses, parasites, and so forth (collectively, germs). Prior to this understanding, lay and professional treatments evolved through a multitude of approaches that were not necessarily scientific and included cultural and often supernatural explanations. One of the earliest attempts to formulate principles of medical treatment based upon rational ideas, natural causes, and rejection of supernatural explanations was made by the Greek physician Hippocrates (400 BC), who is known today for the Hippocratic Oath (the foundation of contemporary medical ethics) that physicians and other health professionals take before entering practice (Weiss & Lonnquist, 2012).

By 1881, the wide acceptance of germ theory was opening a new era in modern medicine (Cockerham, 2012). Attention became focused on recognizing a particular disease based on the recurrent symptoms it produced, identifying the agent that caused the conditions, and discovering ways to eradicate the disease-causing agent and thereby cure the person of the illness. Thus, **modern medicine** evolved into a symptom-based, curative model of health care.

As emphasis on natural causes of disease grew, the human body became an object of observation and analysis. Hospitals, clinics, and schools were established to train physicians and treat patients. "Disease was no longer considered an entity outside of the existing boundaries of knowledge, but an object to be studied, confronted scientifically, and controlled" (Cockerham, 2012, p. 9). The discovery of natural causes of disease led to improvements in public health measures that emphasized unhealthy social conditions and lifestyles that could also lead to a host of negative health outcomes. These advances were furthered by the discovery in 1928 of penicillin, the first antibiotic. Drugs to treat a variety of conditions became mass produced as the primary method to control or cure diseases. By the late 20th century, as chronic diseases replaced infectious diseases as major threats to health, modern medical practitioners were called upon to deal with health problems that extended beyond germs to include additional causal factors—environment, diet, lifestyle, demographic conditions, and genetic predispositions (Cockerham, 2012).

Although modern medicine remains the world's dominant system of health care, the type of health care system found in a particular country is shaped by its social and political culture, history, availability of economic and other resources, and the degree of governmental involvement in the organization and financing of health services. Together, these factors determine how health services are implemented and financed (Sanders, 2002). In some countries health care is believed to be a fundamental right (at least for its citizens), whereas in other countries health care is seen as a service to be purchased, just as any other service (Ogden, 2012). Four very different approaches to organizing and financing health care are now described.

Models of Organizing and Financing Modern Medicine

In his ambitious and influential study of global systems of health care, journalist T. R. Reid (2009) describes four main models of organizing and financing modern health care: (a) the Bismarck model; (b) the Beveridge model; (c) the National Health Insurance model; and (d) the out-of-pocket model. Sorting out the specific differences among these four models and understanding the unique ways they have been modified and combined in different countries is a huge task that is not possible in this chapter. It is helpful to keep in mind several major policy decisions that underlie the design of any particular health care system. First is the issue of universal or targeted coverage. Will all citizens be covered by a particular health system, or will only certain groups be assured access? The United States does not have universal health care, but it does have coverage for everyone age 65 and older (Medicare), and it currently is transitioning to a new publicly mandated system of private insurance that eventually will be available for purchase by nearly all citizens. This scheme, created in 2009 through the Affordable Care Act, is more popularly known as "Obamacare" after its chief sponsor and advocate.

Source: U.S. Bureau of the Census.

A second fundamental issue is how the health care system is financed. In some countries, taxes paid by everyone help to pay for health care; in other places individuals pay out of pocket, or make contributions through their employers. Whether a system is publicly financed or not depends a great deal on whether health care is considered a right or a privilege. In the latter case, individuals are expected to take responsibility for their own health care costs; in the former, some level of public funding guarantees that all citizens have some access to health care. A third feature that distinguishes different approaches to health care is whether there is a single payer. In a single-payer system, one entity (government-run) administers the health care system, collecting all fees and paying all health care costs (PNHP [Physicians for a National Health Program], n.d.). In contrast to a single-payer system, in the United States thousands of entities are involved in the administration of health care, including insurance companies, health care providers, and billing agencies. A fourth distinction among health care systems is the role of private ownership and the possibility of profit. In some countries, health care providers are employed by the government; in other countries, it is possible for individual physicians and for health care organizations like hospitals to compete for customers, set their own prices, and make a profit. Although it is possible to differentiate health care systems along all of these dimensions (and others!), several features are often found in combination. For example, the term national health insurance typically refers to a health system in which health care is considered a right of citizenship, some level of access is guaranteed for everyone, and public funds (gathered through taxation) help to support the system. More fully developed national health care systems often use a single payer.

Reid's (2009) discussion of the four primary models of modern health care gives a more historic picture of the different ways in which health care systems are organized. As we can see in the following sections, whereas many countries have adopted one of these models, the United States is unique in that all four of these models are represented within the American health care system. American military veterans receive care organized similar to the Beveridge model; older people covered by Medicare have a plan that is similar to the National Health Insurance model; Americans with health insurance through their employers are familiar with a form of the Bismarck model; and the rest of the American population is operating on the out-of-pocket system (Reid, 2009). Subsequent sections serve as a brief introduction to each model and how it relates to existing health care systems around the world.

The Bismarck Model

The **Bismarck model** is the oldest health care model. Created and implemented in 1881 by Prussian Chancellor Otto von Bismarck (at the time Prussia was a powerful Germanic state that became a dominant force in the creation of modern Germany), this model was intended as a social insurance plan that would be used to protect all citizens when they became sick, were injured or disabled, or experienced health problems in old age (Cichon & Normand, 1994). Although it was a universal health plan, the model required joint contributions from both employers and employees to create a large pool of money (the sickness fund) that was used to pay expenses of individuals who needed medical attention. These contributions were deducted from employees' payroll checks and matched by their employers.

This may sound a lot like the currently most common health care financing system in America, where a good job might come with health insurance benefits, but it is drastically different. A fundamental difference between the American system and the Bismarck model is that the money allocated to the sickness fund in the latter model is redistributed to cover the health of everyone in the country, not just the worker (and the worker's family members) who paid into the system. This model is consistent with some of the ideas behind a national health insurance approach in that every person has the right to health care, funded not by individuals but through a taxation and redistribution system.

Which countries have health care systems based on this model? Germany, France, the Netherlands, Austria, Belgium, Switzerland, Japan, and even some countries in South America have adopted the Bismarck model as their own (Lameire, Joffe, & Wiedemann, 1999; Reid, 2009). This approach provides everyone with health care, but the overall health care system and health insurance plans do not profit, even though a majority of the hospitals and physicians' offices tend to be private. For example, Japan has more hospitals that are viewed as private than does the United States, even though Japan has a strong collective component to its Bismarck-based model for financing health care (Reid, 2009).

The Beveridge Model

Unlike the employer/employee-financed Bismarck model, the **Beveridge model** offers an alternative to paying for health care (Reid, 2009). Proposed by the British social reformer Lord William Beveridge and implemented shortly after World War II, the U.K. National Health Service (NHS) capitalized on the general postwar collective feeling in Great Britain that helping each other, including providing health care for every citizen, was a political and moral duty. This notion appears to have had its roots in the deep collective commitment to national, rather than individual, survival and well-being the war had required of the British. Enacted in the United Kingdom in 1948, this model of financing and providing health care might be thought of as a fully developed public (or national) health care system (as opposed to national health insurance, in which some level of public funding is mandated but the system might be run by private or public entities), since the government employs most of the care providers and is the only payer. In countries utilizing the Beveridge model, payment for health care is very different from that in systems where patients pay bills upon receiving approved services and are later reimbursed for a percentage set by the government or by an insurance company. For example, some Americans must initially pay for care or medications and later file for reimbursement by their insurance companies. In the British NHS, many types of care (including physician visits, surgical procedures, and diagnostic tests) are free to eligible patients (all citizens and permanent residents); some specialized services such as eye tests, dental care, and, for most people, prescription drugs, and most personal care, carry an additional charge. For services that are free of charge, the patient never receives or even sees a bill.

Since the government pays for the national health care system, it only makes sense that they would also be responsible for deciding what services are offered, who can perform them, and how much they should cost. As a result of the lack of provider competition under this model (in contrast to capitalist, market-based systems where providers compete for clients and set their own prices), the NHS in the United Kingdom and the Beveridge model have been associated with lower costs and are thought by some to be the "epitome of tax-financed public health insurance" plans (Musgrove, 2000, p. 846).

Giving so much control to the government may be unappealing to some whose political beliefs and values lead them to oppose collective solutions to social needs. Government-run national health insurance is also sometimes criticized as providing poor quality care and no choice for consumers. Proponents of this position suggest that the competition among providers in a capitalist system (where they can benefit financially) leads to better quality and faster technological advances. This debate cannot be resolved here, but it is worthwhile to note that citizens of the United Kingdom report very high levels of satisfaction with the care they receive and the system that provides it. Although it might be counterintuitive, it is also worth noting that some private clinics and hospitals do exist in the United Kingdom where consumers may receive private care at generally higher prices and with somewhat shorter waits. Such physicians and hospitals can collect partial reimbursements from the government for selected procedures that meet the service and cost criteria set by the NHS. Otherwise, private patients must pay out of pocket. Even in a country with a universal-coverage system, some degree of medical pluralism is a reality.

If the Beveridge model sounds familiar, it is probably from listening to news about the British royal family—Kate Middleton's pregnancy or Queen Elizabeth's health problems. This system of care may also be familiar in relation to several controversial political conversations surrounding the Obama proposal for health reform in the United States in 2009 and 2010. American conservative politician Sarah Palin coined the term "death panels" in 2009 and claimed the Affordable Care Act would authorize and mandate them to decide who might live and who might die. Although she was quickly proven wrong, she and many other opponents of universal, government-run health insurance continued to perpetuate the myth by insisting it was true. It was shown that she was referring to an early provision of the president's proposal that she claimed originated in Great Britain's NHS. Actually, the group being described was the National Institute on Health and Clinical Excellence, the NHS unit charged with ensuring that all therapies and medications used in the United Kingdom are safe and effective (Oakshott, 2009). Palin viewed this process as tantamount to a government decision to ration care by making it available to only the most worthy. Poorly informed critics of the Affordable Care Act demanded that the government stay out of health care; however, one of the most successful health insurance programs in the United States—Medicare—is precisely that: a government-run, publicly sponsored health care program universally available to all citizens age 65 and older. Although the Beveridge model was originally developed for Great Britain, Italy, Sweden, Spain, Norway, Finland, New Zealand, Hong Kong, and Cuba all have adopted varying versions of this health care model (Lameire, Joffe, & Wiedemann, 1999).

The National Health Insurance Model

Aspects of both the Bismarck and the Beveridge models can be found in the third health care model, known as the **National Health Insurance (NHI) model**. Canada, Taiwan, and South Korea are excellent examples of countries with existing NHI models of care (Reid, 2009). NHI is similar to the Bismarck model in that health providers are private and funding is provided through private, nonprofit insurers, but they differ because the government is the single payer, as in the Beveridge model. Health care professionals do not have to work for the government, although the government does determine what it will pay for care, exercising excellent control over costs. A major advantage of this approach is that it utilizes both the private and public sectors to provide health care to individuals. A major disadvantage, at least in the Canadian system, is unusually long waiting times for some procedures. So cost is controlled but at the expense of access.

The Out-of-Pocket Model

The final form of health care, the **out-of-pocket model**, can be found in most developed countries, at least as an alternative or supplement to the dominant system of payment. This particular model provides care to individuals who can afford to pay for needed health services and procedures, and, of course, it often denies care to those who cannot pay and are not otherwise eligible for the available payment programs.

Paying out of your own pocket can have several meanings depending on the country and culture. In some countries, like the United States, the patient will be billed after receiving care or must pay immediately after the service has been rendered. In other countries, such as India, an individual who is unable to pay in advance and in cash for the cost of an anticipated length of stay in a hospital, plus potential supplies, medicine, and deposits for expected procedures, is refused admission to the hospital. In some parts of the world, most often in rural regions of Africa, Asia, and South America, trained medical professionals are not readily available, and economic resources are often scarce, so paying in cash may seem unreasonable. In such regions, people often seek care from shamans, healers, or other medicine men, or they use homemade treatments that have been passed down from one generation to another. These forms of health care fit the folk and traditional models discussed earlier in this chapter, but they also must be purchased in some manner, with personal resources. Some families in rural areas who do not have money are forced to trade goods, such as animals, textiles, and produce, or to provide labor, such as farming or childcare, in order to repay their debt (Reid, 2009). If one does not have the money and has no goods to trade, then the only alternative is to go without the needed care.

Some would argue that an out-of-pocket model of financing care is unfair to the poor and that individuals should not be turned away from receiving care based solely on the fact that they are unable to pay. Others might say that paying taxes into a general health fund for all citizens is not fair to those who work hard to make sure that they can afford care if they or their family members need it in the future. Regardless of which argument is favored, the important question is what type of health care model offers the best care to the most people at the most reasonable cost. But underneath this question is a set of very challenging decisions: Who defines best care? Who decides which citizens should be covered by the health care system? Who should pay for the cost of care? Cultural values (which vary within and among nations) have helped to fuel ongoing and heated debates about all these questions.

Health care is a topic that touches every single individual, whether you are watching a grandparent or parent being cared for in a hospital; a sibling or friend being taken to a clinic, shaman, medicine man, or healer; or if you are the one waiting in line for care. As a result, all have stories to share about their health and health care experiences. Some are positive stories about quality care or surviving a health crisis; others are negative tales of poor care, suffering, and even an unexpected death. Experiences are shaped by the type of health care available. As educated citizens, imagine that you are future leaders of your nation. Would you make minor tweaks to your current system, or would you pick one of the other models to best serve your nation's needs? You might even challenge yourself to think of a new model, a hybrid of some of the others, which might be a catalyst for change in the way health care is provided in your country. What type of care do you expect such a system would provide the older people in your country?

Health Systems and Older People

It is not obvious how Dunn's scheme for classifying health care into folk, traditional, and modern medicine—or even Reid's four organizational models of modern, biomedical health care—relate to older people. An easy assumption is that older people, especially in developing regions, are drawn to the practice of folk or traditional medicine more than modern medicine. This might be based on the stereotyped connection between old age and old ways, between age and traditional values and practices. Of course, that stereotype, as do all others, possesses a kernel of truth. All of us learn our culture as we grow up and use it throughout our lives, so by late life, it is accepted, practiced, and comfortable. Our commitment to what we know and have lived with for a lifetime—our tradition—is strong, so generation (or cohort) is a far more powerful influence on health behavior than age.

However, the type of health care that is preferred and sought depends far more on what is dominant in our society or tribe, especially as we mature into adulthood (Haug, Wykle, & Namazi, 1989). That is, our birth cohort is far more likely to influence our choice of medical provider than our age. If a trip to the doctor, a referral to a medical specialist, and a stay in the hospital for surgical removal of a diseased body part is what our parents did and what we have done all our lives (i.e., the modern medical model of care), we will not be inclined to seek or accept folk practitioners in later life. An Italian who has benefitted from tonsillectomy and appendectomy in early life is likely to accept hip replacement and cancer chemotherapy in old age. Conversely, an older Mexican farmer who has frequented the local *curandero* (folk healer) all his life is likely to continue to do so and shun trips to town to see a medical doctor. These choices are culture- and nation-specific and also have little to do with age.

It also must be kept in mind that the nature of health problems changes with age, from mostly acute (curable) to mostly chronic (incurable), so the type of care provided may need to change as well. For example, the modern, biomedical model of care, common in economically developed nations, was constructed on principles of cure of acute, infectious diseases and has developed that ability to a high level. An illustration of ways in which a cure model is no longer adequate is provided by the essay at the end of this chapter describing the growth of **palliative care**, which focuses on relieving pain; preventing suffering; and a holistic approach to the medical, social, psychological, and spiritual needs of the patient. Whereas palliative care can be appropriate for any stage of dealing with disease, it is often offered during the last stages of life, and helps to support the patient and the patient's family in their decisions about how to live fully until the very end of life. This is quite a different approach from one focused on treatment and cure.

HEALTH BEHAVIOR OF OLDER PEOPLE

Because many more people in all countries are surviving to old age, medicine is being asked to deal with more chronic conditions that have nothing to do with germs or injuries. Consequently, physicians trained and committed to the cure model, and health care systems built on that model, are finding themselves increasingly ill-equipped to treat the very long-term conditions common in old age. Older people, therefore, are developing a somewhat more skeptical, even negative, attitude toward modern medical practitioners, as they experience less-than-effective care and management of their chronic health problems.

Such skepticism and negative judgment appear to parallel the rise among most Western societies of **medical consumerism**, the active, educated information-seeking and questioning that many people employ when confronted by a health issue. Physicians and other practitioners are no longer automatically revered and implicitly trusted; patients do their own research online (e.g., with the health education websites WebMD or MedlinePlus) before office visits and ask their doctors probing questions about the relative effectiveness of alternative procedures, the likely prognosis, and, of course, the cost. The traditional power differential between doctor and patient and its resulting asymmetrical relationship is fast eroding in developed societies, resulting in three major trends: (a) a rise in alternative health practices and practitioners (so-called **complementary and alternative medicine**, or CAM); (b) greater emphasis on *health promotion and disease prevention*; and (c) a heightened role for educated and empowered consumers to have more responsibility for their health care decisions and actions and for the management and consequences of those actions. We present more about health promotion and *self-care* (also called consumer-directed care) later in this chapter. First we explore how medical pluralism (discussed earlier) is becoming a much more common health care strategy among older people—even as it is for the larger societies in which they live.

Complementary and Alternative Medicine

A clear trend in Western developed societies is toward medical pluralism. With the rise of health consumerism, citizens have become skeptical, even of scientific medicine and its practitioners. As mass communication has become universal in these countries, and information—both true and false—has become instantly available to nearly all, consumers are aware of, and listening to, claims, counterclaims, and new knowledge that supersedes older beliefs about causes, medicines, and practices. It has been learned in recent years that caffeine may be bad for us, may be good for us, or may have little effect on our well-being. The general public has been exposed to every "latest discovery" about cholesterol and heart disease, many of which have contradicted those of just a few years earlier. People have come to doubt even the most authoritative sources broadcasting the new medical truth and to expect another research report shortly that will contradict or dispute it.

In this pluralistic atmosphere, scientific discoveries are considered by many people as no more likely true than nonscientific claims. Under a constant assault of marketing puffery and misleading claims, consumers often do not know whom to believe or what to think. Therefore, many feel free to choose from the marketplace any nostrum, diet, or therapy that appeals to them, even if offered by nonmedical or folk practitioners. Of course, some of these alternative treatments or approaches do have value—although many do not—and the medical establishment (in the United States that is the National Center for Complementary and Alternative Medicine of the National Institutes of Health) is increasingly studying and testing the efficacy and safety of a variety of therapies. These therapies fall into two general categories: natural products such as dietary supplements and mind/body practices such as massage therapy, acupuncture (a traditional medical practice described earlier), massage therapy, and tai chi (U.S. National Center on Complementary and Alternative Medicine, 2008).

CAM and Aging

Having established that age is perhaps the least powerful influence on the choice of health care provider, it should be noted that CAM use is very popular among older people. One study of an American Medicare population (Astin, Pelletier, Marie, & Haskell, 2000) found more than four in ten seniors used at least one of the ten types of CAM the researchers asked about. Some of the conditions for which older people are most likely to use CAM are arthritis, cancer, mental health, and sleep disorders (Arcury et al., 2012).

Consumers who use CAM techniques do not always subscribe to the classical model of patient compliance with doctors' orders. In one study of medication use by older people in Finland (Lumme-Sandt, Hervonen, & Jylha, 2000), "the respondents who talked about the natural products they used seemed to be more active than others with respect to their medication. They said explicitly that they did not obey doctors' orders" (p. 1847). In other words, a segment of older adults in Finland are choosing to go to the doctor for their medical problems but then are deciding for themselves whether to follow a doctor's advice or perhaps self-medicate with some other therapy that was not prescribed. "In the self-help repertoire, the superiority of medical knowledge is challenged directly by introducing alternative drugs and remedies" (p. 1849). Similarly, CAM users in the

Source: Jaylene Liang.

United States do not always report their use of alternative therapies to their physicians. The major reasons for not disclosing CAM use were concern about physicians' negative attitudes regarding such treatment, the fact that physicians do not ask, and the conviction that physicians do not need to know (Arcury et al., 2012).

Cochran (2002, p. 74) suggests that older people, like younger adults, use CAM to assert their beliefs about the ineffectiveness of biomedicine. Further, in his study of two age cohorts of older adults in Georgia (the United States), Cochran found that CAM users were quite similar to people who used biomedicine in that both held a range of views about the nature of health and how to achieve it. He asserts, "The CAM user cannot be characterized as some aberrant lay consumer with beliefs that are divergent from the mainstream; rather, the CAM user is squarely in the mainstream of belief about health" (p. 284). Cochran demonstrates that not only do older people differ in their definitions of health, but they also simultaneously subscribe to alternative means of achieving it, lending further support for our contention that medical pluralism is becoming more common in most Western nations. We can only hypothesize that a similar process of medical pluralism is occurring in developing societies; the increasing acceptance and availability of modern medicine add to the choices that older people have and encourage their involvement in assessing its claims and successes versus traditional and folk medicine. It may be that population aging is presenting all practitioners—biomedical and traditional—with chronic disease challenges that neither so far has been able to solve, or even to manage with only its own toolkit.

Health Promotion and Self-Care

As noted earlier in this chapter, the major health challenge that accompanies global aging is the increased burden of CNCDs. Motivated by the dramatic increase in preventable premature deaths projected to occur as a result of CNCDs, especially in developing countries, an expert panel recently identified the most critical steps that should be taken to solve these important health problems. This grand-challenge exercise resulted in a global health agenda for people of all ages affected by CNCDs. Many of the 20 recommendations are tied directly to the health of older adults, including: (a) promoting healthy lifestyles and choices through education and public engagement; (b) promoting lifelong physical activity; (c) better understanding of environmental and cultural factors that affect health behaviors; and (d) developing strategies to integrate management of CNDCs into health care systems (Daar et al., 2007). The ambitious goals and specific recommendations put forth by this group of experts call for changes at the level of public health, public policy, and health care systems; however, many have implications for individual health behaviors and actions, with a clear focus on helping people live better and healthier, not just longer.

This theme is echoed in several U.S. and international health care initiatives for older adults. Within the United States, a heightened emphasis on health promotion and disease prevention is evidenced in a host of new programs seeking to maximize health by preventing falls, promoting good mental health, and enhancing older people's ability to manage chronic disease. For example, the Stanford Chronic Disease Self-Management Program (CDSMP) is a 6-week program offered to individuals with one or more chronic conditions. The program helps participants learn how to gain (or regain) a sense of control over their health and chronic conditions, which can be a challenge for people dealing with a condition (such as diabetes) that will affect the rest of their lives. This new sense of control is achieved by utilizing personal skills and resources to better manage their chronic condition(s) through (a) understanding their condition, (b) making needed lifestyle changes, (c) setting and achieving personal goals for improving their health, and (d) improving communication with health care professionals. Two components of this program have implications for the health of older adults in all countries: the ability to understand and act on health information (health literacy) and a sense of empowerment and involvement in one's own health care (self-care or self-management).

Health Literacy

The American Medical Association (AMA) defines *health literacy* as a patient's "ability to obtain, process, and understand basic health information and services needed to make appropriate health decisions" (Weiss, 2007, p. 6). These abilities play an essential role in a person's adhering to medical advice, achieving good health-related outcomes, and utilizing health services. Factors such as an individual's age, socioeconomic status, and race/ethnicity all affect that patient's health-literacy level and ability to obtain and utilize basic health care information and services. Increasing health-literacy levels among older adults is imperative to help them manage their chronic diseases. In general, health literacy determines a patient's ability to complete forms, understand medical advice and instructions, and utilize and pay for required therapies. Furthermore, a physician's orders are not always expressed in only words but are often provided in the form of numbers. Examples include the dosage and frequency of taking a medication, the number of units of insulin that a diabetic patient should take for a particular numeric glucose reading, or how often an older adult should have blood work done to check for high cholesterol or even infectious diseases like HIV. Thus, the ability to understand both words (literacy) *and* numbers (numeracy) is important for health outcomes.

The concept of health literacy is embedded in both clinical and public health settings in Europe and North America. Yet, the idea of health literacy and the need to improve it may seem like distant concepts in developing nations where even general literacy is not assured. Countries in the Middle East, south Asia, and Africa currently face such challenges in attempting to increase general literacy rates that it is unlikely they have the resources to focus on improving health literacy as well. Although it is true that developing nations are far behind the developed world, it has been estimated that about 100 million people in *developed* nations are considered to be "functionally illiterate," indicating that this is still a relevant concern for both developed and developing nations (Kickbusch, 2001, p. 290).

Since older adults have high rates of chronic conditions, the ability to understand medical advice, answer providers' questions, take the appropriate dosage of medications, and make decisions about different types of treatment all take on heightened importance. Improving health literacy for older adults would allow them to take a more active role in managing their own chronic conditions, preventing disease-related complications, and decreasing their risk of comorbidities (i.e., multiple chronic conditions). However, although the idea of taking a more active role in one's health may seem empowering, it is not always feasible for an older adult because of physical and cognitive deficits, societal expectations, and even economic dependency. Such factors limit the exercise of personal health autonomy in both developed and less developed countries.

Literacy and numeracy skills are necessary in the complex health care systems in developed nations, but what skills are needed in other countries or cultures where individuals might not be as likely to seek help from a Western medical system? It is important to consider how health communication occurs in non-Western cultures and how such understanding might be used to improve patient adherence and provide health care professionals with an accurate picture of what their patients really understand about their conditions. For example, in public health interventions in China to reduce schistosomiasis, an intestinal parasitic infection from contaminated water, health education programs focus more on improving functional health literacy—that is, knowing how to follow basic instructions to avoid risky behaviors—than trying to explain the scientific basis of the condition or convincing people they should be responsible for their own health by controlling their environment (Wang, 2000).

In countries that tend to be in the earlier stages of the demographic transition, where infections and mortality rates are extremely high, it is more effective to provide information that improves functional health literacy. On the other hand, in more developed countries where chronic conditions are more common and life expectancies longer, both adherence and autonomy are useful. Given physicians' limited ability to treat and even manage many of the interrelated problems of old age and the difficulty and cost of being seen by a doctor in the first place, personal responsibility for managing illnesses and for directing care may be an important component of a healthier, longer life.

Self-Directed Care

Clearly, one of the goals of health literacy is to provide individuals with the tools to be involved in, and to some extent take charge of, their own health care and outcomes. This philosophy and practice can play out in all types of interactions between older adults and the health care system, including learning how to manage a chronic disease such as diabetes, asking more questions of health care providers, using CAM, or even seeking the advice of a traditional healer. The CDSMP mentioned earlier helps people gain information about their conditions (become more health literate) and empowers them to take charge of their own care. Perhaps one of the clearest examples of self-care comes from consumer direction in long-term care. In this model, older adults who need assistance with activities of daily living (ADLs; described in Chapter 5) are able to select, train, and manage the people who provide their care. For older adults who have adequate economic resources, hiring people to provide needed assistance, whether with housework or with ADLs, is a common strategy.

For those without resources, the option to choose their own workers and tell them how the work should be done is not as readily available (Ball & Whittington, 1995).

What is unique about the consumer-directed movement in long-term care is its placement within publicly funded long-term care systems. In the United States, United Kingdom, and many European nations, some older adults are able to use funding from public programs to hire the workers of their choice, including family members. This movement represents an important step in respecting the rights and expertise of older people needing services. Interestingly, although it might seem quite reasonable to expect that older adults would be able to talk about what services they need and express preferences about how and when those services should be offered, the early days of the consumer-directed movement were fraught with controversies and concerns. Critics worried about whether older adults could effectively manage their own care, whether consumer-employed workers would take advantage of them, whether fraud and abuse would increase, and whether health outcomes would be better or worse. Careful research has revealed that self-directed consumers fare quite well: Rates of fraud and abuse are lower, health outcomes are as good or better than those in traditional care, and participants are more satisfied (Carlson, Foster, Dale, & Brown, 2007; Dale & Brown, 2006; Schore, Foster, & Phillips, 2007).

The fact that the idea of consumer-directed care was at first both novel and contested within the United States reflects the dominance of the medical model, the passivity that has been expected from older consumers, some ageism about the ability of older adults to be actively involved in their own care, and paternalism in publicly funded programs that invests rights and responsibilities with the care providers rather than the receivers. Consumer-directed care along with disease self-management programs are slowly but successfully challenging each of these assumptions. Of course, in less developed nations where access to paid assistance for long-term care needs from professionals may not be readily available, consumer responsibility and involvement in self-care, supplemented by family care, have always been the norm.

SUMMARY

Health is important to all of us. Because it is so problematic in old age and is ultimately an existential question, the health of older people is a central concern in all societies. Through history, humans have sought many means of improving their health and delaying the inevitable, but just as modern biomedicine seems to be gaining the upper hand on a broad range of communicable diseases, many of the world's populations are aging and in need of a different sort of health care intervention, one that is just beginning to be understood.

The chronic diseases of late life—heart disease, cancer, diabetes, arthritis, and AD—are so far incurable, but we are learning how to manage them and we know that, through their public health efforts, societies are crucial actors in preventing disease and promoting health. Just as importantly, patients can play a significant role in improving their own quality of care and quality of life (not to mention its quantity), if they will assert their right to do so. Evidence is mounting that personal autonomy is a key element of health and well-being in later life and, indeed, in all of life.

DISCUSSION QUESTIONS

1. Why do you think health is a universal value?
2. Why do we say that chronic (noncommunicable) diseases are the major challenge for health care in the future?
3. What disease (or diseases) place(s) the greatest burden on the country you are from? On the families in your society?
4. Do you think medical pluralism is a good thing?
5. Can you think of examples of folk medicine in your own community?
6. What about examples of traditional medicine?
7. Do you think modern medical practitioners are moving beyond germ theory? In what ways?
8. How do the four models of organizing and financing modern medicine fit with the political labels conservative and liberal?
9. What do dishwashing powder and headache pills have in common in the United States?
10. Have you used WebMD or another health information site online? Was it helpful?
11. Have you ever used a treatment or health promotion practice that might be considered by your physician as an alternative to scientific medicine? What was your experience?
12. How do you feel about patients deciding for themselves what medicine they will take or whether they will refuse certain treatments?

KEY WORDS

Beveridge model
Bismarck model
Burden of disease
Chronic noncommunicable diseases
Complementary and alternative medicine
Epidemiological transition
Folk medicine
Medical consumerism
Medical pluralism

Modern medicine
National Health Insurance model
Out-of-pocket model
Palliative care
Self-directed care
Traditional medicine

Palliative Care: A Global Public Health Initiative to Improve Quality of Life

Jasleen K. Chahal

Prior to the 1960s, medical and public health professionals rarely talked about ways to alleviate the suffering of dying patients. The sole focus was on providing curative treatment. During that pivotal decade the hospice movement, originating in the United Kingdom during a time of civil and consumer rights movements, was the first to place emphasis on relieving unnecessary end-of-life suffering (Beider, 2005). The civil and consumer rights movements of the 1960s and 1970s gave people a new sense of empowerment to question medical authority and to fight for what they felt were basic human rights. Providing a means for patients to die humanely, allowing them to live their last days without experiencing pain and suffering, is only one example of how the movements helped to create societal change. Hospice appeared to be an answer to this call by developing a formal standard of care that helped to give patients more choice in treatment—alleviating pain and addressing end-of-life care issues for both the patients and their families.

Although hospice has commonly been referred to as a last resort to care when treatment fails, the basic principle of hospice is for health care professionals to act as a support system for patients and families throughout the entire dying process—right before, during, and after the death of a patient (Beider, 2005). Whereas it may seem that the hospice movement happened recently and quickly, it is important to acknowledge that the demographic transition (discussed in Chapter 4) and the epidemiological or health transition (discussed in this chapter) have both contributed to the emergence of hospice service. In the past, individuals did not have to worry about experiencing prolonged periods of suffering prior to death, since most deaths resulted from acute infectious diseases rather than chronic conditions and occurred rather quickly. However, as nations began to see improvements in sanitation and nutrition—and advancements in medical treatments and technology—rates of communicable diseases decreased, life expectancy improved, and the prevalence of chronic diseases increased. These transitions influenced medical practitioners to balance their focus on acute care with more interest in preventive and end-of-life care. Additionally, the health care field began to acknowledge the importance of considering medical treatments to improve both the quality and quantity of life.

As a result, palliative care entered the health care field as a new approach to ending suffering much earlier in the chronic or terminal disease–related experience, although still providing comfort care and support for a prolonged period of time. Since palliative care emerged from the hospice movement, the two have continued to have a lasting connection. One of the major benefits of being associated with hospice is that some of its supporters have been quick to advocate for the importance of implementing palliative care throughout the health care continuum. However, the close link to hospice has provided more challenges than opportunities in creating a global standard of care, as a result of existing social stigmas attached to death and dying, economic issues in providing adequate resources, and varying cultural beliefs about end-of-life care.

Discussing death and dying has consistently been a taboo or negative topic within most societies. Even after Elizabeth Kubler-Ross developed a theoretical model for the five stages of coping with dying in her 1969 book, *On Death and Dying*, the topic became only slightly more acceptable for conversation, but is still often avoided (Weitz, 2010). The history of how society has dealt with death throughout the ages has been divided into the following four categories: "The Tame Death" (from pre-Christian Middle Ages), "The Death of the Self" (during the Middle Ages), "The Death of the Other" (post-Middle Ages), and the current period of "The Invisible Death" (Aries, 1981; cited in Meier, 2010, p. 11). Philippe Aries (1981) claimed that the first stage of death was "central, routine, and unpredictable and was tamed through social rituals and codes of behaviors," but then shifted to a belief in an afterlife and a fear of death because of the need to atone for committed sins. The third stage he describes as a time of the dramatization of death and associated emotions with the growing importance of familial relationships. Finally, the current stage shows death as something that an individual can avoid, as a result of progress in public health interventions, medicine, and research (Meier, 2010, pp. 11–12).

Although these previous stages generally apply in most Western cultures, beliefs about death and dying differ among Asian nations. For example, whereas the commonly known Eastern faiths of Islam, Hinduism, and Buddhism have many differences, followers of each of these faiths believe in reincarnation and view death as a natural stage of life that acts as a transition from an individual's current life into a new life (Puchalski & O'Donnell, 2005). Similarly, in Sikhism, a religious group that arose from Hinduism in the 16th century, followers (or Sikhs) also believe in reincarnation in that those who have lived a life without "self-centeredness and spiritual blindness" will be greeted by God after death, whereas others will be reborn because of their karma, or the fate determined by their previous actions (Firth, 2000, pp. 30–31). Additionally, variations in beliefs and values related to dying can also vary across cultures that are found in one nation. A good example of diversity within a national culture is that of India, where Christians, Buddhists, Hindus, Muslims, and many other religious cultures coexist to help create the values of a larger national culture. Therefore, a country's social and cultural values about death and dying may align with either Eastern or Western beliefs, or some combination of both, which in turn can heavily impact the understanding, importance, and delivery of end-of-life care.

People, including researchers and clinicians, tend to confuse palliative care with hospice care, leading ultimately to negative social views of death. However, hospice and palliative care are significantly different, and it is important to distinguish between the two to help minimize the impact of social stigma attached to hospice care. To be eligible for hospice services in the United States, a patient must be diagnosed with a terminal illness, have less than 6 months to live, and be willing to forego further lifesaving treatments. Whereas palliative care does require that an individual have a terminal or chronic condition, it does not put the same restrictions on treatment or life expectancy after the diagnosis or progression of an illness. Palliative care also aims to help enhance the quality of life for an individual with a terminal illness; unlike hospice, however, palliative care can be initiated at any stage of a person's chronic disease continuum. Therefore, the major difference between the two forms of end-of-life care lies in either restricting or providing the choice for continuing curative treatment as individuals and their families slowly face the inevitable.

It is important to note that even if patients decide to utilize palliative care, they still may use hospice services once they meet the eligibility requirements described. Many patients do not realize that by using palliative care they actually have control over whether or not to enter hospice or to stop medical treatments—simultaneously receiving treatments that help manage pain. In addition, CAM—much of which is based on Eastern medical principles and practices and includes such measures as acupuncture, self-hypnosis, group therapy, nerve stimulation, and massage therapy—can be integrated into a palliative care initiative. It is seldom offered, however, or even considered for use within health care settings in developed countries, primarily due to the emphasis placed on Western (cure-oriented) medicine. CAM measures are intended to provide pain relief for patients without prescribing actual medications (Beider, 2005). The integration of both CAM and palliative care can provide a pain-management alternative for patients throughout the health continuum in a manner that supports both Western and Eastern medical practices. The combination of the two may provide an avenue to give patients more control over their end-of-life care based on their cultural, personal, and medical beliefs.

Unfortunately, palliative care is still not as widely accepted within Western medicine as it should be. In 1980, to increase awareness and urge earlier palliative care intervention, based on its own framework for standards of palliative care (see Table E6.1), the World Health Organization (WHO, 2012)

TABLE E6.1 The World Health Organization (WHO) Definition of Palliative Care

• Provides relief from pain and other distressing symptoms
• Affirms life and regards dying as a normal process
• Intends neither to hasten nor postpone death
• Integrates the psychological and spiritual aspects of patient care
• Offers a support system to help patients live as actively as possible until death
• Offers a support system to help the family cope during the patient's illness and in their own bereavement
• Utilizes a team approach to address the needs of patients and their families, including bereavement counseling, if indicated
• Enhances quality of life, and may also positively influence the course of illness
• Is applicable early in the course of illness, in conjunction with other therapies that are intended to prolong life, such as chemotherapy or radiation therapy, and includes those investigations needed to better understand and manage distressing clinical complications

Source: Sepulveda et al. (2002).

created a worldwide public health palliative care initiative (Sepulveda, Marlin, Yoshida, & Ulrich, 2002). Later, the U.S. Institute of Medicine's (IOM) Committee on Care at the End of Life emphasized the importance of incorporating palliative care into the medical model by claiming that "a human care system is one that people can trust to serve them well as they die, even if their needs and beliefs call for a departure from typical practices" (Field & Cassel, 1997). As a result, in North America and Europe, at least, palliative care has slowly come to be considered a humane approach to medicine because, although it does not treat incurable diseases, it does help to comfort patients by alleviating symptoms and side effects.

Despite the efforts of WHO, several countries still do not embrace the palliative care initiative, creating differences in the level of integration of palliative care among countries (see Table E6.2).

Variation in palliative care implementation and allocation of resources differs greatly based on the economic development of a particular country (see Figure E6.1).

For example, although both the WHO HIV/AIDS initiative in Africa and its cancer initiative in Europe focus on providing palliative care services to individuals of all ages, the nature and scope of the intervention depend greatly upon a country's economic climate and its ability to fund them. Some African countries are simply unable to afford palliative care, whereas some European nations face political issues in defending the rationale and benefit of allocating resources to care for the dying (Sepulveda et al., 2002). In other words, developing nations struggle with having

TABLE E6.2 Palliative Care Development and Funding in Nine Countries

Country examples	Summary
Norway Diagnosis-related groups (DRGs)	• Mixed payment system (vulnerable to budget cuts) • 60% from fixed grants, 40% from DRG fees • Provided across levels of care • Home care visits included since 1996
Hungary Average-based reimbursement system	• Palliative care now considered a DRG reimbursement • Physician incentives used to "engage and ensure care" • Covers one third of Hungarians, 100% of home care visits, and 50%–80% of inpatient visits
Spain Cost-saving model	• Rapidly growing—combines cancer and geriatrics care models • Led to reduced emergency admissions and hospital cost-savings
United States Three levels of hospice care payments	• No integration between curative and palliative care • Most care in home (35% of all deaths, 40% of cancer deaths) • Payment based on three levels of care (routine, inpatient, and intensive), in which routine care covers 96% of all days and intensive care is the most expensive
Singapore Cost-sharing model	• Originates in voluntary sector • Rapidly growing, combined with geriatric or older care • Increasing number of older women shifted to this type of model because of user payment and families providing care for loved ones
Australia Needs-based approach	• Australian National Palliative Care Program organized funding to shift from charities to the national health system (1998) • Resources allocated based on need and size of population • Palliative Care Outcomes Collaboration established in 2005 to evaluate outcomes, later intended for benchmarking
Canada Prospective approach	• Covers 81% of palliative care for cancer patients • Publicly funded and prospective needs-based approach, with two thirds of funding related to hospital costs • Costs increase in older versus younger people and at 6 months before death, with highest cost at 2 months before death
Ireland Publicly funded	• 85% government-funded (almost 100% reimbursement) • Geographical variations and highly related to cancer care
United Kingdom Generalist focus	• Covers about 60% of all cancer deaths • Two thirds of palliative care specialist funding from charities and voluntary sector; one third from government funding and increasing • 2008 initiative to allow people to die at home upon their wishes, also looks to improve generalist and specialist palliative care for all, both cancer and noncancer, patients

Adapted from Gomes et al. (2009).

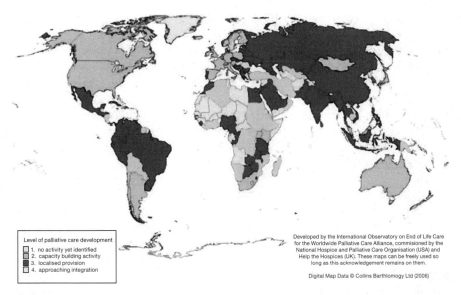

Level of palliative care development
☐ 1. no activity yet identified
☐ 2. capacity building activity
■ 3. localised provision
☐ 4. approaching integration

Developed by the International Observatory on End of Life Care
for the Worldwide Palliative Care Alliance, commisioned by the
National Hospice and Palliative Care Organisation (USA) and
Help the Hospices (UK). These maps can be freely used so
long as this acknowledgement remains on them.

Digital Map Data © Collins Barthlomogy Ltd (2006)

FIGURE E6.1 Global levels of palliative care development illustrating the various levels of palliative care development around the world.
Source: Gomes et al. (2009).

enough money to obtain resources, such as medical supplies and staff, to provide pain relief; developed nations lack the political will to spend so much money on people viewed as unproductive and a burden on society. One study found that the United States (27%–30%), the Netherlands (26%), and Switzerland (18%–22%) had similar percentages of government spending for care during the last year of life in individuals age 65 or older (Shugarman, Decker, & Bercovitz, 2009). Some may argue that all three countries should allocate such resources to improve education for future generations. On the other hand, allotting that many resources to end-of-life care would be rare in such nations as Iraq or Syria, where inpatient palliative care and cancer care units have not been established, mostly due to the continual shortage of trained medical professionals and acceptable forms of morphine to help alleviate pain and suffering (Zeinah, Al-Kindi, & Hassan, 2013).

In addition to facing economic issues (e.g., spending on end-of-life care), countries often face an obstacle of political beliefs or governmental regulations regarding the availability of appropriate medication or interventions used to minimize pain and suffering. In developing countries like India, challenges arise with the accessibility of opioid medication, legislative issues regarding the use of pain-relieving medication, and a lack of both monetary and professional resources for palliative care training. Political issues are not limited to developing countries; similar restrictions have been found in various eastern European countries (Cherny, Catane, & Kosmidis, 2006). In fact, programs such as Medicare (public health insurance for older adults in the United States) have affected the use of particular palliative care approaches. Although hospice benefits were initially provided to individuals in 1983, as of 2005, no benefits existed for reimbursement of other palliative care services (Beider, 2005). Today, individuals with Medicare are covered for spiritual, respite, and medical care, only if they meet the same eligibility requirements as for admission into hospice care: a diagnosis of a terminal illness, acceptance of no future forms of curative treatments, and a life expectancy of fewer than 6 months. In other words, government benefits are not intended to reduce suffering or to improve an individual's quality of remaining life, but solely as a last resort in comforting someone before death.

Political and economic issues are not the only barriers to providing timely palliative care interventions. Differences in cultural beliefs about end-of-life care, based on racial, ethnic, religious, and personal values, also hinder utilization of palliative care. Such cultural beliefs tend to have a major impact on a patient's readiness, willingness, and ability to use palliative care services. In some cases, even if patients meet certain requirements to receive hospice or palliative care, some individuals choose to forego treatments in accordance with their personal belief that it is essential to endure any pain. One such example is that some African Americans believe that death is only a transition and that pain and suffering should not be avoided but tolerated because they represent a divine or spiritual obligation (Crawley et al., 2000). In Spain, a strong Catholic tradition influences the country's palliative care initiative, in that euthanasia is generally rejected in favor of an overwhelming acceptance of sedation as a method of pain relief (Perkins, Geppert, Gonzales, Cortez, & Hazuda, 2002). These cultural, religious, and ethnic differences often result in additional barriers to providing palliative care.

Studies have also shown that cultural beliefs affect the way in which general health care decisions are made. Euro-Americans and African Americans tend to prefer making individual decisions about advance care planning; Mexican Americans and Latino Americans prefer making decisions as a family (Olarte & Guillen, 2001). A similar preference for depending on family members in decision making and providing care is still present in various Asian countries. Families in India are considered a major care network since they are often large and willing to provide various forms of nursing care, ranging from changing dressings to administering injections (Shanmugasundaram, Chapman, & O'Conner, 2006). Meanwhile in Japan, prior to death, support for terminally ill patients is also usually provided by children and siblings in addition to health care professionals (Matsushima, Akabayashi, & Nishitateno, 2002). Such support networks often aid patients in completing depressing tasks, while at the same time enhancing their quality of life. Thus, both social support and cultural beliefs play a major role in advance care planning and the end-of-life care process. Sensitivity to cultural values and potential barriers to end-of-life care would be one of the first steps in opening the door for palliative care in any cultural community.

One subculture that has a major effect on palliative care utilization is that of medicine. The impact of medical culture depends greatly on whether its practices are more aligned with Western or Eastern traditional beliefs about care. The use of medical interventions or pharmaceutical drugs for alleviating pain may not be equally accepted or available in all countries (Cherny et al., 2006). Global differences in the types of interventions and medications available to patients make it increasingly harder for international organizations such as the WHO to create a public health initiative that can provide standardized palliative care measures worldwide. Without international standards, it will be hard to assure the quality of life of older patients and their families if they choose to travel, move closer to loved ones at the end of their lives, or migrate back home to their country of origin.

Professionals are taught with ideologically based terminology and beliefs about death that help create the medical culture as it is today, especially in Western countries. An essential component of the American health care culture is the need to obtain informed consent prior to initiating treatment. By obtaining such consent, physicians can provide or withdraw appropriate treatment to patients. The issue arises when other cultures, such as in China, Bosnia, and even Italy, prefer not to tell terminally ill family members about a terminal diagnosis or treatment because it is viewed as being more humane and a sign of respect for that patient's emotional and physical well-being (Searight & Gafford, 2005). Sometimes the inability to provide information regarding the patient's condition can inhibit the amount of care or the appropriate care that physicians see fit to provide for a particular illness. In order to circumvent this dilemma, physicians in Western countries have been advised to ask patients if they would like to be medically informed regarding their condition and treatments, or if they would like to designate a particular person to be responsible for all decisions (Crawley, Marshall, Lo, & Koenig, 2002). Another important complication is the fact that most physicians are trained to place great importance on saving lives. Therefore, if a patient needs to be referred to palliative care or hospice, physicians may view this as a negative outcome and a personal failure rather than the natural outcome of an illness (Crawley et al., 2002). This sense of defeat may make medical professionals more prone to taking extravagant measures and less likely to refer patients to palliative care.

The medical field should view the integration of complementary and alternative medicine and palliative care as a service that presents suffering patients with a way to minimize pain, and still provides hope for curing their illness. Since end-of-life care has negative connotations in society, there is still a need to differentiate palliative care from hospice in order to maximize utilization. Common misconceptions, economic and governmental constraints, and differing cultures will continue to provide challenges for the future of palliative care in both developed and developing nations. Reevaluation of both governmental drug regulations and health care benefit policies is necessary to furthering the accessibility of palliative care worldwide.

Additionally, more emphasis should be placed on continuing to educate both medical professionals and the general public about the benefits of earlier, culturally sensitive palliative care interventions as a way to promote quality of life. A greater understanding of palliative care and its importance could lead to wider acceptance and utilization of needed end-of-life services, and allow families to care for loved ones in the comfort of their own homes as they continue to age with a chronic, terminal condition.

CHAPTER 7

Long-Term Services and Supports

Robert Applebaum, Emily Robbins, and Anthony Bardo

Most of us go through our day-to-day tasks, from taking a shower, to getting dressed, to making breakfast, without a second thought about the effort required to accomplish them. However, for older adults who may experience significant disability due to injury or disease, these daily activities present challenges that may require ongoing assistance from family members, friends, or a formal care service provider. **Long-term services and supports** (a term that has generally replaced the older phrase **long-term care** [LTC]) enable those who need continual help because of physical, cognitive, or developmental disabilities to accomplish the necessary tasks of daily living. As discussed in Chapter 5, the definition, measurement, and prevalence of disability vary across the globe. For example, in Kenya and Bangladesh, less than 1% of the population experiences a disability, compared to 20% for New Zealand and Australia, and 19% of the population in the United States and Canada (Mont, 2007). A variety of explanations are offered as to why disability rates vary so dramatically among countries, from differences in age distribution, life expectancy, and socioeconomic status, to availability of health care. Unfortunately, there is a lack of reliable data to compare disability rates across nations: It is not really known how prevalence of disability varies across countries. It is clear, however, that virtually every nation in the world has older individuals with disability who need assistance with the basic tasks of daily living. A report by the U.S. Bureau of the Census (Kinsella & He, 2009) estimated that worldwide the number of people over age 80, those most likely to need long-term services, will increase by 233% between 2008 and 2040. How countries are responding to the new and growing challenges of assisting older people with long-term services and supports is the focus of this chapter. As with disability rates that vary widely among countries, such is the case with long-term care (LTC) services designed to support the needs of individuals who require assistance carrying out activities of daily living (ADLs). Definitions and level of support are dependent on a number of factors, such as governmental action and the culture of informal care. In attempting to understand the differences and similarities that exist among nations regarding LTC, this

Source: U.S. Bureau of the Census.

chapter provides a broad outline of the variety of approaches countries take in providing LTC services and supports to those in need.

First, a broad definition of LTC services is provided and a global typology of such services and supports is developed. Since no predominant typology definitively captures the variation in long-term services across the globe, the typology used in this chapter acts as a framework to categorize national LTC systems. Specific examples of how different countries handle LTC tasks are presented to illustrate the range of approaches. These examples are used to help explain some of the complexities that arise when attempting to compare and contrast LTC services on a global scale. Some of the LTC policy issues common to many nations are described in the concluding discussion.

DEFINING LONG-TERM SERVICES AND SUPPORTS

Prior to examining the different approaches used to deliver and finance long-term services, it is important to have a common understanding of what is meant by LTC. As noted, individuals who require long-term services and supports primarily need ongoing assistance with the basic daily tasks of living. In some instances individuals may have acute medical needs as well, but it is the personal tasks of life that define one's level of care needs each day. Thus, help with the personal and instrumental activities of daily living (IADLs), such as dressing, bathing, walking, housekeeping, meals, and laundry, direct the need for assistance. A typical case might involve an older person whose physical and/or mental abilities have declined to the point where the individual can no longer bathe or dress independently, but requires assistance from a personal-care aide. The older adult: (a) cannot shop or cook, so someone else must provide for these needs; (b) has lost the ability to manage finances, so others must pay the bills; and (c) cannot live alone, so someone else must provide housing and supportive services. Such assistance can be provided in a range of environments, from an individual's own home to the home of a friend or relative, an adult day facility, a foster home, or a residential care facility such as an assisted-living community or nursing home. LTC services are often provided informally by family members or volunteers, but in many instances they are delivered with the help of paid staff members. The type and amount of assistance is affected by numerous factors such as one's environment, available technology, geographic area, and level of care needs. An individual's circumstances can exacerbate or mitigate challenges of accomplishing the tasks of everyday living, but the need to provide ongoing long-term services and supports is universal across nations.

Typologies of LTC Services and Supports

Kraus and his colleagues (2010) categorized 21 of the European Union (E.U.) LTC systems using two distinct clustering strategies. One approach focused on LTC system characteristics; the other focused on system use and financing. First, they examined the extent to which a nation's long-term services are *means-tested*—whether they are provided only to individuals without the money (means) to pay the cost themselves—or to all equally as an **entitlement**. They also examined the availability of cash benefits, whether individuals had a choice of provider, the use of a quality assurance system, the amount of public expenditures for LTC as a share of gross domestic product (GDP), and the amount of cost-sharing required by citizens. In this model, access to publicly funded long-term services can be viewed on a spectrum from global entitlement to heavily means-tested. Based on these factors the 21 E.U. countries were categorized into four groups (see Appendix A for listing of countries). The first cluster, including Denmark, Belgium, the Netherlands, Sweden, and France, was characterized as financially generous and having a well-developed LTC system. Cluster 2 included such nations as Italy, England, and Spain and was classified as having medium financial generosity and a moderately developed LTC system. The countries placed in Clusters 3 (Bulgaria, Estonia, and Czech Republic) and 4 (Hungary, Poland, Romania) were classified as having a low amount of resources allocated to LTC. The Cluster 3 group had a more developed LTC system than the countries in Cluster 4.

The second approach focused on public expenditures on LTC as a share of GDP, the share of private expenditures, the proportion of the older population that used formal care, the proportion that used informal care, the level of support for informal caregivers, targeting based on needs of users, and the amount of cash benefits available for home care. Results from this analysis classified Denmark, the Netherlands, and Sweden as high public-spending nations; countries such as France, Finland, and England were in the medium-expenditure group; and Slovakia, Czech Republic, and (somewhat surprisingly) Germany were in the low-spending category.

An analysis conducted by the Organisation for Economic Co-operation and Development (OECD; Colombo, Llena-Nozal, Mercier, & Tjadens, 2011) expanded upon the Kraus typology (see Appendix B for listing of countries). Their classification is based on the funding structure (universal, means-tested, or mixed) and provision of care provided by each LTC system. **Universal systems** provide publicly funded nursing and personal care to all eligible individuals (defined by their level of disability) regardless of income or assets. Within the universal category are three different funding structures: (a) **tax-based**, (b) **social long-term care insurance** (LTCI), and (c) long-term services included as part of overall health coverage. Under a means-tested financing structure, income and/or asset tests are used to determine eligibility for publicly funded LTC services and supports. Means-tested systems are the least accessible and provide services and benefits only to those whose income falls below a defined threshold (sometimes called the poverty level). People in this category are usually referred to as the poor. The third OECD category is a mix of the universal system and the means-tested system. These systems tend to vary greatly in eligibility criteria, individual cost, and services provided. In countries with limited formal service delivery, benefits are often limited to nursing-home care.

A New Typology

Building on previous work, in this chapter a five-category typology to classify approaches to LTC services and supports has been created. As noted, a range of criteria can be considered when assessing and comparing LTC systems at a global level. In addition to the previously identified factors of funding and definition of disability, also included are the supply of LTC services and people's access to them. It is critical to combine the issues of financial and functional disability requirements with the supply, balance, and array of long-term services available. Thus, the classification approach in this chapter draws heavily on the OECD (Colombo et al., 2011) financial categories, universal versus means-tested or mixed, and some of the system classification factors used by Kraus and colleagues (2010), such as the availability of services and the amount of out-of-pocket expenditures by individuals. These factors have been combined with additional delivery system indicators, such as the availability of residential care and the balance of formal and informal LTC services. A description of the categories established and examples of select countries that have been classified in each group are in Table 7.1.

Group 1

Nations in this grouping have developed publicly funded systems that provide universal LTC coverage for older individuals. Using a range of funding sources including a payroll tax, personal income tax, and general revenues (national, regional, and/or municipal), these countries have in common a long-term benefit covering both in-home and institutional services for their

TABLE 7.1 Typology of a Country's Long-Term Care Services and Supports System

Group 1	Group 2	Group 3	Group 4	Group 5
Public insurance funding available for long-term care services	Mixture of public insurance and means-tested funding available	All funding for long-term services is means-tested	Funds are means-tested, but quite limited in availability	No public funds are available for long-term care services
HCBS widely available	HCBS widely available	HCBS commonly available	HCBS limited availability	HCBS not available
Institutional care widely available	Institutional care widely available	Institutional care widely available	Institutional care somewhat available	Institutional care rarely available
Housing with services widely available	Housing with services widely available	Housing with services available	Housing with services limited availability	Housing with services not available
Cash payments often available for long-term services	Cash payments generally available	Cash payments available on a limited basis	Cash payments not available	Cash payments not available
Informal care is one component of the system	Informal care is an important part of the system	Informal care is a critical element of the system	Very heavy reliance on informal care	Exclusive reliance on informal care
Examples: Germany, Japan, Korea, the Netherlands	Examples: France, Ireland, Spain, Switzerland, Australia	Examples: United States, Estonia, Italy, Poland, Romania	Examples: China, Thailand, South Africa, India, Egypt, Mexico, Argentina, Brazil	Examples: Kenya, Nepal, Ghana, Bangladesh

Note: HCBS, home and community-based services.

older populations. These countries have developed systematic approaches to identifying and determining levels of long-term disability and have established an array of service options. Their LTC systems typically include a supportive service option linked to housing and self-directed and cash options for recipients. Although informal caregivers are involved both as unpaid and sometimes paid caregivers, the overall long-term services and supports

Source: U.S. Bureau of the Census.

system of nations in this category is designed to balance the help provided by informal and formal providers. Examples of countries in this group include Germany, Japan, Korea, and the Netherlands.

Germany

In 1995, Germany established a universal, non-means-tested, contribution-based system for funding LTC (*Pflegeversicherung*). The system is funded through employee payroll contributions with matching employer contributions (contributions for unemployed persons are paid for by unemployment insurance). Pensioners pay the entire contribution out of pocket. Since 2008, the contribution rate for individuals has been fixed at 1.95%; for those age 23 and older without children there is an additional 0.25% contribution charge. Those who opt out of the public system can do so if they have higher incomes that meet a strict eligibility standard. However, they are mandated to purchase private LTCI that guarantees at least as much coverage and benefits as the public system.

The German LTCI fund provides for home care (family members or nonprofessional private persons), home help service (professional staff or ambulatory help), and institutional care (Heinicke & Thomsen, 2010). Family caregivers are eligible for 4 weeks of vacation, during which the LTCI fund will cover respite services, as well as provide caregivers with an option for free education and training. Benefits are received as formal services such as personal care, nutrition, transportation, and housekeeping carried out by professional care providers, or beneficiaries can opt for a lump-sum cash allowance that they can use to purchase services from a provider, compensate family caregivers, or spend on something else entirely (care-related or otherwise). The amount of the payment is based on the level of care category under which the beneficiary falls. In general, the system favors community-based care, and individuals using institutionalized care pay a significant co-pay to cover the cost of services that lie outside the scope of the LTCI fund.

Individuals who have a physical illness/disability—or a mental illness or other mental incapacity—who regularly need help with ADLs for a period of at least 6 months and have contributed to the system for a minimum of 2 years are eligible for benefits under the German LTCI system (Schulz, 2010). Although there is no age criterion for eligibility, nearly 80% of beneficiaries are age 65 and older (Rothgang, 2010). The level of benefits received is determined by the care category into which individuals are designated. Determination of care level is done via an examination by a medical review board (*Medizinischer Dienst der Krankenversicherung–MDK*) designated by the insurance fund. Based on the assessment of the review board, individuals are placed into one of three levels of care, ranging from the lowest to the highest level of assistance required. Care *level 1* indicates that the individual requires help with at least two ADLs for at least half an hour per day and requires assistance with household tasks (IADLs) several times a week. A designation of care *level 2* indicates that an individual requires at least three hours of help with ADL tasks at least three times per week and needs assistance with household tasks several times a week. Finally, in care *level 3*, the highest level of need, individuals require a minimum of five hours of assistance with ADL tasks continuously during the day and night.

Since its implementation in 1995, significant criticism of the German LTCI system has been surrounding the lack of adequate coverage provided for individuals with dementia (Rothgang, 2010). Because the definition of dependency, and resulting classification of care level, is limited primarily to assistance with ADLs and IADLs, general supervision (such as what might be required when caring for a person with dementia) is not covered. This leaves many with an unmet need of care. A second criticism of the system is that because of the cap on benefits, individuals who need substantial care must pay a significant portion of the cost themselves. The final major criticism of the German system is that, although the climate of care and the needs of beneficiaries are changing, the benefit structure has not been adjusted. However, Germany has been able to provide some LTC coverage for nearly all citizens. Yet, with approximately 20% of the population age 65 or older, some substantial issues remain that threaten the sustainability of the system in the future (Colombo et al., 2011).

Japan

In April 2000, Japan implemented its national long-term insurance policy (*Kaigo Hoken Ho*), which provided a universal benefit for individuals age 65 and older with severe disability (Yong & Saito, 2011). Today, with more than 23% of Japan's population at or older than age 65 and projected to be as high as one third by 2025 (Muramatsu & Akiyama, 2011), efforts to address the challenges of LTC have attracted national support. The *Kaigo Hoken Ho* law relies on funds from general tax revenues, plan premiums, and co-payments. Half of the program funds come from government: either national, prefectural (prefectures are similar to states in the United States, provinces in Canada, shires in England, and departments in France), or local. The other half of funding comes from individuals, including: (a) Japanese adults between the ages of 40 and 64 who contribute through a payroll tax of 0.9%; (b) those older than age 65 who pay an income-based premium; and (c) co-payment contributions by users who can afford them, equivalent to 10% of the total costs (Yong & Saito, 2011).

The LTCI covers all Japanese people age 65 and older without regard to income. Individuals between the ages of 40 and 64 with severe disability can also qualify for LTCI benefits, but their disabilities must be caused by health-related conditions associated with aging (e.g., early onset of dementia and cerebrovascular strokes) and require assistance with ADLs. Recipients can receive assistance at home through an array of in-home and community-based supports, including basic personal care assistance, rehabilitation and nursing services, and medical day care. The LTCI provides funding for medical equipment, such as an adjustable bed, and minor home renovation, such as a ramp (Yong & Saito, 2011). Institutional care is also covered under the LTCI fund. Nursing homes are placed into three major categories: those serving frail older people, those serving older people with high medical needs, and those emphasizing dementia care.

To determine eligibility for an LTCI benefit the program relies on a structured assessment and eligibility determination process. After a person applies for or is referred to the program, a nurse or social worker employed by the municipality completes an in-home assessment of the individual's physical and mental functioning that also includes a report from the applicant's physician. The assessment information is electronically submitted, and the applicant is then placed into one of six levels of care. The assessment is then reviewed by a care needs certification board of health professionals who review the physician's report and the assessor's notes to make a final decision regarding level of care. Eligible applicants are assigned a case manager, and service dollars are allocated based on the determined level of care. Although a dollar amount is associated with each level of care for planning purposes, the LTCI program does not allow a cash benefit to be paid directly to participants or their families. The case manager assists in developing, implementing, and monitoring the plan of care. A recent report indicated that the program is currently serving more than 4 million participants (about 14% of the age 65+ population; Yong & Saito, 2011).

Reviewers of the implementation experience have identified a series of issues about the LTCI experience (Yong & Saito, 2011). To illustrate, utilization rates, particularly for institutional care, are higher than anticipated. Questions have also been raised about whether the age criterion of 65 and older is the optimum approach. Concerns about the care-management component of the program have also been raised, with concerns about the adequacy of the reimbursement rate and the independence of care managers. Finally, despite efforts to develop a national benefit, service and use patterns vary considerably across the country (Tsutsui & Muramatsu, 2005). As other countries develop efforts to respond to the LTC needs of their citizenry, the experiences of Japan will be quite instructive in efforts to balance a comprehensive benefit with affordability.

Group 2

Nations included in this category have developed systems that rely on a mixture of public insurance and means-tested funding strategies, using a range of financing approaches. For example, some countries provide a universal benefit for certain long-term services, such as nursing-home care, but not for others like assisted-living or in-home services. The nations in Group 2 typically have a wide array of institutional, community-based services, and specialized housing and supportive services. These countries typically have self-directed services available and informal care is an important part of the system. Examples of countries in this group are Switzerland, Australia, Canada, Spain, Ireland, and France.

France

France's LTC system includes a mix of universal and means-tested funding for a wide array of home and community-based services and institutional care. Until the 1990s, LTC was traditionally a family or informal responsibility (Gannon & Davin, 2010). In 1997, France launched its first national LTC program targeted at the age 60+ population. The initial program was a care allowance to support frail older persons in need of ADL and IADL assistance. After much criticism, this initial system was replaced by the Allocation Personnalisee d'Autonomie (APA), which is still in place today (Kraus et al., 2010). The new system is primarily based on a cash benefit. The French system is overseen by the federal government—the main funding source—but divides further fiscal and organizational responsibilities among regional or local departments (subnational governments; Colombo et al., 2011). Eligibility for APA assistance is nationally based and requires that beneficiaries be age 60 or older and meet a high level of dependency for ADLs and IADLs (Kraus et al., 2010).

The **dependency assessment** consists of three steps: (a) a request from the older person in need, (b) an evaluation by an assessment team (medical doctor, nurse, and social worker) that defines the care package, and (c) a final agreement on the care package by the departmental (state) authorities (Kraus et al., 2010). France is one of only a few countries that require a medical doctor to be involved in the assessment and care-package development process (Colombo et al., 2011). The local departmental authorities are responsible for coordinating and partially financing the APA, and they grant final approval for the care services (Kraus et al., 2010).

The APA covers both home and community-based services and institution-based care, but at a progressively reduced rate (Kraus et al., 2010). Every disabled person age 60 and older is eligible for APA benefits, but beneficiaries are compensated based on their income and can expect to pay up to 90% of their LTC costs out of pocket. The monthly cash allowances vary based on level of dependence but are typically between €530 (Euros) and €1,235 (about US$700–US$1,700; Colombo et al., 2011). Therefore, this higher amount is reserved for high-need/low-income individuals. These cash allowances are strictly designated to support any expenses that fall under the approved care plan. In the case of home and community-based services, as in Japan, beneficiaries are prohibited from hiring their spouses or partners, but may engage only accredited and approved providers to deliver care (Colombo et al., 2011). For institutional care, the APA covers only personal and nursing costs and requires users or their families to pay for board and lodging themselves (approximately US$2,000 a month). If the nursing-home residents—and their immediate families—are destitute, they can apply for housing subsidies (that is separate from the APA LTC system) to cover their nursing-home meals and lodging. The average out-of-pocket expense is about 20% of income for home and community-based services and 35% for institutional care (Colombo et al., 2011).

Additional unique LTC options are available in France, such as one of the largest private LTCI markets in Europe, caregiver support programs, and increased attention to dementia-related problems in LTC. The potential for private LTCI has slipped recently and now covers only about 5% of the French market (150,000 individuals) who typically carry LTCI as part of their life insurance policies. This represents quite a small proportion of individuals who may require LTC in the future (Colombo et al., 2011). The APA provides a variety of caregiver programs, such as education, training, and respite care. However, France also provides caregivers with a relatively long (3 months) unpaid leave from work that employers cannot decline, although leave is only available for caregivers of a relative with at least an 80% autonomy loss (OECD, 2011b).

Ireland

Ireland's LTC system also combines a universal and means-tested approach. The development of a formal LTC system is relatively new for Ireland, which launched its first national Office for Older People in 2008 (Colombo et al., 2011). Ireland's LTC system is organized and financed by the national government, through the health service executive (HSE). Until recently, Ireland has had the second lowest LTC expenditure among OECD nations and lately has prioritized LTC planning through a 10-year strategy that began in 2006 (OECD, 2011c). However, the use of formal LTC services remains low, with only about 0.5% of individuals in institutional care, compared, for example, with about 5% in the United States. This low utilization rate reflects the importance placed in Ireland on informal and community-based care, as well as the newness of a more formal LTC system.

In 2009, Ireland initiated **Fair Deal legislation** that states everyone with care needs is eligible for personal care in institutions (this plan, unlike France's, covers room and board; Colombo et al., 2011). This plan requires that all participants contribute 80% of their incomes and 5% of their assets' value toward the cost of their care. However, because the formal LTC system is relatively new, access is limited by resources and has resulted in targeting those most in need. There is a 3-year cap on asset-based contributions (for a total of 15%), and in the case of a couple—when only one of the individuals is residing in an institution—the personal contribution is based on only half of their assets (Colombo et al., 2011).

Despite Ireland's relatively clear-cut institutional LTC plan, several issues surround eligibility and asset protection. Until 2006, there was no national standard for needs assessment, but Ireland is currently using a common assessment report. This report takes ADLs, cognitive needs, and medical requirements into account, and is carried out by a multidisciplinary assessment team (typically consisting of a public health nurse and various other health professionals). A system similar to the U.S. public reverse mortgage program, called the Nursing Home Loan, has been developed. Despite a 3-year cap on asset testing, this program allows individuals to borrow on the equity in their homes to pay for institutional care. This type of program demonstrates the role that the government can play in converting nonfiscal assets into cash to pay for nursing-home care (Colombo et al., 2011).

According to an OECD (2011c) report, an informal care provision in most countries is highly dependent on the health status of the care recipient. Those who have greater ADL limitations are more likely to receive care in an institutional setting. This is not the case in Ireland, however, where no correlation between the health status of care recipients and care setting is found. This is likely related to the strong traditional informal support system in Ireland, as well as the many caregiver support programs. In addition, an array of public training, education, and counseling programs are available for caregivers. Ireland is one of a few nations that allow a long leave from work for caregivers (up to 1 year or more), but this can be refused by employers on certain grounds. The Carer's Allowance (a means-tested government program) provides cash benefits to caregivers and acts like an income support program replacing lost wages or caring expenses (Colombo et al., 2011). The Constant Attendance Allowance (a government program based on compulsory social insurance for employees) is considered more of an income support program than a formal caregiver payment and covers such expenses as travel and utilities (gas and electricity; Colombo et al., 2011). Beyond allowances, Ireland provides a respite care grant that is tax-supported, non-means-tested, and available to all resident caregivers who provide full-time care (OECD, 2011c).

Group 3

Countries in this grouping offer a wide array of long-term services including supportive housing, institutional care, and home and community-based services. Under this model, no public insurance is available to fund LTC. Typically, a range of services is available to low-income persons meeting a high-disability and low-income threshold. Under the approach used in these countries, all LTC is means-tested, and public financing does not begin until consumers have depleted their own resources. Self-directed care is available on a limited basis for some services for certain populations. Informal care is an integral part of this system, with an expectation that family will provide primary assistance prior to using governmental services. Examples of Group 3 countries include the United States, Italy, Poland, Romania, and Estonia.

United States

Because the United States continues to have policy debates and controversy about its overall approach to health care, it is not surprising that it has never designed a system of LTC. In fact, the major program for LTC in the United States—Medicaid, adopted in 1965—did not even include most of the LTC services funded today. Neither the intermediate care nursing-home benefit (added in 1967) nor the home and community-based care benefit (1981) were included in the original legislation. Medicaid accounts for almost 70% of all public LTC services in the United States. It has very strict income and asset criteria and requires the participant to have severe disability. Under no exceptions can individuals receive Medicaid assistance for LTC unless they meet the strict income and disability criteria.

Other sources of revenue for LTC include out-of-pocket payments by individuals (22%), private LTCI (9%), the U.S. Department of Veterans Affairs (VA) (3%), philanthropic organizations (3%), and state-funded programs (3%). The social insurance program covering health care for older people, Medicare, provides a 100% nursing-home rehabilitation benefit for 20 days following a 3-day or longer stay in the hospital, and 80 additional days with a significant co-pay. Medicare also provides home health care coverage, but again it is designed to be delivered in conjunction with an acute care illness, not as a chronic care benefit.

The United States has an extensive array of formal services available to the approximately 6 million older adults with disability, including more than 16,000 nursing homes serving more than 1.5 million individuals. Approximately two thirds of all nursing-home residents are supported by the income-tested Medicaid program, although when residing in the community less than 8% of these individuals were eligible for the program (Stone, 2011). In the United States the majority of nursing homes are for-profit in nature (62%). Additionally, about 800,000 individuals receive home and community-based services provided through Medicaid-waiver programs operated at the state level. The waiver process was allowed in 1981 when the U.S. Congress passed legislation allowing states to waive Medicaid requirements, requiring Medicaid LTC funds to be spent in institutional settings. A sizable private home care market, estimated to be similar in scope to the publicly supported services, also exists for individuals who do not meet the strict Medicaid eligibility criteria for income and severity of disability.

Private-pay individuals and in some states publicly funded participants can self-direct their services, determining both the nature of assistance received and who will provide the necessary assistance. Tested in a research demonstration called the National Cash and Counseling Demonstration and Evaluation (Benjamin & Fennell, 2007), self-direction for Medicaid recipients is now being expanded across the United States.

Housing with supportive services is also an important component of the U.S. long-term services and supports system. In particular, the assisted-living option has expanded rapidly in recent years. Under the assisted-living model used in the United States, an individual with severe disability resides in a small individual apartment with a bathroom and a limited food-preparation area. Residents receive personal care, meals, and housekeeping services directly from the facility; however, home health care is generally provided through an agency as though the individuals were living in the community. More than 800,000 individuals now reside in assisted-living facilities across the United States. Although assisted living is typically privately funded, in recent years the means-tested Medicaid home and community-based waiver program has allowed funds to be used for assisted living.

In many states a not-for-profit network of organizations, termed area agencies on aging, provide case management and coordination for the in-home services network. These agencies often complete eligibility assessments for LTC settings and help ensure that the needed services are provided. These agencies provide information to all older persons, although most of the programs and services are earmarked for low-income individuals.

As a large country with a well-developed services system, the United States spends more than $225 billion annually on LTC. The majority of the nursing homes, assisted-living facilities, and home care agencies are proprietary in nature, and the U.S. delivery system is consistent with the market values of the nation. One of the major challenges faced by the U.S. LTC services and supports system is very high costs that are increasingly being shifted to the public Medicaid program. In many U.S. states, the costs of LTC are becoming one of the highest expenditure categories in state government— rivaling the cost of education—and projections suggest that the current system will be unaffordable in the future (Mehdizadeh et al., 2011).

Estonia

Unlike many countries, due to out-migration, Estonia's population is actually decreasing. This makes LTC for older adults (17% of the total population) even more of a challenge. The goal of LTC in Estonia is to help individuals achieve the best possible quality of life, based on their needs and abilities— remaining at home for as long as possible (Paat & Merilain, 2010). LTC in Estonia is mandated by the Social Welfare Act and is divided between local governments and the individuals needing care. Public health insurance pays for a significant portion of nursing care (financed via a payroll tax). Although LTC services are provided regardless of age, the amount of financial support or welfare services received is means-tested. Preference for funding is

Source: Lawrence Downes.

given to those who remain at home, with allowances for family caregivers provided by local municipalities (OECD, 2011a). Quality of care in institutional settings has been left to the local governments, which until recently have been criticized for not holding facilities to high standards. In many LTC institutions there is a shortage of both beds and space and a lack of quality care (Paat & Merilain, 2010).

An assessment for eligibility for LTC services is conducted by an interdisciplinary team of professionals. Specially trained case managers assess an individual's health and need for personal assistance, guidance, or supervision. Doctors assess an individual's need for nursing care and a local social worker examines an individual's need for welfare services. Estonia's health insurance fund pays for the initial assessment for care need and for nursing care; service users can expect to pay a portion of institutional care, and home health care costs are divided between local governments and the service users (Paat & Merilain, 2010).

Under the current Estonian system, service users can receive benefits from the state (in cash) or from the local government (either in cash or in-kind). In general, the state outlines the minimum requirements for service provisions. Local governments plan, implement, and supervise care services. Several different types of care are recognized by the state, but all are provided by local governments unless otherwise noted. Allowances are provided for care by relatives/informal care and for family care (which can be provided by a nonfamily member). Home services (e.g., household chores) are provided either by the local government or by a private company (OECD, 2011a). Additional types of care include: housing services (providing 24-hour accommodations), a personal assistant, adult day care, institutional care, strengthened support care (which has a goal of improving independence), and strengthened supervision care service (with a goal of maintaining quality of life in an institution; Paat & Merilain, 2010).

A number of challenges are recognized throughout the Estonian LTC system. With little national oversight, quality of care remains a significant issue. Additionally, the current system is rather fragmented with some funds and services provided by the state and some by local governments or private

companies. Finally, although the goal of the LTC system is to promote dom-
iciliary care, the financial support is insufficient (€13–€41 for people older
than age 65; Paat & Merilain, 2010). To address these concerns, the Social
Welfare Act was scheduled to begin making changes to the system in 2013.
The changes have three significant goals: (a) to decrease the state's contribution, (b) to increase individual and local government contributions, and (c) to
further develop housing services (Paat & Merilain, 2010). With a fragmented
system providing less than ideal care, it is clear that the Estonian LTC system
will need to see substantial changes in the coming years in order to meet the
needs of an aging population.

Group 4

Nations included in Group 4 have very limited public funds to support
individuals in need of LTC, but they have begun to see the development
of some private service providers, particularly in the nursing-home and in-
home areas. In Group 4 countries, older people who need such care must rely
on family and friends for the majority of assistance received. Examples of
countries in this group include Thailand, India, Mexico, Brazil, South Africa,
and China. The demarcation of Group 4 and Group 5 (discussed later) is not
always easily discerned because nations with extremely limited LTC funds
may appear to be more similar to nations in Group 5 than those in Group 4.
In their essay at the end of this chapter, Norori, Fredersdorff, and Wilson provide details on Nicaragua, one such nation that is transitioning out of Group
5 and into Group 4.

Thailand

To prepare for population aging and LTC issues, in the 1980s Thailand
established the National Elderly Council (Jitapunkul & Wivatvanit, 2009;
Knodel & Chayovan, 2008). This early action was an attempt to help educate families and the general population about how the shifting demographics could influence their lives and how the government planned to
provide public assistance for aging-related issues that might emerge. It
was not until 15 years later, however, in 1995, that actual legislation was
passed to provide direct support to older people. In 1997, the Thai government mandated that poor individuals age 60 and older had a right to
receive some income assistance from the state (Jitapunkul & Wivatvanit,
2009). This was a substantial move forward for a government with limited
resources and marked a dedication to improving the quality of life for the
poor and disabled older population.

The Thai government continued to recognize the social, cultural, political, and economic impacts of an aging nation. One of the first major concerns was that informal family support for older parents would erode due
to increasingly lower fertility rates and the migration of youth from rural
farming communities to urban centers. AIDS also became a concern, as aging
parents were caring for their infected children, and HIV was increasingly

spreading among the older population itself (Knodel & Chayovan, 2008). These concerns and many more were addressed in numerous political initiatives that recognized the importance of caring for those in need, but did little to establish any formal system to provide such support. For example, the 1999 Declaration of Thai Senior Citizens was primarily concerned with preserving social and cultural values, containing such declarations as: "The elderly ought to live with their families with love, respect, care, understanding, support, and mutual acceptance of the family member roles so as to cherish the bond of contented co-residing" (Jitapunkul & Wivatvanit, 2009, p. 64). It was not until 2003 that legislation was passed to provide more substantive support for older adults, which included tax deductions for children caring for their older parents, and more than doubled the financial support for poor older adults from about US$6 a month to US$14 a month.

As with most countries with very limited funds, Thailand has little formal structure in place for LTC services and supports. There are a few public nursing homes to service older disabled individuals who have no family left and no means to pay for care. A handful of private nursing facilities scattered around Thailand's main urban centers cater to wealthier and often foreign retirees. Nongovernmental organizations (NGOs) and community volunteers play a pivotal role in providing LTC, offering food and companionship programs.

China

With the largest older population in the world (more than 143 million people age 65+), China faces monumental challenges as it addresses the LTC needs of the nation. The aging population in China has increased from 3.6% in 1964 to 8.9% in 2010, and by 2030 the number of older people will more than double (Flaherty et al., 2007). Compounding China's challenges is the now well-known one-child policy. As noted in Chapter 1, it is uncertain whether these adult children will be able to provide the support needed by their aging parents. (See Chapter 9 for discussion of recent changes in this policy.)

Although it was not until the 1990s that institutional care became available in China, by 2006 the country had more than 39,500 institutions with about 1.5 million beds (Flaherty et al., 2007; Zhan, Feng, Chen, & Feng, 2011). Coincidentally, this is the same number of beds available in the United States to serve 100 million fewer older people. Approximately 900,000 beds are in rural areas of China, serving about 0.8% of the total aging population of the country (Flaherty et al., 2007). There are five types of institutions, varying by both the kind and level of disability of the resident and economic resources available (Chou, 2010). Institutions in rural areas tend to offer a lower level of care than urban facilities. These rural homes are also more likely than those in urban areas to be funded by the government (Wu, Mao, & Xu, 2008). These facilities appear to serve a range of residents, from those with minimal impairment to those with high levels of disability (Chou, 2010). In addition to government funding, these institutions are paid for by medical insurance and through private (out-of-pocket) expenditures.

China appears to have a strong commitment to family and community support. The overwhelming majority of older Chinese adults with severe disability receive assistance in their own homes, either from family caregivers or through a live-in maid system, termed *bao mu*. For example, a study in Shanghai found that more than 90% of individuals with dementia were cared for by families at home (Hua & Di, 2002). In fact, the Chinese Constitution states that "Children who come of age have the duty to support and assist their parents" (Chu & Chi, 2008). Although family care is the dominant mode of LTC, China's recent demographic changes in combination with the one-child policy will represent considerable future challenges.

Formal community services are now being developed across China, with estimates identifying more than 900,000 community service centers (Chu & Chi, 2008). A study of community service centers in Shanghai found that these government-funded entities provided such services as LTC, shopping, home maintenance, counseling, and meals (Wu, Carter, Goins, & Cheng, 2005). These centers also help to arrange the *bao mu* (housemaid service) that typically includes personal care services, household chores, shopping, and accompanying seniors to medical visits. The vast majority of the *bao mu* workers are paid out of pocket by older people and their families (Wu et al., 2005).

China certainly recognizes the tremendous challenges it faces in the future. As part of its national strategic plan, the government has set a goal of establishing a comprehensive social care system as the foundation of their LTC system, to be supported by institutional care (Zhang, 2011). The plan also includes a proposal to add 1 million new institutional beds to bring the supply of that resource to 3% of the aged population. Although these changes are in the planning stage, China appears to be on a continuing path to development of a stronger, more comprehensive system of LTC for its rapidly growing older population.

Group 5

Nations falling into this final grouping have a very limited array of formal services available. For the most part, nursing homes do not exist in these countries, and very few in-home services are available. Generally, public funding for support services for older individuals with severe disability does not exist. Families provide the majority of long-term services and supports, and the nations expect they will continue to be responsible for such care. Countries included in this category are Nepal, Kenya, Ghana, and Bangladesh.

Kenya

Until now, the discussion of LTC around the globe has focused on countries with at least some form of organized system for providing such services and supports to older adults. Kenya, unlike the countries previously

Source: Lawrence Downes.

discussed in this chapter, stands in stark contrast, having essentially no formalized LTC system. Moreover, the long-established informal network of social support via family caregivers has undergone significant changes in recent years, leaving many older adults impoverished and with little familial support.

Historically in Kenya, as in most less developed countries, parents provide care for their children until grown, and in return children have a duty to provide care for their parents when they reach old age. However, a number of social and economic factors have caused a change in this structure. On the economic side, in order to explore new job opportunities and advancements, a relatively recent shift toward urban migration for younger adults—rather than remaining in rural farming communities—has left many older adults alone in rural areas to tend the family homestead. This is also happening in many other developing nations, including China, Thailand, and Vietnam.

The most notable social factor remains the HIV/AIDS epidemic that currently affects approximately 6% of the Kenyan population (U.S. CIA World Factbook, 2011). Palliative and LTC services in sub-Saharan Africa are primarily associated with HIV and AIDS, leaving the needs of older adults largely neglected (Bock & Johnson, 2008). Due to the rise in the number of individuals who contract this often-fatal disease, caring roles have become less clear, so many parents are forced to provide care for their adult children who have AIDS. It has been noted that although older adults derive satisfaction from their caregiving roles, many still lack adequate knowledge, skills, and resources for patient care (Juma, Okeyo, & Kidenda, 2004). Additionally, due to the AIDS pandemic, the number of grandparents providing care for grandchildren is also increasing (Bock & Johnson, 2008). Economic, emotional, and physical strain are often associated with becoming, as an older adult, a full-time caregiver for young children.

Although formal social support is still relatively sparse in Kenya, a few organizations like HelpAge International supply economic assistance in some parts of the country to impoverished older adults who provide care for orphaned children (HelpAge International, 2011). On a national level, programs for older adults are coordinated by the Ministry of Gender, Children, and Social Development (MGCSD). In an effort to ease the burden on older adults, beginning in 2004, the Older Persons Cash Transfer (OPCT) Program—targeting individuals over age 65—established a way to provide older adults with essential funds for obtaining necessary provisions such as food, clothes, and adequate shelter (Mwangi, personal communication, February, 2012). In July 2009, Kenya launched a program targeting impoverished older adults with its new pension scheme (HelpAge International, 2009a). Traditionally, the old-age pension in Kenya was tied to employment, with employee contributions to the social security fund accounting for about 5% of their earnings (Social Security Programs Throughout the World, Kenya, 2011). The new pension program, which eliminates the contributory element, makes Kenya one of the few countries in the region to have a noncontributory pension. In December 2009, older citizens (age 65+) in 750 "extremely poor households" in 44 districts received 1,500Ksh (Kenya shillings; approximately US$19.40) per month (HelpAge International, 2009b). Payments are made through mobile phones, post offices, or electronic cards. No data have been collected yet as to the effect of this program on the beneficiaries.

Several policy plans have included provisions for the needs of older persons, although all were broad, general goal statements and took few direct actions (Mbithi & Mutuku, 2010). From 2002 to 2008, The 9th National Development Plan, noting that the disintegration of family support due to urbanization caused undue hardships for many older adults, designed programs to sensitize the public to the needs and rights of older individuals. As another example of national-level policy proposals, The Kenya National Policy on Aging aimed to integrate the needs and concerns of older adults into national policy by ensuring that older people were "reorganized, respected, and empowered to actively and fully participate in society and development" (Mbithi & Mutuku, 2010). Unfortunately, little progress has been made toward implementation of any national policies related to LTC services and supports for older adults in Kenya.

An opportunity exists for the government of Kenya to begin implementing the policies that have been outlined to provide care and funds for older citizens in need. HIV and AIDS education as well as teaching proper caregiving techniques would benefit Kenya's older population; providing them with predictable, adequate levels of support would certainly improve their living, working, and aging conditions.

Nepal

LTC in Nepal is provided by family members rather than governmental agencies or NGOs. Institutional care is practically nonexistent, with less than a handful of old-age homes in the entire country. Nepal has approximately 27 million people, with less than 4% of the population age 65 and older. Yet, life expectancy at birth has been improving for both men and women in Nepal, increasing from age 41 in 1971 to age 61 in 2005—when for the first time life expectancy for women equaled that of men. Approximately 83% of the older population reside with their children in rural areas (Pienta, Barber, & Axinn, 2001). A 1995 study, the Disabled People of Nepal Survey, reported that the prevalence of disability across all age groups was 4.6% (Basnyat, 2010).

Nepal has a small number of old age homes called *Briddha Ashram*. *Pasupati Briddha Ashra* is one of the oldest old-age homes and is funded by the government of Nepal. The *Pasupati Briddha Ashram* is situated near a famous temple, because in Nepal it is a religious and cultural belief that after-death cremation near this temple assures entry to heaven (Basnyat, 2010). Although the capacity of this shelter home is 150 individuals, about 200 older people reside there. Recently, several additional shelter homes for older adults have opened. The *Nisaya Sewa Sadan* (shelter home for the helpless) is partially funded by the government and has 56 residents. It also receives contributions from residents and/or their families, and some funds are provided by additional sources such as voluntary contributions. Siddhi Memorial Old Age Home, a private, nonprofit facility funded by residents' family and friends and a German nonprofit organization, also opened in 2008. This institution targets those older people who can make private out-of-pocket payments for care and appears to be the only such facility in Nepal.

Although Nepal's seniors constitute less than 4% of the population, the country still has more than 1 million individuals age 65 and older. With no formal community-based services and an institutional capacity of less than 1,000 beds nationwide, older persons with disability rely exclusively on family and friends for long-term assistance. Although the country has a long-standing cultural tradition of filial piety, economic and social changes are now presenting major challenges to this approach. As the nation shifts to a more urban economy, as is occurring in China, Kenya, Thailand, and other places, many of the younger family members are migrating to the cities, resulting in higher levels of unmet need for the older population. Because of a weak economy the country has not been able to develop even a basic infrastructure for old-age pensions, and the development of long-term services does not seem to be a high priority. A recent study of Nepali political officials found that the majority of respondents were unaware of problems associated with LTC, and they did not believe that LTC was an important role for government (Basnyat, 2010).

CROSS-CUTTING ISSUES FOR AN AGING PLANET

The examples provided in this chapter indicate the tremendous variation in the ability of countries to address the long-term needs of their citizens. Despite the many differences that exist among nations, a series of LTC policy issues unite them.

Financing

Although it is clear that nations with higher per capita incomes (typically in Groups 1–3) have developed a much more extensive array of long-term services and supports, it is also evident that literally every one of these nations is facing challenges of long-term financing. Even highly resourced nations such as the United States, Japan, and Germany face substantial funding issues as they address the potential needs of their boomer populations. The older population in need of long-term services is projected to more than double in the next 30 years; however, none of these countries has programs ready for the demographic growth they will experience between now and 2040. Some of the countries in Group 4, who now are experiencing rapid economic growth and an evolving LTC system, such as China, India, and Thailand, will also face big future challenges. These nations are still in the process of developing their LTC infrastructure, but they will experience a faster growth rate of their older populations than the previous group of nations. Thus, they will

Source: U.S. Bureau of the Census.

be under pressure to quickly create an adequately financed system for their seniors. Finally, it is the Group 5 nations that may be in for the biggest challenge. With no formal long-term service funding on the horizon, but a recognition that the aging populations will grow substantially, these nations must develop both an infrastructure and financing mechanisms quickly. However, many of these nations do not have basic pension plans in place, making the likelihood remote that planning for long-term services will occur.

Support for Family

Regardless of a nation's resources, LTC of older people is a family issue. Even for those nations with well-developed formal service systems, it is clear that informal supports are critical. However, a consistent theme heard in many countries is that demographic and social changes are placing more pressure on families. Whether it is the one-child policy of China, the migration patterns of rural Kenya and Nepal, or the dual-income worker structure in Europe and the United States, country after country is experiencing changes that are affecting the family's ability to provide assistance. Efforts to develop sound policies to support families in their efforts to assist their loved ones will be a universal challenge in years to come.

Need to Develop an Efficient and Effective LTC System

No nation has yet figured out how to provide all types of long-term services and supports in the most effective and efficient manner possible. Some countries have developed excellent supportive services in housing; others have created well-developed in-home care systems; still others have developed high-quality nursing homes or assisted-living communities. Certain nations are exploring the use of technology to improve service provision; others have developed effective and efficient systems to pay family members and friends for caregiving. Many interesting innovations are appearing, but countries have not done a good job of adopting the most successful approaches of other nations. The LTC challenges that the world faces are so monumental that in years to come it will be necessary that countries share knowledge and take advantage of progress, as we have done in medical research and treatment.

Need for Prevention

A review of global demographic and social changes indicates that the numbers of older people with severe disability will more than double by 2040. Although such growth is a symbol of progress, suggesting many more people are surviving into old age, such changes will also place major financial pressures on all nations. Therefore, substantial efforts aimed at preventive actions will be necessary in four important areas. First, it must be recognized that aging occurs across a life course and that such issues as childhood obesity, malnutrition, and access to adequate health care in early life will significantly affect rates of disability in later life. Second, we must continue to explore and encourage lifestyle changes, including exercise and social engagement, that older individuals can use to help prevent disability in later life. Small delays in disability will have big economic and social consequences. Third, we must encourage environmental changes that can help older individuals optimize the livability of their home settings. Simply improving access to a toilet and ease of use of a kitchen can make a huge difference, allowing a person to manage disability at home. Finally, the development of technology will be necessary. Whether it be more low-technology devices such as water or door sensors (a battery or electronic sensor that would sound an alarm when it detects water or the opening of a door), or high-technology robots or floor sensors (actual monitors built into the floor that could monitor gait and assess potential for a fall), all of us will need the assistance of technical innovation to meet the challenges of our aging populations.

CONCLUSION

As we has been made clear in this chapter, the countries of the world have adopted a variety of fiscal and care system responses to the growing number of older adults who need assistance with ADLs. Based on the type of care provided and the financing structure, and in an effort to more clearly articulate the different approaches to long-term services and supports, a typology of LTC systems has been created, ranging from most to least comprehensive. For countries in Group 1, like Germany, care is widely available and publically supported and funded. Group 2 countries, like France, have a mix of public funding and **means-testing**, and informal care is an important part of the system. For the United States, a country that falls into Group 3, public funding is means-tested, and individuals are expected to be financially responsible for their own LTC. In Group 4 countries like China, funding for care is means-tested and available only on a very limited basis, so older Chinese people rely heavily on informal family care. Finally, for countries like Kenya in Group 5, no public funds are available for care, and older adults must rely almost exclusively on informal care and support networks. All nations must take steps to mitigate the challenges of an aging population by creating sustainable financing systems, finding better ways to support informal caregivers, sharing ideas for best-care practices, and focusing efforts on prevention.

DISCUSSION QUESTIONS

1. Who provides long-term care (LTC), and in what types of settings?
2. Is there a formal LTC system in your country? How is it funded? Who is eligible to receive services?
3. What are the advantages and disadvantages of using means-testing as a way for determining eligibility for publicly funded long-term services

and supports? How do these advantages and disadvantages compare to those for a universal system?

4. Should LTC programs be designed specifically for, and only offered to, older people?

5. Can you see any overlap in the groupings included in the LTC typology? Are there countries that might fit in more than one category?

6. Of the countries you read about in this chapter, which two or three seem to have systems that make sense to you? Would their systems work in your country?

KEY WORDS

Dependency assessment
Entitlement
Fair Deal legislation
Housing with supportive services
Long-term care
Long-term services and supports
Means-testing
Social long-term care insurance
Tax-based systems
Universal systems

APPENDIX A: COUNTRY LIST

The following is an alphabetical list of the 21 European countries included in the Kraus et al. (2010) typology: Austria, Belgium, Bulgaria, Czech Republic, Denmark, England, Estonia, Finland, France, Germany, Hungary, Italy, Latvia, Lithuania, Poland, Portugal, Romania, Slovak Republic, Slovenia, Spain, Sweden.

APPENDIX B: OECD COUNTRY LIST

The following is an alphabetical list of OECD member countries as of July 12, 2012: Australia, Austria, Belgium, Canada, Chile, Czech Republic, Denmark, Estonia, Finland, France, Germany, Greece, Hungary, Iceland, Ireland, Israel, Italy, Japan, Korea, Luxembourg, Mexico, the Netherlands, New Zealand, Norway, Poland, Portugal, Slovak Republic, Slovenia, Spain, Sweden, Switzerland, Turkey, United Kingdom, United States.

Aging in Nicaragua

Milton Lopez Norori, Carmen Largaespada Fredersdorff, and Keren Brown Wilson

OVERVIEW

Nicaragua is one of the poorer countries of Latin America. In 2008, general poverty was estimated at 61.9% of the population; this figure includes 31.9% of the population who live in extreme poverty. Extreme poverty is defined by the World Bank as less than US$1 per day, whereas poverty is defined as income insufficient to purchase a basic shopping basket that includes both food and nonfood items (United Nations, 2010). Three of ten people in Nicaragua live on less than a dollar a day.

Despite its young population, Nicaragua has begun to experience changes in its population structure, due mainly to decreases in the fecundity, morbidity, and mortality rates and an increase in life expectancy. Therefore, Nicaragua's population has begun to age. In 2005 the population age 60 and older was 6.2% of the total; by 2030 this is expected to be about 12%, and by 2050, 18%. Some sociodemographic characteristics of the Nicaraguan population are presented in Table E7.1.

Although most seniors (91%) are not covered by social security, the level of poverty of the older adult population (36%) is considerably less than that of the general population (48.3%). Largaespada (2004) suggests two alternative hypotheses. First, life expectancy may be inversely related to poverty; the poorer you are, the younger you die. A second hypothesis suggests that fewer older adults live below the poverty line because older Nicaraguans work as long as they are able and receive support from their extended families. Analysis of the first hypothesis is still pending, as well as the relationship between work activity and the level of perceived well-being.

Health care is one of the more urgent needs for older Nicaraguans. Although the attention paid to older adults by the public health system has improved, older people in Nicaragua still suffer from lack of affordable or universal access to health services.

TABLE E7.1 Selected Sociodemographic Characteristics of Nicaragua's Population*· **

Total Nicaraguan population	5,142,098 inhabitants
Female population	51% of total
Urban population	56%
Overall rate of fecundity	2.7 children per woman
OLDER POPULATION***	
Population age 60 and older (2005)	6.2%
Female population age 60 and older (2005)	51%
Literacy rate	50.2%
Social Security Institute pension coverage	9%
Older population in extreme poverty	11%

*Nicaragua. National Institute of Statistics and Census. VII Census of Population and VII of Living. INEC (2005).
**Nicaragua. National Institute of Information and Development. Nicaragua Survey of Demographics and Health (2006–2007).
***Nicaragua. National Institute of Statistics and Census. Sociodemographic Situation and the Older Adults in Nicaragua. INEC (2004).

CURRENT SITUATION

The social and economic needs of the older population in Nicaragua increase every year because both their number and percentage of the general population grow. The state, civil society, and the community have been major suppliers of their assistance and care; however, there is major need for improvement.

Nationwide, there are 18 geriatric homes (*hogares*) and 7 meal sites/ social clubs. This represents the entire spectrum of age-related services available to older adults. The residents of *hogares* are typically seniors who do not have family, whose health status is fragile, who suffer from physical and mental disabilities, and who seldom have the material resources to pay for their care. Older persons living in *hogares* represent less than 0.1% of the total number of older citizens in the country, whereas the vast majority are living in their own homes and communities. The cultural mandate still predominant in Nicaraguan society involves a moral duty to take care of older kin within the family context. Culturally, sending one's older relatives to a *hogar* is only justified in extreme need. In familial units without the resources to survive, this duty does lead to older people being abandoned by families. This mandate may also represent an asset for the well-being of seniors in a country with high poverty levels. Its preservation is also an opportunity to build stronger community-based solutions for the care of the older population, both in *hogares* and within their own homes. A new challenge is adult children migrating to cities, leaving older persons stranded in rural communities without the typical familial support systems—a pattern being seen in many areas of the world.

The major source of government financing for geriatric homes is Nicaragua's National Lottery. Most of its earnings are transferred to the Ministry of the Family, the government institution that has the mandate to organize the government's response to the more vulnerable sectors of population in the country. In this context, geriatric homes receive part of this funding, sharing it with other institutions of public welfare such as abandoned, abused, or disabled children's homes.

Given the nation's very limited resources, local communities are the major suppliers of resources in a context of increasing needs, out-migration of young adults, and increased life expectancy and poverty levels. Local governments (municipalities) in many provinces or states of Nicaragua allocate a small fraction of their budgets to help older indigents and support geriatric homes, but high financial deficits still prevail in most homes. Most geriatric homes are managed by private organizations that are also responsible for obtaining the resources required for the care of the residents: the buildings and maintenance, paid caregivers, food, and health needs. Table E7.2 shows other important characteristics of *hogares* in Nicaragua.

COMMUNITY-BASED OLDER CARE: ATTENTION AND SUPPORT STRATEGIES

Nicaragua represents a growing number of countries that are aging rapidly with scarce resources. The work undertaken there for the past decade offers an example of how changing population dynamics may be addressed in other developing areas of the world, with similar characteristics and needs of older citizens, local and national budget limitations, and the richness of social capital. Using asset-based community development principles, the Jessie F. Richardson Foundation, a charitable foundation based in Clackamas, Oregon (United States), in collaboration with local organizations and interested individuals, has been offering immediate aid while designing and implementing capacity-building strategies with a focus on sustainability. Two priorities have guided these efforts:

1. For medium- and long-term results, the first priority has been strengthening the ability of local organizations and individuals to address the issues of seniors living in geriatric homes, as well as in their own communities. Efforts include:
   - Alliances and partnerships with local representatives of organized private groups and individuals (older groups, local churches, community leaders, religious groups), government institutions (Ministry of Health, Ministry of the Family, Nicaraguan Institute of Social Security), and private companies (local banks, microenterprises). One outcome is the development of the Nicaraguan Aging Council that acts to

TABLE E7.2 Selected Characteristics in Six Geriatric Homes in Nicaragua

Physical Characteristics and Architecture*	
Urban location	50.0%
Average number of years in operation	20.5
Average number of residents	30
Physically comfortable homes	28.5%
Homes with sociorecreational aides	45.0%
Homes with prosthetic assistance	39.8%
Homes with adequate signals for orientation	16.6%
Homes that have complete health assistance	31.4%
Staff and Worker Characteristics	
Percentage of women	80.0%
Workers with low educational level (elementary school)	41.4%
Illiterate workers	5.7%
Workers without formal education or training in gerontology	96.0%
Characteristics of the Residents	
Average age of residents	79
Illiteracy rate	69.1%
Residents without pension	95.8%
Residents without family	74.5%
Residents who perceive their health as regular or bad	66.0%
Residents without proper dental attention	100.0%
Residents who are sick or have at least one illness	92.1%

*Average percentage scores based on the scale of the Evaluation System for Nursing Homes (SERA). Ballesteros et al. (1997).

Source: López (2008).

advise, advocate, and support age-related activities, and includes collaborative development with the Jessie F. Richardson Foundation of a National Training Center, the development of recognized standards for LTC in the *hogares*, and focused age-related research.

• Raising awareness and supporting advocacy activities directed to local and national government authorities about feasible strategies for the care of older persons, resulting in additional support by government agencies.

- Technical advice to boards of directors of private organizations and groups who provide care for older citizens aimed at improving the organization and quality of services, as well as the effectiveness of their fund-raising activities.
- Training of staff directly involved in the care of seniors in *hogares*. In a 5-year period, more than 200 direct-care workers have been trained for at least 40 hours each in geriatric care techniques.
- Promotion of intergenerational links between youth and older adults, contributing to a culture of respect and mutual support between the groups.
- Promotion of micro and small-business enterprises in some geriatric homes, thus reducing their economic vulnerability by generating income to support the cost of care.
- Provision of specialized training for health care professionals, first-responders, and others already working with older people in the community.
- Scholarships to Nicaraguan students who are placed as interns in *hogares* to not only learn about senior issues and care but to bring much-needed skills in areas such as accounting, counseling, business development, and nursing.

2. The short-term priority has been to generate rapid responses to unsolved basic needs. Immediate solutions have been given to elementary needs of selected groups of older adultss (all in extreme poverty and vulnerability) through the donation and delivery of health services, medicine, medical supplies, and equipment to geriatric homes, hospitals, and health centers. To date, the Jessie F. Richardson Foundation has provided health services and food to nearly 10,000 seniors living in their own communities and in geriatric homes. Donations account for more than 30,000 pounds of basic materials of health supplies, rehabilitation equipment, medicines, and clothing for older adults. More than 40,000 hours of volunteer labor have been contributed by university students in Nicaragua and from the United States on behalf of older persons and organizations working with them.

Additionally, collaboration and cooperation activities with local partners—the Rotary Club, Nicaraguan YMCA, John XIII Society, Society of St. Vincent DePaul, and Niccabean Company—and U.S.-based partners such as Concepts in Community Living, Marquis Companies, Wilkes Senior Village, and countless business donors have sought to create and strengthen alliances and local networks to care for the Nicaraguan older population. These efforts have improved voluntary work, social cooperation, and sensitivity toward the care of the old in some municipalities of Nicaragua. Relationships between countries and with some universities in the United States—Portland State University in Portland, Oregon, Pacific University in Forest Grove, Oregon, and Concordia University, also in Portland—have been strengthened to the point where joint training, research, and university courses are being developed.

CONCLUSIONS

Throughout this process, activities have been accompanied by a systematic and critical reflection about the results, aiming to understand the substantive lessons learned. Among the most important of these lessons is that for permanent change to be achieved, aid and training alone are inadequate. Aid by itself over long periods of time can foster learned helplessness. To create capacity, training cannot be only topic- or content-based; it must involve long-term, hands-on technical support for adaptation, implementation, and acculturation. Solutions must be locally prioritized and owned by those whose responsibility it will be to maintain them. A final component is developing reliable sources of income apart from traditional donations when government sources are inadequate. The goal is to improve the ability of civil societies to address the increasing needs of the older population and to replicate and expand services to the remaining areas of Nicaragua, as well as in other developing areas of the world where resources are limited.

CHAPTER 8

Work and Retirement

Phyllis Cummins, J. Scott Brown, and Philip E. Sauer

Henning is 60 years old and has been working for 37 years as a vice principal at a German high school. If everything goes as planned and the state does not change regulations, he will retire early at age 62.5 rather than at the mandatory retirement age of 64.5 for civil servants in teaching. *Henning* has a capital life insurance scheme and state-funded extra insurance in addition to his civil servant's pension. He will be working full time for seven eighths of his salary for 7 years in order to retire 2 years early, which will reduce his pension by 3.8%. *Henning's* English wife, *Janice,* is 56 years old; she plans to stop working at age 60. She has worked freelance for the last 33 years in adult education teaching English, and has taught German–English translation courses at a university. She pays annually into a life insurance plan that matures when she turns age 60. She pays into a state-funded insurance scheme (Riester-Rente), and into a small state pension insurance plan. Additionally, she co-owns her parents' house in Britain with her brother, which she rents out to students as an additional financial bonus for when she retires. Near the end of her working life, she does not feel pressured in any way but does feel strange realizing that she is now probably the oldest among her group of colleagues. Working freelance, *Janice* was flexible and able to try to balance the demands of working for certain periods during the week, running a household, and being a mother of two children. Once her children were older, she increased her work hours. Her husband always worked full time. Consequently, she will receive much less than her husband when she stops working. She did not work at all during the year after her first child was born.

Henning and *Janice* will have paid off the mortgage on their house by the time they retire. This also will provide capital for old age if they have to move into a nursing home or assisted living facility. *Henning* feels a certain relief that he will retire before experiencing the full impact of planned structural changes to the school system that will, he feels, produce a decline in quality. Hence, he feels he is retiring at the right time. Regarding their timing of retirement—once *Janice* was diagnosed with multiple sclerosis (MS), they both agreed on trying to go for early retirement. Because they do not know how the disease will progress, they would like to have the chance of spending time together in a relative good state of health. If her health permits, *Janice* will continue to work in adult education for another 2 years, before she stops her freelance work at the age of 60.

As a civil servant in Germany, *Henning's* pension will be taxed. The biggest challenge or disadvantage he can see as a civil servant is that—in spite of getting the best medical care as a private patient— he is concerned with getting old because he will have to pay for all doctors' bills and medication first before getting reimbursed through the state and health insurance. In old age, this means giving access to all of their estate to their children. However, they may have to designate a guardian with access to all of their estate in case their children live too far away from them to look after their affairs and needs on a regular basis. They do not have to worry about long-term care insurance; this is provided by the state. However, they have to be more proactive regarding their wills, and must decide in a living will what treatment is to be applied in case of ill-health. They also must look into making their house more age-friendly or make the decision to move.

Since *Henning's* retirement will be at a relatively early age, he and *Janice* are going to wait for now and become more proactive once retired. They feel the biggest challenge will be to stay independent in spite of possible frailties of old age, and to prepare for their own care so their children will not be burdened by either the costs or the need to look after their ailing parents. *Janice* will have to review her finances and make cutbacks during retirement. She is concerned about whether they, as a couple, will be able to cope in old age with increasing health costs. Due to the Eurozone crisis (also known as the European sovereign debt crisis of 2010–2013 [and counting]), her life insurance will be worth less than originally expected. Generally, the euro crisis is of concern to all Europeans, but it did not have an impact on the timing of retirement for *Henning* and *Janice*. They do not plan to take on paid employment once retired, but wish to be actively engaged as community volunteers.

Janice is apprehensive about stopping work, especially about how she will cope with suddenly no longer having the routine she has lived with for so long. However, she looks forward to being able to choose what she wants to do with her time: enjoy her hobbies; spend more time with people who are important to her; not have to cram everything into the weekend period; travel in the low (off) season; and, finally, find the time and energy to renovate their home and get rid of a lot of clutter that has accumulated over the years. Overall, she is looking forward to retirement with mixed feelings of joy and some apprehension.

Understanding *Henning* and *Janice*'s story of impending retirement requires looking beyond the basics of saving money for old age. Indeed, in addition to purely economic resources, this couple's retirement decisions are also influenced by the support they expect to receive from their family and from the state, as well as the impact their health will have on the quality and location of their retirement. To truly understand such a complex process, one might adopt a life course approach to retirement. The **life course perspective** is a way to study aging that considers human development in the context of historical events, social interactions, individual choice (i.e., human agency), and the effects of early-life experiences in determining later life outcomes (Elder, George, & Shanahan, 1996). Historically in industrialized societies, the life course has been partitioned into three sequential phases: education and training for work, continuous work activity, and retirement. Over the past several decades, age structuring among education, work, and retirement has become less pronounced. Social and cultural understandings of work and retirement vary considerably around the world; age norms for experiencing life events, such as transitioning between work and retirement, are very different in developed nations compared to developing nations. The world's aging population has become increasingly heterogeneous, making it difficult to predict the timing of life's transitions (Dannefer & Settersten, 2010).

DEFINING WORK AND RETIREMENT

From an economic standpoint, **work** can be defined as "activity for another party for compensation" (Cappelli & Keller, 2012, p. 5). Work can have diverse meanings for different people; however, for most it is necessary for human existence by providing funds for basic human needs such as food and shelter. It is also important in determining standing within a community and providing a source of identity—for many, it is the primary source of human interaction. In developed countries, there has been a shift from traditionally defined jobs (those that are full time and long term) to more flexible work arrangements such as contract work and part-time employment. In recent years, those living in developing countries have had access to new types of work such as virtual employment with high-technology, U.S.-based companies (Ardichvili & Kuchinke, 2009).

Defining **retirement** has become more difficult with less standardized life course transitions. Transitions between work and retirement have become increasingly complex; permanent withdrawal from the labor force to a life of

Source: Dr. Sukhminder S. Bhangoo.

retirement and leisure has become less common. Blackwell, Obka, and Casey (1995) describe two broad forms of transition into retirement: (a) a direct move from working to not working, as a consequence of becoming unemployed or disabled, or as a consequence of making a decision to cease working; and (b) a move from a full-time job done for many years, to a part-time, occasional, or otherwise lighter job and only later a complete cessation of work (p. 7). Blackwell et al. (1995) also suggest that a third meaning of retirement is a self-description of being retired, regardless of whether or not a pension is received. **Unretirement** is another possible transition, when an individual shifts from full or partial retirement back to full-time employment (Maestas, 2010). Increased life expectancy has raised the probability for multiple transitions into and out of the labor force (Warner, Hayward, & Hardy, 2010).

Retirement in the United States and other developed nations was uncommon until the early to mid-20th century, and in many developing countries it is still rare. Public and private pensions—especially the growth of defined-benefit pension plans (discussed later), combined with **mandatory retirement**—resulted in retirement becoming a normative phase of the life course in most developed countries. This norm has weakened with the abolition of mandatory retirement and early-retirement incentives offered by both public and private pension plans in some societies. This combination of factors has resulted in increased heterogeneity in retirement patterns (Warner et al., 2010).

A single definition of retirement that applies globally is not realistic. Retirement has differing connotations to people in different countries, and its meaning has become increasingly individualized. In many countries, the

Westernized view of retirement does not exist, and only the most physically disabled and financially destitute are able to leave the workforce. Retirement in the United States is conceptually quite different from retirement in sub-Saharan Africa. Cultural beliefs, societal expectations, and political realities shape how retirement is defined in a given situation.

WHAT GIVES RISE TO RETIREMENT?

Despite the global reach and diversity of retirement across both developed and developing societies, retirement of large segments of national populations is historically relatively recent. Although there were certainly wealthy individuals in the preindustrial world who were able to separate themselves from paid work, such people were very much the exception. Retirement as a life stage that can be expected by substantial segments of the population emerged in the 20th century as a result of changes in demography, the global economy, and government policy.

As we noted in Chapter 4, the 19th and 20th centuries witnessed perhaps the most dynamic changes in human population structure in history. The demographic and epidemiological transitions led to substantial gains in life expectancy; people in many European nations can now expect to live twice as long as their ancestors did in 1900. This massive demographic shift has resulted in growing older populations typically making up one eighth to one fifth of many nations' populations. In industrialized societies, many, if indeed not most, of these individuals reach this old age after working for 30 to 40 years. As such, they have experienced more paid employment than any other generation in history.

These dramatic demographic shifts have been coupled with substantial changes in the global economy over the past two centuries. At the beginning of the 19th century, the overwhelming majority of the world's population worked as farmers (often at only a subsistence level), whereas those who did not farm were frequently artisans, merchants, or involved in cottage industries. The Industrial Revolution changed this arrangement in drastic ways, including massive shifts in occupational structure as people left their farms and moved to more concentrated urban environments that offered the population density required for factory production. Most importantly, for the emergence of retirement, work in an industrial economy often results in a surplus in wealth and production. At the individual level, this transition allowed for a movement from day-to-day subsistence to a lifestyle with the possibility of surplus income, and this allowed for differences in individual and household economies such as increased consumerism and the ability to save resources for future endeavors, including retirement.

At the same time that these demographic and economic changes occurred, substantial changes in government and government policies also emerged. Perhaps most prominently, this period saw the emergence of the modern social democracies across the industrialized world. The importance of the rise

Source: Lawrence Downes.

in democratic government for work and retirement should not be underestimated; it is within this form of government that labor unions first arose and workers began to bargain for higher wages and other fringe benefits such as retirement pensions and health care. It is also within this form of government that welfare programs such as **public pensions** were established (see Chapter 3 for a more detailed description of the emergence of the welfare state). Although these changes occurred in North America and most of Europe in the 19th and early 20th centuries, similar demographic, economic, and political changes have continued in the developing world up to the present day—often in different combinations and at different (usually more rapid) rates.

WHAT DRIVES INDIVIDUAL RETIREMENT?

Retirement ages vary throughout the world; some countries have mandatory retirement age policies, supported by their public pension eligibility rules (e.g., full benefits may be conveniently available from the public pension plan at age 65, which just happens to be the mandatory retirement age). In other countries, however—primarily developing nations—the concept of retirement may not exist. Health and functional limitations also play a role in individual retirement decisions. Availability of pensions and personal savings are also considerations in retirement timing, whereas some people may retire strictly for personal reasons, such as the desire to travel or spend more time with friends and family.

Bureaucratic Rules

In developed countries, both country- and company-level rules affect the age at which an individual can or must withdraw from the labor market. Cross-country variations in retirement age are often influenced by an individual's financial incentive to retire. Both companies and countries have offered financial incentives to retire early, but that trend is changing with pension reform and related increases in normal retirement ages. In 1986, the United States became one of the first countries to abolish mandatory retirement at any age (for most occupations) and other countries, such as Canada and New Zealand, soon implemented similar regulations. Mandatory retirement is permitted in Japan, France, and Sweden, but the minimum permitted retirement age varies among these countries. In Japan, the minimum permitted mandatory retirement age increased from age 60 to age 65 in 2013; in Sweden the minimum mandatory retirement is age 67. Ireland permits mandatory retirement but allows employers to make retirement-age decisions; minimum retirement ages are not set by government policy (Wood, Robertson, & Wintersgill, 2010).

The age of eligibility for pension benefits varies widely throughout the world and also varies by gender (see Table 8.1). The most common eligibility age for full retirement is age 65; the most common age for early retirement is age 60. Several countries, including Iceland, Norway, and the United States, have changed their public pension full retirement to age 67, and more countries are expected to make similar adjustments. Several countries have lower eligibility ages for women: Turkey's early retirement age for women is age 58; for men it is age 60. China also has gender-specific retirement ages. Early retirement ages range from age 55 in Australia and China (age 50 for women) to age 65 in Iceland (OECD, 2011d). Normal retirement ages vary from age 55 for women in China and Saudi Arabia to age 67 in Iceland and Norway. Some countries prefer not to spend money on retraining older workers and, as a result, some retire early due to lack of employment opportunities.

Functional and Health Limitations

As we can see in the story of *Janice* at the beginning of this chapter, health can have a significant impact on the decision to retire. Indeed, employment in physically demanding jobs has been a cause of early retirement for many older workers; however, over the past several decades—as industrialized economies have shifted to postindustrial employment dominated by service sector occupations—jobs have become less physically demanding and have tended to rely more on cognitive ability and interpersonal skills. Lower skilled and more physically demanding jobs are often occupied by those with less education and lower socioeconomic status. Men, manual laborers, and blue-collar workers are more likely than other groups to retire prior to their normal retirement age due to poor health or functional limitations. Poor health can result in the inability to perform work-related tasks, but it also

TABLE 8.1 Pension Systems and Eligibility Ages in Selected Countries

	Pension scheme types			Eligibility age			
	Public	Mandatory private	Voluntary DC	Early		Normal	
				M	F	M	F
Australia		X		55[1]	55[1]	65[2]	65[2]
Chile	X	X		–	–	65	60
China	X			55[3]	50[3]	60	55[4]
France	X			–	–	60	60
Germany	X		X	63	63	65[5]	65[5]
Greece	X			60[6]	60[6]	65	65
Iceland	X	X		65	65	67	67
Japan	X			–	–	65	65
Mexico	X	X		60	60	65	65
Norway	X	X	X	62	62	67	67
Russian Federation	X	X		–	–	65	60
Saudi Arabia	X			–	–	60	55
South Africa	X			–	–	60	60
Turkey	X			60	58	65	65
United Kingdom	X		X	–	–	65[7]	60[7]
United States	X		X	62	62	66[8]	66[8]

Notes: DC, defined contribution; F, female; M, male.
Sources: OECD (2011d); OECD (2012b).

[1] Early pensions are only available from mandatory private plans; age is increasing to 60 over the next several years.
[2] Pension age for women becomes 65 in 2014 and will increase to 67 for both men and women by 2017.
[3] Pension age is 55 for men and 50 for women if they are involved in physically demanding work.
[4] Pension age for blue-collar women is 50.
[5] Pension age will increase to 67 for those born in 1964 or later.
[6] Early (full) pension for those with 37 years of work and with some reduction at age 60 for those with at least 15 years of work.
[7] Pension age for women will reach 65 by 2020 and will increase to 68 for both men and women by 2046.
[8] Pension age increases to 67 for those born in 1960 or later.

may cause a person to value leisure time more. Employers will sometimes offer older workers the option of less physically demanding work or shorter hours or provide special equipment so that they can remain employed (Boockmann, Fries, & Gobel, 2011). Exiting the labor market due to health limitations can result from either physical deterioration, such as worsening arthritis, or from a health or disability shock, such as a stroke or automobile accident; deteriorating health is more common than a health shock. Variations in country-level policies on disability benefits affect continued employment. Countries with more liberal disability benefits are likely to experience higher levels of labor market exit for health reasons.

Economic conditions can also affect the timing of labor market exit for those with health limitations. In the United States, applications for Social Security Disability Insurance experienced a substantial increase during the Great Recession. If individuals with physically demanding jobs become unemployed, their physical limitations may limit their reemployment options. European countries, Japan, the United States and many other developed nations provide long-term disability benefits prior to eligibility for a public pension, but eligibility requirements and actual benefits vary considerably (OECD, 2011d). Depending on age and availability of early retirement benefits from either public or private pensions, an individual may choose retirement rather than remain in a physically demanding job.

Financial and Personal Reasons

Availability of pension income from private and/or public sources affects the timing of retirement. A high **replacement rate** (i.e., pension income is not substantially less than income from employment) could result in an individual retiring sooner than a person with a low replacement rate. Personal savings or availability of income from family members also impacts retirement timing. The Great Recession caused a decline in the value of pension accounts and savings for many of those approaching retirement age in developed nations, resulting in retirement delays to allow time to rebuild assets.

Financial status varies by gender and impacts the timing of retirement. Women typically have substantially lower retirement benefits than men and, as a result, labor-force participation rates for older women have increased over the past several decades. Women often hold lower paying jobs and have intermittent careers due to family responsibilities; therefore, many need to remain in the workforce at older ages in order to avoid poverty in retirement. In some countries such as China, Vietnam, and Indonesia, public pensions play a small role and individuals, especially women, rely on family members for support (Song, Li, & Feldman, 2012).

Individuals also retire for personal reasons, such as a desire to spend more time in leisure activities or with family and friends. Personal reasons also include a desire to leave a stressful job or devote more time to volunteering. Couples often prefer to retire at the same time; however, age differences between spouses and age for benefit eligibility determine whether this is possible. In the United States, joint retirement is difficult unless spouses are about the same age. Alternatively, in countries like Austria, where the normal retirement age for men is age 65 and for women it is age 60, joint retirement is only possible if the husband is older than the wife (Szinovacz & Davey, 2005).

PRIVATE PENSION SYSTEMS

Historically, a retiree living in a social democracy had three sources of retirement income: a public pension, a defined-benefit private pension (described later), and personal savings. This is often referred to as a **"three-legged stool"** of retirement income. In recent years and especially since the Great Recession, individuals living in industrialized countries are increasingly expected to rely mainly on pension benefits from private rather than public sources (OECD, 2012b). In many countries, pensioners rely only on a public pension and personal savings that might be in the form of a defined-contribution plan (also discussed later). The third leg, if it exists, might be from earnings or funds from family members. Availability of private pension plans generally is limited to those living in industrialized nations; people in developing countries typically do not participate in private pension plans but instead rely on informal support from their families and communities (Vlachantoni & Falkingham, 2011). Within industrialized nations, the proportion of labor-force participation in private pensions varies widely: For example, 93.4% of workers in the Netherlands have an occupational pension, whereas in Germany only 51.6% and in the United States only 56.7% have such a pension (OECD, 2012b).

Private pension plans are mandatory in some countries, such as Chile, Australia, Mexico, and Sweden (OECD, 2012b). Private pensions are typically categorized as either **defined-benefit** (DB) or **defined-contribution** (DC) plans. Within DB plans, there are both traditional and hybrid variants. In traditional DB plans, pension payments are determined by a formula that considers salary and length of employment, along with other factors. DB pension benefits result from retirement, disability, or survivorship (i.e., a spouse or dependent child receives benefits following the pensioner's death) and generally are paid out as a fixed monthly payment over the life of the pensioner (or beneficiary) rather than as a lump-sum distribution. In a DB plan, the employer bears the risk of investing funds in the retirement account to ensure that balances will be adequate to pay all future pension liabilities. Hybrid pension plans combine elements of DB and DC plans so that longevity and investment risk are shared by the employer and employee. These plans often occur as a way for employers to transition out of DB plans.

DC plans (typically known as 401(k) plans in the United States) are retirement accounts established by employers but owned and controlled by the employees. In the United States and most developed countries, contributions to these DC plans are voluntary (OECD, 2012b). Employers often subsidize DC plans through matching a portion of the employees' contributions. To illustrate, if employees contributed 10% of their income to their 401(k) account, the employer might match up to 3%, so the employees actually are saving 13% per year for retirement. In DC plans, however, all the risk lies with the employee. The employers make contributions, but their liability is limited to current costs. In that sense, a DC plan is the same as a savings account that can grow in value—or decline over time—and can lose buying power due to inflation.

Over the past three decades, employers in industrialized countries have been shifting from DB plans to DC plans for three main reasons: (a) they were facing an increasing number of retirees; (b) those retirees were living longer and thus drawing more monthly checks; and (c) the benefit formulas that most DB plans had originally promised seemed overly generous. Each of these factors contributed to larger annual pension payouts and obligations than employers had planned for. Hence, many plans were beginning to run out of money, or they could project a shortfall in the foreseeable future. As noted earlier, the move to DC plans placed more of the risk on the employee than on the employer. Figure 8.1 provides information about net pension replacement rates in selected countries from both public and private sources. It is interesting to contrast Greece and Mexico: Pension replacement rates in Greece are entirely from public sources and are well over 100%, whereas in Mexico they are about 30% and primarily from mandatory private pensions.

For companies that offer DB plans, everyone has the same plan, whereas DC plans take many different forms. Two people working for the same company and earning the same amount of money with the same years of service will have identical pension benefits under a DB plan. Alternatively, if the same two people work for a company with a DC plan, different investment decisions can result in substantially different retirement benefits. In addition to stocks, bonds, and standard bank savings alternatives (e.g., fixed interest accounts), DC plans often offer additional investment options, including employee stock ownership plans and employee savings and investment plans, which can involve purchasing stock in the employer's company. If employees choose to invest retirement funds in their employer's stock,

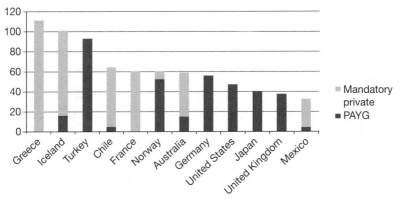

FIGURE 8.1 Net pension replacement rates from PAYG* and mandatory private pensions for average earners in selected countries.

*PAYG (or PAYGO) stands for pay as you go, and refers to public pension plans that tax workers to pay current benefits to retirees. As described in Chapter 3, "The Welfare State and Global Aging," no funds are saved or set aside to pay future benefits. The U.S. Social Security system is a good example of a PAYG plan.

Source: OECD (2011d).

substantial, even catastrophic, risk can be involved should the employer experience financial problems. Enron, a U.S. energy company, is a prime example: When Enron went out of business, many employees lost both their jobs and most, if not all, of their retirement savings.

Retirement plans for public employees (civil servants) are sponsored by governmental entities, such as federal, state, or local governments. To distinguish them from public plans discussed earlier in the welfare state chapter, they are referred to here as public employee pensions (PEPs). About half of the countries in the world—including some large developing countries such as Brazil, China, and India—have separate pension plans for civil service employees. In some more affluent OECD countries, spending on pensions for civil servants constitutes up to about 25% of total pension spending, whereas in developing countries the proportion is much higher, creating a substantial fiscal problem for some nations (Palacios & Whitehouse, 2006).

Unlike retirement plans sponsored by private employers, few public employee plans have transitioned from DB plans to DC plans. Unfunded pension liabilities have been a problem for states, counties, and cities throughout the United States; unfunded liabilities for PEPs are a problem for many developed countries (Fong, Piggott, & Sherris, 2012). In some countries such as Germany, civil servants do not make contributions to their retirement plans; retirement benefits are considered part of their compensation (Müller, Raffelhüschen, & Weddige, 2009).

The shift from DB to DC plans also has increased concerns about economic security in retirement for women and minorities. Women tend to realize lower investment returns in their DC plans than do men, primarily because they are more conservative investors. This disadvantage is compounded at retirement because women typically have lower wages and more intermittent work histories than men and, thus, may have lengthy periods of low or no contributions to their DC plan. Racial and ethnic minorities and low-income earners often experience the same issues. As wage inequality has increased, so has pension inequality, especially with the advent of DC plans. By way of example, from 1993 to 1994, only one third of female retirees in the United Kingdom received pension income, whereas three fourths of male pensioners received such income (Bardasi & Jenkins, 2010). These risks are increased in countries that have fully or partially replaced their public pensions with private savings accounts (Orenstein, 2011).

DIFFERENT FORMS OF RETIREMENT

Population aging, changing family structures, and globalization have resulted in increased complexity in transitions to retirement. Unlike most retirements in earlier years that involved an abrupt departure from work at a fixed age (age 65 in the United States), exits from the labor market in developed countries today are quite varied and include early retirement, delayed retirement, phased retirement, unretirement, and partial retirement that may combine receipt of pension income with part-time work. Figure 8.2 provides

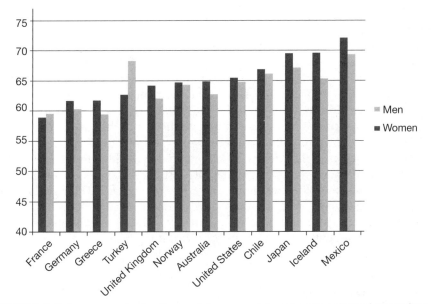

FIGURE 8.2 Average age of retirement for men and women in selected countries: 2004–2009.
Source: OECD (2012a).

information on average retirement ages in selected countries. It is interesting to note that in several countries average retirement ages differ from early or full retirement ages (see Table 8.1).

Early Retirement

Early retirement is characterized by exiting the labor force and collecting pension benefits earlier than normal retirement age. Individuals who have more education, have had multiple jobs, have children at older ages, and have experienced late divorces are less likely to retire early. Those with less education, physically demanding work, and poor health are more likely to retire early (Damman, Henkens, & Kalmijn, 2011). Early retirement can be either voluntary or involuntary. Voluntary early retirement is characterized by a preference for leisure activities as opposed to continued work. Alternatively, involuntary retirement is often unexpected and can result from events such as corporate downsizings or plant closures. Involuntary retirement also can result from poor health or family caregiving obligations. Although involuntary retirement has increased as a result of the Great Recession, it is still relatively uncommon in the United States, Canada, Denmark, and Norway as compared to Germany, where more than half of early retirements are involuntary. Some European countries have age restrictions on new hires, making it quite difficult for older workers who become unemployed to find new jobs, thus forcing them to retire early (Dorn & Sousa-Poza, 2007).

European labor markets are characterized by low labor-force participation at older ages, primarily because of the structure of their pension systems that provide monetary incentives to exit the labor force early. Over the past several decades, governments in several European countries have implemented early retirement programs that allow workers to retire and receive pension benefits prior to the mandatory retirement age. Countries in central and southern Europe have high levels of wage replacement in their public pensions, encouraging early retirement; this is not the case in the United Kingdom or the United States. In recent years, European Union (E.U.) countries have increased their focus on keeping older workers in the labor force in order to maintain the financial viability of their pension systems. In 2001, the E.U. established the Stockholm and Barcelona targets: Their goals are to increase employment rates for those age 55 to age 64 (Stockholm target) and to increase effective retirement ages (Barcelona target). Although these programs have met with some success, the Great Recession has resulted in most countries falling short of their targets (Rix, 2011).

Delayed Retirement

Individuals who decide to retire later and receive their pension benefits later than their normal retirement age have delayed their retirement. Most industrialized countries have attempted to adjust retirement ages to be more in line with increased life expectancy; examples include Australia, Germany, the United States, and the United Kingdom (see footnotes to Table 8.1). In the United States, phased increases in the normal retirement age to receive full Social Security benefits, combined with financial incentives to defer retirement, have caused some people to work past their normal retirement age. The Great Recession has resulted in some people deferring their retirement to make up for losses in their retirement accounts. Elimination of mandatory retirement in the United States has also been a factor in people working at older ages, as has the shift to DC pension plans and less generous pensions. Characteristics of individuals who delay their retirement are good health, less physically demanding work, and higher levels of education. Efforts have also been made to improve working conditions and job quality to encourage working at older ages (Pollak & Siven, 2011), but many Europeans remain reluctant to delay retirement. In order to encourage work at older ages, it may be necessary to implement policies such as flexible work arrangements and to provide training to upgrade skills (Winkelmann-Gleed, 2012).

Over the past several decades, labor-force participation rates at older ages increased in most countries, and the rates of increase have been greater for women than men. Figures 8.3 through 8.6 show changes in labor-force participation rates for men and women age 55 to age 64, and age 65 and older between 2000 and 2011. It is interesting to note that Greece has one of the lowest rates of labor-force participation rates at older ages, whereas Iceland has the highest rates. Ages for pension eligibility for both early and normal retirement are higher in Iceland, which results in higher labor-force participation rates at older ages.

Japan's retirement age is among the highest in the OECD countries: The average retirement age between 2004 and 2009 was age 69.7 for men and age 67.3 for women. Japan has one of the highest life expectancy rates in the world, which partially explains the relatively high retirement ages. The

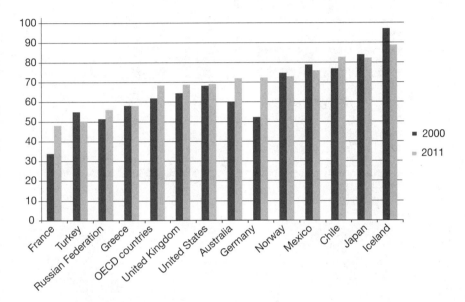

FIGURE 8.3 Labor-force participation rates in selected countries for men age 55–64.
Source: OECD (2012c).

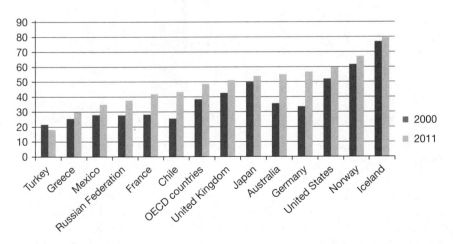

FIGURE 8.4 Labor-force participation rates in selected countries for women age 55–64.
Source: OECD (2012c).

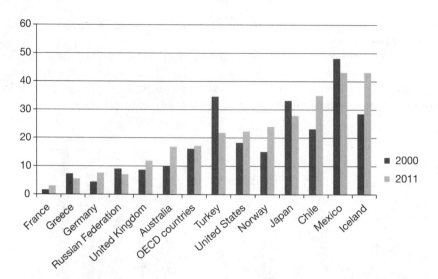

FIGURE 8.5 Labor-force participation rates in selected countries for men age 65 and older.
Source: OECD (2012c).

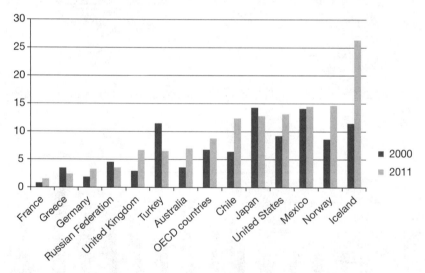

FIGURE 8.6 Labor-force participation rates in selected countries for women age 65 and older.
Source: OECD (2012c).

Japanese government has encouraged firms to increase their mandatory retirement to age 65 or older, or to eliminate mandatory retirement entirely. Although many in Japan retire at age 65, it is common for individuals to be rehired by the same firm or become employed by another firm through an introduction by their career employer (Shimizutani & Takashi, 2010).

Source: U.S. Bureau of the Census.

Partial Retirement and Return to Work

Partial retirement includes several different types of retirement transition, including phased retirement, part-time work while collecting pension income, and bridge jobs. Only about one fourth of career employees leave their career jobs and the labor force simultaneously (Cahill, Giandrea, & Quinn, 2012). Phased retirement involves a gradual transition into retirement rather than an abrupt shift from full-time employment to full-time retirement. It does not necessarily involve a change of employers, but it can be simply a reduction of work hours with the same employer. Formal phased retirement policies are uncommon, but employers sometimes negotiate working arrangements on an informal basis, especially for employees who have specialized skills (Hutchens, 2010). In the United States, pension regulations can restrict access to pensions unless there is a change in employers. Thus, it may be necessary to change employers in order to receive pension benefits. Data suggest that most employers in the United States are unwilling to allow their employees to switch to part-time employment (Even & Macpherson, 2004). On the other hand, Germany and Italy have had work-sharing programs for several decades (Baker, 2011) that provide a mechanism for older workers to remain in the workforce on a part-time basis.

Returning to the labor force following retirement, or unretirement, has become more common since the Great Recession, especially for those with DC plans. In many respects, returning to the labor force is similar to partial retirement. About 25% of Americans with career jobs (i.e., they worked full time for the same employer for at least 10 years) returned to the workforce following retirement. Those who returned to the workforce tended to be in good health and to have a desire to remain active and productive but also to have a less stressful job. Although some retirees return to the workforce for financial reasons, in most cases they either did not find retirement satisfying or they anticipated returning to the workforce at the time of their retirement (Maestas, 2010). In Japan, whereas most individuals are rehired on a full-time basis, either by their career employer or another employer, in some cases they shift to part-time work or to self-employment. Transitioning to part-time work is more common for Japanese women than men (Shimizutani & Takashi, 2010).

In the United States, the shift from DB to DC pension plans has caused many workers to either delay retirement or return to the labor force if they had retired already. The Great Recession resulted in a significant loss of value (and therefore the payouts) of many DB plans. Baby boomers born after 1950 have been the group most affected by the transition to DC plans; therefore, the trend of working at older ages, either on a full-time or part-time basis, is likely to continue. Indeed, given the financial crisis of many state-sponsored public pension plans and the likely greater reliance on the private pension "leg" of the stool for old-age financial well-being mentioned in Chapter 3, it is likely that many nations will experience an increase in the diversity of partial retirement and continued labor-force engagement of their older citizens.

RETIREMENT IN DEVELOPING NATIONS

The earlier discussion focuses more heavily on issues of work and retirement in developed nations because these countries have the longest experience with retirement, and the most developed social policies and private sector involvement in financial support in old age. However, most of the global population lives in the developing world where the notion of retirement ranges from an emerging social reality to a nearly nonexistent concept. Indeed, the range of economies and demographic realities affecting retirement and work are far more diverse in the developing world than in the industrialized nations.

Liang's essay at the end of this chapter provides an excellent example of the more economically affluent portion of the developing world spectrum. The essay discusses the potential oncoming crisis that China faces due to its rapid reduction of fertility, rising life expectancy, and rising economic quality of life. Simply put, if no changes are made in the near future, China will soon face an enormous retired population compensated through an antiquated retirement policy from the 1940s that was never meant to serve such a large segment of its population. Similar crises have already occurred in places like Latin America, where the solution has often been to privatize public pension programs, although this strategy has produced only limited success. These wealthier developing nations soon will have populations that are nearly as old as their developed counterparts; however, they will face

Source: Dr. Sukhminder S. Bhangoo.

this situation with far fewer financial resources in either the government or the private sector.

In these wealthier developing nations, at least, retirement from work in later life is a possibility for some portion of their populations. In the poorest of developing nations, like Haiti in the Caribbean or Sierra Leone in west Africa, retirement is a concept largely absent from the experiences of everyday people. Adulthood permits only three phases: work, dependency, and death. Life and retirement in developed—and, increasingly, developing—countries may not be easy or simple or even secure, but it is much more desirable than that in the poorest nations. There, the work one does as a young adult likely will be the same as in middle age and, if one is lucky enough to enjoy a long life, in old age as well. No promotions, raises, career changes, early retirement, delayed retirement, pension benefits, old-age security, disability payments, leisure time, life insurance, or death benefits can be expected. These are all concepts and opportunities available through the welfare state and advanced economies of developed countries.

Where extreme poverty is common, and working often consists of laboring in subsistence agriculture, no surplus income is available to save for retirement; although some governments are beginning to provide small public assistance/pensions for their older citizens (e.g., see the discussion of Kenya in Chapter 3), these are typically far too small to live on without supplementing them with substantial time working. Interestingly, in nations such as these, the very nature of work leads to an unexpected gender equality in labor-force participation. Specifically, due to the need for the participation of all able-bodied family members in many subsistence agricultural economies, the labor-force participation rate for women is often quite high, even rivaling that of men in these societies. Nevertheless, such high participation rates have little bearing on the old-age security outlook for older women (or men) in these nations.

CONCLUSIONS

Understanding work and retirement in the global context is a tricky business. What would seemingly be the simple task of defining retirement becomes quite complex, once we begin to understand the considerable heterogeneity in retirement experiences. Indeed, the stereotypical view of a retiree as an elder who has fully disengaged from the workforce is quite flawed, and in many national contexts may well be in the minority of retirement experiences. With widely varying public pension support, private savings and employer-sponsored pensions are quite important for retirement security in developed nations. Older people in these places who come up short in one of these three areas of financial security often find that they must continue or return to some type of paid employment, even after normal retirement ages.

Work appears to be a universal cultural experience, despite a wide variation in forms and rewards. Retirement, however, is a modern, Western social invention that is permitted by economic plenty. As poorer societies develop economically, they probably will also create both public and private pension systems to ensure economic security in old age, and they will invent their own social arrangements to guide and support retirees' use of their new-found leisure time. Whether they will learn from the successes and failures of those who have traveled this road earlier—or whether the West may learn lessons from these new retirement societies —remains to be seen.

DISCUSSION QUESTIONS

1. Does every society divide adulthood into work and retirement?
2. Why do people work?
3. Why do people retire?
4. At what age should people retire? Why?
5. What is the difference between a defined-benefit (DB) plan and a defined-contribution (DC) plan?
6. What is retirement like in developing countries for the people who experience it and for their families and their governments?
7. If retirement is a period of extended leisure without productive labor, how does this benefit society?

KEY WORDS

Defined-benefit plan
Defined-contribution plan
Life course perspective

Mandatory retirement
Public pensions
Replacement rate
Retirement
Unretirement
Three-legged stool
Work

Retirement in China

Jiayin (Jaylene) Liang

DEMOGRAPHIC PROFILE OF THE PEOPLE'S REPUBLIC OF CHINA

Global aging has become one of the most popular buzzwords since the United Nations General Assembly declared the year 1999 as the International Year of Older Persons (IYOP). Worldwide, we now are confronted with the challenges posed by the increasing older population. In fact, the developing world is facing even bigger challenges because of two major considerations. First, both the size of the older population and the pace of growing older in developing countries exceed those in developed countries. Second, the level of economic progress in developing countries does not allow them to provide appropriate support systems of health care and pension plans for their older populations. How to make up for this structural lag is the key to overcoming the challenges of population aging.

When considering global aging, China definitely deserves the world's attention because it has the largest population of older people in the world and is aging more rapidly than other developing countries. In the IYOP (1999), China announced its entry into an aging society. The number of older adults (people age 60 and older) in China reached 143 million, 11% of the total population as of 2005 (Li, 2007). It is projected that by 2040 China will have 430 million older adults—one out of four Chinese, compared with one out of ten in 1980 (Li, 2007). One consequence of population aging is the growing number of retirees. China is soon to become no longer the "world's factory," offering a cheap, young workforce.

China had completed her demographic transition by the end of the 20th century (Zhu, 2009). According to the *China Statistical Yearbook 2000*, China's fertility rate was as high as 6.14 after the founding of the People's Republic of China in 1949; however, there has been an extreme decrease since the late 1970s, to a large degree due to the family planning program started in 1973 (Information Office of the State Council of the People's Republic of China, 1995) and the one-child policy implemented in the late 1970s. As noted by Peng (2009), "China's total fertility rate dropped to below replacement level in the 1990s and has remained there since." Meanwhile, life expectancy in China has increased tremendously. According to the *China Human Development Report 2007–2008*, China's average life expectancy has increased from age 57 in 1957 to age 72.4 in 2005 (United Nations Development Program: China & China Institute for Reform and Development, 2009). Similar to most of the industrialized world, Chinese women have a longer life expectancy than men. During the period of 2005 to 2010, women's life expectancy at birth was age 74.8, whereas men's life expectancy was age 71.3 (United Nations Statistics Division, 2010). This significantly prolonged life expectancy has increased the years in retirement for Chinese elders.

However, the mandatory retirement system has not been changed much since 1949. Generally, legal retirement is age 60 for male workers and government officials, age 50 for female workers, and age 55 for female government officials. For those who are working in arduous conditions, men can retire at age 55 and women can retire at age 45 (Chen, 2010). In reality, people might retire even earlier than the mandatory retirement age. In 2000, average retirement was age 51.2 (Anonymous, *China Daily*, 2006). Women's relatively longer life expectancy and earlier retirement age compared to their male counterparts in China mean that women will spend more years in retirement. Until recently, no major change has been made since the mandatory retirement system took effect after the founding of the People's Republic of China. Realizing the potential burden of a national pension, the debate over increasing the mandatory retirement age has been brought into focus. However, according to a recent official announcement, China will not postpone the retirement age in the foreseeable future (Chen, 2010).

CURRENT STATUS OF RETIREMENT STUDIES IN CHINA

With prolonged life expectancy and extended postretirement years, the study of retirement in China is becoming increasingly important but so far has received little attention. Most of the national or large-scale studies in China focus on persons age 60 and older. Recently, China has made some advances in this area through the China Health and Retirement Longitudinal Studies (CHARLS), an international collaboration targeting the Chinese population age 45 and older. The second International Conference on Health and Retirement in China—to generate awareness of the research opportunities regarding retirement in China and introduce the newly released dataset—was held in Beijing in July 2009.

The pilot survey of CHARLS was conducted in two provinces—Zhejiang (a rich, coastline province) and Gansu (a poor, inland province)—in 2008. The samples were first stratified by province and then further stratified by urban and rural areas. The questionnaire covers information on household demographics, family transfers, health status, health care, employment, income, consumption, and assets, as well as health facilities in local areas (China Center for Economic Research, 2009). It is hoped that the findings from CHARLS will be helpful in understanding how retirement decisions are influenced by structural forces that shape the average standard of living, health care policy, and pension plans, and how the changing demographic and economic realities have created for the current aging population a situation unlike previous generations in China. However, the economic aspects are less than sufficient to capture the whole picture of retirement in China.

Family remains the major support in old age in China, yet the government has begun efforts to expand pension and health care benefits for workers in nonstate sectors and farmers in the countryside (Zhao & Sheng, 2009). In rural areas, lack of care in old age caused by the out-migration of adult children is an important issue to be addressed. Different structures in rural and urban areas should be a great consideration when it comes to retirement studies in China. The urban dwellers are "entitled to more social services such as favorable social security assistance, more and better education resources, lower income taxes (relative to the agricultural taxes and miscellaneous tolls on farmers), and many other privileges" (Su, Shen, & Wei, 2006, p. 383). As to the unequal development between urban and rural populations, more detailed information and data can be found in the *China Human Development Report 2005* (United Nations Development Program: China & Development Research Center of State Council, 2005).

Traditionally, elders are looked after by their children, but such an arrangement is becoming increasingly difficult or even impossible as economic development has increased mobility among the younger generation. Empty-nesters make up about half of the 143 million Chinese age 60 and older (Li, 2007). One study showed that Chinese seniors have genuine fun in attending to and playing with grandchildren (Su et al., 2006). However, because of prolonged schooling, late job entry, and postponed marriage and childbearing, especially among the one-child generation, the aging parents might not have grandchildren to look after when they retire. Therefore, how to improve the quality of retirement life is obviously an important issue in China, although it has not been studied much. "What is problematic about retirement is not that work is always better but that the abundance of free time in late life is not adequately structured for any larger social purpose or meaning" (Moody, 2000, p. 268). How to fill up that free time and live a meaningful retirement life is becoming a big concern for older individuals in China.

THE RELEVANCE OF CULTURAL AND SOCIAL REALITIES

From reviewing the gerontology literature in the United States, "being productive" is often regarded as the value model of a good retirement life (Caro, Bass, & Chen, 1993), what Ekerdt (1986) has referred to as "the busy ethic." However, whether and how the gerontology literature in the United States might be useful in studying the aging experience in China is unknown. Cultural meaning plays a crucial role in the retirement process (Luborsky, 1994;

Luborsky & LeBlanc, 2003), so understanding Chinese cultural and social realities is essential to defining good retirement life in China. For example, Confucianism places a great emphasis on the interdependence between the old and the young in a family and encourages the young to show respect for the seniors in the society. Another traditional body of Chinese thought, Taoism, points to the natural law of growing old, stresses the balance between mind and body, and reveals the benefits of introspection. These ideas are very different from the model of successful aging applied commonly in the United States that is, to a large degree, based on the value judgment of elders' usefulness through productivity and consumption.

In my recent phenomenological study about what constitutes a good retirement life, I conducted in-depth interviews with 10 people who were born in the 1950s, the first generation of baby boomers in China (Li, 2007, p.17). People from this cohort are the parents of the first one-child generation. They have less family support, especially filial care, in later life as a result. This cohort is now in their "third age" (Siegel, 1990); most of them are healthy. Also, they are generally financially better-off compared with previous generations. This is because of the economic achievement of China's reform and opening-up policy since 1978. In general, their material life has been greatly improved with national economic growth, except for the laid-offs.[1] In terms of what makes a good retirement life for them, four themes have emerged in my study: (a) cohort identification and formative experiences, (b) family orientation with a special focus on the only child, (c) pursuit of a balanced state of mind in the face of challenges, and (d) leisure without self-indulgence (Liang, 2011). These themes tentatively suggest that culture plays a significant role in defining a good retirement life in China, although further research is needed.

In the United States, people born between 1946 and 1964 are defined as baby boomers. In 2011 the oldest of that group turned age 65, so sometime between 2020 and 2025 boomers will become a majority of the U.S. aging population. An historical and comparative approach investigating the phenomenon of aging in China can produce great insights into global aging research. In comparison, family structure would be a significant variable, considering the effect of China's unique one-child policy, as would be the publicly funded support systems of the two countries—exemplified in the United States by programs such as Medicare (the federal health insurance program for older adults) and Medicaid (a joint federal–state program to provide health care for the poor). Both have profoundly affected the aging experience of the U.S. baby boomer cohort. These social structures and historical backgrounds must serve as a comparative horizon for retirement studies in either country. In China, aging is a more recent phenomenon, and the

---

[1]*Note*: Among this urban cohort, some of them have experienced *Xia Gang*—being laid-off from money-losing state enterprises in the 1990s.

society grows older before it grows richer. Thus, how to face the challenge of population aging—drawing on experiences and lessons from the United States and, at the same time, reflecting on China's own unique economic and social realities—should be put at the top of the cross-cultural gerontological research agenda. In addition, how the value systems in the two countries differently shape the expectations and preferences about a good retirement life is well worth exploration.

CHAPTER 9

Families, Caregiving, and Community Support Systems

Jennifer M. Kinney, Suzanne R. Kunkel, Jasleen K. Chahal, and Frank J. Whittington

Family Tree
by John Forster and Tom Chapin
©1988 Limousine Music Co. & The Last Music Co. (ASCAP)

Before the days of Jello
Lived a prehistoric fellow,
Who loved a maid and courted her
Beneath the banyan tree.
And they had lots of children,
And their children all had children
Until one of them had me!
Chorus

We're a family and we're a tree.
Our roots go deep down in history
From my great, great, Granddaddy
Reaching up to me,
We're a green and growing family tree.

My Grandpa came from Russia;
My Grandma came from Prussia;
They met in Nova Scotia,
Had my Dad in Tennessee.
Then they moved to Yokohama
Where Daddy met my Mama.
Her Dad's from Alabama
And her Mom's part Cherokee.
Chorus

Well one fine day I may go
To Tierra Del Fuego.
Perhaps I'll meet my wife there
And we'll move to Timbuktu.
And our kid will be bilingual,
And though she may stay single,
She could, of course, comingle
with the King of Kathmandu.
Chorus

The folks in Madagascar
Aren't the same as in Alaskar:
They've got different foods, different
 moods
And different colored skin.
You may have a different name,
But underneath we're much the same,
You're probably my cousin
And the whole world is our kin.
Chorus

The lyrics quoted above from a wonderful song by John Forster and Tom Chapin—which folksinger Chapin performed while also using American sign language for the deaf—describe a new genetically and ethnically mixed and blended family, created by the global migration and amalgamation of people. The "different foods, different moods, and different colored skin" are hypothesized as only cosmetic shells under which are very similar members of the same megatribe, *homo sapiens*. Yet, it is known that smaller tribes have invented different, persistent ways of creating society, including marriage, family relations, and economic partnerships. So, before accepting Forster and Chapin's observation that all persons are basically the same "under the skin," there must be an exploration of how their beliefs, values, and lives remain different.

AN AMERICAN FAMILY

In an Inauguration Day article in the January 21, 2013, issue of the *Washington Post* newspaper, Krissah Thompson painted a glowing portrait of the Obama family and their public image during the past 4 years living in the White House—Mom and Dad, their two well-behaved, yet normal teenage daughters, and Mom's mom. Mom and Grandmom stay at home (mostly) to see to the girls' care and raising. Dad works at running the country but, since his office is in his house, he's home for dinner most nights. All in all, the Obamas have been able to present the image of an ideal American family, although living their lives in a fishbowl of media scrutiny. More importantly, Thompson conveyed the belief that their image was, in fact, reality and that the family was pretty much the same in private as they appeared to the public. The headline of the story summed up the point of the story: "The family next door." In case the message was not clear, the subhead expanded: "Despite living in the White House, the Obamas seem normal—and that resonates with Americans."

Of course, this says as much about politics in the United States as it does about American families. We elect leaders—and their families—who appear to be the best of us, who seem able to master the challenges of life, while at the same time dressing, acting, and relating like (almost) perfect people—like we ourselves would do if we could. The Obamas are an intact, nuclear family, with two children, a dog, and a mother-in-law. They live in a large, white four-story house surrounded by a beautiful, secure, wooded estate with a classy address in a very safe neighborhood. They are the American dream family. But what about the rest of the world? Is there a Korean dream family? Or an Argentinian dream family? What about the ideal family in Gabon or Guinea?

THE UNIVERSAL CONCEPT OF FAMILY

Families are at the heart of every culture and every society. They vary considerably in size, structure, and specific expectations about who does what. Across those variations, however, the family is universally identified as the social unit responsible for several important functions, including facilitating procreation, caring for and raising children, socializing its members to cultural values and practices, and managing the ways in which households produce or purchase the goods and services its members need (Horwitz, 2005). There are many other purposes that families can, should, should not, or sometimes do fulfill, but that discussion is beyond the scope of this chapter. One extremely important role held by families today in all corners of the globe should be added: providing care and support for older adults. Longer lives have created new stages of life, including the potential for a stage of frailty and declining health when family help is needed and given. Noting that "[P]roviding care to an older family member is an activity that spans time, place, and cultures," Gitlin and Schulz (2012) reinforce the position taken by Kendig, Hashimoto, and Coppard two decades earlier:

> Worldwide the family is the primary caregiver to the elderly. This reality transcends culture, politics, and economic circumstances in spite of wide variations in the way care is provided in different societies. Especially for developing countries where elderly populations are increasing very rapidly, families play a critical role. But in all societies families are typically generous in providing care, and those receiving care usually want care first from those with whom they are most intimate. (1992, p. ix)

As a student of global aging, you can imagine that the specific types of support and care that families provide for their older members vary across cultures; indeed, that is one of the topics that this chapter explores. But two other aspects of family life deserve attention: (a) the contributions that older kin make to their families, including financial support and caregiving for children; and (b) the other sources of support that are available to older people as their needs change, including extended kin, neighbors, informal community organizations, and nongovernmental organizations (NGOs). Any one of these topics could fill its own chapter (or book). Our goal here is to provide an overview of the ways that older people, their families, and their communities give to and receive from each other across the life course. First, it is necessary to establish what is meant by family and how its forms vary across the globe.

EVOLVING DEFINITIONS OF THE FAMILY

Definitions of family are contested almost as soon as they are written down. One of the earliest comprehensive studies of families in different cultures resulted in the conclusion that a "family . . . includes adults of both sexes, at least two of whom maintain a socially approved sexual relationship, and one or more children, own or adopted, of the sexually cohabiting adults" (Murdock, 1949, p. 1). Newer definitions reflect significant structural diversities, as illustrated in Bedford and Blieszner's (1997) statement that a family is "a set of relationships determined by biology, adoption, marriage and in some societies, social designation and existing even in the absence of contact

Source: U.S. Bureau of the Census.

or affective involvement and, in some cases, even after the death of certain members" (p. 526). Perhaps an equally inclusive, more efficient definition that captures the structural diversity of families is Leeder's (2004) definition of a **family** as "a group of people who have intimate social relationships and have a history together." Across definitions, contemporary scholars study the things that family members do for one another out of a sense of obligation and the things they want to do with and for each other (Ross, Stein, Trabasso, Woody, & Ross, 2005).

Capturing the continually evolving idea of what constitutes a family, a very popular current television show in the United States, *Modern Family*, builds its episodes around three families, all related. Jay, in his 60s, is currently married to Gloria, who has a child from her first marriage; Gloria and Jay welcomed their new son in the 2012–13 season of the show. Jay has two other children: Claire and Mitchell. Claire's household consists of her husband and their three children. Mitchell lives with his life partner Cameron, and their adopted daughter, Lily. Complicated? Perhaps. But the popularity of this television show in the United States definitely reflects an American recognition and acceptance of a variety of family forms—the modern family.

Kinship Ties

Another way to think about families is to consider who is considered to be part of which family, and how they are related. This genealogically based idea is **kinship**—the ties that are claimed by people who consider themselves to be related (Leeder, 2004, p. 2800). Kinship is a very complicated concept and is the topic of extensive anthropological and sociological research, but three main ideas are important here: (a) kinship systems (who is related to whom and how) are culturally defined; (b) different terms are used for people, depending on how genealogically distant they are; and (c) cultures vary in how broadly or narrowly they use terms to distinguish people of the same lineage and generation.

There are two basic ways to classify relatives. As explained by Stanton (2006), in a classificatory system, a large number of people are put into a single category such as brother or mother. Stanton's example of this is the Hawaiian kinship system, in which all adults in the target person's parental generation are called mother or father; all members of the target person's generation are called sister or brother; and all members of the generation of the target's children are called daughter or son. In a descriptive system such as the Sudanese kinship system, there are separate terms for the target's parents, the parents' siblings, and for each set of cousins (Stanton, 2006).

Other kinship systems fall between these two extremes. For example, in the United States, the terms sister and brother are reserved for biological or adoptive siblings. In many Spanish-speaking countries, aunts and uncles would all be called *tía* or *tío*, regardless of whether they are father's or mother's sister or brother. In Indian culture, the term "cousin-brother" describes a broader category for people who share generation but slightly different genealogies. In other cultures, such as in Punjab, a northern state in India, although everyone is considered an uncle or an aunt, there is a clear distinction in how that uncle or aunt is related to you. To illustrate, your father's younger brother would your *chacha ji*, but your father's older brother would be your *thaya ji*. These different names not only suggest whether these individuals are maternal or paternal relatives; they also help to show the level of authority, respect, and/or rank that individual has within the hierarchical family structure. The names used for grandmother, and who gets called by that name, are interesting examples of how kinship terms vary across cultures.

What Do You Call Your Grandmother?

In every society, grandmothers and grandfathers assume a new status, identity, and name when they become grandparents. In most languages, grandparents have prescribed names that almost everyone uses (see Figure 9.1). In some cases, there are several choices, depending on whether it is the paternal

FIGURE 9.1 Grandmother names around the world.
Source: www.grandparents.com

(your father's) or maternal (your mother's) grandparent or on whether the speaker wants to make a formal address or an informal one. The formality generally depends on the speaker's relationship to the grandperson or on the social situation.

If one is lucky enough to have a grandmother—or two—or knew her before she died, her real name is probably known, but more familiar is the name used to speak to her and refer to her in conversations with others. In the United States, there is a limited supply of official words (both formal and informal) to apply to grandmothers, although many families depart from the limited choices and customize their own names. Many people have different names for their paternal and maternal grandmothers, as a way to distinguish between them. In rural Swaziland—where extended families are the norm and different combinations of families share land but have different dwellings on the homestead—every grandmother is called *Gogo*. It is quite difficult for outsiders to get a clear sense of which *Gogo* belongs to which children and which grandchildren. For Swazis, it is not a problem to articulate how each grandmother is connected to the extended family.

AGING FAMILIES

Expanded life expectancies also have broadened definitions of what families are and what they do. The possibility of interactions across four generations within a family creates new possibilities for what families look like. Aging not only happens to individuals but to all family members—and to the unit as a whole (Hargrave & Anderson, 1992). Given the interdependencies between and among family members, two distinct processes are always operating: Aging is affecting what happens in a particular family and, at the same time, the family is affecting how it (and its members) age(s) (Blieszner & Bedford, 2012). Blieszner and Bedford (2012) emphasize the importance of appreciating that older adults and their families grow old together: They individually grow old in the context of their family relationships, and they ultimately become the members of the oldest living generation within their family.

Kinship systems, along with a host of other cultural values and norms, play an important role in expectations about support, family roles, and families' decisions about their household structures and living arrangements. In a lineal kinship system (in which relationships are based on a common ancestor), family members have explicit expectations about living arrangements; for example, in patrilineal systems (where kinship ties are based on lines of masculine descent), women join their husband's father's household. Lineal systems also tend to grant seniors a position of authority. In contrast, in bilateral kinship systems in which connections are traced through both mother and father, there is far more choice concerning household structure and far more flexibility in the roles available to older persons.

Household Structures and Living Arrangements

Older adults' living arrangements vary widely within and across countries as a function of kinship system, marital status, availability of kin, health, wealth, individual and family preferences, and cultural norms.

In most societies, older adults who are married typically live with their spouses; those who lack spouses either reside alone (the tendency in developed countries) or with kin (the tendency in developing countries), but the

Source: Dr. Sukhminder S. Bhangoo.

actual proportions vary by country and gender. A greater percentage of the world's older women than older men live alone (United Nations Department of Economic and Social Affairs, 2005). Research in many cultures consistently shows that older persons, including those who live alone, prefer this living arrangement (Kinsella & He, 2009). Although the trend is for fewer multi-generational households in developed countries, two- and three-generation households are still the norm in developing countries (Kinsella & He, 2009). Obviously, the presence of kin influences living arrangements, and residing with kin is common in most countries in Africa, Asia, Latin America, and the Caribbean, where more than 60% of older adults live with children and/or grandchildren (Bongaarts & Zimmer, 2002; United Nations Department of Economic and Social Affairs, 2005). To illustrate this point, co-residence of older adults with their adult children and/or grandchildren ranges from 4% in Denmark to 90% in Bangladesh. Nonetheless, co-residence can vary widely, even within geographic regions. For example, co-residence is 85% in the African country of Guinea and only 50% in nearby Gabon; in Europe, the percentages range from the aforementioned 4% in Denmark to 43% in Spain (United Nations Department of Economic and Social Affairs, 2005).

It is important to realize that co-residence benefits members of all generations, and the flow of resources across generations is not unidirectional (e.g., United Nations Population Fund, 2012). In fact, many researchers (cf. Albertini, Kohli, & Vogel, 2007; Lee & Mason, 2011) estimate that the flow of resources from older generations to younger ones exceeds flow in the opposite direction. Just as co-residence of generations does not signal the direction of the resources that are exchanged, lack of co-residence does not suggest the absence of intergenerational transfers, a topic discussed later.

Of course, household structures and living arrangements depend in part on individual and family preferences and social norms, which are not static. One contemporary trend in several parts of the world is a decrease in intergenerational households that has been reported in many European countries (Kinsella & He, 2009), the United States (Ruggles, 2007), and some countries in Asia as well (Takagi, Silverstein, & Crimmins, 2007). A second trend is **skipped-generation households**, in which older and younger generations of a family live together in the absence of a member of the middle generation (Merli & Palloni, 2006). This is seen in sub-Saharan Africa, where Zimmer (2007) estimates that approximately 14% of older adults live in a skipped-generation household. It is also seen in subsets of families in developed nations where the middle generation is missing. Beyond actual co-residence, Luo, LaPierre, Hughes, and Waite (2012) found that in the United States between 1998 and 2008, 60% of grandparents provided care to grandchildren, and 70% did so for more than 2 years; higher percentages of African American than white grandparents assumed this responsibility.

Two additional phenomena have the potential to erode patterns of co-residence in later life families: *childlessness* (which is increasing in the developed world and predicted to increase in the developing world) and *migration* (Frankenberg & Thomas, 2011). Rates of childlessness are as high as 15% in some industrialized societies, including Germany and Britain (Basu, 2004; Simpson, 2006). Similar trends are anticipated in Latin America and southeast Asia (Frankenberg & Thomas, 2011), and more than one third of European adults between the ages of 18 and 39 in Germany, the Netherlands, Finland, and Poland either intend to remain childless or are considering it (Sobotka & Testa, 2006).

Increasing childlessness and migration are global phenomena, although the particular context in which each occurs influences its motivations, mechanics, and consequences. For example, reasons for childlessness can be voluntary or involuntary, lifelong or imposed in later life. Obviously, the availability of children affects intergenerational transfers (Indrizal, Kreager, & Schroeder-Butterfill, 2009; Kreager & Schroeder-Butterfill, 2005). In China, intergenerational co-residence is declining because the one-child policy of the 1960s, 1970s, and 1980s ensures that most young couples will be the sole support for up to four parents and potentially eight grandparents (Frankenberg & Thomas, 2011)! This 4:2:1 family structure (four grandparents, two married adult children, 1 child) has implications for household structure, but it has even more serious consequences for long-term care, as was seen in Chapter 7. In November 2013, the Chinese government announced that it will relax the one-child policy nationwide so that couples in which either the husband or wife is an only child will be allowed to have two children, as most rural families are already (Buckley, 2013). The long-term effects of this policy shift on co-residence are impossible to predict.

In many rural environments, members of the younger generation move away from the rural family homeplace to find paid work in locations with better economic opportunities. This migration also reduces co-residence.

In these situations, the older parents are "left behind" to support and care for themselves (Du & Yang, 2009), but many of them receive some help from financial remittances that their children dutifully send home from their paychecks. This situation is becoming common in China, Vietnam, the Philippines, Kenya, and several other countries (United Nations Population Fund, 2012). The United Nations Population Fund (2012) identifies Kyrgyzstan as "one of the most remittance-dependent countries" (p. 80) and cites research by Nasretdinova and Schenkkan (2012) that found that more than half of migrants' families include grandparents and grandchildren.

When the migration is to another area within the same country, this creates a **trans-local family**. When the migration is to another country, this creates a **trans-national family**. A trans-national family is "generally one where core members are distributed in two or more nation–states but continue to share strong bonds of collective welfare and unity [and] is a strategic response to the changing social, economic, and political conditions of a globalizing world" (Asis, Huang, & Yeoh, 2004, p. 199). Economic necessity and changing patterns of transportation and communication have created trans-local and increasingly trans-national communities (Baldassare, Baldock, & Wilding, 2007; Calasanti & Kiecolt, 2012). Return migration of adults after extended periods of employment in other countries can result in intergenerational alienation and can create family and community stress (Lamb, 2009; Zhang, 2009).

Intergenerational Transfers

In contrast to popular stereotypes, substantial numbers of older adults across the globe contribute financial support to younger generations of their families and to their communities by paying taxes (United Nations Population Fund, 2012). The National Transfer Accounts (NTA) project examines the transfer of economic resources from one age group to another at the aggregate level (National Transfer Accounts, 2013). The lead institutions for the NTA project are the University of California at Berkeley and the East-West Center in Honolulu, Hawaii. Regional centers are located in Tokyo (Japan), Santiago (Chile), Nairobi (Kenya), Stockholm (Sweden), and Vienna (Austria). Research teams in more than 30 countries work together with the lead institutions to analyze and interpret the macroeconomics of population aging around the world.

The NTA project documents that, within families, older adults typically give more to younger generations of their families than they receive. For example, older adults in Brazil, Mexico, the United States, and Uruguay, among other countries, give far more to their younger family members than they receive from them (Lee & Mason, 2011). Survey data indicate that 55% of older adults in Thailand provide financial assistance to their adult children, as do 67% of older parents in the Philippines (Chan, 2005).

Whereas the contributions that older adults make to their younger family members are significant, in many developing countries, private transfers from family or social network members constitute the main source of support for older adults (Agree, Biddlecom & Valente, 2005; Biddlecom, Ofstedal, & Chayovan, 2002; United Nations Population Fund, 2012). Types of support include financial payments (money or transfers of assets) and/or in-kind transfers such as food, clothing, shelter, or caregiving. Familial transfers are especially important to the very old in Asia and Latin America, but not as important at any age in Europe and the United States because of well-developed society security systems (Lee & Mason, 2011). In fact, in Europe and the United States, older parents are more likely to provide assistance to adult children than to receive it (U.S. National Institute on Aging, 2007). The difference, according to Frankenberg and Thomas (2011), is because of public policies that promote saving for old age in developed countries.

The probability that older adults will receive support is greater when they live with their children or other family members than if they live alone (Vos, Ocampo, & Cortez, 2008). Researchers predict that decreasing family sizes, the increasing number of older adults who live alone, and changing attitudes toward older adults are trends likely to result in decreases in within-family transfers to older adults (Vos et al., 2008). Family transfers to older adults in Japan, the Republic of Korea, and Taiwan have declined in the past several decades, and data from the NTA program suggest that interfamily transfers to older adults decrease as a function of development (Lee & Mason, 2011).

Older Adults as Caregivers

Throughout the world, families rely on their older members, especially older women, to assist with childcare. Grandmothers and, to a lesser extent, grandfathers provide care to their grandchildren for a variety of reasons. They care for their grandchildren while parents are at work locally and when work requires parents to migrate either within their home country (e.g., from a rural area to a city where there are more work opportunities) or beyond. Even in countries that provide state-sponsored childcare, grandparents often participate in raising their grandchildren. For example, in Denmark and the Netherlands, more than 60% of grandmothers and 40% of grandfathers between ages 60 and 65 provide care for their grandchildren (Croda & Gonzalez-Chapela, 2005). Grandparents in rural China care for almost two-fifths of children under age 5 whose parents have migrated to work in urban areas (China Development Gateway, 2008), and 70% of Bolivians who migrated to Spain left their children at home, the majority with grandparents (Asociación de Cooperación Bolivia España, 2008).

Grandparents also provide care for grandchildren when parents are unavailable to provide care due to their incarceration, serious illness, or death. Worldwide, the most common reason for these "skipped generation" situations is HIV/AIDS among the middle (i.e., parental) generation. The HIV epidemic is the most serious contemporary health crisis; it is estimated that in 2011, 34 million individuals were living with the virus (United Nations Population Fund, 2012). Older family members (primarily grandmothers) are estimated to care for 40% to 60% of children in eastern and

Source: U.S. Bureau of the Census.

southern Africa whose parents are no longer able to care for them, either due to severe impairment or death (UNICEF, 2006). Data also indicate that 81% of orphans in Zimbabwe are cared for by older people (Beegle, Filmer, Stokes, & Tiererova, 2008). Increasingly, throughout the world older adults are making substantial contributions to their families and communities.

CULTURAL VALUES ABOUT OLDER ADULTS AND FAMILY RELATIONSHIPS

Underlying kinship ties, household structures/living arrangements, and the role of older adults in family life are cultural values about seniors and family relationships. There is a fairly pervasive "urban legend" (a modern myth, usually with an underlying negative and sometimes fear-based message that is based on hearsay and often on stereotypes) that goes something like this: In Western societies traditional family values have eroded to the point that "families aren't what they used to be." Proponents point to changes in family structure, geographic mobility, and technological advances and conclude that families have abandoned their older members, dumping them into nursing homes or other care facilities and forcing them to rely on social programs for their care and security. Further, the legend continues, as developing nations become more Westernized, family members' attitudes and behaviors toward older adults become less positive and supportive. In some versions of the legend, filial piety (i.e., a child's duty of respect, obedience, and care for older family members, discussed later), which is characteristic of most Asian cultures, is threatened by the rugged individualism that is said to characterize the United States. Finally, the legend concludes, in the absence of formal support systems for older adults in developing nations, their older members will be left with virtually no resources.

Although this set of beliefs is grounded in modernization theory (Burgess, 1960; Cowgill, 1972, 1974), that theory has been discredited on both empirical and conceptual grounds. In addition, a score or more of studies in the United States, the United Kingdom, and other Western countries have documented the strong commitment of family members to take care of their parents and other older members, as well as their actual personal caregiving behavior (Agree & Glaser, 2009; Herlofson, Hagestad, Slagsvold, & Sørensen, 2011). Children in developed countries want to be responsible for the care of their parents, and they willingly assume that burden when necessary, often to their own detriment. The burdens (and rewards) of family caregiving are among the most frequently researched issues in gerontology (cf., Pinquart & Sörensen, 2003, 2005, 2007; Pruchno & Gitlin, 2012). So, like most legends, the one about Western families abandoning their elders simply is not true.

A leading African gerontologist, Isobel Aboderin (2005), warns against dichotomizing the developing world and the Western industrial world as two distinct, homogeneous entities. Doing so, she maintains, obscures "the tremendous cultural, social, economic, and demographic differences and the great diversity in family functions, forms, and relationships that exist between regions, countries, and societies" (p. 469). Although Aboderin made her comment in the context of family trends in developing countries, it applies to cultural values about older people and family relationships across all countries. It is important to be aware of and appreciate that differences exist in these values about families within and across both developing and industrialized countries.

Whereas Aboderin (2005) focuses on heterogeneity within all countries, a second inaccuracy in the stereotype of developed societies is that it overlooks commonalities in developing and industrialized countries. One example is the common assumption that filial piety is unique to countries in Asia (e.g., China, Japan, Korea, Vietnam; Sung, 2001). Filial piety is based in Confucianism; although often thought of as a religion, Confucianism is more accurately characterized as a set of values that instructs individuals how to live in harmony with one another. Nonetheless, as pointed out by Eun (2003), Hashimoto and Ikels (2005), and others, virtually all religions (including Buddhism, Christianity, Islam, and Judaism) teach some degree of filial responsibility. It is a value that is observed and practiced in both developing and developed nations. When a class of students is asked to identify ethnic groups with particularly strong family ties and solidarity, answers often include: Asians, Italians, Jews, Latin Americans, and African Americans. But these same students are unwilling to concede that strong family feeling in their own ethnic groups is nonexistent or even weaker than the groups they portrayed as having especially strong family ties. Perhaps beliefs about one's own culture—as well as others—are informed more by stereotype than by fact.

So the urban legend about Western families is inaccurate; we have a tendency to both ignore differences between nations at the same level of development and overlook commonalities across nations at different levels of development. A legitimate question is whether families throughout the world share any key values that characterize and/or distinguish their relationships with older adults. Although this is an ambitious undertaking, decades of research have resulted in a set of core concepts that assist in this task. Among these concepts are interdependence, filial piety and filial responsibility, intergenerational solidarity, and the emerging concept of family integrity. Each of these concepts is discussed in this chapter.

Interdependence

In their discussion of family support for older adults throughout the world (i.e., in English-speaking and European countries, the Middle East and Africa, Latin America, and Asia and the Pacific), Hashimoto and Kendig (1992) maintain that support between younger and older family members is best characterized as a two-way interdependency rather than a unidirectional dependency of the old on the young. This **interdependence**, defined as each generation needing, accepting, and giving support to the others, acknowledges older adults' contributions earlier in life (e.g., raising children and/or caring for their own older kin) or more recent contributions within the family (e.g., intergenerational financial transfers and caregiving, as discussed earlier) or community, both of which entitle them to receive care in later life.

Despite Hashimoto and Kendig's (1992) emphasis on interdependence within families throughout the world, other researchers (e.g., Aboderin, 2004; Harding, 1981; Pyke & Bengtson, 1996; Reykowski & Smolenska, 1993) point to variability in the extent to which families (and the societies in which they exist) embrace interdependence between older adults and their family members. For example, Weibel-Orlando (2009) describes diverse strategies used by contemporary families in Tuscany, Italy, to respect their older members' autonomy and also meet their needs for care. Among the strategies were increased monitoring of older adults who remained in their long-time homes; creating three-generational households; having older family members stay with different family members for extended periods of time and, despite a value of family care for older relatives, hiring professional caregivers to assist in the home; and developing community strategies for older adults who do not have family members who are able/willing to provide care to them.

Filial Piety and Filial Responsibility

A concise definition of **filial piety** is "the practice of respecting and caring for one's parents in old age, based on a moral obligation that children owe their parents" (Hashimoto & Ikels, 2005, p. 437). This reverence for parents is said to be the basis for all human relationships in East Asian cultures (Sung, 2001). Rooted in Confucianism, traditional filial piety in East Asia has reinforced hierarchies based on gender (male dominance) and age (elder dominance). For decades, the Confucian principles of filial piety were used to maintain social order, provide a moral and spiritual foundation, and assure social control. In recent decades, distinct demographic, social, and legal mandates have changed the practice of filial piety in many East Asian countries, including China, Japan, and Korea (Eun, 2003; Koyano, 2003). Hashimoto and Ikels (2005) believe that the future of filial piety is uncertain, due to both social policy changes within specific countries and to global concerns with individual rights and autonomy.

Similar to filial piety, but without the deep philosophical underpinnings associated with Confucianism and ties to Asian society, **filial responsibility** "represents the extent to which adult children feel obligated to meet the basic needs of their aging parents" (Katz et al., 2003, p. 308). A large body of contemporary research (conducted primarily in the United States) documents that, in general, the norm of filial responsibility is strong, although it differs according to sociodemographic characteristics such as age, gender, ethnicity, socioeconomic status, and whether families live in urban or rural areas (Katz et al., 2003). The bottom line is that the stereotype that Western, industrial societies such as the United States have weak families and little value for filial responsibility simply is not true.

Intergenerational Solidarity–Conflict

Lowenstein (2005) posed the question of how the phenomenon of global aging is reflected at the level of the family. The intergenerational solidarity model (e.g., Bengtson & Roberts, 1991; Bengtson, Rosenthal, & Burton, 1996; Silverstein & Bengtson, 1997) can help answer this question (see Table 9.1). Bengtson and his colleagues define **intergenerational solidarity** as positive interactions, cohesion, and sentiments between parents and their children and between grandparents and their adult children. Over time, Bengtson and his colleagues incorporated conflict as one dimension in the model, reflecting negative aspects of intergenerational family relationships (e.g., Bengtson et al., 1996). Table 9.1 presents the different types of solidarity described by Bengtson and his colleagues.

Family Integrity

A new concept, family integrity (King & Wynne, 2004), has the potential to increase our understanding of later life families throughout the world. King and Wynne defined **family integrity** as the "ultimate, positive outcome of an older adult's developmental striving toward meaning, connection, and continuity within his or her multigenerational family" (p. 7). Family integrity consists of three interrelated competencies of the family as a system. First, relationships change over time in response to changing life cycle needs of the individual family members, such as when a child grows up, marries, and the parents must now accept their child in a new independent role. Second, families must find resolution or acceptance of past losses and/or conflicts with both the living and the deceased ("My father never told me he loved me, but he worked hard to send me to college, so I know he did"). Finally,

TABLE 9.1 Dimensions of Intergenerational Solidarity

Dimension of solidarity	Description
Affectual	Type and degree of positive sentiments/emotional closeness held about family members and the degree of reciprocity of these sentiments
Associational	Frequency and patterns of interactions among family members
Consensual	Degree of agreement on values, attitudes, and beliefs among family members
Functional	Degree of instrumental and emotional support given and received among family members
Normative	Strength of commitment to norms and expectations regarding the performance of familial obligations (e.g., filial and parental responsibilities)
Structural	Opportunities for intergenerational relationships based on the number, type, and geographic proximity of family members
Conflict	Tension or disagreement among family members, even if not explicitly expressed

Adapted from Bengtson & Roberts (1991) and Giarrusso et al. (2005).

families must create shared meaning through legacies across the generations. The focus here may be on family history, genealogy, and shared characteristics or activities ("All our ancestors were farmers, and I am proud to be a farmer, too"). The processes of family integrity occur at multiple levels. At the individual level, family integrity provides older adults with a sense of completeness and/or satisfaction in their family relationships. At the family level, the ability of family members to get along with each other and meet each other's needs provides older adults with an important sense of meaning, purpose, and connection with others in the family. At the societal level, publicly acknowledged values (as when societal leaders verbalize the importance of seniors to society and to family life) and oft-rehearsed rituals ("Grandpa always carves the turkey at Thanksgiving dinner") influence the extent to which older individuals experience meaning and purpose within their intergenerational families.

The family integrity perspective has been used to examine the role of material inheritance in the construction of family integrity among later life Portuguese families (Patrao & Sousa, 2009) and as an alternative to traditional conceptualizations of later life as a time of disconnection and alienation from the family (Sousa, Silva, Marques, & Santos, 2009). For example, Patrao and Sousa found that the presence of a future material inheritance challenged family members to: (a) transform relationships so the older adult is cared for without disrupting the family hierarchy and power structure (i.e., children must try to provide care while allowing the parent to retain as much

Source: U.S. Bureau of the Census.

autonomy and control as possible); (b) maintain family harmony by preventing and/or resolving conflicts associated with the inheritance (e.g., potential heirs who are too disruptive or unpleasant may be "written out of the will"); and (c) come to an understanding of what the legacy means for the family ("This is Daddy's money [land, house]. He and Mama worked hard for it, and he wants us all to share in their legacy to us.")

The family integrity perspective is important because it is one of only a few perspectives that offer a model to help us think about how families typically evolve and change as their members (and the family unit itself) grow older. Explorations of family integrity in different cultural contexts will provide important comparative information on later life families throughout the world.

WHO PROVIDES CARE FOR OLDER PEOPLE?

From the preceding sections, it is clear that older people are part of interdependent family systems, giving and receiving support of all types, and performing important functions for their families. What any one of us needs and gives to our family support unit depends on many things, including stage of life. If and when poor health, frailties, or declining physical reserves interfere with individuals' regular activities, they need assistance. This help, along with some protections against age discrimination and economic insecurity, is more likely to be needed in later life. A number of factors determine where that help will come from. The beginning of this chapter provided evidence for the fact that families are universally the bedrock of senior caregiving; in developing countries, families are also an important source of economic security for older people.

However, there are other sources of assistance for older adults. As seen in Chapter 3, when societies go through the changes that typically accompany economic development (such as industrialization and urbanization), the traditional family institution becomes less able to address all the needs of its members. Out of this combination of demographic, economic, and social change, the welfare state arises—a system of public programs and policies that supplant, or at least complement, some of the roles fulfilled by families in earlier times. Formal policies and programs that are government-sponsored (or state-funded, using the broadest sense of the word) are most definitely an important piece of the puzzle in providing support and protections for the older population. Medicare (publicly financed health insurance for older people in the United States) is an excellent example of a government program that makes a significant difference in the lives of older adults.

In addition to family and government aid, community organizations and NGOs (defined and discussed later) provide crucial scaffolding to the support network for older adults. An example of such community organizations is the "old-age clubs" in India. Housed in centers run by voluntary organizations with some support from the government, these clubs provide opportunities for socialization and some limited access to health education and services (Prakash, 1999). An example of an NGO that has a strong presence in providing support for older people in developing nations is HelpAge International (also further discussed later in this chapter), which helps older people overcome poverty and live healthy lives.

Comparing the systems of support and protection available to older persons in different countries reveals unique blends of family, government, community, and NGO assistance. Although it is the case that an old-age welfare state dominated by publicly sponsored programs is more common in developed Western nations than in developing countries, it is also the case that families, the state, communities, and NGOs are part of the support network for older adults in every aging society. In an effort to explain cross-country variation in care for vulnerable older citizens, Hashimoto and Kendig (1992) describe a framework anchored at one end by family support and by state support at the other. They point out that in between these two support systems are community and neighborhood supports (either individual or organizational, such as churches or voluntary organizations) that can supplement or substitute for family and state support systems. In the essay at the end of this chapter, Samuel Mwangi illustrates this point very nicely, describing the ways in which families, government, and informal social connections combine in support of seniors in Kenya. By providing important contextual information about changing demographics and a predominantly agricultural economy, Mwangi suggests some of the factors that shape the system of care in his country.

Understanding who provides what types of care, and why, in different cultures is a complicated task. One of the fundamental issues underlying systems of care is the culturally specific ideology about who *should* provide care. The discussions about filial piety in this chapter illustrate how deeply those values are held and how powerfully they can be challenged by shifting economic and demographic realities. An in-depth analysis of how systems of care evolve is beyond the scope of this book. It is useful to keep in mind, however, a message that has been repeated throughout this text: economic development, social change, and demographic change all influence the experiences of aging. In the remainder of this chapter, the role of families in providing care, and the growing position of international and local-level NGOs in the formal and informal networks of support for older persons is touched on briefly.

Informal and Formal Systems of Support

One way the "who and what" of types of care are distinguished is along a continuum of formal and informal support. **Formal support** is typically provided for pay by an agency or individual whose work is clearly specified and often governed by regulations about payment and standards about how care must be provided. In the United States, for example, formal home health care services are provided by agencies that are certified by state and federal agencies; the work itself, and the training required for workers who provide the services, are carefully spelled out in formal documents. **Informal support** is nicely defined in a publication of the National Health Committee (NHC) of New Zealand as "caring for a friend, family member, or neighbor who . . . can't manage everyday living without help . . . . [It] is not usually based on any formal agreement or service specification. Informal caregiving is characterized by relationships and social expectations" (Goodhead & McDonald,

2007, p. 4). Payment for services and some sort of contractual arrangement are the two distinguishing features of formal care, whereas informal care is typically unpaid, and the arrangements for support arise out of a nonbusiness relationship. This distinction provides some language with which to talk about who provides what type of care for what reasons. However, even these distinctions are getting blurrier; many Western nations are adopting models of publicly funded paid care in which the recipient of services can hire a friend or family member (Meiners, Mahoney, & Shoop, 2002; Nadash & Crisp, 2005). Some of these issues (who pays for care, who provides care, what type of care is provided) were discussed in Chapter 7. That chapter also described publicly funded, formal systems of long-term care. To balance that part of the picture, the remainder of this chapter focuses on informal care provided by families and the middle ground of support offered by local, national, and international NGOs.

Variations in Systems of Support and Care

Extending the work of Hashimoto and Kendig (1992) mentioned earlier, other researchers have studied care arrangements for older adults in different cultural contexts. The OASIS study (Old Age and Autonomy: The Role of Intergenerational Solidarity and Service Systems; Katz et al., 2003) used the intergenerational solidarity model to study family norms and preferences regarding intergenerational relations in five countries—Spain, Israel, Germany, Norway, and the United Kingdom. The purpose of the research was to document norms and preferences regarding intergenerational relations and the balance of family and state responsibility for older adults.

The results revealed both commonalities and differences across the countries, which the researchers attributed to interactions between variations in family and cultural norms and behaviors at the individual level and in the social policies of each country (Katz et al., 2003). For example, in Spain the role of the family in caring for older adults is stronger than in the other four countries, and policy reform reinforces family care. The high centrality of family combined with a well-developed welfare state in Israel results in the interesting combination of strong filial obligation but a preference for formal services. A majority of older adults in Norway prefer help from formal services rather than their families, reflecting the expanding social democratic welfare regime that characterizes Norway and other Scandinavian countries (Daatland, 1990, 1997). Families in Germany believed that families and the welfare state should share responsibility for older adults. The preferences of participants from the United Kingdom fell between those found among Germans and Norwegians.

Bengtson and colleagues (2000) and Bengtson and Putney (2000) summarized the differences between Asian and Western countries with respect to who provides care for older adults. They cited the speed of population aging (as discussed in Chapter 4) as one of the factors that influences systems of support. The very rapid population aging being experienced by developing nations often competes with the demands of economic growth. Western Europe and the United States have had decades to adapt to population aging by creating infrastructures for formal support services; however, nations in the developing world must adapt much more quickly, at the same time that their economies are being built. "While the United States, Europe, and Japan all became affluent societies before they became aging societies, Latin America may grow old before it grows rich" (Jackson, Strauss, & Howe, 2009, p. 1). This "old before rich" circumstance magnifies the challenges of allocating family and government resources to a growing population of older people requiring assistance, and also needing to invest in the infrastructures that support economic growth, including education and labor-force development. Another difference noted by Bengtson and colleagues (2000) between Asian and Western nations are the cultural and historical traditions that involve older adults. For example, although filial piety is seen in both Asian and Western cultures, it is most often associated with Confucianism in Asian societies.

In a discussion of future public policy directions of Asian and Western nations, Putney and Bengtson (2003) point to the importance of acknowledging culture and history, in addition to demography, economics, and political arrangements, when exploring questions about who provides care for older adults. They propose that a greater role for the state in Asian nations, a diminished role in Western nations, and—across both Asia and the West—an increase in shared responsibility between families and the state will be seen. The role of government in providing care for older adults has increased in China. A nation that once relied heavily on "filial piety," so much so that it is included in the nation's constitution, is now being forced to provide government-funded services, such as nursing-home care, due to the one-child policy that resulted in smaller families, fewer younger individuals, and inadequate resources to provide senior care (Chu & Chi, 2008).

By now it should be clear that government support versus family support, or formal versus informal care, is not an either/or situation in which one type of care substitutes for the other; the reality is that the two types of care are complementary and both are supplemented by community care. This issue was central in the first United Nations World Assembly on Aging, convened in 1982 in Vienna. The gathering brought together policy makers from around the world who agreed on six main points: (a) in-home care and support of older adults is preferable to institutionalization, which should be the option of last resort; (b) family must remain an important component of society even in the face of industrialization, urbanization, and geographic dispersion; (c) there is gender inequality in later life; (d) the contributions that older adults make to their families and societies are frequently overlooked; (e) we need more data about older adults throughout the world; and (f) NGOs play an important role in the well-being of older adults, and that role is likely to increase in the future (Oriol, 1982). These points of agreement were used to develop the Vienna International Plan of Action on Aging (United Nations, 1983), which gave aging advocates in every country a global statement of policy to guide and bolster their own local efforts.

COMMUNITY CARE: NGOs

The agenda that emerged from the Vienna World Assembly on Aging underscores a theme that ripples through this chapter: interdependency. Dispelling the myth that "families aren't what they used to be," we have seen examples of the many ways in which younger and older family members both ask for and provide assistance to each other. But families don't operate in isolation. Just as each individual is embedded in a family, each family is embedded in a community, and communities organize themselves in many ways to provide care for older citizens when it is needed. Such **community care** includes services and supports to supplement and fill the gap between family and governmental efforts; it is considered a type of formal support because it is organized and programmatic, although not connected with the government. Worldwide, one of the most important community resources supporting older adults and their families are **nongovernmental organizations (NGOs)**, defined as:

> any nonprofit, voluntary citizens' group that is organized on a local, national, or international level. Task-oriented and driven by people with a common interest, NGOs perform a variety of service and humanitarian functions, bring citizen concerns to governments, advocate and monitor policies, and encourage political participation through provision of information. Some are organized around specific issues, such as human rights, environment, or health. They provide analysis and expertise, serve as early-warning mechanisms, and help monitor and implement international agreements. (United Nations, n.d.)

NGOs "have become major international players in developing and implementing policies related to the environment, women's rights, and poverty. . . . [An important question is] whether civil society organizations, including NGOs, might meaningfully supplement the family and the state in addressing the needs of growing older populations" (Angel, 2011, p. 557).

As a reminder, one of the six points of agreement among attendees at the Vienna World Assembly was that NGOs play an important role in the well-being of older adults, and it was predicted at the time that this role likely would increase (Oriol, 1982). These claims have proven to be true. NGOs educate older people about their human rights and entitlements and lobby policy makers and service providers for improvements. NGOs, working individually and with governmental agencies, provide education, counseling, and assistance to caregivers in countries with high rates of HIV/AIDS, fight against abuse of older persons and family violence, and develop disaster response strategies that address the specific vulnerabilities of older adults (United Nations Population Fund, 2012).

NGOs not only work on behalf of older adults; they also work *with* older adults who possess local knowledge that benefits their communities. For example, to identify impending local weather patterns, one international

NGO relies on Chamani seniors' observations of the nest-building patterns of birds in the lowlands of Bolivia and by observation of patterns of the sun, moon, and trees by older Kenyans (HelpAge International, 2009c). The areas of expertise of some older persons extend beyond what might be considered folk knowledge. A quote attributed to a resident of rural Ethiopia highlights the important role of older adults in their communities: "Socially, older people play leading roles at the community level and are a bridge between the government, NGOs, and the community in all necessary aspects, political and social, and in realizing development interventions" (United Nations Population Fund, 2012, p. 142).

Expanding Role of NGOs: The Madrid Plan

Twenty years after the first World Assembly on Aging, the United Nations convened the Second World Assembly on Aging in 2002. Delegates from more than 160 governments and intergovernmental and nongovernmental organizations came together in Madrid to develop a new plan to respond to the opportunities and challenges presented by global aging in the 21st century (United Nations Economic and Social Commission for Asia and the Pacific, n.d.). One principle that guided the delegates was that adults throughout the world must have the opportunity to age with dignity and security and be accorded all human rights and fundamental freedoms. This was the first time that many governments linked aging and human rights. The resulting *Political Declaration and Madrid International Plan of Action on Ageing*—subsequently adopted by the United Nations and often called simply the Madrid Plan, or MIPAA—is a comprehensive plan that calls for changes in attitudes, policies, and practices to assure that older adults of all nations are active participants in society. The ultimate goal was to create a "society for all ages" with the broad aim of "ensur[ing] that people everywhere are able to age with security and dignity and to continue to participate in their societies as citizens with full rights" (United Nations Economic and Social Commission for Asia and the Pacific, n.d., paragraph 10).

The Madrid Plan provides a blueprint for how governments, the international community, and civil society can create a society for all ages by focusing on three priority areas: (a) older persons and development, (b) advancing health and well-being into old age, and (c) ensuring enabling and supportive environments. Within each priority area are specific objectives and action steps. Across the three major priority areas, the blueprint identifies 18 areas of concern or issues for older adults (see Table 9.2) and makes 239 specific recommendations (United Nations Department of Economic and Social Affairs, 2002).

As we can see in the table, the scope of the Madrid Plan extends well beyond families, but it certainly has implications for the role of older members within the family. Mirroring one of the themes of this chapter, the plan calls for "provision of a continuum of care and service for older persons from various sources and support for caregivers" (United Nations Department of Economic and Social Affairs, 2002, paragraph 105). Of additional relevance for this

TABLE 9.2 Priority Directions and Issues Identified in the International Plan of Action on Ageing and the Political Declaration (Madrid, 2002)

Older Persons and Development
Issue 1: Active participation in society and development (2 objectives, 13 actions)
Issue 2: Work and the ageing labor force (1 objective, 14 actions)
Issue 3: Rural development, migration, and urbanization (3 objectives, 20 actions)
Issue 4: Access to knowledge, education, and training (2 objectives, 14 actions)
Issue 5: Intergenerational solidarity (1 objective, 7 actions)
Issue 6: Eradication of poverty (1 objective, 8 actions)
Issue 7: Income security, social protection/social security, and poverty prevention (2 objectives, 13 actions)
Issue 8: Emergency situations (2 objectives, 18 actions)
Advancing Health and Well-Being Into Old Age
Issue 1: Health promotion and well-being throughout life (3 objectives, 27 actions)
Issue 2: Universal and equal access to health care services (4 objectives, 22 actions)
Issue 3: Older persons with HIV/AIDS (3 objectives, 9 actions)
Issue 4: Training of care providers and health professionals (1 objective, 3 actions)
Issue 5: Mental health needs of older persons (1 objective, 10 actions)
Issue 6: Older persons and disabilities (1 objective, 10 actions)
Ensuring Enabling and Supportive Environments
Issue 1: Housing and the living environment (3 objectives, 17 actions)
Issue 2: Care and support for caregivers (2 objectives, 14 actions)
Issue 3: Neglect, abuse, and violence (2 objectives, 12 actions)
Issue 4: Images of ageing (1 objective, 8 actions)

chapter is the inclusion of intergenerational solidarity (social cohesion or integration among generations) as Issue 5 under the priority area of older persons and development. As explained in the document, "Solidarity between generations at all levels—in families, communities, and nations—is fundamental for the achievement of a society for all ages" (United Nations Department of Economic and Social Affairs, 2002, paragraph 42). The report continues:

> At the family and community level, intergenerational ties can be valuable for everyone. . . . Despite geographic mobility and other pressures of contemporary life that can keep people apart, the

great majority of people in all cultures maintain close relations with their families throughout their lives. These relationships work in both directions, with older persons often providing significant contributions both financially and, crucially, in the education and care of grandchildren and other kin. (United Nations Department of Economic and Social Affairs, 2002, paragraph 43)

As noted earlier, the ultimate goal of MIPAA was to ensure the full rights of older people to participate in society with security and dignity. Anyone familiar with human rights in general might question why we even needed the Madrid Plan. After all, the Universal Declaration of Human Rights (UDHR), which was adopted by the United Nations General Assembly in 1948, proclaims: "All human beings are born free and equal in dignity and rights" (article 1). Further:

Everyone is entitled to all the rights and freedoms set forth in this Declaration, without distinction of any kind, such as race, colour, sex, language, religion, political or other opinion, national or social origin, property, birth or other status. Furthermore, no distinction shall be made on the basis of the political, jurisdictional or international status of the country or territory to which a person belongs, whether it be independent, trust, non-self-governing or under any other limitation of sovereignty. (United Nations General Assembly, 1948, article 2)

Isn't this enough to protect older adults? Unfortunately it is not. Despite its assurances, the UDHR does not specify age as a protected category; furthermore, the declaration is characterized as "soft" international law, which means that although it is aspired to, it is not legally binding. Nonetheless, in the years since the UDHR was adopted, it generally has become customary law (i.e., widely accepted norms and practices that eventually are considered legally binding; Fredvang & Biggs, 2012).

The Madrid Plan, which is another example of soft law, specifically addresses human rights for older adults. Since adopting the plan, the UN General Assembly has passed resolutions to reaffirm the plan multiple times (United Nations General Assembly, 2013). In 2009, the Committee on Economic, Social, and Cultural Rights, an independent group of experts who monitor certain UN activities, "highlighted the need to address discrimination against unemployed older persons in finding work, or accessing professional training or retraining, and against older persons living in poverty with unequal access to universal old-age pensions due to their place of residence" (United Nations Economic and Social Council, 2009, p. 8). In 2011, United Nations resolution 65/182 established the Open-Ended Working Group on Ageing to advance the principles of the Madrid Plan, "encouraging Governments to mainstream ageing issues into poverty eradication strategies and national development plans. States should reaffirm the role of United Nations focal points on ageing, enhance technical cooperation and expand regional commissions' role on such matters" (United Nations General Assembly, 2012, no page).

These ongoing endorsements of the Madrid Plan are necessary because large numbers of older adults throughout the world "face challenges such as discrimination, poverty and abuse that severely restrict their contribution to society" (Fredvang & Biggs, 2012, p. 5). But this situation appears to be changing. Focus groups with older people who reside in rural and urban areas in 37 countries reveal that seniors' relationships with their families and communities are characterized by reciprocity or interdependency. Families and communities provide for their older members. But, in turn, older adults also support themselves, their families, and their communities. Much of this work is done through organized groups of older persons, and their efforts result in economic and social benefits, increased respect from their families and communities, and realization of their increasing political power (United Nations Population Fund, 2012).

At the same time that these efforts are underway, NGOs are actively advocating for a stronger human rights instrument to protect the rights of older populations. One of the best-known NGOs that works on behalf of older citizens is HelpAge International. HelpAge was founded in 1983 when five organizations in Canada, Colombia, Kenya, India, and the United Kingdom came together to create a network to support older adults worldwide. Today, HelpAge has six regional development centers and an office in London, works in more than 65 countries, and has 100 affiliates and 180 other partners across all continents. HelpAge International "helps older people claim their rights, challenge discrimination and overcome poverty, so that they can lead dignified, secure, active and healthy lives" (HelpAge International, n.d.a).

Among HelpAge International's many activities is Age Demands Action (ADA), which began in 2007 as a worldwide "grassroots campaign to fight age discrimination and combat the perception that older people are not important" (HelpAge International, n.d.b). For example:

> In 2011, citizens in 59 countries participated in ADA, and it is
> anticipated that by 2013 at least 10.5 million older adults will benefit
> from this campaign. ADA's possibly most ambitious initiative to
> date is advocating for an International Convention on the Rights
> of Older People. Such a convention will advance the universal
> position that age discrimination and ageism are morally and legally
> unacceptable and must be combatted; clarify governments' human
> rights obligations toward older adults; establish a mechanism to
> hold people accountable for their actions toward older adults;
> and recognize and promote the role of older adults as responsible,
> contributing members of their communities (as opposed to recipients
> of welfare programs). (HelpAge International, n.d.b)

Families and Social Support Today: Updates to the Madrid Plan

Ten years after adoption of the Madrid Plan in 2002, the United Nations Population Fund (2012) published *Aging in the Twenty-first Century: A Celebration and a Challenge*. This report gives us a contemporary snapshot of aging and who provides care for older people throughout the world. Included in the report are: (a) a summary of specific governmental policies and programs to support informal caregivers, and (b) updates from the United Nations Regional Commissions that include key caregiving facts and issues and documents progress that nations are making in implementing and monitoring the Madrid Plan. Tables 9.3 and 9.4 present examples of specific national policies and programs to support informal caregivers and promote a continuum of care for dependent older adults, respectively. As can be seen in the tables, these programs and policies tend to be found in developed countries.

In addition to the governmental policies and programs listed in the tables, the report identified caregiver support services such as counseling, training, and education that are typically provided by voluntary organizations and NGOs (Colombo, Llena-Nozal, Mercier, & Tjadens, 2011). The report specifically mentions the important role that NGOs play in countries that have high rates of HIV/AIDS. Another important trend mentioned in the report is the increasing availability of community care systems to supplement or take the place of family care.

The report also includes updates from five U.N. Regional Commissions: Economic Commission for Africa (ECA), Economic Commission for Europe (ECE), Economic Commission for Latin America and the Caribbean (ECLAC), Economic and Social Commission for Asia and the Pacific (ESCAP), and Economic and Social Commission for Western Asia (ESCWA). Each of these

TABLE 9.3 Recent Programs and Policies to Support Informal Caregivers

Type of national program/policy	Implementing government(s)
Strategy for caregivers	Australia, New Zealand, United Kingdom
Laws to support caregivers	Japan, Finland, Sweden
Training program for caregivers	Hungary
Caregiver allowances (to balance caregiving with paid work)	Canada, Russian Federation, Slovak Republic, Turkey, United Kingdom
Tax benefits for caregivers	Canada, Thailand
Protocols to assess caregivers' needs and sources of stress	Australia, Sweden, United Kingdom

Adapted from United Nations Population Fund (2012).

TABLE 9.4 Examples of Policies That Promote a Continuum of Care

Country	Policies
Australia	Assistance directly and through caregivers (2010 Carer Recognition Bill, Home and Community Care Act of 1985 [revised 2007], National Respite for Caregivers Programme, National Carer Counselling Programme, Carer Advisory Service, grants for caregivers)
Canada	Financial assistance through taxes (2011 Family Caregiver Tax Credit, enhanced Medical Expenses Tax Credit, and Infirm Dependent Tax)
Finland	Provides a care allowance and services (e.g., respite) to support caregivers and care recipients (2006 Act on Support for Informal Care, 2004 voucher system allows caregivers to select service providers)
Hungary	Training for caregivers and those who receive an allowance for caregiving (2009 One Step Forward Programme)
Japan	Provides support to informal caregivers due to high turnover (2008 Act to Amend Part of Long-Term Care Insurance Act on Social Welfare Service for Elderly & Act on Improvement of Treatment of Long-Term Care Workers Aiming at Securing Human Resources of Long-Term Care Workers; 2006 Elder Abuse Prevention and Caregiver Support)
New Zealand	Provides support to caregivers to assure a continuum of care (2005 Caregivers' Strategy and Five-Year Action Plan)
Singapore	National grants for training for informal caregivers
United States	Financial support for community-based programs and services (e.g., adult day care, home health care)

Adapted from United Nations Population Fund (2012).

updates provides a far-reaching description of later life families in the region. Several commonalities across geographic regions should become apparent as they are reviewed briefly.

As reported by the ECA, family support is strong in African countries, but both outmigration of young adults and HIV/AIDS are changing traditional support patterns within families. The number of skipped-generation households is growing, and older women who have little or no formal support typically serve as primary caregivers within the family. The ECE reports a similar pattern of skipped-generation households in European countries where working-age adults migrate to western Europe or the Russian Federation. Rapid population aging in Europe is resulting in increases in the proportion and absolute number of the oldest-old. Demand is growing for home- and community-based (as opposed to residential) long-term care services. Unfortunately, a continuum of care is not always available, and the services that are available are often of poor quality and/or not affordable for many later life families.

According to the ECLAC, in Latin America and the Caribbean, family size is decreasing, family structures are becoming more diverse, an increasing percentage of households include older adults, and, as national governments have grown weaker, families are assuming more responsibility for their older members. Based on the ESCAP and ESCWA summaries, older women across countries in Asia are particularly disadvantaged; this reflects the lifelong consequences of low education and little paid work and their frequent role as informal family caregivers. Similar to other geographic regions, families in Asian countries are experiencing the consequences of outmigration of working-age members and the impact of HIV/AIDS. Like many European countries, those in Asia lack a well-developed continuum of care. For example, in the Arab countries, care is traditionally welfare-based and does not seek to empower its recipients. In western Asia, home care services are not widely available; when they are, they are not affordable, and consumers are often stigmatized for using them.

Looking across the five regional reports that span Africa, Europe, Latin America and the Caribbean, Asia and the Pacific, and western Asia, we can see that traditional later life families have been particularly affected by outmigration of young adults (for purposes of employment opportunities or because of the devastation of HIV/AIDS) that results in skipped-generation households headed by older women with few resources. Further, demographic changes necessitate a continuum of care that is not readily available in most countries. In each of the five regions, efforts are underway to address the needs of later-life families. For example, the ECA recommends research that can support the development of effective policy; efforts are underway in Europe to support family caregivers by enhancing inter- and intragenerational solidarity; and in most English-speaking countries in Latin America and the Caribbean (e.g., Aruba, Belize, Saint Lucia, Saint Vincent, Grenadines, Trinidad, Tobago), training is available for family caregivers. In addition, China's 12th Five-Year Plan (2011–2015) has a national priority to establish a comprehensive care and social service system for older adults, and ESCWA recommends either subsidies or tax reductions for families who care for older adults.

CONCLUSION

It should be clear by now that families are a central social institution in all societies, and they provide their older members with two important resources: (a) social identity and roles, and (b) economic support and physical care. In every society, families are the primary recipient of older people's emotional and productive contributions, and families are the bedrock of belonging and sustenance for older people. Yet it is also clear that families often cannot fulfill these functions without help from both their governments and from NGOs. As economic development allows, nations are moving toward establishing public systems of economic and health support to supplement the efforts of family units.

It is not yet clear whether societies in the developing world will tend to copy the social care systems so far created by Western, industrialized nations—embodied in the welfare state (Chapter 3) and formal long-term care systems (Chapter 7)—or whether they will invent or adapt their own culturally appropriate systems. Developing nations are struggling mightily to join a globalizing economy and increase their usable resources, while being pulled between the growing educational and health requirements of their youth and the growing needs of their aging populations. Although Western nations have a long head start in dealing with their own aging societies, there is no perfect system. Both developing and developed nations continue to face challenges in balancing the educational and health requirements of their citizens. As suggested in the next chapter, a swiftly aging world challenges us to learn from each other and to acknowledge the older people among us as a common bond and perhaps, in our response to them, a key to realizing the global centrality of the family.

DISCUSSION QUESTIONS

1. Is family more important in the developed world or in the developing world?
2. Are families more valued among some ethnic groups than others? Which ones?
3. Whom do you consider to be members of your family? How do you decide?
4. What functions does your family perform in your life?
5. Do you know any people who live in skipped-generation families? How is life in those families the same and different from that in other families?
6. Can you think of examples in your community of trans-local and trans-national families?
7. Do you think Americans value filial piety?
8. Give your opinion of how older people are treated in your country.
9. What public policy changes should be made in your country to help or support older people and their families?
10. What do you think is your personal responsibility in caring for your grandparents? Your parents?
11. Do you know of NGOs that operate in your community to help or support older people? What type of services do they provide?
12. React to the statement: "It takes a village to care for an older person."

KEY WORDS

Community care
Family
Family integrity
Filial piety
Filial responsibility
Formal support
Informal support
Interdependence

Intergenerational solidarity
Kinship
Nongovernmental organizations (NGOs)
Skipped-generation households
Trans-local family
Trans-national family

Social Support Systems for Rural Older Adults in Kenya

Samuel M. Mwangi

Contemporary Kenyan family structure is changing drastically as a result of modern economic, social, and political changes that have continued to weaken extended family systems (Kinsella, 1992; Nyambedha, Wandibba, & Aagaard-Hansen, 2001). This observed trend is explained in terms of two important processes: rural-urban migration of younger adults moving to the cities in pursuit of education and employment, leaving older adults isolated and poor in the rural areas; and a decline in the traditional kinship-based support of older people as a result of economic hardships experienced by people across all the age groups. The latter has been exacerbated by the effects of the recent global economic meltdown, leaving older adults further impoverished and with significant unmet health care, social, and economic needs. The scenario is further complicated by the impacts of HIV/AIDS where older adults, despite meager resources, provide care for their ailing adult children as well as their orphaned grandchildren. These realities have psychological, economic, and social consequences (Menken & Cohen, 2006), further driving seniors into hopelessness and destitution in most rural villages of Kenya. Formal social support systems are still almost nonexistent, although a few donor-funded initiatives do reach a handful of older persons. For instance, HelpAge International has projects in several districts of Kenya that provide economic security in the form of cash handouts for impoverished older people caring for orphaned children. Through a combination of such small bits of formal support and their natural resilience in hard times, Kenyan elders seem to find ways of adapting and surviving.

Against this backdrop of diminishing support from kin and increasing social isolation in rural villages brought by the processes of modernization, rapid urbanization, formal education and employment, and Westernization, in this essay I identify the resources, structures, and systems that provide social and economic support to the older people in rural parts of Kenya to meet their everyday needs. Three crucial sources of formal and informal support are discussed in their order of importance to Kenyan seniors: subsistence farming, social networks within their rural communities, and the recently introduced government-sponsored and donor-funded cash transfer programs.

FARMING

Traditionally, rural communities in Kenya and elsewhere in Africa have relied predominantly on subsistence farming (Nyambedha et al., 2001), with little or no external support from government. Governments have perennially marginalized rural subsistence farming, which in turn has hindered economic and agricultural development of rural Africa, leading to a low asset base and variable incomes (Omiti & Nyanamba, 2007). Thus, subsistence farming to some extent can be seen as perpetuation of a "hunting and gathering" way of life. This is because this type of farming has not lifted rural communities out of deprivation and chronic poverty. On the contrary, dependency on subsistence farming exposes rural communities to vulnerabilities and adversities such as crop failure due to unreliable weather patterns and the collapse of market prices due to surplus commodities or constrained purchasing capabilities (Omiti & Nyanamba, 2007).

Despite the shortcomings mentioned, subsistence farming remains the most common and significant way of providing basic necessities to the rural older adults in sub-Saharan Africa. This includes both food crops, such as corn/maize, beans, roots, and vegetables, and a few cash crops, such as coffee, tea, pineapples, sugarcane, sisal, and pyrethrum, and rearing livestock (e.g., cattle, sheep, goats, chickens, pigs) to feed their families and sell the surplus in the local market. The money raised in selling such commodities is used in meeting other needs, such as sending children to school, improving homesteads, and buying medicines and nonperishable food items (e.g., cooking fat/oil, sugar, salt, flour, tea leaves, etc.), although in most cases the money is inadequate to meet all the needs for many rural households. In other cases, goods are used in informal barter trade, where commodities are exchanged for others in place of monetary resources as a medium of exchange. For instance, one would exchange cattle fodder (e.g., a stack of African napier grass) for a pint of milk (i.e., about half a liter). Therefore, subsistence farming is an important part of the fabric of social support systems in rural communities of Kenya. It is especially important for older adults who have no formal education or previous employment histories to entitle them to formal pensions and employment-based health insurance coverage.

SOCIAL NETWORKS

Closely related in importance to subsistence farming are social support networks within rural communities of Kenya. Prior to colonialization in Africa, communities held resources communally and created strong, ingrained networks. These networks were instrumental in buffering people from adversities associated with low economic resources, sickness, and death. In other words, the community provided a social safety net in times of hardship. However, colonialism disintegrated the existing community structures, and many young people and the economic elite adopted new ways and modern lifestyles and sought education. Colonialism further weakened the social support systems through the infamous "divide and rule" approach used by British colonial authorities to conquer African territories and impose their rule in the late 19th and early 20th centuries (Christopher, 1988).

In the rural parts of postindependent Kenya, however, social support networks have remained a significant resource because community members have a strong social fabric—as opposed to individualistic culture—that has emerged in the urban areas. A significant proportion of older adults live in the rural areas in Kenya as elsewhere in Africa (Kinsella, 1992) where they benefit from the community resources in the form of social support networks. But this support is strained by the responsibilities and burdens of grandparenting due to the effects of HIV/AIDS and the rising mortality of elders resulting from unmet medical/health needs.

GOVERNMENT SUPPORT

Social protection is defined as the range of public actions carried out by the state and others (e.g., community-based organizations and NGOs) in response to vulnerability, poverty, hunger, sickness, and risk (Mbithi & Mutuku, 2010; Omiti & Nyanamba, 2007). They seek to guarantee relief from destitution for vulnerable populations who, for reasons beyond their control, are not able to meet their own basic needs. This approach is gaining importance as a tool for older people in developing nations burdened with social, economic, and health needs. Social protection has been successfully implemented in other developing regions of Asia and Latin America, and it is steadily taking root in Africa. According to HelpAge International, African governments and policy makers have recently been involved in creation of social protection programs and strategies as part of their development agenda. These efforts have been responses to the two global plans of action on aging, the Madrid and Vienna International Plans of Action on Aging, and the African Union's framework on aging policy in Africa (HelpAge International, 2006).

The Kenyan government, through various ministries, departments, and agencies, has instituted a process of putting in place policy and structures necessary for the development, coordination, and implementation of national social protection programs (Omiti & Nyanamba, 2007; Mbithi & Mutuku, 2010). Programs for older people are coordinated by the Ministry of Gender, Children, and Social Development (MGCSD) in collaboration with HelpAge Kenya, a nonprofit organization (Mbithi & Mutuku, 2010). An interim National Social Protection Secretariat was established at the MGCSD to oversee these processes. The secretariat is headed by a social protection advisor to provide leadership and coordination to this structure. One of the various cash transfer initiatives introduced by the government is the Older Persons Cash Transfer (OPCT) Program that targets adults older than age 65. OPCT was developed and implemented through partnership with development partners such as the United Kingdom's Department for International Development (DfID) and the World Bank (Government of Kenya, 2008).

The program was started in 2004 on a pilot basis in three districts: Nyando, Busia, and Thika (HelpAge International, 2006). MGCSD and its social protection partners (i.e., bilateral donors, NGOs, and other government ministries) have been expanding the program. Currently, there is coverage in 44 districts countrywide, more in those with especially high poverty levels in northern Kenya as well as in urban slums (Maina, personal communication, December 29, 2010). Approximately 750 older persons in each covered district benefit from this program; this translates to 33,000 households nationally. In the fiscal year 2009–2010, the government allocated 550 million Kshs (Kenya shillings; i.e., US$7.1 million) for this program. Each household received a total of 2,000 Kshs (US$24) per month. By Kenyan living standards in rural areas, this amount is modest to meet the needs of older adults for supplementing food gained from subsistence farming and buying medications. However, in some rural areas—due to poor infrastructure and lack of basic services such as communication and banking—OPCT has not reached the targeted number of beneficiaries. Additionally, the administration of social protection programs is fragmented, thus marginalizing the needy and deserving individuals (Mbithi & Mutuku, 2010). Further, the Kenyan media have reported unsubstantiated cases of embezzlement of funds, although government sources and partners in these programs have not raised a red flag about the alleged malpractices.

The benefits of social protection programs for the older adults in several countries in the southern part of Africa have been documented through evaluation projects. In Kenya, however, the evaluation of the impact of this program is just underway. In addition to the challenges cited earlier, barriers to effective implementation of the program include: (a) lack of knowledge among the potential beneficiaries about the existence of such programs, (b) irregular and unpredictable support, and (c) inadequate data on utilization of the program (Omiti & Nyanamba, 2007).

CONCLUSION

In conclusion, both formal and informal social support systems exist in rural Kenya. Subsistence farming and social support networks are the informal systems that have traditionally provided support to rural families, especially to uneducated and unemployed middle-aged and older adults. These two systems will continue playing very crucial roles. Recently, formal government efforts through social safety nets have started taking shape. Social protection mechanisms have been implemented following the government's recognition of need to provide assistance to vulnerable groups such as older adults, orphaned children, women-headed households, people with disabilities, and people living with HIV/AIDS. The importance of the formal social safety nets for elders is yet to be determined as the government rolls out this program. However, the three pillars of support—farming, social networks, and social protection—provide necessary and complementary sustenance for poor Kenyan elders as the pressure of population aging grows.

CHAPTER 10

Global Aging and Global Leadership

If a man takes no thought about what is distant, he will find sorrow near at hand.

Confucius

Some readers may be quite knowledgeable about what is called local aging—the shape and implications of the aging process for individuals and the impact of an aging population on the society in which they live. If so, they know that aging per se is not scary or depressing, although it can have those effects on some people. Many readers also probably know that the processes of aging—physical, psychological, social, and economic—are a complex web of reality, a puzzle that can stimulate minds and capture attention in ways only the deepest, most fundamental human questions can. Where else but in the field of gerontology can one of the oldest mysteries of our species be addressed: Why do people get old and die? Where else but in gerontology or geriatrics can preparation be made to answer that question and its partner: What can I do about it?

This book focuses on aging as a global phenomenon and attempts to take local knowledge on the road: to see how it plays in Indonesia or Bolivia, to compare what is thought to be known about our own ageways with what can be learned about the thoughts of other cultures on the subject. One of the basic insights of this study so far is that aging is not the same for everyone; culture, politics, religion, and economic realities, among other factors, shape the internal biological process far more than might be thought. Despite the constraints of limited data about aging in many countries, inability to access local sources, and the space limitations of this textbook, readers now should be aware of the endless variety of aging experiences in the world. It is hoped, too, that they are now a little more intrigued with that variety and the promise for learning about biology, culture, politics, and society that it offers.

A second major understanding that we hope has emerged from reading this book is that the life course is a powerful force in all our lives: What happens to us early in life, and through adulthood, is one of the most powerful influences on how people age *and* how we experience later life. Children who are malnourished, poorly educated, or deprived of fundamental

Source: Dr. Sukhminder S. Bhangoo.

human needs such as security and affection will suffer the effects of those deprivations throughout their lives, and their old age is likely to bear the marks of those early limitations. Evidence of this fact is both plentiful and unequivocal, at least in Western, developed countries. We are just beginning to accumulate the data to show the applicability of the life course perspective in many regions of the world, however, so we still must approach it as a powerful theory awaiting proof.

A third and final proposition that weaves through the text is: Although aging can appear to play out quite differently in various people and diverse societies, individuals experience both body and life changes that bear a remarkable similarity to those being felt by every member of the human species—in the remotest reaches of the world, in deserts, jungles, urban slums, farmhouses, and castles. Age (or aging) works somewhat mysteriously through the cells and DNA to control what can be done at a given age and how people feel. It is closely related to mechanisms that control the bodily functions and the very life force. Age doesn't cause people to die, but in a very obvious way it is quite highly correlated with death in all populations in all parts of the world. Age also affects the brain and nervous system and, through them, the very center of individuals' beings, minds, and spirits. Age is a powerful social timing device that determines when people are protected and when they are expected to fend for themselves; when they receive education and when they are considered to have completed it; and when (or if) they may marry, have children, vote, work, or stop working. The magic of age is that it is both ubiquitous and invisible. Some think about it to the point of obsession, but also try (and usually succeed) to ignore it in their daily lives. It works its way so gradually into the bones and muscles and mind that we cannot see and feel it happening; we only experience the result. A common late-life question is: When did I become old? The final happy, somewhat reassuring fact is that aging links us inextricably with every other human being; it really does give all of us a common life experience that could form the basis for mutual understanding—if we focused on it.

THEMES WORTH REMEMBERING

Throughout this book, we have mentioned several important truths about global aging that bear repeating here. As this book took shape, we interviewed three experts on global aging—Zachary Zimmer (the United States), Dorly Deeg (the Netherlands), and Karel Joyce Kalaw (the Philippines)—to learn their thoughts about *aging as a global topic*. Therefore, to conclude, we present 13 themes that have emerged from both the book and conversations with these scholars.

1. *The world continues to be divided into developed and developing nations.* This obvious fact can escape memory at the worst times, such as when people wish to generalize about the effects of aging on family life or retirement. Some things are generalizable, but it is well to remember that economic resources are one key to health and well-being in late life, and all the world does not share in the same bounty as the developed world. On the other hand, developing nations may have stronger family and community support systems than those more economically developed.

2. *Globalization is continuing and the gap between the haves and many of the have-nots is shrinking.* Through swift scientific and engineering advances in communication, transportation, and medicine, through the expanding value placed on education and open borders and open trade, the people of the world are becoming less diverse and foreign to each other. This trend is being fed by personal and population mobility and not a little by the economic interdependence on which the growing number of multinational corporations are dependent. For better or worse, mass popular culture (i.e., the movies; music; personalities; and lifestyles of Western, developed nations) is more accessible and valued throughout the world today than ever before and seems to be growing in popularity, even as local competition seems stronger in Latin America, Africa, India, China, Korea, and Japan. Some observers are even postulating that a broad, long-term political convergence—toward liberal democracy—is underway, although it is hard to discern what is the real, underlying trend of the tumultuous change we—and every other world citizen served by television or the Internet—see daily on our screens. The panel of global aging experts (Deeg, Kalaw, and Zimmer) agree that the impact of globalization on both individual older people and on aging societies will increase.

3. *Human health is improving and longevity is increasing.* These facts have been demonstrated beyond question (see Chapters 4 and 5). This is certainly

a result of the growth and improvement of modern medical science and the triumph of public health practice (see Chapter 6). It is, of course, also due to the expansion globally of wealth and scientific investment, the fruits of the pursuit of discovery. Most people alive today have benefited from the health explorations and interventions of earlier centuries. Many would not, in fact, have been born if their grandmothers and grandfathers, and their parents also, had not been able to survive childbirth and childhood because scientists discovered the danger of germs and how to kill them and had not physicians begun to adopt antiseptic practices when they did in the 19th century. It's a provable fact: no grandmother, no you. But since your grandmother survived and lived so long, you now have a chance of beating her record.

We should keep in mind, however, both the limitations of Western medicine (acute care bias at the expense of chronic and palliative care) and the value of culturally appropriate care. As our Dutch colleague Dorly Deeg (personal communication, 2011) has suggested, however, "The question is not who has the best medical model, developed or developing nations, but how can a global society gain by integrating the best of both?"

4. *World and national populations are aging* (see Chapter 4). These changes are the result of effective population control and better health across the lifespan for more of the world's people. In turn, the aging of populations means that older people are becoming more visible and more available to all of us. Children are increasingly growing up with living grandparents and great-grandparents, which can be expected to alter markedly their views on old age. Stereotypes of older people as decrepit and out of touch cannot survive a trip to the circus or a football match with grandma and grandpa. And even family holiday gatherings are very different events when older members are there, mingling with the young and teaching them the family and community traditions.

5. *Public opinion is changing toward older people.* Certainly, ageism still is common in nearly all societies, but it may be—and can be expected to continue—declining as more realistic models of the old are available. This does not mean all aging people are healthy and happy—that would be a stereotype of a different sort. It just means that societies are beginning to see both possibilities for people in later life: health, financial security, and productivity as well as frailty, poverty, and institutionalization. This is beginning to be true (or at least more common) in many, many parts of the world.

6. *The family still is the core and most important social setting for aging.* One of the clear conclusions of the information presented in this book is that family life is necessary to our birth; it sustains and guides us as we mature; it is the cornerstone on which our adult lives are built; and it is our shelter and emotional center in old age. This is true to some extent in nearly all cultures and probably will continue to be (see especially Chapter 9). A related core truth—as both Zimmer and Deeg confirm—is that care of the older population is largely a family affair. Without both nuclear and

extended family support—financial, personal, and emotional—old age would be a bleak prospect, indeed.

Likewise, the tension between independence (autonomy) and family or community control of one's choices in late life remains in all cultures. The panel offers no predictions, however, on how the balance between these values may change as population aging becomes a larger reality in more countries. Some hint that the developing world is beginning to mimic the wealthier nations as families become smaller, more women work outside the home, and the government is forced to take on a greater role in elder care. Yet, established culture dies hard; the value of family care—and family control—will not go away simply because the children (or child) work(s) long hours in a factory or lives far away from the parents. Deeg notes, in addition, that, even in the Netherlands, the burden of bureaucracy discourages many older people from applying for direct government cash that would increase their ability to choose and pay for formal care. They seem to prefer to rely on their families, where fewer choices are available.

7. *Work and productivity are universal human values.* All but the super-rich must work to live, and even many of them continue working far beyond their actual need. Humans seem either genetically or culturally wired to want to produce things, whether products, food, services, ideas, or art. The creative push is both universal and powerful, and it does not seem to diminish much in old age—unless the culture works hard to extinguish it by fostering the stereotype of old age as a time of rest and leisure. That desire to work, to be productive, is probably a good thing, since most of us are required to do it anyway. People might be better off if they live to work, rather than if they merely work to live. On the other hand, according to our American global aging expert Zach Zimmer (personal communication, 2012), older people probably are going to be asked to work longer, both to reduce pressure on public pension systems and to continue contributing their experience and knowledge to the workforce.

8. And yet, *retirement is becoming more common, even in developing countries.* Despite their apparent need to work, people seem also to have a need for leisure and fun. Once the idea of retirement as a normal life stage becomes culturally accepted, most people seem to adapt to it and even look forward to it. But the habits of a lifetime, rising early to produce something valuable and socially important, can interfere with adjustment, and the need to be useful sometimes reasserts itself.

9. *Older adults are becoming more involved in community affairs.* As postretirement health is extended, a growing number of older people seek outlets for their productive urge in community organizations and volunteer efforts. Tasks that formerly might have been performed by nonworking women (i.e., housewives whose children were in school) are increasingly falling to retirees, as more women have entered the workforce. School and library volunteers, fundraisers for charities, and political activists, at least in many Western nations, are all likely to be well over age 60

Source: Dr. Sukhminder S. Bhangoo.

these days. Some social clubs that formerly depended on older women for membership (e. g., Daughters of the American Revolution, garden clubs) are finding their rolls dwindling as older women move into more socially engaged volunteer roles.

10. *Most national governments are beginning to recognize their senior population and enact policies to support them.* Zimmer notes that such policies represent a major accomplishment for both advocates and governments. Still, the developed nations are far ahead of the rest of the world due to their greater economic resources. But even some poor countries, like Kenya, are establishing old-age pensions for their older citizens. Still quite small and inadequate to sustain life, these payments represent a commitment and a down payment on the intergenerational debt that is owed to all our parents and their generation. As nations modernize and populations are exposed to the ways of other, richer countries, expectations begin to rise and, with them, demands that government step in where families—too busy working or simply nonexistent—are unable to provide the traditional support.

11. *Older people are actively driving much of the change.* In country after country, including some less developed ones, older people are discovering a new, more assertive social (and political) role for themselves. In some cases, the urge for meaningful use of free time leads them into advocacy for themselves and other seniors. This certainly has been true in the United States, with the rise of AARP (the age-based organization that was formerly known as the American Association of Retired Persons). With about 36 million members among the age 50+ population, their advocacy messages certainly reach a sizable audience and probably influence them on important policy issues affecting seniors, such as Social Security, Medicare, and the way health care is delivered and paid for. Many seniors find advocacy for the older population, whether through AARP or otherwise, to be a particularly satisfying way to remain socially active.

12. *A global aging science is emerging, along with a global network of caring professions.* We have called this a "virtual scientific network" because it is largely populated by professionals who do not know each other personally and may never actually meet (Whittington & Kunkel, 2013b). This network is emerging through its members' research and its publication in scholarly journals and books that now need not wait to be shipped abroad, but can be accessed electronically, downloaded to a computer, or printed for convenient reading and study later. The modernization of globalization is creating unanticipated marvels of scientific understanding in all parts of the educated world, and that definitely includes the lone scientist working in poor conditions with inadequate tools and support, far from the nearest hospital or modern university. With Internet access—admittedly not yet a universal reality—both Nobel Prize winners and unknowns can communicate with others on the cutting edge and, if not literally together, certainly can work in concert toward the same solution to a common human problem.

We also are seeing the emergence of a global, mobile workforce of professional caregivers who will leave their home countries, where few jobs are available and the population so far has not aged into dependence, for better paid, elder care work abroad. Our Filipino colleague Karel Joyce Kalaw (personal communication, 2011) has spoken eloquently about the family and community impact of the migratory Philippine workforce (including her own father) who leave their home country for the better economic prospects of the developed world, especially for jobs in the long-term care industries of Spain, Italy, Canada, the United States, New Zealand, and Japan, all rapidly aging societies. Zimmer underscores the negative effects of this global trend on the older generations who remain behind as the younger family members become economic migrants in such less developed Asian countries such as Cambodia, Laos, and Myanmar.

13. *In difference is possibility.* As we argued in the introduction to this chapter, much about aging is universal; and—in many more ways than the typical collection of international photos of older people in native dress and hairdo might lead us to think—older people are probably more alike than different. Yet the differences persist, and we do well to note and study them. If our ethnocentrism tends to get in the way, valuable avenues of learning are closed off. We cannot learn what we already know; we can learn only what we do not know. What possibilities await global inquiry? What local solutions are to be found far from home? We can only imagine the answers that may be offered us, if we attend to global differences and ask global questions.

BECOMING A GLOBAL LEADER

We conclude this book with a simple suggestion. If thinking globally appeals to you, and if you imagine some form of global work may be in your future, why not aspire to a leadership role? Despite the seeming rush of individuals and organizations to become "global," few will follow through, and fewer still will truly succeed. We commend to you these following thoughts about how to become a global leader.

Ángel Cabrera, president of George Mason University, has studied closely the process of globalization, as well as global organizations and the personal characteristics it takes to manage them well. He and his co-author, Gregory Unruh, have summarized their theories in a recent book entitled *Being Global: How to Think, Act, and Lead in a Transformed World* (Cabrera & Unruh, 2012). Their views are contained in two broad conclusions: (a) on balance, globalization is good; and (b) a certain type of leader is needed to make globalization work better.

Certainly, they argue, globalization has some negative consequences. Among them are pandemic diseases, terrorism, long-range war and nuclear threats, and the international trade in drugs, guns, and human beings (so-called human trafficking, which is another term for slavery). Scientific advances, modern transportation systems, nearly instantaneous communication, and the global marketplace all have permitted and supported these scourges on all our societies. These activities must be inhibited and their tragic impact limited.

However, globalization is fundamentally about freedom, argue Cabrera and Unruh—the freedom to travel, to associate, to communicate, to buy and sell, and to learn. They are vastly more optimistic about the positive consequences of opening global markets and new cultural exchanges than they are worried about the negative side of the shift. But they also posit that certain qualities are necessary for leaders to function productively in a global environment. First, they say, leaders must have a *global mindset*. This means that individuals should value the world outside their own narrow slices of it. Tribal forces—those that command loyalty and obedience only to one's own racial, ethnic, or national group—tend to inhibit and counter globalization. Ethnocentrism (the belief that one's own culture is best) is the enemy of globalization. They admit that suspending judgment of outsiders and learning to tolerate the ambiguity that accompanies the confrontation with difference is hard. They speak of some people having the cognitive architecture to handle it, implying that others may not. The goal of the global mindset is connection with the rest of the world: its people, its places, its ways of living. They observe that globally minded people possess a desire for knowledge of the things of the world, the achievement of which increases their intellectual capital. They also believe that persons with a global mindset are likely to accumulate many friends and contacts around the world, establishing for themselves a global social network, constituting a sort of social capital. Neither intellectual nor social capital is a new concept, but they are handy

Source: Jiayin (Jaylene) Liang.

tools to help us think about what it takes to become a global leader. But, of course, having a global mindset is not enough if it is not used.

Thus, the second major trait of an effective global leader is *global entrepreneurship*, the ability to see possibilities, make connections, and make things happen. Global entrepreneurship is similar to the local, economic kind, except it is not limited to starting a business and making money. It can encompass almost any endeavor, from working on the ground as a Peace

Source: The World Bank.

Corps volunteer, to creating or expanding an international nonprofit organization, to studying in another country with a goal of learning a better way of solving problems than one's fellow citizens have devised at home. It may be shocking to realize that the way Americans think about aging, provide for elder care, and utilize their abilities to solve other social problems leaves much to be desired. *Social entrepreneurship* across national borders is in its infancy, especially in the field of aging; it is on the cutting edge of all that is modern and exciting and *cool*.

But even more *cool* is what Cabrera and Unruh suggest as the third, quite essential, item in the global leader's toolkit: *global citizenship*, which they define as the understanding that all people and all nations are connected and that what is good for one is good for all—and the actions that flow from that understanding. That is, what is good for older Latvians and the caregiving children of aging Kenyans is good also for our older citizens—and for us. They invite a Buddhist way of thinking about social relations and how to live one's life, which, finally, suggests that it is rational to show compassion because it will benefit you and those close to you. Global citizenship, then, is the highly desirable, ultimate expression of global thinking and global entrepreneurship. It is a values-laden approach to global issues, global problems, and globalization itself. These three elements of a global person, if it can be called that, will prepare any of us to become effective leaders in an increasingly globalized world.

Returning to the questions we posed at the beginning of this chapter: Why do people get old and die? And what can I do about it? We suggested that gerontology and geriatrics are perfect fields in which to explore the existential mysteries of the life course and, as this book has made clear, how aging is embedded in every society, every community, every family, and every person in the world—including you. Can you imagine a more fundamental or universal or worthwhile set of problems? . . . . Just a thought.

ABOUT THE EXPERT PANEL

Zachary Zimmer is a professor in the Department of Social & Behavioral Sciences, School of Nursing at the University of California–San Francisco (nursing.ucsf.edu/faculty/zachary-zimmer). His main research focus is health and other aspects of well-being among older persons in developing countries, particularly those experiencing rapid social change.

Dorly Deeg is a professor in the Department of Epidemiology and Biostatistics at Vrije University in Amsterdam, the Netherlands (www.vumc.com/branch/epidemiology-biostatistics/research/5346012). Her research activities focus on changes in, and the experience of, the health and daily functioning of older people and both determinants of health, function and perception, and the consequent use of care.

Karel Kalaw is a doctoral candidate in the social gerontology program at Miami University in Oxford, Ohio (www.scripps.muohio.edu/node/469). Her research is focused in areas that will allow the Filipino community to better understand issues of families and older family members in the Philippines.

Web Resources for Further Information

AARP Public Policy Institute

www.aarp.org/research/ppi

The Public Policy Institute of AARP informs and stimulates public debate on the issues people face as they age. The institute promotes development of sound, creative policies to address common needs for economic security, health care, and quality of life.

Age Data

www.census.gov/population/www/socdemo/age.html

This is a linked website maintained by the U.S. Bureau of the Census. It provides access to national, state, or local sources of information on demography from the Census Bureau. International data are also available. In general, the census provides both statistics on current populations and projections for population change/growth through these sites and their printed publications.

Agingstats Site

www.agingstats.gov

The Federal Interagency Forum on Aging-Related Statistics (Forum) was initially established in 1986, with the goal of bringing together federal agencies that share a common interest in improving aging-related data. The Forum has played a key role by critically evaluating existing data resources and limitations, stimulating new database development, encouraging cooperation and data-sharing among federal agencies, and preparing collaborative statistical reports. In addition to the original three core agencies (National Institute on Aging, National Center for Health Statistics, and Census Bureau), the organizing members of the Forum now include senior officials from the Administration on Aging, Agency for Healthcare Research and Quality, Bureau of

Labor Statistics, Centers for Medicare and Medicaid Services, Department of Veterans' Affairs, Environmental Protection Agency, Office of Management and Budget, Office of the Assistant Secretary for Planning and Evaluation in HHS, Social Security Administration, and the Substance Abuse and Mental Health Services Administration.

Employment Benefit Research Institute

www.ebri.org

The mission of the Employee Benefit Research Institute (EBRI) is to contribute to, encourage, and enhance the development of sound employee benefit programs and sound public policy through objective research and education.

European Health & Life Expectancy Information System

www.eurohex.eu/index.php

EurOhex is a website that provides access to research on health expectancies in Europe. It includes a database on health indicators comprising life expectancies and Healthy Life Years (HLYs) for 27 European countries.

European Social Survey

www.europeansocialsurvey.org

The European Social Survey (ESS) is an academically driven social survey designed to chart and explain the interactions among Europe's changing institutions and the attitudes, beliefs, and behavior patterns of its diverse populations.

Frontline: *Sick Around the World*

www.pbs.org/wgbh/pages/frontline/sickaroundtheworld

Online documentary produced in 2008 by the Public Broadcasting System (PBS) of the United States. The program focuses on how health care is provided and paid for in five capitalist democracies around the world—the United Kingdom, Switzerland, Germany, Taiwan, and Japan. Highlights the differences in structure and outcome in an effort to draw lessons for the United States.

Gapminder

www.gapminder.org

Established by Hans Rosling, this interactive website allows the user to observe and customize graphs and charts showing worldwide trends in population growth, aging, and economic trends. Rosling demonstrates the many ways that demographic data are useful, lively, and essential for understanding the complexities of national and worldwide trends.

HelpAge International

www.helpage.org/Home

HelpAge International is a global network of not-for-profit organizations with a mission to work with, and for, disadvantaged older people worldwide to achieve a lasting improvement in the quality of their lives. Their website provides the reader with access to a vast array of reports about aging around the world and information about current projects that HelpAge is working on, research and policy, and news. You can watch videos, view photos, retrieve reports, and hear stories from older people around the world. It also provides an in-depth overview of worldwide emergencies and helpful resources. HelpAge has organizational affiliates in 50 countries.

International Data Base (IDB) from U.S. Bureau of the Census

www.census.gov/ipc/www/idbnew.html

If you ever want to know what population pyramids will look like for Albania, Guatemala, or Sierra Leone in 2025, this is the website for you. Visiting the IDB site provided by the U.S. Bureau of the Census will enable you to look at projections for population and detailed characteristics of various countries or regions of the world. Choose from a large number of countries and look at the aging rates of the populations (via population pyramids) or at statistics in tables. It is also possible to download IDB data, but review the requirements in advance and be prepared for a large data set!

The International Handbook on Aging (3rd ed.). Erdman B. Palmore, Frank Whittington, and Suzanne Kunkel, Editors

www.abc-clio.com

In this book a global team of contributing gerontologists and geriatricians examines the aging-related challenges facing many countries of the world. The handbook collects and summarizes information on education, research, and policy in aging in 47 countries where substantial work is underway. Chapters on individual countries facilitate comparisons of population aging and societal responses via a standard format that identifies population characteristics, training programs in gerontology and geriatrics, principal research issues and findings, and public policy issues. The book also contains a chapter of nongovernmental organizations (NGOs) concerned with aging and an international directory of gerontological and geriatric associations.

International Social Security Association

www.issa.int

The ISSA Social Security web portal provides comprehensive information, news, data, and analysis on social security developments worldwide.

International Social Science Programme

www.issp.org

The ISSP is a continuing annual programme of cross-national collaboration on surveys covering topics important for social science research. It brings together preexisting social science projects and coordinates research goals, thereby adding a cross-national, cross-cultural perspective to the individual national studies. The ISSP researchers especially concentrate on developing questions that are meaningful and relevant to all countries and can be expressed in an equivalent manner in all relevant languages.

Luxembourg Income Study

www.lisproject.org

The Luxembourg Income Study is a cross-national data center that serves a global community of researchers, educators, and policy makers. LIS acquires datasets with income, wealth, employment, and demographic data from a large number of countries, harmonizes them to enable cross-national comparisons, and makes them available for public use by providing registered users with remote access.

Organisation for Economic Co-operation and Development (OECD) StatExtracts

stats.oecd.org

OECD.StatExtracts includes data and metadata for OECD countries and selected nonmember economies.

OECD Pensions Glossary

www.oecd.org/insurance/privatepensions/2496718.pdf

In order to develop a common understanding and vocabulary, under the aegis of the Working Party on Private Pensions (WPPP), ongoing work on the OECD Pensions Glossary includes an expanded list of terms, proposed definitions, and related vocabularies.

Population Reference Bureau

www.prb.org

The Population Reference Bureau, funded by government agencies, foundations, universities, and nonprofit organizations, makes available a range of demographic data, including a page on Aging. Articles, reports, and datasheets change over time but focus on the size, diversity, and characteristics of the older population and the baby boomers in the United States and the world.

REVES Network on Health Expectancy

reves.site.ined.fr/en

Réseau Espérance de Vie en Santé (REVES) is an international organization that promotes the use of health expectancy as a population health indicator. Disability-free life expectancy was one of the first measures developed for cross-national comparisons of the health of populations. It is a widely used metric for health comparison. REVES members are involved in the definition, measurement, and comparison of disability globally.

Survey of Health, Ageing, and Retirement in Europe. 2013

www.share-project.org

United Nations Programme on Aging

www.un.org/esa/socdev/ageing

The United Nations has a multifaceted agenda to promote dignity, independence, and security for older persons in all countries, as embodied in their slogan, "Towards a Society for All Ages." This website describes major U.N. initiatives, such as the Policy Framework for a Society for All Ages. The site includes a wide variety of other resources, including the list of U.N. Principles for Older Persons, a summary of the Madrid International Plan of Action, and a document that describes links to other sites on a range of topics related to global aging, include links to publications about population aging, income transfer programs, older rights, retirement, civic engagement, and toolkits for practitioners and policy makers interested in implementation of the International Plan of Action on Ageing policy reports from countries and regions.

United Nations Statistics Division

unstats.un.org/unsd/methods/inter-natlinks/sd_natstat.htm

The UNSD provides a web page that links to selected national statistics offices. Each of the country statistical information is unique, but may be useful for international comparisons on aging issues. Nations are organized alphabetically by continent.

Urban Institute: Retirement and Older Americans

www.urban.org/retirees/index.cfm

The Urban Institute has done extensive work on retirement policy, covering the many ways the aging of America will trigger changes in how we work, retire, and spend federal resources.

U.S. Census Disability Overview

www.census.gov/hhes/www/disability/overview.html

U.S. Department of Health and Human Services, Office for Human Research Protection Regulations

www.hhs.gov/ohrp/humansubjects/index.html

Social Security Programs Throughout the World

www.ssa.gov/policy/docs/progdesc/ssptw

This publication highlights the principal features of social security programs in more than 170 countries. Published in collaboration with the International Social Security Association (see above), one of four regional volumes is issued every 6 months.

World Health Organization: Ageing and Life Course

www.who.int/ageing/en

In their WHO Active Ageing agenda, the World Health Organization emphasizes the positive contributions that older people can make to their communities up until the very ends of their lives. Their approach focuses on strategies for prevention of chronic disease, access to age-friendly primary health care, and creation of age-friendly environments (including age-friendly cities). This website describes the WHO strategies and provides links to information and resources related to these initiatives, as well as resources and general information about aging and the life course.

The World Health Organization Quality of Life Project

www.who.int/mental_health/publications/whoqol/en/index.html

Quality of life is an important measure used in studies of aging and health. The World Health Organization has developed and validated an instrument that can be used to assess this important indicator in different countries, and for comparative research. This website includes the instrument itself, special modules about spirituality and personal beliefs, and provides documentation about how the assessment was developed.

World Values Survey

www.worldvaluessurvey.org

The World Values Survey (WVS) is a worldwide network of social scientists studying changing values and their impact on social and political life. The WVS in collaboration with the European Values Study has carried out representative national surveys in more than 100 countries containing almost 90% of the world's population. These surveys show pervasive changes in what people want out of life and what they believe. In order to monitor these changes, the EVS/WVS has executed six waves of surveys, from 1981 to 2013.

References

Aboderin, I. (2004). Modernisation and ageing theory revisited: Current explanations of recent developing world and historical Western shifts in material family support for older people. *Ageing & Society, 24*(1), 29–50. doi:10.1017/S0144686X03001521

Aboderin, I. (2005). Changing family relationships in developing nations. In M. L. Johnson, V. L. Bengtson, P. Coleman, & T. Kirkwood (Eds.), *The Cambridge handbook of age and ageing* (pp. 469–475). Cambridge, England: Cambridge University Press.

Agree, E. M., Biddlecom, A. E., & Valente, T. W. (2005). Intergenerational transfers of resources between older persons and extended kin in Taiwan and the Philippines. *Population Studies, 59,* 181–95.

Agree, E. M., & Glaser, K. (2009). Demography of informal caregiving. In P. Uhlenberg (Ed.), *International handbook of population aging* (Vol. 1, pp. 647–668). Dordrecht, The Netherlands: Springer Science.

Ahmed, F. E. (2006). Women, gender, and reproductive health: South Asia. In S. Joseph (Ed.), *Encyclopedia of women and Islamic cultures* (Vol. III). Leiden, The Netherlands: Brill Academic Publishers.

Albertini, M., Kohli, M., & Vogel, C. (2007). Intergenerational transfers of time and money in European families: Common patterns—different regimes? *Journal of European Social Policy, 17*(4), 319–334.

Alessio, H. (2001). The physiology of human aging. In L. A. Morgan & S. Kunkel (Eds.), *Aging: The social context* (2nd ed., pp. 107–137). Thousand Oaks, CA: Pine Forge Press.

Alzheimer's Association. (2013). *2013 Alzheimer's disease facts and figures.* Chicago, IL: Author.

Alzheimer's Disease International. (2010). *World Alzheimer report 2010: The global impact of dementia.* London, England: Author.

Angel, R. (2011). Civil society and elder care in posttraditional society. In R. Settersten & J. Angel (Eds.), *Handbook of sociology of aging* (pp. 549–562). New York, NY: Springer Publishing.

Anonymous. (2006, November 28). Pension fund woes could mean rise in retirement age. *China Daily.* Retrieved from http://www.chinadaily.com.cn

Arcury, T., Bell, R., Altizer, K., Grzywacz, J., Sandberg, J., & Quandt, S. (2012). Attitudes of older adults regarding disclosure of complementary therapy use to physicians. *Journal of Applied Gerontology, 32*(5), 627–645.

Ardichvili, A., & Kuchinke, K. P. (2009). International perspectives on the meanings of work and working: Current research and theory. *Advances in Developing Human Resources, 11*(2), 155–167. doi:10.1177/1523422309333494

Aries, P. (1981). *The hour of our death*. London, England: Penguin.

Asis, M. M. B., Huang, S., & Yeoh, B. S. A. (2004). When the light of the home is abroad: Unskilled female migration and the Filipino family. *Singapore Journal of Tropical Geography, 25*, 198–215.

Asociación de Cooperación Bolivia-España. (2008). *Situación de familias de migrantes a España en Bolivia*. Madrid, Spain: Author; La Paz, Asociación de Migrantes Bolivia-España.

Astin, J. A., Pelletier, K. R., Marie, A., & Haskell, W. L. (2000). Complementary and alternative medicine use among elderly persons: One-year analysis of a Blue Shield Medicare supplement. *Journal of Gerontology: Medical Sciences, 55a*, M4–M9.

Baistow, K. (2000). Cross-national research: What can we learn from inter-country comparisons? *Social Work in Europe, 7*(3), 8–13.

Baker, D. (2011). *Work sharing: The quick route back to full employment*. Washington, DC: Center for Economic and Policy Research.

Baldassare, L., Baldock, C., & Wilding, R. (2007). *Families caring across borders: Migration, ageing and transnational caregiving*. London, England: Palgrave-Macmillan.

Ball, M. M., & Whittington, F. J. (1995). *Surviving dependence: Voices of African American elders*. Amityville, NY: Baywood Publishing Co.

Ballesteros, R. F., Izal, M., & Montorio, I. (1997). System of evaluation of homes for the elderly–SERA–Technical Documents. Managua, Nicaragua: National Institute for Social Services.

Bardasi, E., & Jenkins, S. P. (2010). Gender gap in private pensions. *Bulletin of Economic Research, 62*(4), 343–363. doi:10.1111/j.1467-8586.2009.00336.x

Basnyat, K. (2010). Decision-makers' perception and knowledge about long-term care in Nepal: An exploratory study. Master's Thesis, Miami University, Oxford, Ohio.

Basu, A. M. (2004). *On the prospects for endless fertility decline in South Asia*. Report of the United Nations Expert Group Meeting on Completing the Fertility Transition. March 11–14, 2002, New York, NY. Retrieved from http://www.un.org/esa/population/publications/completingfertility/4RevisedBASUpaper.PDF

Beard, R. J. (1963). A theory of mortality based on actuarial, biological and medical considerations. In *Proceedings of the International Population Conference* (Vol. 1, New York, NY, 1961). London, England: International Union for the Scientific Study of Population.

Bedford, V. H., & Blieszner, R. (1997). Personal relationships in later-life families. In S. Duck (Ed.), *Handbook of personal relationships* (2nd ed., pp. 523–539). Chichester, England: John Wiley.

Beegle, K., Filmer, D., Stokes, A., & Tiererova, L. (2008). *Orphanhood and the living arrangements of children in sub-Saharan Africa* (Policy Research Working Paper WPS4889). Washington, DC: World Bank. Retrieved from http://www-wds.worldbank.org/servlet/WDSContentServer/WDSP/IB/2009/07/24/000112742_20090724110307/Rendered/PDF/WPS4889.pdf

Beider, S. (2005). An ethical argument for integrated palliative care. *eCAM, 2* (2), 227–231.

Bengtson, V. L., Kim, K.-D., Myers, G. C., & Eun, K.-S. (Eds.). (2000). *Aging in East and West: Families, states, and the elderly.* New York, NY: Springer.

Bengtson, V. L., & Putney, N. M. (2000). Who will care for tomorrow's elderly? Consequences of population aging East and West. In V. L. Bengtson, K.-D. Kim, G. C. Myers, & K.-S. Eun (Eds.), *Aging in East and West: Families, states, and the elderly* (pp. 263–285). New York, NY: Springer.

Bengtson, V. L., & Roberts, R. E. L. (1991). Intergenerational solidarity in aging families: An example of formal theory construction. *Journal of Marriage and the Family, 53,* 856–870.

Bengtson, V. L., Rosenthal, C. J., & Burton, L. M. (1996). Paradoxes of families and aging. In R. H. Binstock, & L. K. George (Eds.), *Handbook of aging and the social sciences* (4th ed., pp. 253–282). San Diego, CA: Academic Press.

Benjamin, A. E., & Fennel, M. (2007). Putting consumers first in long-term care: Findings from the Cash and Counseling Demonstration and Evaluation. Special Issue of *Health Services Research, 4*(1), Part II, 353–361.

Biddlecom, A., Ofstedal, M. B., & Chayovan, N. (2002). Intergenerational support and transfers. In A. I. Hermalin (Ed.), *The well-being of the elderly in Asia: A four-country comparative study* (pp. 185–207). Ann Arbor: University of Michigan Press.

Blackwell, J., Obka, M., & Casey, B. (1995). *The transition from work to retirement* (Social Policies Studies No. 16). Paris, France: OECD.

Blieszner, R. & Bedford, V. H. (2012). The family context of aging. In R. Blieszner, & V. H. Bedford (Eds.), *Handbook of families and aging* (2nd ed., pp. 3–12). Santa Barbara, CA: Praeger.

Bloom, D. E., Boersch-Supan, A., McGee, P., & Seike, A. (2011). *Population aging: Facts, challenges, and responses* (Working Paper No. 71, Harvard University Program on the Global Demography of Aging). Retrieved September 19, 2013, from www.hsph.harvard.edu/pgda/working.htm

Bock, J., & Johnson, S. E. (2008). Grandmothers' productivity and the HIV/AIDS pandemic in sub-Saharan Africa. *Journal of Cross-Cultural Gerontology, 23,* 1–22.

Bongaarts, J., & Zimmer, Z. (2002). Living arrangements of older adults in the developing world: An analysis of demographic and health survey household surveys. *Journal of Gerontology: Social Sciences, 57*(1), S145–S157.

Boockmann, B., Fries, J., & Gobel, C. (2011). *Specific measures for older employees and late career employment.* Tubingen, Germany: Institute for Applied Economic Research.

Börsch-Supan, A., Brandt, M., Hunkler, C., Kneip, T., Korbmacher, J., Malter, F., & Zuber, S. (2013). Data resource profile: The survey of health, aging, and retirement in Europe (SHARE). *International Journal of Epidemiology*, 1–10.

Brown, J. S. (2005). Examining the adoption of old-age security programs in the developing world. *Sociological Perspectives, 48*, 505–529.

Buckley, C. (2013). China to ease longtime policy of 1-child limit. *New York Times*, November 15. Retrieved from http:// www.nytimes.com/2013/11/16/ world/asia/china-to-loosen-its-one-child-policy.html

Burgess, E. W. (1960). *Aging in western societies*. Chicago, IL: University of Chicago Press.

Cabrera, A., & Unruh, G. (2012). *Being global: How to think, act, and lead in a transformed world*. Cambridge, MA: Harvard Business Review Press.

Cahill, K. E., Giandrea, M. D., & Quinn, J. F. (2011). *How does occupational status impact bridge job prevalence?* (BLS Working Paper 447). Washington, DC: Bureau of Labor Statistics.

Cahill, K. E., Giandrea, M. D., & Quinn, J. F. (2012). Older workers and short-term jobs: Patterns and determinants. *Monthly Labor Review, 135*(5), 19–32.

Calasanti, T., & Kiecolt, K. J. (2012). Intersectionality and aging families. In R. Blieszner & V. H. Bedford (Eds.), *Handbook of families and aging* (2nd ed., pp. 398–434). Santa Barbara, CA: Praeger.

Cameron, L. J., Kabir, Z. N., Khanam, M. A., Wahlin, A., & Streatfield, P. K. (2010). Earning their keep: The productivity of older women and men in rural Bangladesh. *Journal of Cross-Cultural Gerontology, 25*(1), 87–103.

Campbell, B. C., Gray, P. B., & Radak, J. (2011). In the company of men: Quality of life and social support among the Ariaal of Northern Kenya. *Journal of Cross-Cultural Gerontology, 26*(3), 221–237.

Cappelli, P., & Keller, J. R. (2012). Classifying work in the new economy. *Academy of Management Review*. doi:10.5465/amr.2011.0302

Carlson, B. L., Foster, L., Dale, S. B., & Brown, R. (2007). Effects of cash and counseling on personal care and well-being. *Health Services Research, 42*, 467–487.

Carmel, S., & Lowenstein, A. (2007). Addressing a nation's challenge: Graduate programs in gerontology in Israel. *Gerontology & Geriatrics Education, 27*(3), 49–63.

Caro, F. G., Bass, S. A., & Chen, Y. P. (1993). Introduction: Achieving a productive aging society. In H. R. Moody (Ed.), *Aging: Concepts and controversies* (pp. 277–281). Thousand Oaks, CA: Sage.

Cash, R., Wikler, D., Saxena, A., & Capron, A. (2009). *Casebook on ethical issues in international health research*. Geneva, Switzerland: World Health Organization.

Chan, A. (2005). Formal and informal intergenerational support transfers in South-Eastern Asia. In *Proceedings of the United Nations expert group meeting on social and economic implications of changing population age structures* (pp. 331–338). New York, NY: United Nations Department of Economic and Social Affairs. Retrieved from http://www.un.org/esa/population/ meetings/Proceedings_EGM_Mex_2005/

Chen, X. (2010, September 17). Government denies immediate plan for retirement age rise. *China Daily*. Retrieved from http://www.chinadaily.com.cn

Cherny, N. I., Catane, R., & Kosmidis, P. A. (2006). Problems of opioid availability and accessibility across Europe: ESMO tackles the regulatory causes of intolerable and needless suffering. *Annals of Oncology, 17*(6), 885–887.

Chesnais, J.-C. (1992). *The demographic transition. Stages, patterns, and economic implications.* Oxford, England: Oxford University Press.

Chi, I. (2011). Cross-cultural gerontology research methods: Challenges and solutions. *Ageing and Society, 31*(3), 371.

China Center for Economic Research. (2009). *China health and retirement longitudinal studies.* Retrieved from http://charls.ccer.edu.cn/charls/

China Development Gateway. (2008). *"Left-behind" rural children numbered at 58 million.* Retrieved February 28, 2008, from www.chinagate.cn/news/2008-02/28/content_10958410.htm

Chou, R. J. (2010). Willingness to live in eldercare institutions among older adults in urban and rural China: A nationwide study. *Ageing & Society, 30,* 583–608.

Christopher, A. J. (1988). "Divide and rule": The impress of British separation policies. *Area, 20,* 233–240.

Chu, L. W., & Chi, I. (2008). Nursing homes in China. *Journal of American Medical Directors Association, 9,* 237–243.

Cichon, M., & Normand, C. (1994). Between Beveridge and Bismarck: Options for health care financing in central and eastern Europe. *World Health Forum, 15*(4), 323–328.

Clinton, H. R. (1996). *It takes a village: And other lessons children teach us.* New York, NY: Simon & Schuster.

Coale, A. (1964). How a population ages or grows younger. In R. Friedman (Ed.), *Population: The vital revolution* (pp. 47–58). Garden City, NY: Anchor Books.

Cochran, R. A. (2002). The meaning of health: Differences between cohorts and between users of biomedicine and complementary/alternative medicine. Ph.D. Dissertation, Georgia State University, Atlanta, Georgia.

Cockerham, W. C. (2012). *Medical sociology.* Upper Saddle River, NJ: Prentice Hall.

Colombo, F., Llena-Nozal, A., Mercier, J., & Tjadens, F. (2011). *Help wanted? Providing and paying for long-term care.* OECD Health Policy Studies, OECD Publishing. Retrieved from http://dx.doi.org/10.1787/9789264097759-en

Cowgill, D. O. (1972). A theory of aging in cross-cultural perspective. In D. O. Cowgill & L. D. Holmes (Eds.), *Ageing and modernization* (pp. 1–14). New York, NY: Appleton-Century-Crofts.

Cowgill, D. O. (1974). Aging and modernization: A revision of the theory. In J. F. Gubrium (Ed.), *Late life* (pp. 123–145). Springfield, IL: Thomas.

Cowgill, D. O., & Holmes, L. D. (1972). Summary and conclusions: The theory in review. In D. O. Cowgill & L. D. Holmes (Eds.), *Aging and modernization* (pp. 305–323). New York, NY: Appleton-Century-Crofts.

Crawley, L., Payne, R., Bolden, J., Payne, T., Washington, P., & Williams, S. (2000). The initiative to improve palliative and end-of-life care in the

African-American community. *Journal of the American Medical Association,* *284,* 2518–2521.

Crawley, L. M., Marshall, P. A., Lo, B., & Koenig, B. A. (2002). Strategies for culturally effective end-of-life care. *Annals of Internal Medicine, 136*(9), 673–679.

Croda, E., & Gonzalez-Chapela, J. (2005). How do European older adults use their time? In A. Borsch-Supan, A. Brugiavini, H. Jurges, A. Kapteyn, J. Mackenbach, J. Siegrist, & G. Weber (Eds.), *Health, aging and retirement in Europe: First results from the survey of health, ageing and retirement in Europe* (pp. 265–271). Manheim, Germany: MEA. Retrieved from www.share-project.org/uploads/tx_sharepublications/CH_5.6.pdf

Daar, A., Singer, P., Persa, D., Pramming, S., Matthews, D., Beaglehole, R., . . . Bell, J. (2007). Grand challenges in chronic noncommunicable diseases. *Nature, 450*(22), 494–496.

Daatland, S. O. (1990). What are families for? On family solidarity and preferences for help. *Ageing and Society, 10,* 1–15.

Daatland, S. O. (1997). Family solidarity, popular opinions and the elderly: Perspectives from Norway. *Ageing International, 1,* 51–62.

Dale, S., & Brown, R. (2006). Reducing nursing home use through consumer-directed personal care services. *Medical Care, 44,* 760–767.

Damman, M., Henkens, K., & Kalmijn, M. (2011). The impact of midlife educational, work, health, and family experiences on men's early retirement. *The Journals of Gerontology, Series B: Psychological Sciences and Social Sciences, 66*(5), 617–627. doi:10.1093/geronb/gbr092

Dannefer, D., & Settersten, R. A. (2010). The study of the life course: Implications for social gerontology. In D. Dannefer & C. Phillipson (Eds.), *The Sage handbook of social gerontology* (pp. 3–19). Thousand Oaks, CA: Sage.

Denton, T. (2007). Unit of observation in cross-cultural research. *Cross-Cultural Research, 41*(1), 3–31.

DeStatis [Federal Statistical Office of Germany]. (2011). Retrieved March 2013, from https://www.destatis.de/EN/FactsFigures/NationalEconomy Environment/LabourMarket/Employment/LabourForceSurvey/ LabourForceSurvey.html

Diamond, L. (2007). A giant among teachers: An appreciation of the original "political man." Hoover Institution, Stanford University. Retrieved from www.hoover.org/publications/hoover-digest/article/6041

Do, Y. K., & Malhotra, C. (2012). The effect of co-residence with an adult child on depressive symptoms among older widowed women in South Korea: An instrumental variables estimation. *The Journals of Gerontology Series B: Psychological Sciences and Social Sciences, 67*(3), 384–391.

Dorn, D., & Sousa-Poza, A. (2007). *'Voluntary' and 'involuntary' early retirement: An international analysis* (IZA Discussion Papers, No. 2714). Bonn, Germany: Institute for the Study of Labor (IZA).

Du, P., & Yang, H. (2009). China. In E. B. Palmore, F. Whittington, & S. Kunkel (Eds.), *International handbook on aging: Current research and developments* (3rd ed., pp. 145–157). Westport, CT: Praeger.

Duda, R., Anarfi, J., Adanu, R., Seffah, J., Darko, R., & Hill, A. (2011). The health of the "older women" in Accra, Ghana: Results of the women's health study of Accra. *Journal of Cross Cultural Gerontology, 26*, 299–314.

Dunn, F. L. (1976). Traditional Asian medicine and cosmopolitan medicine as adaptive systems. In C. M. Leslie (Ed.), *Asian medical systems: A comparative study* (pp. 133–158). Berkeley: University of California Press.

Ekerdt, D. J. (1986). The busy ethic: Moral continuity between work and retirement. *The Gerontologist, 26*(3), 239–244.

Elder, G. H., George, L. K., & Shanahan, M. J. (1996). Psychosocial stress over the life course. In H. B. Kaplan (Ed.), *Psychosocial stress: Perspectives on structure, theory, life-course, and methods* (pp. 247–292). San Diego, CA: Academic Press.

Ember, C. R., & Ember, M. (2009). *Cross-cultural research methods* (2nd ed.). Lanham, MD: AltaMira Press.

Esping-Andersen, G. (1990). *The three worlds of welfare capitalism.* Princeton, NJ: Princeton University Press.

Esping-Andersen, G. (1999). *The social foundations of postindustrial economies.* Oxford, England: Oxford University Press.

Eun, K.-S. (2003). Changing roles of the family and state for elderly care. In V. L. Bengtson & A. Lowenstein (Eds.), *Global aging and challenges to families* (pp. 253–271). New York, NY: Aldine De Gruyter.

Eurostat. (2011a). *Active ageing and solidarity between generations.* Luxembourg City, Luxembourg: Author.

Eurostat. (2011b). *Healthy life years and life expectancy at age 65, by gender* [Excel file]. Retrieved February 1, 2012, from http://epp.eurostat.ec.europa.eu/tgm/download.do?tab=table&plugin=0&language=en&pcode=tsdph220

Eurostat. (2013). *Proportion of population aged 65 and over* [Excel file]. Retrieved March 7, 2013, from http://epp.eurostat.ec.europa.eu/portal/page/portal/population/data/main_tables#

Even, W. E., & Macpherson, D. A. (2004). *Do pensions impede phased retirement?* (IZA Discussion paper series, No. 1353). Bonn, Germany: Institute for the Study of Labor (IZA).

Field, M. J., & Cassel, C. K. (1997). *Approaching death: Improving care at the end of life.* Washington, DC: National Academy Press.

Firth, S. (2000). Approaches to death in Hindu and Sikh communities in Britain. In D. Dickenson, M. Johnson, & J. S. Katz (Eds.), *Death, dying, and bereavement.* London, England: Sage.

Flaherty, J. H., Liu, M. L., Ding, L., Dong, D., Ding, Q., Li, X., & Xiao, S. (2007). China: The aging giant. *Journal of the American Geriatrics Society, 55*, 1295–1300.

Fong, J. H., Piggott, J., & Sherris, M. (2012). *Public sector pension funds in Australia: Longevity selection and liabilities* (Working Paper No. 2012/17). Sydney, Australia: ARC Centre of Excellence in Population Ageing Research.

Frankenberg, E., & Thomas, D. (2011). Global aging. In R. H. Binstock & L. K. George (Eds.), *Handbook of aging and the social sciences* (7th ed., pp. 73–89). San Diego, CA: Academic Press.

Fredvang, M., & Biggs, S. (2012). The rights of older persons: Protection and gaps under human rights law. *Social Policy Working Papers, 16*, 1–21. Retrieved April 7, 2013.

Freedman, V. A., Crimmins, E., Schoeni, R. F., Spillman, B. C., Aykan, H., Kramarow, E., . . . Waidman, T. (2004). Resolving inconsistencies in trends in old-age disability: Report from a technical working group. *Demography, 41*(3), 417–441.

Friedland, R. B., & Summer, L. (1999). *Demography is not destiny*. Washington, DC: National Academy on Aging; Gerontological Society of America.

Friedland, R. B., & Summer, L. (2005). *Demography is not destiny, revisited*. Georgetown University Commonwealth Publication, No. 789. Washington, DC: Center on Aging Society.

Fries, J. F. (1980). Aging, natural death, and the compression of morbidity. *New England Journal of Medicine, 303*(3), 130–135.

Gannon, B., & Davin, B. (2010). Use of formal and informal care services among older people in Ireland and France. *European Journal of Health Economics, 11*, 499–511.

Gerontology Research Group. (2006). *Homepage*. Retrieved from http://www.grg.org/

Giarrusso, R., Silverstein, M., Gans, D., & Bengtson, V. L. (2005). Ageing parents and adult children: New perspectives on intergenerational relationships. In M. L. Johnson (Ed.), *The Cambridge handbook of age and aging* (pp. 413–421). New York: Cambridge University Press.

Gitlin, L. N., & Schulz, R. (2012). Family caregiving of older adults. In T. Prohaska, L. Anderson, & R. Binstock (Eds.), *Public health of an aging society* (pp. 181–204). Baltimore, MD: Johns Hopkins University Press.

Goldstein, J. (2009). How populations age? In P. Uhlenberg (Ed.), *International handbook of population aging* (Vol. 1, Part 1, pp. 7–18). Retrieved from http://www.springerlink.com/context/x40621714xhwt753/fulltext.pdf

Gomes, B., Harding, R., Foley, K. M., & Higginson, I. J. (2009). Optimal approaches to the health economics of palliative care: Report of an international think tank. *Journal of Pain and Symptom Management, 38*(1), 4–10.

Gompertz, B. (1825). On the nature of the function expressive of the law of human mortality, and on a new mode of determining the value of life contingencies. *Philosophical Transactions of the Royal Society of London, 115*, 513–585.

Goodhead, A., & McDonald, J. (2007). *Informal caregivers literature review: A report prepared for the National Health Committee*. Wellington, New Zealand: Health Services Research Center. Retrieved from http://nhc.health.govt.nz/system/files/documents/publications/informal-caregivers-literature-review.pdf

Government of Kenya. (2008). *National Social Protection Policy*. Nairobi, Kenya: MGCSD.

Goyal, R. S. (1989). Some aspects of aging in India. In R. N. Pati & B. Jena (Eds.), *Aged in India: Socio-demographic dimensions* (pp. 19–36). New Delhi, India: Ashish Publishing House.

Graunt, J. (1662). *Natural and political observations mentioned in a following index and made upon the bills of mortality*. No location: No publisher.

Guardiancich, I. (2011). Pan-European pension funds: Current situation and future prospects. *International Social Security Association, 64*(1), 15–36. doi:10.1111/j.1468-246X.2010.01382.x.

Hamilton, B., Martin, J., & Ventura, S. (2010). Births: Preliminary data for 2008. *National Vital Statistics Reports, 58*(16), 1–6.

Hank, K., & Stuck, S. (2008). Volunteer work, informal help, and care among the 50+ in Europe: Further evidence for "linked" productive activities at older ages. *Social Science Research, 37*(4), 1280–1291.

Hantrais, L. (2009). *International comparative research: Theory, methods and practice*. Basingstoke, England: Palgrave Macmillan.

Harding, S. (1981). Family reform movements: Recent feminism and its recent opponents. *Feminist Studies, 7*, 57–75.

Hargrave, T. D., & Anderson, W. T. (1992). *Finishing well: Aging and reparation in the intergenerational family*. New York, NY: Brunner/Mazel.

Hashimoto, A., & Ikels, C. (2005). Filial piety in changing Asian societies. In M. L. Johnson (Ed.), *The Cambridge handbook of age and aging* (pp. 437–442). Cambridge, England: Cambridge University Press.

Hashimoto, A., & Kendig, H. L. (1992). Aging in international perspective. In H. Kendig, A. Hashimoto, & L. C. Coppard (Eds.), *Family support for the elderly: The international experience* (pp. 3–14). New York, NY: Oxford University Press.

Haub, C. (2007). Global aging and the demographic divide. *Public Policy & Aging Report, 17*(4), 1–6.

Haug, M. R., Wykle, M. L., & Namazi, K. H. (1989). Self-care among older adults. *Social Science and Medicine, 29*, 171–183.

Heinicke, K., & Thomsen, S. (2010). *The social long-term care insurance in Germany: Origin, situation, threats and perspectives*. Center for European Economic Research (Discussion paper no. 10-012). Retrieved December 1, 2011, from ftp://ftp.zew.de/pub/zew-docs/dp/dp10012.pdf

Helman, C. (1984). *Culture, health and illness: An introduction for health professionals*. Boston, MA: John Wright-PSG.

HelpAge International. (2006). *Social cash transfers for Africa: A transformative agenda for the 21st century*. Intergovernmental Regional Conference Report. Livingstone, Zambia, 20–23 March.

HelpAge International. (2008). *Protecting the rights of older people in Africa*. Retrieved from http://www.helpage.org/publications/?ssearch=Prote cting+the+Rights+of+Older+People+in+Africa&adv=0&topic=0&regio n=0&language=0&type=0

HelpAge International (2009a). Practical issues in ageing & development. *Ageing & Development*, Issue 26.

HelpAge International (2009b). Practical issues in ageing & development. *Ageing & Development*, Issue 27.

HelpAge International. (2009c). *Witness to climate change: Learning from older people's experience*. London, England: Author. Retrieved from http://www.helpageusa.org/what-we-do/climate-change/witness-to-climate-change-learning-from-older-peoples-experience/

HelpAge International. (2011). *Development*. Retrieved December 20, 2011, from www.oecd.org/health/longtermcare

HelpAge International. (n.d.a). Retrieved from http://www.helpage.org/what-we-do/rights/towards-a-convention-on-the-rights-of-older-people/

HelpAge International. (n.d.b). Retrieved from http://www.helpage.org/get-involved/campaigns/what-is-age-demands-action/

Herlofson, K., Hagestad, G., Slagsvold, B., & Sørensen, A. M. (2011). Intergenerational family responsibility and solidarity in Europe. Oslo, Norway: Norwegian Social Research (NOVA). Retrieved from http://www.multilinks-project.eu/uploads/papers/0000/0038/herlofson_deliverable.pdf

Hinrichs, K. (2000). Elephants on the move: Patterns of pension reform in OECD countries. *European Review, 8*(3), 353–378.

Horwitz, S. (2005). The function of the family in the great society. *Cambridge Journal of Economics, 29*, 669–684.

Hsiao, W. C., & Shaw, R. P. (Eds.) (2007). Social health insurance for developing nations. Washington, DC: World Bank.

Hua, F., & Di, X. (2002). Case-study: China. In J. Brodsky, J. Habib, & M. Hirschfeld (Eds.), *The World Health Organization Collection on Long-Term Care: Long-Term Care in Developing Countries*. Geneva, Switzerland: World Health Organization.

Huber, B. (2005). *Implementing the Madrid Plan of Action on Aging*. United Nations Department of Economic and Social Affairs. Retrieved from http://www.un.org/esa/population/meetings/EGMPopAge_21_RHuber.pdf

Huff, R. M. (2002). Folk medicine. In L. Breslow (Ed.), *Encyclopedia of public health*. New York, NY: Macmillan Reference.

Human Mortality Database. (2011). University of California, Berkeley (USA), and Max Planck Institute for Demographic Research (Germany). Retrieved October 2011, from www.mortality.org or www.humanmortality.de

Hutchens, R. (2010). Worker characteristics, job characteristics, and opportunities for phased retirement. *Labour Economics, 17*, 1010–1021. doi:10.1016/j.labeco.2010.02.003

Ikels, C. (1993). Chinese kinship and the state: Shaping of policy for the elderly. In G. L. Maddox & M. P. Lawton (Eds.), *Annual Review of Gerontology and Geriatrics: Focus on kinship, aging, and social change* (Vol. 13, pp. 123–146). New York, NY: Springer.

Indrizal, E., Kreager, P., & Schroeder-Butterfil, E. (2009). The structural vulnerability of older people in a matrilineal society: The Minangkabau of West Sumatra, Indonesia. In J. Sokolovsky, (Ed.), *The cultural context of aging: Worldwide perspectives* (3rd ed., pp. 383–394). Westport, CT: Praeger.

Information Office of the State Council of the People's Republic of China. (1995). *Family planning in China* (Government white paper). Retrieved

June 18, 2009, from http://www.china.org.cn/e-white/familypanning/index.htm

International Social Security Agency. (2010). *Country profile: Sweden. Reforms.* Retrieved February 3, 2012, from http://www.issa.int/Observatory/Country-Profiles/Regions/Europe/Sweden/Reforms2 on

Ipsos-MORI. (2008). Frontiers of performance in the NHS II. London, England: National Health Service.

Jackson, J. S. (2002). Conceptual and methodological linkages in cross–cultural groups and cross–national aging research. *Journal of Social Issues, 58*(4), 825–835.

Jackson, R., Strauss, R., & Howe, N. (2009). *Latin America's aging challenge: Demographics and retirement policy in Brazil, Chile, and Mexico.* Washington, DC: Center for Strategic and International Studies. Retrieved from http://csis.org/files/media/csis/pubs/090324_gai_english.pdf

Jagger, C., & Fouweather, T. (2012). *Cross-sectional analysis of health expectancies in 2008: Evaluation of the 2008 implementation of the greater harmonisation of the Mini European Health Module.* EHELEIS Technical Report 2012_5.1.

Jahan, R., & Germain, A. (2004). Mobilizing support to sustain political will is the key to progress in reproductive health. *Lancet, 364,* 742–744.

Jemal, A., Center, M., DeSantis, C., & Ward, M. (2010). Global patterns of cancer incidence and mortality rates and trends. *Cancer Epidemiology, Biomarkers, and Prevention, 19,* 1893–1907.

Jitapunkul, S., & Wivatvanit, S. (2009). National policies and programs for the aging population in Thailand. *Ageing International, 33,* 62–74.

Juma, M., Okeyo, T., & Kidenda, G. (2004). *Our hearts are willing, but . . . Challenges of elderly caregivers in rural Kenya.* Nairobi, Kenya: Population Council; Horizons Research Update.

Katz, R., Daatland, S. O., Lowenstein, A., Bazo, M. T., Ancizu, I., Herlofson, K., . . . Prilutzky, D. (2003). Family norms and preferences in intergenerational relations: A comparative perspective. In V. L. Bengtson & A. Lowenstein (Eds.), *Global aging and challenges to families* (pp. 305–326). New York, NY: Aldine De Gruyter.

Katz S., Ford A. B., Moskowitz R. W., Jackson, B. A., & Jaffe, M. W. (1963). Studies of illness in the aged. The index of the ADL: A standardized measure of biological and psychosocial function. *Journal of the American Medical Association, 185,* 914–919.

Kendig, H. L., Hashimoto, A., & Coppard, L. C. (1992). Preface. In H. Kendig, A. Hashimoto, & L. C. Coppard (Eds.), *Family support for the elderly: The international experience* (pp. ix–x). New York, NY: Oxford University Press.

Kickbusch, I. S. (2001). Health literacy: Addressing the health and educational divide. *Health Promotion International, 16*(3), 289–297.

King, D. A., & Wynne, L. C. (2004). The emergence of "family integrity" in later life. *Family Process, 43*(1), 7–21.

Kinsella, K. (1992). Aging trends in Kenya. *Journal of Cross-Cultural Gerontology, 7,* 259–268.

Kinsella, K. (2009). Global perspectives in the demography of aging. In J. Sokolovsky (Ed.), *The cultural context of aging: Worldwide perspectives* (3rd ed, pp. 13–29). Westport, CT: Praeger Publishers.

Kinsella, K., Beard, J., & Suzman, R. (2013). Can populations age better, not just live longer? *Generations, 37*(1), 19–26.

Kinsella, K., & He, W. (2009). An aging world: 2008. In U.S. Bureau of the Census (Ed.), *International population reports P95/09-1.* Washington, DC: U.S. Government Printing Office. Retrieved from https://www.census .gov/prod/2009pubs/p95-09-1.pdf

Kinsella, K., & Phillips, D. R. (2005). Global aging: The challenge of success. *Population Bulletin, 60*(1), 3–42.

Knodel, J., & Chayovan, N. (2008). *Population ageing and the well-being of older persons in Thailand.* Research Report 08-659. Ann Arbor: Population Studies Center, University of Michigan, Institute for Social Research.

Kohn, M. L. (1987). Cross-national research as an analytic strategy: American Sociological Association, 1987 presidential address. *American Sociological Review, 52*(6), 713–731.

Komp, K. (2013). Political gerontology: Ageing populations and the state of the state. In K. Komp & M. Aartsen (Eds.), *Old age in Europe: A textbook of gerontology* (pp. 59–78). Dordrecht, The Netherlands: Springer.

Komp, K., & Aartsen, M. (2013). Introduction: Older people under the magnifying glass. In K. Komp & M. Aartsen (Eds.), *Old age in Europe. A textbook of gerontology* (pp. 1–14). Dordrecht, The Netherlands: Springer.

Komp, K., & Béland, D. (2012). Balancing protection and productivity: International perspectives on social policies for older people. *International Journal of Social Welfare, Supplement, 1*(21), S1–S7.

Korpi, W., & Palme, J. (1998). The paradox of redistribution and strategies of equality: Welfare state institutions, inequality, and poverty in the Western countries. *American Sociological Review, 63*(5), 661–687.

Koyano, W. (2003). Intergenerational relationships of Japanese seniors: Changing patterns. In V. L. Bengtson & A. Lowenstein (Eds.), *Global aging and challenges to families* (pp. 272–302). New York, NY: Aldine De Gruyter.

Kraus, M., Riedel, M., Mot, E., Willeme, P., Rohrling, G., & Czypionka, T. (2010). *A typology of long-term care systems in Europe.* European Network of Economic Policy Research Institutes. Assessing Needs of Care in European Nations (ANCIEN).

Kreager, P., & Schroeder-Butterfill, E. (Eds.). (2005). *Ageing without children: European and Asian perspectives.* Oxford, England: Berghahn.

Kruse, A., & Schmitt, E. (2009). Germany. In E. Palmore, F. Whittington, & S. Kunkel (Eds.), *International handbook on aging: Current research and developments* (3rd ed., pp. 221–237). Santa Barbara, CA: Praeger.

Kubler-Ross, E. (1969). *On death and dying.* New York, NY: Simon & Shuster.

Kumar, S. (2003). Economic security for the elderly in India. *Journal of Aging and Social Policy, 15*(2/3), 45–65.

Kumar, V. (2003). Health status and health care services among older persons in India. *Journal of Aging and Social Policy, 15*(2/3), 67–83.

Kunkel, S. R. (2008). Global aging and gerontology education: The international mandate. *Annual Review of Gerontology and Geriatrics, 28*, 45–58.

Kunkel, S., & Subedi, J. (1996). Aging in south Asia: How "imperative" is the demographic imperative? In V. Minichiello, N. Chappell, H. Kendig, & A. Walker (Eds.), *Sociology of aging* (pp. 459–466). Melbourne, Australia: International Sociological Association; Toth.

Lamb, S. (2009). Elder residences and outsourced sons: Remaking aging in cosmopolitan India. In J. Sokolovsky (Ed.), *The cultural context of aging: Worldwide perspectives* (3rd ed., pp. 418–440). Westport, CT: Praeger.

Lameire, N., Joffe, P., & Wiedemann, M. (1999). Healthcare systems—An international review: An overview. *Nephrology Dialysis Transplantation, 14*(suppl 6), S3–S9.

Largaespada Fredersdorff, C. (2004). *The aging of Nicaragua*. PowerPoint Presentation. Seminar about the Aging in Latin America. INAPAM-RIICOTEC, Mexico.

Lawton, M. P., & Brody, E. (1969). Assessment of older people: Self-maintaining and instrumental activities of daily living. *The Gerontologist, 9*, 179–186.

Lee, R., & Mason, A. (2006). What is the demographic dividend? *Finance and Development, 43*(3), 1–9.

Lee, R., & Mason, A. (2011). Population aging and the generational economy: Key findings. In R. Lee & A. Mason (Eds.), *Population aging and the generational economy* (pp. 3–31). Northampton, MA: Edward Elgar.

Leeder, E. (2004). *The family in global perspective: A gendered journey.* Thousand Oaks, CA: Sage.

Leibfried, S., & Obinger, H. (2000). Welfare state futures: An introduction. *European Review, 8*(3), 277–290.

Liang, J.-Y. (2011). Components of a meaningful retirement life—A phenomenological study of the 1950s birth cohort in urban China. *Journal of Cross-Cultural Gerontology, 26*(3), 279–298.

Liebig, P. (2003). Old-age homes and services: Old and new approaches to aged care. *Journal of Aging & Social Policy, 15*(2/3), 159–178.

Lien, S.-C., Zhang, Y. B., & Hummert, M. L. (2009). Older adults in prime-time television dramas in Taiwan: Prevalence, portrayal, and communication interaction. *Journal of Cross-Cultural Gerontology, 24*(4), 355–372.

Lloyd, L. (2012). *Health and care in ageing societies: A new international approach.* Bristol, England: The Policy Press.

López Norori, M. (2008). *Evaluation of homes for the elderly of Central and Northern Nicaragua.* Investigative Report. Managua, Nicaragua: Author.

Lowenstein, A. (2005). Global ageing and challenges to families. In M. L. Johnson (Ed.), *The Cambridge handbook of age and aging* (pp. 403–412). Cambridge, England: Cambridge University Press.

Luborsky, M. R. (1994). The retirement process: Making the person and cultural meanings malleable. *Medical Anthropology Quarterly, 8*(4), 411–429.

Luborsky, M. R., & LeBlanc, I. M. (2003). Cross-cultural perspectives on the concept of retirement: An analytic redefinition. *Journal of Cross-Cultural Gerontology, 18*, 251–271.

Lumme-Sandt, L., Hervonen, A., & Jylha, M. (2000). Interpretive repertoires of medication use among the oldest-old. *Social Science and Medicine, 50,* 1843–1850.

Luo, Y., LaPierre, T. A., Hughes, M. E., & Waite, L. J. (2012). Grandparents providing care to grandchildren: A population-based study of continuity and change. *Journal of Family Issues, 33*(9), 1143–1167.

Luxembourg Income Study. (n.d.). *Home page.* Retrieved from http://www.lisproject.org/

Lynch, J. (2001). The age-orientation of social policy regimes in OECD countries. *Journal of Social Policy, 30*(3), 411–436.

Lynch, S. M., & Brown, J. S. (2010). Generating multistate life table distributions for highly refined subpopulations from cross-sectional data: A Bayesian extension of Sullivan's method. *Demography, 47*(4), 1053–1077.

Maestas, N. (2010). Back to work: Expectations and realizations of work after retirement. *The Journal of Human Resources, 45*(3), 718–748.

Marshall, P. S. (2006). Informed consent in international health research. *Journal of Empirical Research on Human Research Ethics, 1*(1), 25–41.

Mathers, C. D., Murray, C. J. L., Lopez, A. D., Salomon, J. A., Sadana, R., Tandon, A., . . . Chatterji, S. (2001). Estimates of healthy life expectancy for 191 countries in the year 2000: Methods and results. *Global Programme on Evidence for Health Policy Discussion Paper No. 38.* Geneva, Switzerland: World Health Organization.

Matras, J. (1990). *Dependency, obligations, and entitlements: A new sociology of aging, the life course, and the elderly.* Englewood Cliffs, NJ: Prentice Hall.

Matsushima, T., Akabayashi, A., & Nishitateno, K. (2002). The current status of bereavement follow-up in hospice and palliative care in Japan. *Palliative Medicine, 16,* 151–158.

Mbithi, L. M., & Mutuku, M. (2010). *Social protection status in developing countries: The case of Kenya.* Draft paper prepared for ERD regional conference on promoting resilience through social protection in sub-Saharan Africa.

McDonald, G. (2000). Cross-cultural methodological issues in ethical research. *Journal of Business Ethics, 27,* 89–104.

McFalls, J. A. (1998). Population: A lively introduction. *Population Bulletin, 53*(3). Washington, DC: Population Reference Bureau.

McLuhan, M. (1962). *The Gutenberg galaxy: The making of typographic man.* Toronto, Ontario, Canada: University of Toronto Press.

Mehdizadeh, S., Applebaum, R., Nelson, I., & Straker, J. (2011). *Coming of age: Tracking the progress and challenges of delivering long-term services and supports in Ohio.* Scripps Gerontology Center, Miami University, Oxford, Ohio.

Meier, D. E. (2010). The development, status, and future of palliative care. In D. E. Meier, S. L. Isaacs, & R. G. Hughes (Eds.), *Palliative care: Transforming the care of serious illness* (pp. 11–12). New York, NY: Jossey Bass.

Meiners, M., Mahoney, K., & Shoop, D. (2002). Consumer direction in managed long-term care: An exploratory survey of practices and perceptions. *The Gerontologist, 42*(1), 32–38.

Menken, J., & Cohen, B. (2006). *Aging in sub-Saharan Africa: Recommendations for furthering research.* Washington, DC: National Academies Press.

Merli, M. G., & Palloni, A. P. (2006). The HIV/AIDS epidemic, kin relations, living arrangements and the African elderly in South Africa. In B. Cohen & J. Menken (Eds.), *Aging in sub-Saharan Africa: Recommendations for furthering research* (pp. 117–165). Washington, DC: National Academies Press.

Miller-Loessi, K., & Parker, J. N. (2003). Cross-cultural social psychology. In J. Delamater (Ed.), *Handbook of social psychology* (pp. 529–553). New York, NY: Kluwer Academic Plenum.

Mont, D. (2007). *Measuring disability prevalence.* Disability & Development Team HDNSP. Washington, DC: The World Bank.

Montanari, I. (2001). Modernization, globalization, and the welfare state: A comparative analysis of old and new convergence of social insurance since 1930. *British Journal of Sociology, 52*(3), 469–494.

Moody, H. R. (2000). Is retirement obsolete? In H. R. Moody (Ed.), *Aging: Concepts and controversies* (3rd ed., pp. 263–276). Thousand Oaks, CA: Pine Forge Press.

Morgan, L. A., & Kunkel, S. R. (2011). *Aging, society, and the life course,* 4th ed. New York, NY: Springer.

Muir, D. M., & Turner, J. A. (2011). Constructing the ideal pension system: The visions of ten country experts. In D. M. Muir & J. A. Turner (Eds.), *Imagining the ideal pension system: International perspectives* (pp. 1–17). Kalamazoo, MI: W.E. Upjohn Institute for Employment Research.

Müller, C., Raffelhüschen, B., & Weddige, O. (2009). *Pension obligations of government employer pension schemes and social security pension schemes established in the EU countries.* Freiburg, Germany: Research Center for Generational Contracts.

Muramatsu, N., & Akiyama, H. (2011). Japan: Super-aging society preparing for the future. *The Gerontologist, 51,* 425–432.

Murdock, G. (1949). *Social structure.* New York, NY: Free Press.

Muruthi, J. R. (2012). *Perceptions of economic security in old age: The case of rural elders of Maraigushu, Kenya* (Master's thesis, Miami University, Oxford, Ohio).

Musgrove, P. (2000). Health insurance: The influence of the Beveridge report. *Bulletin of the World Health Organization, 78*(6), 845–846.

Mwangi, S. (2010). *Development of palliative care around the world: An examination of standards and guidelines.* Paper presented at the Annual Meeting of the Gerontological Society of America, New Orleans, LA, November 20–23.

Mwangi, S. M. (2009). Kenya. In E. B. Palmore, F. Whittington, & S. Kunkel (Eds.), *The international handbook on aging: Current research and developments* (3rd ed., pp. 331–341). Santa Barbara, CA: Praeger.

Myers, G. C. (1990). Demography of aging. In R. H. Binstock & L. K. George (Eds.), *Handbook of aging and the social sciences* (3rd ed., pp. 19–44). New York, NY: Academic Press.

Myers, G. C., Lamb, V. L., & Agree, E. M. (2003). Patterns of disability change associated with the epidemiologic transition. In J. M. Robine, C. Jagger, C. Mathers, E. Crimmins, & R. Suzman (Eds.), *Determining health expectancies* (pp. 59–74). Chichester, England: John Wiley & Sons.

Nadash, P., & Crisp, S. (2005). *Best practices in consumer direction.* Cambridge, MA: Thompson Medstat. Retrieved from http://www.cms.gov/Medicare/Demonstration-Projects/DemoProjectsEvalRpts/downloads/Section648_Report.pdf

Nagi, S. Z. (1976). An epidemiology of disability among adults in the United States. Health and society. *Milbank Memorial Fund Quarterly, 54*, 439–467.

Nasretdinova, E., & Schenkkan, N. (2012). *A portrayal of absence: Households of migrants in Kyrgyzstan.* Bishkek, Kyrgyz Republic: HelpAge International.

National Institute on Aging & U.S. Department of State. (2007). *Why population aging matters: A global perspective.* Retrieved from: http://www.nia.nih.gov/researchinformation/extramuralprograms/behavioralandsocialreresearch/globalaging.htm

National Transfer Accounts Project. (2013). Retrieved from http://www.ntaccounts.org/web/nta/show/

Nguyen, H. M., & Cihlar, V. (2013). Differences in physical fitness and subjectively rated physical health in Vietnamese and German older adults. *Journal of Cross-Cultural Gerontology, 28*(2), 181–194.

Nyambedha, E. O., Wandibba, S., & Aagaard-Hansen, J. (2001). Policy implications of the inadequate support systems for orphans in Western Kenya. *Health Policy, 58*, 83–96.

Oakshott, I. (2009). Hospitals to be told to make patients happy. *Sunday Times* (London), September 13.

OECD. (2005). *Private pensions: OECD classification and glossary.* Retrieved from http://www.oecd.org/insurance/privatepensions/2496718.pdf

OECD. (2011a). Estonia long-term care. In *Help wanted? Providing and paying for long-term care*, Paris, France. Retrieved November 2, 2012, from www.oecd.org/health/longtermcare and www.oecd.org/health/longtermcare/helpwanted

OECD. (2011b). France long-term care. In *Help wanted? Providing and paying for long-term care.* Paris, France. Retrieved November 2, 2012, from www.oecd.org/health/longtermcarde and www.oecd.org/health/longtermcare/helpwanted

OECD. (2011c). Ireland long-term care. In *Help wanted? Providing and paying for long-term Care*, Paris, France. Retrieved from www.oecd.org/health/longtermcare and www.oecd.org/health/longtermcare/helpwanted

OECD. (2011d). *Pensions at a glance 2011: Retirement-income systems in OECD and G20 countries.* Paris, France: Author.

OECD. (2012a). *Ageing and employment policies: Statistics on average effective age of retirement in OECD countries.* Retrieved October 18, 2012, from http://www.oecd.org/els/employmentpoliciesanddata/ageingandemploymentpoliciesstatisticsonaverageeffectiveageofretirement.htm

OECD. (2012b). *OECD pensions outlook 2012*. Paris, France: Author. Retrieved from http://dx.doi.org/10.1787/9789264169401-en

OECD. (2012c). StatExtracts. Retrieved October 18, 2012, from http://www.stats.oecd.org

OECD. (2013). *Social expenditures–aggregate data* [Excel file]. Retrieved March 8, 2013, from http://stats.oecd.org/Index.aspx?DataSetCode=SOCX_AGG on

Ogden, L. L. (2012). Financing and organization of national healthcare systems. In B. J. Fried & L. M. Gaydos (Eds.), *World health systems: Challenges and perspectives* (2nd ed., pp. 49–70). Chicago, IL: Health Administration Press.

Olarte, J. M., & Guillen, D. G. (2001). Cultural issues and ethical dilemmas in palliative and end-of-life care in Spain. *Cancer Control, 8*(1), 46–54.

Omiti, J., & Nyanamba, T. (2007). *Using social protection policies to reduce vulnerability and promote economic growth in Kenya.* Nairobi: Research Paper Series for Kenya Institute for Public Policy Research and Analysis (KIPPRA).

Omran, A. (1971). The epidemiological transition: A theory of the epidemiology of population change. *Milbank Memorial Fund Quarterly, 49,* 509–538.

Orenstein, M. A. (2011). Pension privatization in crisis: Death or rebirth of a global policy trend? *International Social Security Review, 64*(3), 65–80. doi:10.1111/j.1468-246X.2011.01403.x

Oriol, W. E. (1982). *Aging in all nations: A special report on the United Nations World Assembly on Aging, Vienna, Austria, July 26–August 6, 1982.* Washington, DC: National Council on Aging.

Paat, G., & Merilain, M. (2010). *Long-term care in Estonia.* European Network of Economic Policy Research Institutes. ENEPRI Research Report No. 75. Retrieved December 20, 2011, from http://aei.pitt.edu/14682/

Palacios, R., & Whitehouse, E. (2006). *Civil-service pension schemes around the world* (Social Policy Discussion Paper No. 0602). Washington, DC: World Bank; Santa Monica, CA: Rand Center for the Study of Aging.

Palmore, E. B. (1983). Cross-cultural research: State of the art. *Research on Aging, 5*(1), 45–57.

Palmore, E. B., Whittington, F., & Kunkel, S. (2009). *The international handbook on aging: Current research and developments,* 3rd ed. Santa Barbara, CA: Praeger.

Pampel, F. C., & Williamson, J. B. (1989). *Age, class, politics, and the welfare state.* Cambridge, England: Cambridge University Press.

Paris, V., Devaux, M., & Wei, L. (2010). *Health systems institutional characteristics: A survey of 29 OECD countries* (OECD Health Working Papers No. 50). Paris, France: Organisation for Economic Cooperation and Development.

Patrao, M., & Sousa, L. (2009). Material inheritance: Constructing family integrity in later life. In L. Sousa (Ed.), *Families in later life: Emerging themes and challenges* (pp. 49–74). Fargo, ND: Nova Science.

Peng, X. Z. (2009). *Fertility transition in China over the last 30 years.* International Institute of Social Studies (ISS) of Erasmus University Rotterdam.

Retrieved September 7, 2009, from http://www.iss.nl/DevISSues/Articles/Fertility-transition-in-China-over-the-last-30-years

Perkins, H. S., Geppert, C. M. A, Gonzales, A., Cortez, J. D., & Hazuda, H. P. (2002). Cross-cultural similarities and differences in attitudes about advance care planning. *Journal of General Internal Medicine, 17*, 48–57.

Pichardo, A. (2009). Mexico. In E. B. Palmore, F. Whittington, & S. Kunkel (Eds.), *The international handbook on aging: Current research and developments* (3rd ed., pp. 383–388). Santa Barbara, CA: Praeger.

Pienta, A. M., Barber, J. S., & Axinn, W. G. (2001). Social change and adult children's attitudes toward support of elderly parents: Evidence from Nepal. *Hallym International Journal of Aging, 3*, 211–235.

Pinquart, M., & Sörensen, S. (2003). Associations of stressors and uplifts of caregiving with caregiver burden and depressive mood: A meta-analysis. *Journal of Gerontology: Psychological Sciences, 58B*, P112–128.

Pinquart, M., & Sörensen, S. (2005). Ethnic differences in stressors, resources, and psychological outcomes of family caregiving: A meta-analysis. *The Gerontologist, 45*, 90–106.

Pinquart, M., & Sörensen, S. (2007). Correlates of physical health of informal caregivers: A meta-analysis. *Journal of Gerontology, Series B: Psychological Sciences and Social Sciences, 62*, P126–137.

Pitt, M., Cartwright, J., & Khandker, S. R. (2006). Empowering women with microfinance: Evidence from Bangladesh. *Economic Development and Cultural Change, 54*, 791–831.

PNHP [Physicians for a National Health Program]. (n.d.). About PNHP. Retrieved December 10, 2013, from http://www.pnhp.org/about/about-pnhp

Pollak, C., & Siven, N. (2011). *The social economy of ageing: Job quality and pathways beyond the labour market in Europe* (CES Working Paper No. 2011.66). Paris, France: Travail du Centre d'Economie de la Sorbonne.

Population Reference Bureau. (2009). Social security systems around the world. *Today's Research on Aging, 15*.

Population Reference Bureau. (2010a). World population highlights: Key findings from PRB's 2010 World Population Data Sheet. *Population Bulletin, 65*(2).

Population Reference Bureau. (2010b). China's rapidly aging population. *Today's Research on Aging, 20*. Retrieved from http://www.prb.org/pdf10/TodaysResearchAging20.pdf

Population Reference Bureau. (2012). *More U.S. children raised by grandparents.* Retrieved December 1, 2012, from http://www.prb.org/Articles/2012/US-children-grandparents.aspx

Prakash, I. J. (1999). *Ageing in India.* Geneva, Switzerland: World Health Organization. Retrieved from http://whqlibdoc.who.int/hq/1999/WHO_HSC_AHE_99.2.pdf

Pruchno, R., & Gitlin, L. N. (2012). Family caregiving in later life: Shifting paradigms. In R. Blieszner & V. H. Bedford (Eds.), *Handbook of families and aging* (2nd ed., pp. 515–541). Santa Barbara, CA: Praeger.

Puchalski, C. M., & O'Donnell, E. (2005). Religious and spiritual beliefs in end of life care: How major religions view death and dying. *Techniques in Regional Anesthesia & Pain Management, 9*, 114–121.

Putney, N., & Bengtson, V. L. (2003). Intergenerational relations in changing times. In J. T. Mortimer & M. J. Shanahan (Eds.), *Handbook of the life course* (pp. 149–164). New York, NY: Kluwer Academic/Plenum.

Pyke, K. D., & Bengtson, V. L. (1996). Caring more or less: Individualistic and collectivist systems of family eldercare. *Journal of Marriage and Family, 58*(2), 379–392.

Reid, T. R. (2009). *The healing of America: A global quest for better, cheaper, and fairer health care.* New York, NY: Penguin Press.

Reykowski, J., & Smolenska, Z. (1993). Collectivism, individualism, and interpretations of social change: Limitations of a simplistic model. *Polish Psychological Bulletin, 24*, 89–107.

Rix, S. E. (2011). Employment and aging. In R. H. Binstock & L. K. George (Eds.), *Handbook of aging and the social sciences* (7th ed., pp. 193–206). Burlington, MA: Academic Press.

Robertson, A. (1991). The politics of Alzheimer's disease: A case study in apocalyptic demography. In M. Minkler & C. Estes (Eds.), *Critical perspectives on aging: The political and moral economy of growing old* (pp. 135–152). Amityville, NY: Baywood.

Rodman, H. (1963). The lower-class value stretch. *Social Forces, 42*, 205–215.

Rosow, L., & Breslau, N. (1966). A Guttman health scale for the aged. *Gerontology, 21*, 556–559.

Ross, H., Stein, N., Trabasso, T., Woody, E., & Ross, M. (2005). The quality of family relationships within and across generations: A social relations analysis. *International Journal of Behavioral Development, 29*, 110–119.

Rothgang, H. (2010). Social insurance for long-term care: An evaluation of the German model. *Social Policy and Administration, 44*, 436–460.

Rubin, G. S., Roche, K. B., Prasada-Rao, P., & Fried, L. P. (1994). Visual impairment and disability in older adults. *Optometry and vision science: Official publication of the American Academy of Optometry, 71*(12), 750–760.

Ruggles, S. (2007). The decline of intergenerational coresidence in the United States, 1850–2000. *American Sociological Review, 72*, 964–989.

Russell, A., & McWhirter, N. (1987). *1988 Guiness book of world records.* New York, NY: Bantam Books.

Sanders, J. (2002). Financing and organization of national health systems. In B. J. Fried & L. M. Gaydos (Eds.), *World health systems: Challenges and perspectives* (2nd ed., pp. 25–38). Chicago, IL: Health Administration Press.

Sanderson, W., & Scherbov, S. (2008). Rethinking age and aging. *Population Bulletin, 63*(4), 3–16.

Schore, J., Foster, L., & Phillips, B. (2007). Consumer enrollment and experiences in the cash and counseling program. *Health Services Research, 42*, 446–466.

Schulz, E. (2010). *The long-term care system in Germany.* DIW Berlin (European Network of Economic Policy Research Institute Research Report No. 78). Retrieved from http://aei.pitt.edu/14680/

Searight, H. R., & Gafford, J. (2005). Cultural diversity at the end of life: Issues and guidelines for family physicians. *American Academy of Family Physicians, 71*(3), 515–522.

Sepulveda, C., Marlin, A., Yoshida, T., & Ulrich, A. (2002). Palliative care: The World Health Organization's global perspective. *Journal of Pain and Symptom Management, 24*(2), 91–96.

Shanmugasundaram, S., Chapman, Y., & O'Connor, M. (2006). Development of palliative care in India: An overview. *International Journal of Nursing Practice, 12*, 241–246.

Shimizutani, S., & Takashi, O. (2010). New evidence on initial transition from career job to retirement in Japan. *Industrial Relations: A Journal of Economy and Society, 49*(2), 248–274. doi:10.1111/j.1468-232X.2010.00598.x

Shrestha, S., & Zarit, S. H. (2012). Cultural and contextual analysis of quality of life among older Nepali women. *Journal of Cross-Cultural Gerontology, 27*(2), 163–182. doi:10.1007/s10823-012-9167-0

Shugarman, L. R., Decker, S. L., & Bercovitz, A. (2009). Demographic and social characteristics and spending at the end of life. *Journal of Pain and Symptom Management, 38*(1), 15–26.

Siegel, J. S. (1990). Review of *A fresh map of life: The emergence of the Third Age*, by P. Laslett. *Population and Development Review, 16*(2), 363–367.

Silverstein, M., & Bengtson, V. L. (1997). Intergenerational solidarity and the structure of adult child-parent relationships in American families. *American Journal of Sociology, 103*, 429–460.

Simpson, R. (2006). *Childbearing on hold: Delayed childbearing and childlessness in Britain.* Centre for Research on Families and Relationships (Research Briefing 29). Retrieved from http://www.crfr.ac.uk/briefinglist.htm#rb29

Sirven, N., & Debrand, T. (2008). Social participation and healthy ageing: An international comparison using SHARE data. *Social Science & Medicine, 67*, 2017–2026.

Sobotka, T., & Testa, M. R. (2006). *Childlessness intentions in Europe: A comparison of Belgium (Flanders), Germany, Italy, Poland.* Paper presented at the 2006 European Population Conference, Liverpool, England. Retrieved from http://www.oceaw.ac.at/vid/download/epc_sobotka.pdf

Song, L., Li, S., & Feldman, M. W. (2012). Out-migration of young adults and gender division of intergenerational support in rural China. *Research on Aging, 34*(4), 399–424. doi:10.1177/0164027511436321

Sousa, L., Silva, A. R., Marques, F., & Santos, L. (2009). Constructing family integrity in later life. In L. Sousa (Ed.), *Families in later life: Emerging themes and challenges* (pp. 163–184). Fargo, ND: Nova Science.

Stanton, M. E. (2006). Patterns of kinship and residence. In B. B. Ingoldsby & S. D. Smith (Eds.), *Families in global and multicultural perspective* (2nd ed., pp. 79–98). Thousand Oaks, CA: Sage.

Stone, R. (2011). *Long-term care for the elderly.* Washington, DC: The Urban Institute Press.

Su, B. R., Shen, X. Y., & Wei, Z. (2006). Leisure life in later years: Differences between rural and urban elderly residents in China. *Journal of Leisure Research, 38*(3), 381–397.

Subedi, J. (1989). Modern health services and health care behavior: A survey of Kathmandu, Nepal. *Journal of Health and Social Behavior, 30*, 412–420.

Subedi, J., & Subedi, S. (1993). The contribution of modern medicine in a traditional system: The case of Nepal. In P. Conrad & E. B. Gallagher (Eds.), *Health and health care in developing countries: Sociological perspectives.* Philadelphia, PA: Temple University Press.

Sullivan, D. F. (1971). A single index of mortality and morbidity. *HSMHA Health Reports, 86*(4), 347–354.

Sung, K. T. (2001). Elder respect: Exploration of ideals and forms in East Asia. *Journal of Aging Studies, 15*, 13–26.

Survey of Health, Ageing, and Retirement in Europe (2013). *Home page.* Retrieved from http://www.share-project.org/

Szinovacz, M. E., & Davey, A. (2005). Retirement and marital decision making: Effects of retirement satisfaction. *Journal of Marriage and Family, 67*(2), 387–398. doi:10.1111/j.0022-2445.2005.00123.x

Takagi, E., Silverstein, M., & Crimmins, E. (2007). Intergenerational coresidence of older adults in Japan: Conditions for cultural plasticity. *Journal of Gerontology: Social Sciences, 62*(5), S330–S339.

Tausig, M., Subedi, S., Broughton, C., Subedi, J., & Williams-Blangero, S. (2003). Measuring community mental health in developing societies: Evaluation of a checklist format in Nepal. *International Journal of Social Psychiatry, 49*(4), 269–286.

Thompson, K. (2013, January 21). The family next door. *The Washington Post,* AA14.

Treas, J. (1995). Older Americans in the 1990s and beyond. *Population Bulletin, 50*(2), 2–46.

Trydegard, G.-B., & Thorslund, M. (2010). One uniform welfare state or a multitude of welfare municipalities? The evolution of local variation in Swedish elder care. *Social Policy and Administration, 44*(4), 495–511.

Tsutsui, T., & Muramatsu, N. (2005). Care-needs certification in the long-term care insurance system of Japan. *Journal of the American Geriatrics Society, 53*, S22–S27.

United Nations. (1983). *Vienna International Plan of Action on Ageing.* New York, NY: Author. Retrieved from http://www.un.org/es/globalissues/ageing/docs/vipaa.pdf

United Nations. (2001). *World population ageing: 1950–2050.* New York, NY: Author.

United Nations. (2002). *World population ageing: 1950–2050.* Department of Economic and Social Affairs, Population Division. New York, NY: Author.

United Nations. (2003). *International plan of action on ageing.* Retrieved from http://www.un.org/esa/socdev/ageing/ageipaa1.htm

United Nations. (2009). *World population ageing.* New York, NY: Author. Retrieved from http://www.un.org/esa/population/publications/WPA2009/WPA2009_WorkingPaper.pdf

United Nations. (2010). *World population ageing 2009.* ST/ESA/SER.A/295. New York, NY: Author.

United Nations. (n.d.). *Definition of NGOs.* Retrieved from http://www.ngo .org/ngoinfo/define.html

United Nations Department of Economic and Social Affairs. (2002). *Political declaration and Madrid International Plan of Action on Ageing.* New York, NY: United Nations. Retrieved from http://social.un.org/index/Age-ing/Resources/MadridInternationalPlanofActiononAgeing.aspx or the English version http://social.un.org/index/Portals/0/ageing/docu-ments/Fulltext-E.pdf

United Nations Department of Economic and Social Affairs. (2005). *Living arrangements of older persons around the world.* New York, NY: United Nations. Retrieved from http://www.un.org/esa/population/publica-tions/livingarrangement/report.html

United Nations Department of Economic and Social Affairs. (2009). *World population ageing 2009.* New York, NY: Author.

United Nations Department of Economic and Social Affairs. (2011). *World population prospects: The 2010 revision.* New York, NY: Author.

United Nations Development Program: China & Development Research Center of State Council. (2005). *China human development report 2005.* Retrieved June 11, 2009, from http://www.undp.org.cn/downloads/nhdr2005/NHDR2005_complete.pdf

United Nations Development Program: China & China Institute for Reform and Development. (2009). *China human development report: 2007–2008.* Retrieved June 11, 2009, from http://hdr.undp.org/en/reports/nationalreports/asiathepacific/china/China_2008_en.pdf

United Nations Development Programme. (2005). *Human development report.* Oxford, England: Oxford University Press.

United Nations Development Programme. (2011). *Human development report, 2011.* Oxford, UK: Oxford University Press.

United Nations Economic and Social Commission for Asia and the Pacific. (n.d.). *What is MIPAA?* Retrieved from http://www.unescap.org/sdd/issues/ageing/mipaa.asp

United Nations Economic and Social Council. (2009). *Committee on Economic, Social and Cultural Rights, forty-second session, Geneva, 4-22 May, 2009. Agenda item 3,* General Comment No. 20.GE 09-43405 E 090709. Retrieved from http://idsn.org/fileadmin/user_folder/pdf/New_files/UN/CESCR_GR20.pdf

United Nations General Assembly. (1948). *Universal declaration of human rights.* Retrieved from http://www.un.org/en/documents/udhr/index .shtml

United Nations General Assembly. (2010). *Follow-up to the Second World Assembly on Ageing: Report of the Secretary-General.* Retrieved from http://daccess-dds-ny.un.org/doc/UNDOC/GEN/N02/439/32/PDF/N0243932.pdf?OpenElement

United Nations General Assembly. (2012). *General Assembly GA/11331.* Sixty-seventh General Assembly Plenary, 60th Meeting. Retrieved from http://www.un.org/News/Press/docs/2012/ga11331.doc.htm

United Nations General Assembly. (2013). *A/RES/67/143.* 67th Session Agenda Item 27 c. February 21, 2013. Retrieved from http://www.un.org/en/ga/67/resolutions.shtml

UNICEF. (2006). *State of the world's children report 2007: Women and children, the double dividend of gender equality.* New York, NY: Author. Retrieved from http://www.unicef.org/publications/files/The_State_of_the_Worlds_Children__2007_e.pdf

United Nations Office of the High Representative for Least Developed Countries. (2010). *Criteria for identification of LDCs.* Retrieved from http://www.unohrlls.org/en/ldc/related/59/

United Nations Population Fund. (2012). *Ageing in the twenty-first century: A celebration and a challenge.* New York, NY: Author. Retrieved from http://www.helpage.org/resources/ageing-in-the-21st-century-a-celebration-and-a-challenge/

United Nations Statistics Division. (2010). *Life expectancy at birth (women and men, years).* Retrieved August 13, 2010, from http://data.un.org/CountryProfile.aspx?crName=China

U.S. Central Intelligence Agency. (2013). *World fact book.* Retrieved March 7, 2013, from https://www.cia.gov/library/publications/the-world-fact-book/index.html

U.S. CIA World Factbook. (2011). *Kenya.* Retrieved February 2, 2012, from https://www.cia.gov/library/publications/the-world-factbook/geos/ke.html, Kenya

U.S. Department of Health and Human Services. (n.d.). *HHS: What we do.* Retrieved from http://www.hhs.gov/about/whatwedo/html

U.S. National Center on Complementary and Alternative Medicine (2008). *Complementary, alternative, or integrative health: What's in a name?* Retrieved August 4, 2013, from http://nccam.nih.gov/health/whatiscam

U.S. National Institute of Aging. (2007). *Why population aging matters: A global perspective.* Washington, DC: U.S. Department of State. Retrieved from http://www.nia.nih.gov/sites/default/files/WPAM.pdf

U.S. Social Security Administration (2011). *Social security programs throughout the world: Kenya.* Retrieved February 2, 2012, from http://www.ssa.gov/policy/docs/progdesc/ssptw/2010-2011/africa/kenya.html

U.S. Social Security Administration, Office of Research, Evaluation and Statistics (1999). *Social security programs throughout the world.* Washington, DC: U.S. Government Printing Office.

Vaupel, J. W., Manton, K. G., & Stallard, E. (1979). The impact of heterogeneity in individual frailty on the dynamics of mortality. *Demography, 16,* 439–454.

Verbrugge, L. M., & Jette, A. M. (1994). The disablement process. *Social Science & Medicine, 38*(1), 1–14.

Vlachantoni, A., & Falkingham, J. (2011). *Exploring gender and pensions in Japan, Malaysia and Vietnam* (CRA Discussion Paper No. 1101). Southampton, England: Centre for Research on Ageing, School of Social Science, University of Southampton.

Vos, R., Ocampo, J. A., & Cortez, A. L. (2008). *Aging and development.* New York, NY: United Nations.

Wang, R. (2000). Critical health literacy: A case study from China in schistosomiasis control. *Health Promotion International, 15*(3), 269–274.

Warner, D. F., Hayward, M. D., & Hardy, M. A. (2010). The retirement life course in America at the dawn of the twenty-first century. *Population Research and Policy Review, 29,* 893–919. doi:10.1007/s11113-009-9173-2

Weibel-Orlando, J. (2009). La cura degli nostri cari anziani [Family and community elder care roles in contemporary Italy]. In J. Sokolovsky (Ed.), *The cultural context of aging: Worldwide perspectives* (3rd ed., pp. 536–549). Westport, CT: Praeger.

Weiss, B. D. (2007). *Health literacy and patient safety: Help patients understand: Manual for clinicians,* 2nd ed. Chicago, IL: American Medical Association Foundation.

Weiss, G. L., & Lonnquist, L. E. (2012). *The sociology of health, healing, and illness.* Upper Saddle River, NJ: Prentice-Hall.

Weitz, R. (2010). *The sociology of health, illness, and health care,* 5th ed. Belmont, CA: Thomson Wadsworth.

White, A., & Ernst, E. (2004). A brief history of accupuncture. *Rheumatology, 43,* 662–663.

Whittington, F. J., & Kunkel, S. R. (2013a). Think globally, act locally: The maturing of a worldwide science and practice of aging. *Generations, 37,* 6–11.

Whittington, F. J., & Kunkel, S. R. (Eds.) (2013b). Our world growing older: A look at global aging. Special issue of *Generations, 37.* San Francisco, CA: American Society on Aging.

Winkelmann-Gleed, A. (2012). Retirement or committed to work? Conceptualizing prolonged labour market participation through organisational commitment. *Employee Relations, 34*(1), 80–90. doi:10.1108/01425451211183273

Wongboonsin, K., Guest, P., & Prachuabmoh, F. (2005). Demographic change and the demographic dividend in Thailand. *Asian Population Studies, 1*(2), 245–256. Retrieved from http://pdfserve.informaworld.com/707869_727239124.pdf

Wood, A., Robertson, M., & Wintersgill, D. (2010). *A comparative view of international approaches to mandatory retirement* (Research Report No. 674). Norwich, England: Department for Work and Pensions.

World Bank. (2010). *Long-term care policies for older populations in new EU member states and Croatia: Challenges and opportunities.* Washington, DC: Author.

World Bank Development Group. (2012). Retrieved from http://data.worldbank.org/indicator/SI.POV.GINI

World Health Organization. (2006). *The top ten causes of death.* Retrieved from www.who/int/mediacentre/factsheets/fs310/en/index2.html

World Health Organization. (2008). *Traditional medicine: Fact sheet.* Retrieved from http://www.who.int/mediacentre/factsheets/fs134/en/

World Health Organization. (2010). *Older people and primary health care.* Retrieved from http://who.int/ageing/primary_health_care/en/index.html

World Health Organization. (2011). *Global status report on non-communicable diseases 2010.* Retrieved from www.who.int/nmh/publicaitons/ncd_report2010/en/index.html

World Health Organization. (2012). *Palliative care.* Retrieved from www.who.int/cancer/palliative/en

World Health Organization. (2013). *Noncommunicable diseases fact sheet.* Retrieved from www.who.int/mediacentre/factsheets/fs355/en/

World Health Organization and National Institute on Aging. (2011). *Global health and aging.* Retrieved from www.who.int/ageing/publications/global_health/en/

World Health Organization (n.d.). The top ten causes of death. Retrieved from http://www.who/int/mediacentre/factsheets/fs310/en/index2.html

Wu, B., Carter, M. W., Goins, R. T., & Cheng, C. (2005). Emerging services for community-based long-term care in urban China: A systematic analysis of Shanghai's community-based agencies. *Journal of Aging & Social Policy, 17*, 37–60.

Wu, B., Mao, Z., & Xu, Q. (2008). Institutional care for elders in rural China. *Journal of Aging & Social Policy, 20*, 218–239.

Yaukey, D. (1985). *Demography: The study of human population.* Prospect Heights, IL: Waveland Press.

Yin, S., & Kent, M. (2008). *Kenya: The demographics of a country in turmoil.* Retrieved from http://www.prb.org/Articles/2008/kenya.aspx

Yong, V., & Saito, Y. (2011). National long-term care insurance policy in Japan a decade after implementation: Some lessons for aging countries. *Ageing International.* doi:10.1007/s12126-011-9109-0

Zeinah, G. F., Al-Kindi, S. G., & Hassan, A. A. (2013). Middle East experience in palliative care. *American Journal of Hospice & Palliative Medicine, 30*, 94–99.

Zhan, H. J., Feng, Z., Chen, Z., & Feng, X. (2011). The role of the family in institutional long-term care: Cultural management of filial piety in China. *International Journal of Social Welfare, 20*, S212–S134.

Zhang, H. (2009). The new realities of aging in contemporary China: Coping with the decline in family care. In J. Sokolovsky (Ed.), *The cultural context of aging: Worldwide perspectives* (3rd ed., pp.196–215). Westport, CT: Praeger.

Zhang, Y. (2011). *China's long-term care strategy for the elderly* (EAI Background Brief No. 668).

Zhao, L.-T., & Sheng, S.-X. (2009). *Old age care in China.* East Asia Institute at National University of Singapore. Retrieved from http://www.eai.nus .edu.sg/BB432.pdf

Zhu, Y. (2009). Transition and challenge: China's population at the beginning of the 21st century. *Journal of Population Research, 26*(1), 103–105.

Zimmer, Z. (2007). *HIV/AIDS and the living arrangements of older persons across the sub-Saharan African region* (University of Utah Institute of Public and International Affairs Working Paper, 21 November).

Index

active life expectancy (ALE), 111, 115

Activities of Daily Living (ADL), 40, 112–118, 121, 151, 163, 169, 170, 171, 173, 185. *See also* disability; Instrumental Activities of Daily Living (IADL)

Affordable Care Act (ACA), 142

Africa, 4, 11, 12, 57, 64, 87, 91–93, 98, 120, 132, 143, 149, 157, 197, 226–227, 229, 231, 245–246

Age Demands Action (ADA), 244. *See also* HelpAge International

age discrimination, 11, 236, 244. *See also* Age Demands Action

aged dependency ratios, 8, 83, 93, 94

ALE. *See* active life expectancy

Australia, 4, 14, 60, 78, 83, 105, 120, 130, 158, 199–200, 202–203, 205–208, 245–246

Ayurveda. *See* India, traditional medicine

baby boomers, 76, 85, 96, 97, 210, 217, 271

Bangladesh, 5, 23-26, 28. *See also* single-nation global aging research

basic activities of daily living, 113. *See also* disability, definition

Beveridge model, 138, 141–142. *See also* Bismarck model; National Health Insurance (NHI) model; out-of-pocket model
adoption, 142

and the Affordable Care Act (ACA), 142

and American military veterans, 140

Bismarck model, 138, 140. *See also* Beveridge model; National Health Insurance (NHI) model; out-of-pocket model

and the National Health Insurance (NHI) model, 143

Cabrera, Angel, 262–264

CAM. *See* medicine, complementary and alternative (CAM)

Canada, 68, 75, 83, 105, 120, 142, 158, 199, 205, 244–246, 261

Chapin, Tom, 219–220

caregiving, 7, 16, 55, 165, 167, 168–169, 172, 173, 176, 179, 180–181, 184, 221, 229, 231, 232, 236, 237

childlessness, 227

China
culture, 6
development of the welfare state, 13
fertility drop, 214–215
health care system, 8
limited infrastructure for older people, 7
current developments, 7
one-child policy, 6 (*see also* fertility rate, in China)
family support for the elderly, 7

population pyramids, 2010 vs.
2050, 6
retirement, 214–218
China (*cont.*)
cultural and social realities,
216–217
tradition of filial piety, 15
possible redefinition, 15–16 (*see also*
value stretch)
traditional culture, 15
China Health and Retirement
Longitudinal Studies (CHARLS),
215–216
China's 12th Five-Year Plan
(2011–2015), 247
civic engagement
in Germany, 9–10
Madrid International Plan of Action
on Ageing (MIPAA), 18
in the U.S., 9–10
civil rights movement, 154
cognitive impairment, 122
communication, intergenerational, 28
comparative research in social sciences
and humanities, 36, 45
comparative studies of global aging,
28–45. *See also* global patterns
research; single-nation global
aging research
challenges inherent in
conceptualization and
measurement, 40–42
getting valid data, 42–43
respecting participants, 43–45
unit of analysis, 35–40
distinctive goals, challenges, and
value of, 29
importance of, 29–33
trade-off with in-depth focus on
uniqueness, 30
Confucianism, 15, 217
consumer rights movement, 154
cross-cultural research. *See* comparative
studies of global aging
Cuba, 47–52
cultural values, 15, 17, 37
culture
analysis in comparative research, 36
definition, 36–37
differences in comparative studies, 34

shaping the experiences of aging, 6,
29 (*see also* comparative studies of
global aging)
transmission of, 37

demographic data, 95–96
demographic divide, 81–82
demographic dividend(s), 83–84
second, 84
in Thailand, 83
demographic transition. *See also* fertility;
mortality; population pyramids
in China, 6, 214 (*see also* China,
one-child policy)
in developed compared to developing
nations, 82
in developing countries, 14
earlier stages of, 150
emergence of hospice service and, 154
in Kenya, 11
and mandatory retirement, 7
and the nature of mortality
changes, 80
and population aging, 111
second stage, 80
varying speeds in different countries
of, 83
in Vietnam, 83
in Western Europe, 79
demographic transition theory, 77–81,
93–94
mortality and fertility decline, 77
and industrialization, 77
strengths and weaknesses, 80
demography. *See also* demographic
transition
of aging, xiii, 27, 75–97
and changes in age structure, 111
changes in, and retirement, 197
and mortality, 100, 114
depression, 28, 32, 126
developing nations
age, gender, and power, 5
aging population
challenges of, 3
lack of adequate programs for, 2
unique challenges posed by, 2
challenges, 10
development of the welfare state, 15
lack of adequate programs, 2

life expectancies, 2
proportion of older people, 1
proportion of world's population, 2
rate of aging, 4
Second World Assembly on
    Ageing, 17
social and economic transformation, 20
disability-free life expectancy (DFLE).
    See active life expectancy (ALE)
disabled life expectancy (DLE), 115
disability
    and active life expectancy, 109–127
    comparative measurement of,
        114–117
    definition, 112–114
    in the developed world, 118–119
    in the developing world, 120
    relevance for global aging,
        111–112
disability-adjusted life year (DALY), 117
disease
    prevention, 9, 50, 145, 148
    shift from infectious to chronic, 21, 27

Economic and Social Commission for
    Asia and the Pacific (ESCAP),
    245, 247
economic development
    and aging, 3, 237
    and care of older people, 216, 247–248
    and changes in functions of
        traditional family, 236
    China's one-child policy and, 6
    and demographic dividends, 83
    and the epidemiological transition, 130
    in global patterns research, 27
    interactions of policies, cultures,
        and, 29
    in Kenya, 11–12
    and the Madrid International Plan of
        Action on Ageing (MIPAA), 18
    and palliative care, 39, 157
    and population aging, 76, 79
    and population pyramids, 87, 89
    and social status of older people,
        31–32
    and the welfare state, 13, 15, 236
English Longitudinal Study of Ageing,
    41. *See also* comparative studies of
    global aging

entitlements to LTC services and
    support, 165
epidemiological transition, 130, 197
    second, 111–112
European Health Expectancy
    Monitoring Unit (EHEMU), 118.
    See also disability
exotic other, 20

fallacy of the demographic imperative,
    96. *See also* demographic data
families, caregiving, and community
    support systems, 219–254
    cultural values, 230–236
families, intergenerational, 227–228,
    233–234, 242–243
family care, traditional system of, 15
family (families)
    aging, 225–230
    and household structures,
        225–228
    and intergenerational
        transfers, 228
    and other adults as caregivers, 229
    evolving definitions of, 221–225
    integrity, 233–236
    meaning of, in African American
        community, 15 (*see also* value
        stretch)
    ties, in Confucianism, 15
    universal concept of, 220–221
    values, 6, 230–233
fertility. *See also* demographic divide;
    mortality
    developed vs. developing nations,
        changes in, 82–83
    decline in, 77, 79
    high, in developing countries, 2–3
    rate
        in Bangladesh, 25
        in China, 6, 214–215 (*see also* China,
            one-child policy)
        in Germany, 8
    revised patterns of, 21
    of young societies, 76
filial piety
    and Confucianism, 231
    definition, 37
    and filial responsibility, 232
    tradition of, in China, 15

fitness
mental, 122
physical, 32
folk medicine, 134–135
Forster, John, 219–220
France
Bismarck model, 140
comparative TLE, 119
public pension systems, 63
replacement income calculation, 67
self-perceptions of aging in Morocco vs., 28
speed of population aging, 82
functional limitation, 114, 118, 198, 199. *See also* disability

gamma-Gompertz model, 102–103. *See also* Gompertz's law
generational equity, 9. *See also* Germany, values in
geriatric medicine, 8, 50, 264
Germany
aged dependency ratio, 8
baby boom in the 1950s and 1960s, 8
comparative study of Vietnam and, 32
and development of the welfare state, 13
inverted population pyramid, 8
pension system, 8
population pyramids, 2010 and 2050, 8
shrinking labor force, 8
sustained low fertility, 8
values in, 9
gerontologists, 48
gerontology, 21, 31, 35, 264
global citizenship, 264
global entrepreneurship, 263–264
global leadership, 262, 265
global mindset, 262
global patterns research, 27
global village, 19
globalization, 257, 261, 262–265
Gompertz's law, 100–102. *See also* gamma-Gompertz model
Great Recession of 2008–2009, 67

Haiti, 4
handicapped, 109. *See also* disability
harmonization, 41. *See also* comparative studies of global aging

health
and behavior of older people, 145–146
decline of, as a result of aging, 32
focus in Kenya on, 12
and health care systems, 129–162
insurance, 13, 53 (*see also* Medicare)
literacy, 149–151
promotion, 51, 145, 148–151 (*see also* disease prevention; self-care)
health-adjusted life expectancy (HALE), 117. *See also* healthy life expectancy (HLE)
data in industrialized nations, 117
in developed and developing nations, 120
health care
free, in Cuba, 49
system(s), 97, 129–152
in China, 8
and older people, 144–145
types of, 134–138
in the U.S., 60 (*see also* Medicare)
unequal access to, for older people, in Kenya, 11–12
Health and Retirement Survey, 41. *See also* comparative studies of global aging
healthy life expectancy (HLE), 74, 116. *See also* health-adjusted life expectancy (HALE)
healthy life years (HLYs), 118, 119, 268. *See also* disability, and healthy life expectancy
and total life expectancy (TLE), 118–119
HelpAge International, 11, 109, 181, 236, 241, 244, 250, 252. *See also* Age Demands Action; NGOs
HIV/AIDS epidemic
in Africa, 11
and focus on end-of-life care, 39 (*see also* palliative care)
in Kenya, 11
hospice, 28, 154–156, 160, 161. *See also* palliative care
Human Development Index, 42
Human Mortality Database (2011), 103

illiteracy, 11, 76, 190
incarceration, 11, 229. *See also* skipped-generation households

income inequality
  gini coefficient as measure of, 103
  and heterogeneity in mortality
    patterns, 100–107
income security, 54
  in Chinese pension system, 7
  lack of, in Kenya, 11–12
  recommendations related to, 17
India
  compared to the U.S., 76–77
  competition for mass popular
    culture, 258
  co-residence and family
    caregiving, 16
  diverse culture, 156
  growth of older population, 1
  HALE at age 60, 120
  health care focus, 76
  illiteracy, 76
  kinship ties, 223
  NGOs in, 236, 244 (*see also* HelpAge
    International)
  out-of-pocket system, 143
  palliative care, 159
  pension plans for civil service
    employees, 204
  proportion of older people, 2
    vs. the U.S., 76
  role of families, 160
  role of old-age homes, 16–17
  traditional medicine, 135–136
  type of LTC services and supports,
    177, 183–184
Industrial Revolution
  and emergence of welfare state, 57
  and shifts in occupational
    structure, 197
  and role of family and religious
    organizations, 56
industrialization
  lack of causal connections between
    demographic trends and, 79
  and modernization of societies, 31
    (*see also* modernization
    theory)
  and the welfare state, 13, 57
inheritance
  and family integrity, 234–235
  protection for older people, 11
    in Kenya, 11

Instrumental Activities of Daily Living
    (IADL), 40, 113–114, 124–125,
    164, 169, 171. *See also* Activities of
    Daily Living (ADL)
interdependence between the old and
    the young in a family, 232
  emphasis of Confucianism on, 217
  in Nepal, 40
intergenerational solidarity conflict,
    233–234
intergenerational solidarity model,
    233, 238
intergenerational transfers, 228–229
International Handbook on Aging
    (Palmore, Whittington, &
    Kunkel), 47, 50
International Year of Older Persons
    (IYOP), 17, 214. *See also* aging,
    international initiatives on
IRBs (institutional review boards), 44
Israel, 21, 41, 238
Italy
  aged dependency ratio, 8
  aging index, 93
  and the Beveridge model, 142
  and the convergence hypothesis, 14
  growth of older population, 1, 97
  as the oldest country in Europe, 71
  and terminally ill persons, 161
  type of LTC services and supports,
    165, 173–174

Japan
  aged dependency ratio, 8
  and blood pressure, 132
  and the Bismarck model, 140
  breast cancer in women, 133
  challenges related to aging, 3, 8
  and the convergence hypothesis, 14
  dependency ratio, 93
  economic development and
    population aging, 80
  economic troubles, 107
  growth of older population, 1, 90,
    91, 97
  HALE values at age 60, 120
  hospice development in South Korea,
    Taiwan, and, 28
  life expectancy, 91
  LTC services and supports, 169–171

Japan (*cont.*)
  mortality, 103
  proportion aged 65 or older,
    89–90
  support for the terminally ill, 160
  TLE of women, 121
  traditions, 55–56
Joint Action European Health & Life
    Expectancy Information System
    (JA:EHLEIS), 118. *See also*
    disability

Kenya
  constitutional rights of older
    population, 12
  and development of the welfare state, 13
  eligibility for old-age pension, 12
  health-related trends and
    challenges, 11
  life expectancy at birth, 12
  national policy on aging and older
    persons, 11–12
  population pyramids for 2010 and
    2050, 10
  poverty and health challenges, 10
  problems faced by older people, 11
  social support systems for rural older
    adults, 250–254
  World Health Organization's Quality
    of Life (WHOQOL) project, 42

life course perspective, 36, 58, 195–196,
    221, 255–256
life expectancy, 91–92, 114. *See also*
    active life expectancy (ALE);
    demographic divide; population
    aging, measures of; total life
    expectancy (TLE)
  achievement of maximum, 67–68
  in China, 210, 215
  in Cuba, 47, 51
  and the demographic divide, 81
  and disability rates, 163
  and economic inequality, 80
  and the epidemiological transition,
    130, 154
  gender differences, 91–92, 114–115
  increasing, 27, 112, 154
    adjustment of retirement ages
      to, 206

and the labor force, 197 (*see also*
    retirement)
  in Germany, 8
  in India, 76
  in Japan, 207
  in Kenya, 11, 12 (*see also* HIV/AIDS
    epidemic)
  as measure of population aging, 84
  in Nepal, 182
  in Nicaragua, 187, 189
  and palliative care, 156
  and pension age, 60
  and prospective age, 95
  race/ethnic differences, 114–115
  speed of population aging and, 82
  in Swaziland, 91
  in Sweden, 63, 74
  in Thailand, 91
lifelong learning, 9–10
life span, 21, 91. *See also* life
    expectancy; population aging,
    measures of
living arrangements, 32, 225–228
  among older people, 27
  and filial piety, 37
location. *See also* nation-state
  as proxy for culture, 37
  as unit of analysis in comparative
    research, 36 (*see also* comparative
    studies of global aging,
    challenges inherent in)
long-term care (LTC) services and
    supports, 163–192. *See also*
    Medicaid
  cross-cutting issues for an aging
    planet, 183–185
  definition, 164–165
  and dependency assessment, 171
  entitlements to, 165
  and Fair Deal legislation, 173
  typologies of, 165–182
  universal systems of, 166
    social long-term care insurance
      (LTCI), 166, 168–169,
      170–172, 174
    taxed-based, 166
Luxembourg Income Study, 27. *See also*
    research, global aging, types of
    investigation in the study of;
    global patterns research

Madrid International Plan of Action on Ageing (MIPAA), 17–18, 241–247, 252. *See also* NGOs, expanding role of; aging, international initiatives on
Madrid Plan, *See* Madrid International Plan of Action on Ageing (MIPAA)
Malaysia, 120
means-testing, 185
Medicaid, 54, 175
    and LTC in the U.S., 174
    and Medicare, 217
medical consumerism, 145
medical pluralism, 134, 142, 145, 148
Medicare, 53–54, 60, 76, 138, 174, 217, 236, 261
    and the Affordable Care Act, 142
    and the National Health Insurance (NHI) model, 140
    palliative care approaches, 160
medicine
    complementary and alternative (CAM), 145–146
        and aging, 146–148
    folk, 134–135, 137, 148
    modern, 137–138
        models of organizing and financing, 138–144
    traditional, 135–137
Mexico, 19
    folk medicine, 135
    gerontology, 21
    type of LTC services and supports, 177
migration
    in China, 6–7, 15
    and the welfare state, 13
    global, 220
    importance in age and gender structure, 85
    and industrialization, 57
    in Japan, 56
    in Kenya, 180, 184, 250
    in Nepal, 184
    out of Estonia, 175
    patterns, 38
    and patterns of co-residence, 227
    and population pyramids, 84–85, 86
    and the status of older people, 31
    in Thailand, 177

MIPAA. *See* Madrid International Plan of Action on Ageing
modern medicine, 137–138
modernization theory, 31–32, 231
Morocco, 28
mortality. *See also* Gompertz's law
    and economic inequality, 81
    improvements in, 81
    infant, in Cuba, 49, 51
    low, in China, 6
    in Kenya, as a result of HIV/AIDS, 11

nation-state, in comparative research, 37–38. *See also* comparative studies of global aging, challenges inherent in
National Cash and Counseling Demonstration and Evaluation, 175. *See also* long-term care (LTC) services and supports
National Council on Aging (NCOA), 48
National Health Insurance (NHI) model, 138, 142–143. *See also* Bismarck model; Beveridge model; out-of-pocket model
    and Medicare, 140
NGOs, and support to older people, xiv, 221, 236–237, 238, 239, 240–241, 246. *See also* HelpAge International
    in Bangladesh, 25
    expanding role of, 241–245
    in India, 236, 244
    in Kenya, 109, 252, 253
    in Nepal, 182
    in Thailand, 178
Nepal
    functional health, 40
    interdependence, vs. independence, 40
    methodological problems measuring psychiatric disorders in the U.S., 124–127
Nicaragua, 187–192

Obama family, 220
out-of-pocket model, 138, 143–144. *See also* Bismarck model; Beveridge model; National Health Insurance (NHI) model
    in the U.S., 140, 143

palliative care, 39, 145, 154–162.
See also disease, burden of,
shift from infectious to
chronic
as a global public health initiative,
152–162
and religious beliefs, 155–156
and the World Health Organization
(WHO), 157
Palmore, Erdman B., 29
pension replacement rates, 201, 203
pension system(s). See also
welfare state
age eligibility in, 60, 199
in China, 7
changes in financing due to shifting
age structures, 7
citizen entitlement to, 59–61
defined-benefit (DB) plan, 196, 202
defined-contribution (DC)
plan, 202
distribution of program types, 62–63
earnings-related entitlement to, 59, 61,
62, 63, 64, 68
emergence of, in developing
nations, 17
in Germany, 8
need-based eligibility in, 60, 61
pay as you go, 7
pensionable age in, 63 (see also
pension systems,
retrenchment of)
private, 202–204
the "three-legged stool" of
retirement income, 202
privatized, 58, 64, 65
provident funds in, 61, 64
replacement income, 68
retrenchment of, 58, 63–64
and pronatalist considerations, 64
sustainability and shrinking labor
force, 8
in the U.S.,
funding of, 59
universal, 58, 59, 61, 68
Philippines
comparative HALE at age 60, 120
financial assistance to adult
children, 228
urban migration, 228

physical impairment, 114, 122. See also
disability; cognitive impairment
and functional deficit, 109
shift from early to late life of, 111
population aging. See also population
pyramids
culture, social change, and, 4–6
demands placed on society by, xiii
balance of family, community, and
government involvement, 13, 16
(see also value stretch)
education of citizens about aging, xiii
in France, 82
measures of, 84–95
aging index, 92–93
dependency ratios, 93–95
life expectancy, 91–92 (see also HIV/
AIDS epidemic)
median age, 90–91
population pyramids, 84–89
prospective age, 84, 95
proportion aged, 89–90
speed of, 82–83, 97
in South Korea, 82
in Sweden, 82
in Thailand, 82
in the U.S., 82
universality of, xiii, 4
population pyramid(s), 6
of China, 6 (see also China, one-child
policy)
for Germany for 2010 and 2050, 8
inverted, 8, 10 (see also pension
system)
of Kenya for 2010 and 2050, 10
of United Arab Emirates for 2010, 87
of United States for 2010 and 2050, 86
prospective age, 84, 95

racism, 20
Republic of Korea. See South Korea
research, global aging
cross-national comparative research,
28–33
and global leadership, 255–265
tourist approach to study of, 20
types of investigation in, 27–29
cross-national comparative
research, 28–45
global patterns research, 27

single-nation research, 28
studies within a country, 28
retirement. *See also* work and retirement
causes of, 197–201
and the Industrial Revolution, 197
in China, 7, 214–218
in developing nations, 210–212
different forms of, 204–210
inadequacy of pensions, 7
mandatory, 193, 196, 198, 199, 206, 208
and unretirement, 196, 204, 209
and the welfare state, 12
retrenchment, 58, 63–64
Rodman, Hyman, 15. *See also* "value
stretch" phenomenon

safety net. *See* welfare state
sample design, 43
Second World Assembly on Ageing, 17,
241. *See also* aging, international
initiatives on; United Nations
World Assembly on Ageing
2010 follow-up to, 19
secondary data, 28, 42
self-care, 129, 145, 148–151 (*see also*
health, promotion)
self-directed care. *See* self-care
single-nation global aging research, 28.
See also global patterns research;
cross-national comparative global
aging research
skipped-generation households, 11
Social Security system (U.S.). *See* U.S.
Social Security system
social services
in Kenya, 11
in urban China, 216
solidarity
intergenerational, 232, 238,
242–243, 247
intragenerational, 247
South Korea, 19
children caring for aging parents, 32
comparative study of hospice in
Japan, Taiwan, 28
depression, 28, 32
National Insurance (NHI) model, 142
speed of population aging, 82
type of LTC services and supports,
166–168

Stanford Chronic Disease Self-
Management Program (CDSMP),
148, 151. *See also* medicine,
complementary and alternative
(CAM)
state socialism, 57. *See also* welfare
state, history
stereotypes
about countries, 5
about erosion of family values,
230–233
about intergenerational transfers, 228
about older people, 50, 109, 144,
258, 259
Supplemental Security Income (SSI), 59
support systems for older adults
community care and, 239, 240–247
formal, 231, 239, 240
informal, 173, 184, 202, 237
in Kenya, 250–254
Survey of Health, Ageing, and Retirement
in Europe (SHARE), 21, 41
Swaziland, 43, 65, 87–94, 225
Sweden
challenges and opportunities for the
welfare state, 73–74
description of the welfare state, 72
older citizens' direct participation in
parliament, 73
proportion of older people, 71
as a role model of welfare states,
71–74
workforce participation among older
citizens, 73

Taiwan, 48, 142, 229
Thailand
adjustment to hyperlongevity, 68
age 60 HALE value, 120
demographic dividends, 83
government-sponsored program,
19 (*see also* aging, international
initiatives on)
HIV/AIDS, 177–178
informal family support, 177
life expectancy, 91
National Elderly Council of, 177
NGOs, 178
speed of population aging, 82, 97
state income assistance, 177

themes in the study of global aging, 257–261

"three-legged stool" of retirement income, 202

total life expectancy (TLE), 115. *See also* disability, and active life expectancy
   data for Japanese women, 121
   healthy life years (HLY), 118–119

tourist approach to the study of global aging, 20

traditional medicine, 135–7

transfers, intergenerational, 39, 226, 227, 228–229, 232

unemployment benefits, 13. *See also* welfare state

unit of analysis in comparative studies of global aging, 35–38
   Denton's definition of, 38

unit of observation in comparative studies of global aging, 38–40
   Denton's definition of, 38

United Arab Emirates population pyramid, 87

United Kingdom, 21, 56, 104, 119, 138, 141–142, 151, 154, 158, 200, 203–208, 231, 238, 244, 245, 253

United Nations
   categorization of countries, 4
   First World Assembly on Ageing, 17 (*see also* aging, international initiatives on)
   Madrid Plan of Action on Ageing, 18
   Statistics Division, 3

United Nations World Assembly on Ageing, 17, 239.

United States, 10, 29, 30, 34–36
   births in 1957 vs. 2008, 96
   breast cancer, 133
   budget for social issues, 72
   the "busy ethic," 216
   compared to India, 76
   decline in ADL disability, 121
   delayed retirement, 206
   dependency ratio, 93–95
   disability, 163
   dominant cultural value, 37
   filial responsibility, 233
   fiscal challenge, 7

formal home health care services, 237

gender difference in life expectancy, 92

gerontology, 21

grandparents providing care to grandchildren, 227

growing rate of cognitive impairment, 122

growth of older population, 97

HALE values at age 60, 120

health care system, 140

health promotion and disease prevention, 148

hospice services, 156

importance of independence, 15, 37

increase of retirement age, 64

income inequality, 107

individualism, 230

intergenerational transfers, 228–229

involuntary retirement, 205

life expectancy, 47

and migration, 85

loss of home values, 67

pension regulations, 209

population older than age 65, 47

population pyramid, 85–87

private pensions, 202

public pension programs, 62

public pension system, 59

rates of functional impairment in Nepal, 40–41

relations between Cuba and the, 47–49

retirement, 196–197, 199, 204

skipped-generation households, 11

Social Security Disability Insurance, 201

speed of population aging, 82

type of LTC services and supports, 174–175

use of formal LTC services, 172

variability in mortality rates, 103

welfare, 12

Unruh, Gregory, 262–264

urbanization, 13, 56
   development of the welfare state, 13, 56
   disintegration of family support, 181
   and economic development, 236
   and the family, 239
   in Kenya, 250

and stages of demographic
transition, 79
U.S. Social Security system, 7
Uzbekistan, 20

"value stretch" phenomenon, 15. *See also*
welfare state, and the role of the
family, in China
Vienna International Plan of Action on
Ageing, 17, 239–240, 252. *See also*
aging, international initiatives on;
NGOs, expanding role of
Vietnam, 32, 34
demographic dividends, 83
filial piety, 231
financial remittances, 227
migration, 180
public pensions, 201

welfare state
global aging, 12–18, 53–74
the future of, 64–68
broader than safety-net programs, 12
as collection of social-assistances
policies, 12
concept of, to analyze nations, 12
convergence
lack of evidence for, 14 (*see also*
United States, lack of national
health policy)
unlikelihood of, 17
definition, 55
development of, 13–14

history, 55–58
the Catholic Church, 55
model, dependency on factors among
different nations, 13–14, 15
old age, 12
program types and eligibility, 58–62
role of the family, 14–17
in China, 15
in Sweden, 71–74
traditional values and
modernization, 17
in the United Kingdom, 56
World Bank
calculation of gross national income, 3
categorization of countries, 3
commonly used alternative to, 4
World Health Organization (WHO)
guidelines for ethical research in
cross-cultural studies, 44
longitudinal study of global aging
and adult health, 21
World Health Organization-Composite
International Diagnostic
Interview (WHO-CIDI), 125
World Health Organization's Quality of
Life (WHOQOL) project, 41–42
use in Kenya, 42
work and retirement, 193–218
definition, 195–197
life course perspective, 195–196
unretirement, 196, 204, 209
workplace injuries, compensation for,
13. *See also* welfare state